A Messianic Jewish Siddur for Shabbat and Festivals

A Translation by Rabbi Barry A. Budoff

ר׳ בצלאל אברם בן־יעקב הלוי זצ״ל

Edited by Rabbi Kirk Gliebe

ר׳ שאול בן־יוסף

Editorial Committee:

*Rabbi Seth Klayman, Rabbi Howard Silverman,
Rabbi Matthew Gliebe, Rabbi Eric Meiri*

First Edition   July 23, 1999
Second Edition   July 20, 2006
Third Edition   March 23, 2011
Fourth Edition   December 14, 2017
Fifth Edition   February 13, 2023
                2nd Printing - December 13, 2024

Published by

DEVAR EMET MESSIANIC Jewish Outreach
7800 NILES AVENUE • SKOKIE, IL 60077
847.674.9146 • DEMJO.ORG

ISBN 979-8-9878279-0-1

ISBN: 979-8-9878279-0-1

Note: *the Hebrew on the cover means "The Almighty watching over me is awesome."* ‏(שדי ישמרני כירא)‏

This work is dedicated to the bride of my youth, Dyann Budoff. Had it not been for her love and support, there would have been no way this Siddur could have been written.

Thank you, my love!
—Barry

The 4th & 5th Editions of the Budoff Siddur are dedicated to the life and ministry of my mentor and friend, Rabbi Barry Betzalel Budoff. Rabbi Budoff served as one of the founding leaders of the modern Messianic Jewish Congregational Movement and his passion for Messiah Yeshua and desire to encourage traditional Jewish observance among Messianic Jews was an inspiration for his entire generation.

May his memory remain as a blessing!
—Rabbi Kirk Gliebe

Table of Contents

An Introduction

There are very few things that can be said to bind the Jewish people together. One of them is the Siddur. It is an order of service comprised of ancient prayers that are recited in virtually every synagogue, shul and temple in the Jewish world. While some of the melodies might differ, as do some of the traditions surrounding the reciting of these prayers, if one were to go into any Jewish congregation the basic structure of the service would be the same.

This is a Messianic Jewish Siddur, and as such we felt it needed to reflect that aspect of our faith. As a result, there are portions of texts from the B'rit Chadashah interspersed through the text of the Siddur. However, we felt it just as important that the general integrity and flow of the traditional Jewish Shabbat service not be changed in any drastic manner. As a result, the portions that have been inserted were carefully chosen to fit within the context of the existing service, and to reflect the same sense of the portion of the service into which they were placed.

While we continue to hope and believe that one day the majority of the Messianic Jewish community will be Hebrew literate, currently this is still not the case. As a result we have included a transliteration of those portions of the Hebrew text that are most likely to be used from week to week, during services. This will allow those who don't read Hebrew, as well as those who are unfamiliar with the form and structure of a traditional Jewish service to participate in the service itself.

Finally, you will note that at the beginning of this Siddur there is a brief set of notes. These are not by any means a full explanation of the purpose, function or form of the various prayers found in this Siddur. They are, however, meant to give the reader, and the user, some sense of how and why a particular prayer is used and what its historical roots are said to be. We have always found that this kind of information allows us all to better connect to the text and to the rest of the Jewish community, as we join in praying these beautiful and ancient words.

Rabbi Barry Budoff & Rabbi Kirk Gliebe

Introduction to Shabbat and Festival Services

It is important to recognize that this is not simply a traditional Siddur. This is a Messianic Jewish Siddur. As such, it must speak clearly of the supremacy of our Messiah, the Lord Yeshua, and not merely by inference or through some secret code that only *we* recognize. To accomplish this, we have included a number of passages from the B'rit Hadashah as an integral part of this Siddur. Some were chosen because they highlight the same truths that are seen throughout non-Messianic Jewish siddurim, others were chosen because they clearly and eloquently exalt our Redeemer, the Holy One of Israel. These readings are by no means comprehensive, but instead, provide a starting point in the recognition of the cultural and theological continuity that must exist in our worship as Messianic Jews.

At the same time, this Messianic Jewish Siddur also allows us to express our unique responsibility as Jewish people to faithfully follow the Torah, G-d's covenant with Israel, as our covenantal way of life. In this Siddur where the Hebrew word תורה (Torah) is referring to this unique covenant relationship, we leave the word untranslated. Where the Hebrew word Torah conveys a wider understanding of God's general revelation in the Scriptures both for Jews and Gentiles the word is translated *instruction*.

Preliminary Psalms and Readings: *(Pages 12-23 & 50-73)*

When we enter the synagogue to pray, we bring the world and all of its troubles in with us. The preliminary Psalms help us shift the focus from ourselves and *our* concerns, to God and *His* concerns. The Psalms may be incorporated as readings, or they may be used to augment the music and free worship of our congregations.

An additional reading for the Kabbalat Shabbat Service is ***L'kha Dodi***. L'kha Dodi was written in the middle of the sixteenth century by Rabbi Solomon Alkabets, and is composed almost entirely of passages from the Bible. The only potentially controversial concept found in this prayer is the personification of the Sabbath as a bride. However, this idea is presented in much the same way that Israel is portrayed as a bride in Jeremiah 2:2. The last stanza of L'kha Dodi is said while standing and facing toward the entrance of the sanctuary, again, alluding to the welcoming of the bride to the wedding ceremony and feast.

During the Shaharit Shabbat Service there are also additional readings that are included in this section. They include ***Barukh Sh'amar, 1 Chronicles 16:8-36, Rom'mu, Revelation 4:2-11, Y'hi K'vod Adonai*** and ***Nishmat***.

Shokhein Ahd *(Page 72)*

Shokhein Ahd is a prayer that moves the congregation from a place of praise and thanksgiving to the portion of the Shaharit service that declares God's nature and purposes. It is usually chanted by the hazan, and serves as a transition into the Half Kaddish.

Bar'khu *(Pages 24 & 74)*

The Bar'khu is traditionally used as a call to worship, but is omitted when praying without a minyan. According to some commentaries, its origin can be traced as far back as the Temple, where singers used it at the beginning of each day's service. It should be seen as a point of transition between the Psalms of praise and thanksgiving to a portion of the service that declares the unique purposes and nature of our God.

During the chanting of the Bar'khu, the hazan and congregation stand and face east toward Jerusalem or face the open doors of the ark. The hazan chants the initial line while bowing first at the knees and then at the waist. The congregation responds with the second line of the Bar'khu, bowing in the same manner. Finally, the hazan repeats the second line, thus joining himself with the community in blessing God.

Following this is a short, silent meditation which *(as with all "silent" meditations)*, is said in a quiet undertone by each individual congregant. This meditation was originally added to the Bar'khu to affirm the One True God, and to counter a growing Gnostic influence within the Jewish community. As such we can heartily join the rest of our people as we declare "the name of the Lord is to be blessed, both now and forever."

Ahavat Olam *(Page 24)*

Ahavat Olam is one of two preliminary prayers, which precede the reciting of the Shema. The focus of Ahavat Olam, as demonstrated in the first and last lines, is God's love for His people, Israel. As a result of the fact that He loved and loves us, we declare our joy in the hearing and doing of His Torah. We recognize that they are not arbitrary commands, but words that speak life to us. Therefore, we "will meditate on them day and night."

Or Hadash *(Page 78)*

Or Hadash is a profound prayer, beseeching God to send a "new Light to shine upon Tsiyon." As Messianic Jews, we cannot neglect to both recognize and acknowledge its indelible fulfillment in Yeshua, the Light of the World. Our hope is that His light would break forth as a New Light upon our people, Israel. While Or Hadash may be recited or chanted in unison by the hazan and congregation, it is particularly beautiful when each line is first chanted by the hazan and then echoed by the congregation.

Shema & Its Blessings *(Pages 26 & 80)*

The Shema is actually made up of three passages of Scripture, each of which builds upon the other. The first portion, from Deuteronomy 6:4-9, is both a command to love our God, as well as a response to the declaration of God's love for us, as expressed in Ahavat Olam. After all, if He loves us, shouldn't we respond in kind? Hence, the command to love the Lord our God with all of our heart, soul and strength. Moreover, we are commanded to transmit our love of God to our children by both our deeds and by our words.

The second passage, Deuteronomy 11:13-21, reminds us that God is the giver of blessing to His people. If we would see that blessing we must remember that He, and He *alone,* is God. This passage ends with a restatement of the words from Deuteronomy 6:5-9, and a final reminder that God is the giver of life and the keeper of His promises.

The third and final passage, Numbers 15:37-41, speaks to us of the need to wear tsitsit (fringes). Traditionally, the knots, twists and ties of the tsitsit represent the number of positive commandments in the Torah. We are commanded to look at the fringe so that we will be reminded to do what the Word of God commands. It is stated in many commentaries that if we busy ourselves in doing what God has commanded we will never have time to do that which He has forbidden (the negative commands).

Mi Khamokha *(Pages 30 & 84)*

The first part of this magnificent prayer is drawn directly from the Torah (Exodus 15:11). The final segment, a blessing to God for redeeming His people, Israel, is recited only on Erev Shabbat, and finds its origin in Jeremiah 31:11. During the Shaharit Shabbat Service the words which transition us from passage to passage are slightly different. God is still seen as our Redeemer, and as such we recognize Him as the Stronghold of Israel, the Lord of Hosts, and the Holy One of Israel. Mi Khamokha precedes the Amidah, and, as is the case with much of Jewish liturgy, has a variety of melodies.

V'shamru *(Pages 32, 88 & 112)*

V'shamru is one of the many portions of traditional Jewish liturgy which is almost entirely composed of Scripture. In it, we are commanded to keep the Shabbat throughout our generations as a sign of our covenant with God. It has many melodies and is often sung while standing.

Amidah *(Pages 34-39, 86-91, 136-143, 144-163, 166-179)*

There are several different versions of the Amidah (also referred to as the Shemoneh Esreh) included in this Siddur. The Amidah for Erev Shabbat is comprised of seven blessings, or benedictions. The first three and the last three are the same as those recited during the Shaharit Shabbat service. It is the middle benedictions that distinguish the Erev Shabbat Amidah from the Shaharit Shabbat Amidah. The Shabbat Amidah as well does not contain any prayers of supplication (asking for things), as it is the day of rest. Once again, the focus is the nature of our King and the relationship we have with Him. The Amidah is always said while standing and facing east or toward an open ark. During Shaharit and Minha services it is traditionally recited first quietly by the individual members of the congregation as a "silent" meditation, then repeated out loud by the hazan, but only when praying with a minyan. The Musaf Amidah, a "second offering" during the Shabbat and Festival services, a complete version of the weekday Amidah, useful for all three traditional daily services, and the Amidah for Festivals, are all included toward the back of this Siddur. We would like to point out a unique translation in the Modim Anahnu prayer that Rabbi Barry Budoff insisted on keeping in the English translation, the phrase, *"to the end of the age, and until"*. He liked his unconventional translation as he felt it to better relate the mystical unknown of the timing for the coming of Messiah Yeshua and his Kingdom.

Kriat HaTorah *(Pages 92-105)*

While the Torah service is composed of segmented elements, the following is a basic overview of the service from Ashkenazi Jewish tradition. The first major portion in the Kriat HaTorah is ***Ein Kamokha (There is None Like You)***. The congregation may chant it either in unison or responsively. At the conclusion of Ein Kamokha the congregation stands as the ark is opened. The hazan then leads the congregation in singing ***Vay'hi Binso'ah (And it Came to Pass)***. Included in this Siddur is a small portion of the liturgical piece ***Zohar Vayankel*** on the top of page 94\95 which contains perhaps the most vital statement in this part of the service, "In Him I put my trust!"

With the conclusion of Zohar Vayankel the Torah is removed from the ark. The hazan continues the liturgical recitation, beginning with 'Shema...' Again, as with much of the liturgy, the next three lines are particularly effective and beautiful when performed in a call and response fashion. After the third line, the congregation responds by singing L'kha Adonai, followed by the procession of the Torah through the congregation. Upon undressing the Torah, it is placed on the bima (reading table), and congregants may choose to sit or stand through the reading of the parasha. The oleh (individual called up for the reading) chants the opening blessing before reading the Torah portion, and the closing blessing upon completion of the reading. Following the closing blessing is Hagba'ah (the lifting of the Torah before the assembly), and G'lila (the dressing of the Torah scroll). In most traditional congregations, the Torah scroll is not returned to the ark until after the reading of the Haftarah, B'rit Hadashah, and the giving of the drash (D'var Torah). In some congregations, however, the Torah is returned to the ark prior to the drash. In either case, the curtain of the ark should be closed first, followed by the closing of the ark's doors, and the reciting of Ne'eman Atah Hu (You are He Who is Faithful).

Aleinu *(Pages 40 & 106)*

Rav Hai Gaon, the last of the Babylonian Gaonim, believed that Joshua composed this prayer as he led the people of Israel into the land God had promised them. The Aleinu is a prayer that emphatically states that because we have been called by God to be His people, we are different from the nations around us. The Aleinu is divided into two parts. The first is a reminder that our God is the only true God, and that apart from Him nothing truly matters. Everything we see around us, the whole creation, exists because our God keeps it. The second part of the Aleinu begins with "Therefore...". In essence, because the first part is true, we can trust that the second part will be made true as well. The focus of this section is the redemption of the world and the establishment of God's kingdom upon the Earth. The Aleinu is recited at the conclusion of virtually every service, the congregation standing and facing the ark, its doors and curtains opened. The first part of the Aleinu is chanted by the hazan together with the congregation. The second part is usually a "silent" meditation.

When it becomes clear that the majority of the congregation has completed the reading, the hazan chants the last two lines of the Aleinu. Upon concluding the prayer, the ark is closed and the congregation may sit.

Kaddish *(Pages 32, 74, 96, 202)*

There are five different forms of the Kaddish that are said in a traditional Jewish service. Two of these, the Half-Kaddish and the Full Kaddish, are used at points of transition within this Siddur, moving us from one major portion of the service to another.

Mourner's Kaddish *(Pages 42, 50 & 108)*

Mourners recite the Mourner's Kaddish during the first eleven months of bereavement and after that, on the anniversary (yartseit) of the death of their loved one. The Mourner's Kaddish is recited for a spouse, a sibling, a parent or a child, and is only said when a minyan is present (traditionally 10 adult Jewish men). An invitation should be given for anyone who is in mourning to stand and recite this form of the Kaddish. This is *not* a prayer for the dead. Rather, it is a prayer for the living; a reminder to everyone, including the mourner, that even in death God is to be praised. The Kaddish on page 50 is slighly different, expressing the Messianic expectation of the Sephardic Jewish community.

Adon Olam *(Pages 44 & 110)*

Adon Olam is attributed to the great medieval poet, Solomon Ibn Gabriol. An unequalled declaration of faith, it is treasured for the great truths of God which it declares. It is commonly recited at the end of the service and there are many melodies to choose from, both Ashkenaz and Sephard, so enjoy!

Shalom Aleikhem *(Page 46)*

Kabbalists first introduced this portion of the service almost three hundred years ago. It was based on a Talmudic passage that speaks of a good and an evil angel who accompany each person home from synagogue on Friday night. If things are found in order when they enter the home, the good angel imparts a blessing. On the other hand, if all is not in order the evil angel speaks a curse on the home. Whether or not you hold to this persuasion, the words and sentiment expressed in this very beautiful prayer should remain a part of our Shabbat tradition. Though Shalom Aleikhem is usually sung upon returning home from the synagogue, it makes for a beautiful blessing at the end of an Erev Shabbat service.

The Kiddush *(Pages 48 & 112, 190)*

Following the Erev Shabbat and Shabbat Morning Services, it is traditional to recite the Kiddush over a cup of wine, and often also over two loaves of challah. The reason two loaves are used is to remind us of the double portion of manna that was gathered by our people before the Shabbat began. What is true for the Shabbat is also true for the Festivals, so the traditional Festival Kiddush is also included under Additional Readings and Blessings providing the unique blessings associated with the individual Festivals.

Havdalah *(Page 114)*

When Shabbat begins we recite the Kiddush, which sets the Shabbat apart from the other days of the week. In a similar manner, when the Shabbat comes to an end we recite Havdalah. Like the Kiddush, Havdalah *(distinction or separation)* is said to have been written by the men of the Great Assembly *(500-300 B.C.E.)*.

Havdalah consists of four blessings; one over wine, one over fragrant spices, one over fire and one concerning the distinction between the holy and the profane. According to the Rambam *(Rabbi Moshe ben Maimon)* the spices are used to cheer the soul which is saddened at the departure of Shabbat. The wine for Havdalah is allowed to overflow the glass, symbolizing the overflowing blessings expected in the coming week. The Havdalah candle is made up of several wicks that are braided together. This is because the blessing speaks of "lights of fire." It is traditional to hold your hands around the fire and in so doing to be able to see the distinction "between light and darkness" in the reflection and the shadow. Following the recitation of Havdalah it is traditional to sing Ha'Mavdil and other songs.

Birkat HaMazon *(Pages 118)*

Birkat HaMazon *(sometimes called benshen)* is a series of blessings that are said after a meal that included bread. This tradition is based on the passage from Deuteronomy 8:10, which says: "When you eat and are satisfied you will bless the Lord your God for the good land He has given you." Included in this section is the complete traditional version as well as one which is abridged.

Birkat HaMazon consists of four sections. According to a statement found in ***Babylonian Talmud Berachot 48b*** the first paragraph was composed by Moses, the second by Joshua, the third by David and Solomon and the fourth by the sages. The first paragraph acknowledges God as the sustainer of all who live. The second paragraph blesses God for giving the Torah and the Land to His people, Israel. The third paragraph is a prayer for the restoration of Tsiyon and the rebuilding of Jerusalem. The last paragraph contains a number of biblical quotations that focus on the fact that those "who seek the Lord shall want for no good thing."

Additional Readings & Blessings *(Page 128 and following)*

We have in this section additional blessings, prayers and readings, including the Shabbat Musaf Amidah, a full Weekday Amidah followed by an abridged version of Taḥanun, a Festival Amidah and additional Festival liturgy including the Hallel, the Prayer for Rain at Shemini Atseret and the Hakafot for Simḥat Torah. Enough liturgy is now included to make it possible for most within the Messianic Jewish movement to comfortably use the Budoff Siddur for daily Jewish prayer and during the Festivals, excluding Rosh Hashanah and Yom Kippur. Two unique services, one Remembering the Death of Messiah Yeshua and another for Tevilah, allow us as Messianic Jews the opportunity to express these New Testament practices of our faith in Yeshua within a clearly Jewish context.

Using the Budoff Siddur for Daily Prayer

The three traditional times of Jewish prayer are ***Maariv*** (evening), ***Shaḥarit*** (morning) and ***Minḥah*** (afternoon). The outline of major prayers remains the same for all three services, except for the addition of the reading of the weekly Torah portion on Monday and Thursday mornings during Shaḥarit, the omission of the recitation of the Bar'khu and Shema during Minḥah, and the omission of the service leader's repetition of the Amidah during Maariv.

Our suggested approach for a traditional weekday prayer service would be to begin with the blessings for the preparation for prayer found on page 128, to then choose one of the preliminary Psalms such as Psalm 150 on page 70 (Shaḥarit) or Psalm 145 on page 66 (Minḥah), followed by the Bark'hu and Shema (but not at Minḥah), then inserting the full daily Amidah followed by Taḥanun (but not at Maariv) starting on page 144 in place of either the Erev Shabbat or Shabbat morning Amidah. During Shaḥarit the Torah service is added on Mondays and Thursdays, followed by the Full Kaddish, Aleinu and Mourners Kaddish. Certain of these prayers require by tradition a minyan to recite. We encourage you to consult your Rabbi or a Madrikh for advice or to contact us if you have questions.

Hebrew Transliteration Guide:

Hebrew Consonants	Transliteration	Sound
ח	ẖ (see dot below "h")	**Ch**anuka
כ,ך,כּ	kh	Baru**kh**
כּ,ק	k	**K**ippa
שׁ	sh	**Sh**abbat
שׂ	s	**S**amuel
צ,ץ	ts	**Ts**'daka
ה	h	**H**alleluya

Hebrew Vowels	Transliteration	Sound
אָ	a	**Aw**e
אַ	a	**A**pple
אִ	i	B**ee**
אֵ	ei	L**ay**
אֶ	e	B**e**d
אֹ or וֹ	o	R**o**w
אֻ or וּ	u	B**oot**
אְ		sometimes e or sometimes ' like b**e**d. When silent or ending a syllable its a '.

קבלת שבת

Psalm 95

לְכוּ נְרַנְּנָה לַיְיָ נָרִיעָה לְצוּר יִשְׁעֵנוּ. נְקַדְּמָה פָנָיו בְּתוֹדָה בִּזְמִרוֹת נָרִיעַ לוֹ. כִּי אֵל גָּדוֹל יְיָ וּמֶלֶךְ גָּדוֹל עַל כָּל אֱלֹהִים. אֲשֶׁר בְּיָדוֹ מֶחְקְרֵי אָרֶץ וְתוֹעֲפוֹת הָרִים לוֹ. אֲשֶׁר לוֹ הַיָּם וְהוּא עָשָׂהוּ וְיַבֶּשֶׁת יָדָיו יָצָרוּ. בֹּאוּ נִשְׁתַּחֲוֶה וְנִכְרָעָה נִבְרְכָה לִפְנֵי יְיָ עֹשֵׂנוּ. כִּי הוּא אֱלֹהֵינוּ וַאֲנַחְנוּ עַם מַרְעִיתוֹ וְצֹאן יָדוֹ הַיּוֹם אִם בְּקֹלוֹ תִשְׁמָעוּ. אַל תַּקְשׁוּ לְבַבְכֶם כִּמְרִיבָה כְּיוֹם מַסָּה בַּמִּדְבָּר. אֲשֶׁר נִסּוּנִי אֲבוֹתֵיכֶם בְּחָנוּנִי גַּם רָאוּ פָעֳלִי. (Reader) אַרְבָּעִים שָׁנָה אָקוּט בְּדוֹר וָאֹמַר עַם תֹּעֵי לֵבָב הֵם וְהֵם לֹא יָדְעוּ דְרָכָי. אֲשֶׁר נִשְׁבַּעְתִּי בְאַפִּי אִם יְבֹאוּן אֶל מְנוּחָתִי.

Psalm 96

שִׁירוּ לַיְיָ שִׁיר חָדָשׁ שִׁירוּ לַיְיָ כָּל הָאָרֶץ. שִׁירוּ לַיְיָ בָּרְכוּ שְׁמוֹ בַּשְּׂרוּ מִיוֹם לְיוֹם יְשׁוּעָתוֹ. סַפְּרוּ בַגּוֹיִם כְּבוֹדוֹ בְּכָל הָעַמִּים נִפְלְאוֹתָיו. כִּי גָדוֹל יְיָ וּמְהֻלָּל מְאֹד נוֹרָא הוּא עַל כָּל אֱלֹהִים. כִּי כָּל אֱלֹהֵי הָעַמִּים אֱלִילִים וַיְיָ שָׁמַיִם עָשָׂה. הוֹד וְהָדָר לְפָנָיו עֹז וְתִפְאֶרֶת בְּמִקְדָּשׁוֹ. הָבוּ לַיְיָ מִשְׁפְּחוֹת עַמִּים הָבוּ לַיְיָ כָּבוֹד וָעֹז. הָבוּ לַיְיָ כְּבוֹד שְׁמוֹ שְׂאוּ מִנְחָה וּבֹאוּ לְחַצְרוֹתָיו. הִשְׁתַּחֲווּ לַיְיָ בְּהַדְרַת קֹדֶשׁ חִילוּ מִפָּנָיו כָּל הָאָרֶץ. אִמְרוּ בַגּוֹיִם יְיָ מָלָךְ אַף תִּכּוֹן תֵּבֵל בַּל תִּמּוֹט יָדִין עַמִּים בְּמֵישָׁרִים. (Reader) יִשְׂמְחוּ הַשָּׁמַיִם וְתָגֵל הָאָרֶץ יִרְעַם הַיָּם וּמְלֹאוֹ. יַעֲלֹז שָׂדַי וְכָל אֲשֶׁר בּוֹ אָז יְרַנְּנוּ כָּל עֲצֵי יָעַר. לִפְנֵי יְיָ כִּי בָא, כִּי בָא לִשְׁפֹּט הָאָרֶץ, יִשְׁפֹּט תֵּבֵל בְּצֶדֶק, וְעַמִּים בֶּאֱמוּנָתוֹ.

1 Timonthy 3:16

אָכֵן גָּדוֹל סוֹד הַחֲסִידוּת. הִתְגַּלָּה בַּבָּשָׂר, הֻצְדַּק בָּרוּחַ, נִרְאָה לַמַּלְאָכִים, הֻגַּד בַּגּוֹיִם, הֶאֱמִינוּ בּוֹ בָּעוֹלָם, הַעֲלָה לַמָּרוֹם בְּכָבוֹד.

Revelation 19:5-6

וְקוֹל קֹרֵא יָצָא מִן הַכִּסֵּא לֵאמֹר הַלְלוּ אֶת אֱלֹהֵינוּ כָּל עֲבָדָיו וִירֵאָיו הַקְּטַנִּים עִם הַגְּדוֹלִים. וָאֶשְׁמַע כְּקוֹל הָמוֹן רַב וּכְקוֹל מַיִם רַבִּים וְכִשְׁאוֹן רַעַם חָזָק קֹרֵא הַלְלוּיָהּ כִּי מָלַךְ אֱלֹהֵינוּ יְהוָֹה אֵל שַׁדָּי.

Kabbalat Shabbat

Psalm 95

Come, let us sing to the Lord; let us acclaim the Rock of our salvation. Let us come before His face with thanksgiving, let us acclaim Him with songs. For God is a great Lord. He is a great King over all gods, in whose hands are the foundations of the earth; the highest heights are His as well. The sea belongs to Him who made it, whose hands formed the dry land. Come, let us humble ourselves and bow down; let us bend the knee to the Lord, our Maker, for He is our God and we are the people of His pasture, the sheep of His hand. Today if you would listen to Him do not harden your hearts as at Meriba; as on the day of testing in the wilderness, when your fathers tried Me. Although they had seen My deeds, they tested Me. For forty years I argued with that generation, and I said of them, "They are a people who err in their hearts; they have not come to know My ways." Therefore, I swore in My wrath, "They shall not enter My rest."

Psalm 96

Sing to the Lord a new song; sing to the Lord all the earth. Sing to the Lord, bless His Name; proclaim His salvation from day to day. Tell the nations of His glory, the peoples of His wonders, for great is the Lord and His praise is great. He is to be feared above all gods, for the gods of the peoples are idols, but the Lord made the heavens. Glory and majesty go before His face; strength and beauty are seen in His sanctuary. Ascribe to the Lord, you families of peoples, ascribe to the Lord honor and strength; ascribe to the Lord the glory of His Name. Come to His courts bringing an offering; worship the Lord arrayed in holiness. Let all the earth tremble before His countenance. Let it be said among the nations, "The Lord is King!" The world is firmly established, it cannot be shaken; He judges the peoples with righteousness. The heavens will be glad and the earth will rejoice; the sea and all its fullness will roar, the fields and all that is in them will exult. Then the trees of the forest will sing for joy before the Lord who comes - who comes to rule the earth. He will rule the earth in righteousness, and the peoples in His faithfulness.

1 Timothy 3:16

Great indeed, we confess, is the mystery of our faith: He was manifested in the flesh, vindicated in the Spirit, seen by angels, proclaimed among the nations, believed on in the world, taken up in glory.

Revelation 19:5-6

And a voice came out from the throne, saying, "Praise our God, all you His servants, and you that fear Him, both small and great." And I heard as it were the voice of a great multitude, like the voice of many waters, and like the voice of mighty thundering, saying, "Halleluyah! For the Lord God Omnipotent reigns."

Psalm 97

יְיָ מָלָךְ תָּגֵל הָאָרֶץ יִשְׂמְחוּ אִיִּים רַבִּים. עָנָן וַעֲרָפֶל סְבִיבָיו צֶדֶק וּמִשְׁפָּט מְכוֹן כִּסְאוֹ. אֵשׁ לְפָנָיו תֵּלֵךְ וּתְלַהֵט סָבִיב צָרָיו. הֵאִירוּ בְרָקָיו תֵּבֵל רָאֲתָה וַתָּחֵל הָאָרֶץ. הָרִים כַּדּוֹנַג נָמַסּוּ מִלִּפְנֵי יְיָ מִלִּפְנֵי אֲדוֹן כָּל הָאָרֶץ. הִגִּידוּ הַשָּׁמַיִם צִדְקוֹ וְרָאוּ כָל הָעַמִּים כְּבוֹדוֹ. יֵבֹשׁוּ כָּל עֹבְדֵי פֶסֶל הַמִּתְהַלְלִים בָּאֱלִילִים הִשְׁתַּחֲווּ לוֹ כָּל אֱלֹהִים. שָׁמְעָה וַתִּשְׂמַח צִיּוֹן וַתָּגֵלְנָה בְּנוֹת יְהוּדָה לְמַעַן מִשְׁפָּטֶיךָ יְיָ. כִּי אַתָּה יְיָ עֶלְיוֹן עַל כָּל הָאָרֶץ מְאֹד נַעֲלֵיתָ עַל כָּל אֱלֹהִים.

(Reader) אֹהֲבֵי יְיָ שִׂנְאוּ רָע שֹׁמֵר נַפְשׁוֹת חֲסִידָיו מִיַּד רְשָׁעִים יַצִּילֵם. אוֹר זָרֻעַ לַצַּדִּיק וּלְיִשְׁרֵי לֵב שִׂמְחָה. שִׂמְחוּ צַדִּיקִים בַּיְיָ וְהוֹדוּ לְזֵכֶר קָדְשׁוֹ.

Psalm 98

מִזְמוֹר, שִׁירוּ לַיְיָ שִׁיר חָדָשׁ כִּי נִפְלָאוֹת עָשָׂה הוֹשִׁיעָה לוֹ יְמִינוֹ וּזְרוֹעַ קָדְשׁוֹ. הוֹדִיעַ יְיָ יְשׁוּעָתוֹ לְעֵינֵי הַגּוֹיִם גִּלָּה צִדְקָתוֹ. זָכַר חַסְדּוֹ וֶאֱמוּנָתוֹ לְבֵית יִשְׂרָאֵל רָאוּ כָל אַפְסֵי אָרֶץ אֵת יְשׁוּעַת אֱלֹהֵינוּ. הָרִיעוּ לַיְיָ כָּל הָאָרֶץ פִּצְחוּ וְרַנְּנוּ וְזַמֵּרוּ. זַמְּרוּ לַיְיָ בְּכִנּוֹר בְּכִנּוֹר וְקוֹל זִמְרָה. בַּחֲצֹצְרוֹת וְקוֹל שׁוֹפָר הָרִיעוּ לִפְנֵי הַמֶּלֶךְ יְיָ. יִרְעַם הַיָּם וּמְלֹאוֹ תֵּבֵל וְיֹשְׁבֵי בָהּ.

(Reader) נְהָרוֹת יִמְחֲאוּ כָף יַחַד הָרִים יְרַנֵּנוּ. לִפְנֵי יְיָ כִּי בָא לִשְׁפֹּט הָאָרֶץ יִשְׁפֹּט תֵּבֵל בְּצֶדֶק וְעַמִּים בְּמֵישָׁרִים.

Revelation 19:11-16

וָאֵרֶא אֶת הַשָּׁמַיִם נִפְתָּחִים וְהִנֵּה סוּס לָבָן וְהָרֹכֵב עָלָיו נִקְרָא נֶאֱמָן וְיָשָׁר וּמִשְׁפָּטוֹ וּמִלְחַמְתּוֹ בְּמֵישָׁרִים. עֵינָיו כְּלַהֲבוֹת אֵשׁ וַעֲטָרוֹת רַבּוֹת עַל רֹאשׁוֹ וְעָלָיו שֵׁם חָקוּק אֲשֶׁר לֹא יֵדַע אֹתוֹ אִישׁ מִלְבַדּוֹ. וְהוּא עֹטֶה לְבוּשׁ מְאָדָּם בְּדָם וּשְׁמוֹ נִקְרָא דְּבַר הָאֱלֹהִים. וּצְבָא הַשָּׁמַיִם רֹכְבִים אַחֲרָיו עַל סוּסִים לְבָנִים מְלֻבָּשִׁים בִּגְדֵי בוּץ זַךְ וְנָקִי. וְחֶרֶב חַדָּה יֹצֵאת מִפִּיו לְהַכּוֹת בָּהּ אֶת הַגּוֹיִם וְלִרְעֵם בְּשֵׁבֶט בַּרְזֶל וְהוּא דֹרֵךְ גַּת יֵין הַחֵמָה וְהַזַּעַף לֵאלֹהִים אֵל שַׁדָּי. יָעַל בִּגְדוֹ וְעַל יְרֵכוֹ כָּתוּב שֵׁם מֶלֶךְ הַמְּלָכִים וַאֲדֹנֵי הָאֲדֹנִים.

Psalm 97

From the beginning the Lord was King; the earth rejoiced, the many isles were glad! Clouds and darkness surround Him; righteousness and justice are the foundations of His throne. Fire goes out from Him and burns round about His enemies. His lightning enlightens the world which has seen it and trembles. The mountains melted like wax before the face of God - before the face of the Lord of the whole earth. The heavens declared He is just, and all the peoples have seen His glory. Those who serve images, who make their boast in idols, will be put to shame; all their gods are cast down before Him. Lord, Tsiyon has heard and was glad and the daughters of Judah rejoice in Your judgments. Lord, You are supreme over all the earth; You are high above all gods. You who love the Lord, hate evil! He preserves the soul of those who are His; He delivers them from the hand of the wicked. Light is given to the righteous, and to the upright in heart, joy. You who are righteous, rejoice in the Lord, and give thanks at the remembrance of His holiness.

Psalm 98

A song: Sing a new song to the Lord, for He has done wondrous things. His right hand saves; His holy arm has brought Him victory. The Lord has made His salvation known; He has revealed His righteousness in the sight of the nations. He has remembered His lovingkindness and His faithfulness to the house of Israel; all the ends of the earth have seen the salvation of our God. Shout to the Lord, all the earth, give voice to your gladness, and rejoice and sing. Sing to the Lord with the harp - with the harp and the voice of song. Shout before the Lord, the King, with trumpets and the sound of the shofar. The sea and all its fullness will roar; the world and those who dwell upon it. The rivers will clap their hands before the Lord, and the mountains will sing with them, for He is coming to judge the earth. He will judge the world with righteousness and the peoples with uprightness.

Revelation 19:11-16

And I saw the heavens opened, and behold a white horse; and He that sat upon him was called Faithful and True, and in righteousness He judges and makes war. His eyes were as a flame of fire, and on His head were many crowns; and He had a name written, that no man knew, but He Himself. And He was clothed with a vesture dipped in blood; and His name was called the Word of God. The armies which were in the heavens followed Him upon white horses, clothed in fine linen, white and clean. And out of His mouth came a sharp sword, that with it He might smite the nations; and He will rule them with a rod of iron, as He treads the wine press of the fierceness and wrath of the Almighty God. And He has on His clothing and on His thigh a Name that is written: King of kings and Lord of lords.

Psalm 99

יְיָ מָלָךְ יִרְגְּזוּ עַמִּים, יֹשֵׁב כְּרוּבִים תָּנוּט הָאָרֶץ. יְיָ בְּצִיּוֹן גָּדוֹל וְרָם הוּא עַל כָּל הָעַמִּים. יוֹדוּ שִׁמְךָ גָּדוֹל וְנוֹרָא קָדוֹשׁ הוּא. וְעֹז מֶלֶךְ מִשְׁפָּט אָהֵב אַתָּה כּוֹנַנְתָּ מֵישָׁרִים מִשְׁפָּט וּצְדָקָה בְּיַעֲקֹב אַתָּה עָשִׂיתָ. רוֹמְמוּ יְיָ אֱלֹהֵינוּ וְהִשְׁתַּחֲווּ לַהֲדֹם רַגְלָיו קָדוֹשׁ הוּא. מֹשֶׁה וְאַהֲרֹן בְּכֹהֲנָיו וּשְׁמוּאֵל בְּקֹרְאֵי שְׁמוֹ קֹרְאִים אֶל יְיָ וְהוּא יַעֲנֵם.

(Reader) בְּעַמּוּד עָנָן יְדַבֵּר אֲלֵיהֶם שָׁמְרוּ עֵדֹתָיו וְחֹק נָתַן לָמוֹ. יְיָ אֱלֹהֵינוּ אַתָּה עֲנִיתָם אֵל נֹשֵׂא הָיִיתָ לָהֶם וְנֹקֵם עַל עֲלִילוֹתָם. רוֹמְמוּ יְיָ אֱלֹהֵינוּ וְהִשְׁתַּחֲווּ לְהַר קָדְשׁוֹ כִּי קָדוֹשׁ יְיָ אֱלֹהֵינוּ.

Colossians 1:15-20

וְהוּא צֶלֶם שֶׁל הָאֱלֹהִים הַבִּלְתִּי נִרְאֶה, בְּכוֹר כָּל בְּרִיאָה; כִּי בּוֹ נִבְרָא כָּל אֲשֶׁר בַּשָּׁמַיִם וַאֲשֶׁר בָּאָרֶץ, מַה שֶּׁנִּרְאֶה וּמַה שֶּׁבִּלְתִּי נִרְאֶה, גַּם כִּסְאוֹת וְרָשֻׁיּוֹת וְגַם מֶמְשָׁלוֹת וְשִׁלְטוֹנוֹת. הַכֹּל נִבְרָא בְּאֶמְצָעוּתוֹ וּלְמַעֲנוֹ, וְהוּא קוֹדֵם לַכֹּל וְהַכֹּל קַיָּם בּוֹ. הוּא הָרֹאשׁ שֶׁל הַגּוּף, כְּלוֹמַר, שֶׁל הַקְּהִלָּה. הוּא הָרֵאשִׁית, בְּכוֹר מִבֵּין הַמֵּתִים, לְמַעַן יִהְיֶה רִאשׁוֹן בַּכֹּל, כִּי כֵן הָיָה רָצוֹן לְשַׁכֵּן בּוֹ אֶת כָּל הַמְּלוֹא וּבְאֶמְצָעוּתוֹ לְרַצּוֹת אֶל עַצְמוֹ אֶת הַכֹּל. הֵן מַה שֶּׁבַּשָּׁמַיִם וְהֵן מַה שֶּׁבָּאָרֶץ, בְּאֶמְצָעוּתוֹ, בַּעֲשִׂיַּת שָׁלוֹם בְּדָמוֹ עַל הַצְּלָב.

Psalm 29

מִזְמוֹר לְדָוִד הָבוּ לַיְיָ בְּנֵי אֵלִים הָבוּ לַיְיָ כָּבוֹד וָעֹז. הָבוּ לַיְיָ כְּבוֹד שְׁמוֹ הִשְׁתַּחֲווּ לַיְיָ בְּהַדְרַת קֹדֶשׁ. קוֹל יְיָ עַל הַמָּיִם אֵל הַכָּבוֹד הִרְעִים יְיָ עַל מַיִם רַבִּים. קוֹל יְיָ בַּכֹּחַ קוֹל יְיָ בֶּהָדָר. קוֹל יְיָ שֹׁבֵר אֲרָזִים וַיְשַׁבֵּר יְיָ אֶת אַרְזֵי הַלְּבָנוֹן, וַיַּרְקִידֵם כְּמוֹ עֵגֶל לְבָנוֹן וְשִׂרְיוֹן כְּמוֹ בֶן רְאֵמִים. קוֹל יְיָ חֹצֵב לַהֲבוֹת אֵשׁ, קוֹל יְיָ יָחִיל מִדְבָּר, יָחִיל יְיָ מִדְבַּר קָדֵשׁ.

(Reader) קוֹל יְיָ יְחוֹלֵל אַיָּלוֹת וַיֶּחֱשֹׂף יְעָרוֹת וּבְהֵיכָלוֹ כֻּלּוֹ אֹמֵר כָּבוֹד. יְיָ לַמַּבּוּל יָשָׁב וַיֵּשֶׁב יְיָ מֶלֶךְ לְעוֹלָם. יְיָ עֹז לְעַמּוֹ יִתֵּן יְיָ יְבָרֵךְ אֶת עַמּוֹ בַשָּׁלוֹם.

אָנָּא בְּכֹחַ גְּדֻלַּת יְמִינְךָ תַּתִּיר צְרוּרָה. קַבֵּל רִנַּת עַמְּךָ שַׂגְּבֵנוּ טַהֲרֵנוּ נוֹרָא. נָא גִבּוֹר דּוֹרְשֵׁי יְחוּדְךָ כְּבָבַת שָׁמְרֵם. בָּרְכֵם טַהֲרֵם רַחֲמֵם צִדְקָתְךָ תָּמִיד גָּמְלֵם. חֲסִין קָדוֹשׁ בְּרֹב טוּבְךָ נַהֵל עֲדָתֶךָ. יָחִיד גֵּאֶה לְעַמְּךָ פְּנֵה זוֹכְרֵי קְדֻשָּׁתֶךָ. שַׁוְעָתֵנוּ קַבֵּל וּשְׁמַע צַעֲקָתֵנוּ יוֹדֵעַ תַּעֲלוּמוֹת. בָּרוּךְ שֵׁם כְּבוֹד מַלְכוּתוֹ לְעוֹלָם וָעֶד.

Psalm 99

From the beginning God was King; the peoples tremble. He is enthroned upon the Keruvim; the earth is shaken. The Lord is great in Tsiyon; He is high above all the peoples. They shall render praise to Your great and awesome Name, for He is holy. The King's strength is His love of justice; You have established uprightness. You have established justice and righteousness in Jacob. Exalt the Lord our God and bow yourselves before His footstool, for He is holy. Moses and Aaron among His priests, and Samuel in calling on His Name, called upon the Lord and He heard them. He spoke to them from a pillar of cloud; they kept the testimonies and the statutes which He gave them. Lord our God, You answered them; to them You were the God who forgives, although You exacted justice for their misdeeds. Exalt the Lord our God, and bow yourselves before His holy mountain, for the Lord our God is holy!

Colossians 1:15-20

He is the image of the invisible God, the firstborn of all creation. For in him all things were created, in heaven and on earth, visible and invisible, whether thrones or dominions or principalities or authorities - all things were created through him and for him. He is before all things, and in him all things hold together. He is the head of the body, the congregation. He is the beginning, the firstborn from the dead, that in everything he might be preeminent. For in him all the fullness of God was pleased to dwell, and through him to reconcile to himself all things, whether on earth or in heaven, making peace by the blood of his execution.

Psalm 29

A psalm of David. Ascribe to the Lord, you who have been given strength, ascribe to the Lord glory and might. Ascribe to the Lord the glory due His Name; bow yourselves before the Lord who is arrayed in holiness. The voice of the Lord is upon the waters; it is the God of glory thundering, the Lord upon vast waters. The voice of the Lord is powerful. The voice of the Lord is filled with majesty. The voice of the Lord breaks the cedars; the Lord shatters the cedars of Lebanon. He makes them skip like calves, Levanon and Sir'yon like young bulls. The voice of the Lord stirs up flames of fire. The voice of the Lord makes the wilderness tremble, just as the Lord caused the wilderness of Kadesh to tremble. The voice of the Lord causes the hind to birth, even as it strips the forest bare, and in His temple everything cries, "Glory!" The Lord sat upon His throne during the flood; indeed, the Lord sits as King forever. The Lord will give strength to His people. The Lord will bless His people with peace.

Please, by the power of Your right hand, set those in captivity free. Revered One, receive the words of your people; be our cleansing and our strength. Please, Almighty One, guard those who seek you as You would the apple of Your eye. Bless them, cleanse them, have compassion on them; may Your truth be ever before them. Holy One, in Your great goodness guide Your people. Exalted One, turn Your face to Your people who declare Your holiness. May You who know our innermost thoughts, hear our prayer and listen to our cry. Blessed is His glorious name, whose kingdom is forever and ever.

לכה דודי

לְכָה דוֹדִי לִקְרַאת כַּלָּה.   פְּנֵי שַׁבָּת נְקַבְּלָה.
L'khah dodi likrat kallah. P'nei Shabbat n'kabe'lah.

שָׁמוֹר וְזָכוֹר בְּדִבּוּר אֶחָד, הִשְׁמִיעָנוּ אֵל הַמְּיֻחָד.
יְיָ אֶחָד וּשְׁמוֹ אֶחָד, לְשֵׁם וּלְתִפְאֶרֶת וְלִתְהִלָּה.
Shamor v'zakhor b'dib-bur ehad, hish'mianu eil ham'yuhad.
Adonai ehad ush'moh ehad, l'sheim ul'tiferet v'lithillah.

לְכָה דוֹדִי לִקְרַאת כַּלָּה.   פְּנֵי שַׁבָּת נְקַבְּלָה.
L'khah dodi likrat kallah. P'nei Shabbat n'kabe'lah.

לִקְרַאת שַׁבָּת לְכוּ וְנֵלְכָה, כִּי הִיא מְקוֹר הַבְּרָכָה.
מֵרֹאשׁ מִקֶּדֶם נְסוּכָה, סוֹף מַעֲשֶׂה בְּמַחֲשָׁבָה תְּחִלָּה.
Likrat Shabbat l'khu v'neihlkhah, kee hee mekor hab'rakhah.
Meihrosh mikehdem n'sukhah, sof maaseh bemahashava tehillah.

לְכָה דוֹדִי לִקְרַאת כַּלָּה.   פְּנֵי שַׁבָּת נְקַבְּלָה.
L'khah dodi likrat kallah. P'nei Shabbat n'kabe'lah.

מִקְדָּשׁ מֶלֶךְ עִיר מְלוּכָה, קוּמִי צְאִי מִתּוֹךְ הַהֲפֵכָה.
רַב לָךְ שֶׁבֶת בְּעֵמֶק הַבָּכָא, וְהוּא יַחֲמוֹל עָלַיִךְ חֶמְלָה.
Mikdash melekh ir melukhah, kumi tse'i mi'tokh ha-ha'feikhah.
Rav lakh shevet be'ei'mehk habakhah, v'hu yahamol alayikh hem'lah.

לְכָה דוֹדִי לִקְרַאת כַּלָּה.   פְּנֵי שַׁבָּת נְקַבְּלָה.
L'khah dodi likrat kallah. P'nei Shabbat n'kabe'lah.

הִתְנַעֲרִי מֵעָפָר קוּמִי, לִבְשִׁי בִּגְדֵי תִפְאַרְתֵּךְ עַמִּי.
עַל יַד בֶּן יִשַׁי בֵּית הַלַּחְמִי, קָרְבָה אֶל נַפְשִׁי גְאָלָה.
Hit'na'ari mei'afar kumi, liv'shi big'dei tif'ar'teikh ami.
Al yad ben Yishai beit halah'mi, kar'vah el naf'shi ge'alah.

לְכָה דוֹדִי לִקְרַאת כַּלָּה.   פְּנֵי שַׁבָּת נְקַבְּלָה.
L'khah dodi likrat kallah. P'nei Shabbat n'kabe'lah.

L'kha Dodi

Come my beloved to meet the bride; let us welcome the Shabbat!

In a single command, the One God announced to us:
"Observe" and "Remember"
The Lord alone and His Name alone, for renown,
and for glory and for praise.

Come my beloved to meet the bride; let us welcome the Shabbat!

Let us go together to meet the Shabbat
for it is a source of blessing.
From the very beginning it was set forth;
last in creation, first in thought.

Come my beloved to meet the bride; let us welcome the Shabbat!

Sanctuary of the King; royal city, arise!
Come forth from your ruins.
You have dwelt too long in the vale of tears!
And He will have compassion on you.

Come my beloved to meet the bride; let us welcome the Shabbat!

Shake off your dust; arise!
My people, be clothed with your garments of glory.
Through the hand of the son of Jesse, the giver of bread,
draw near; bring redemption to my soul.

Come my beloved to meet the bride; let us welcome the Shabbat!

הִתְעוֹרְרִי הִתְעוֹרְרִי, כִּי בָא אוֹרֵךְ קוּמִי אוֹרִי.
עוּרִי עוּרִי שִׁיר דַּבֵּרִי, כְּבוֹד יְיָ עָלַיִךְ נִגְלָה.

Hit'or'ri hitor'ri, ki va oreikh kumi ori.
Uri Uri shir da'bei'ri, kevod Adonai ala'yikh nig'la.

לְכָה דוֹדִי לִקְרַאת כַּלָּה. פְּנֵי שַׁבָּת נְקַבְּלָה.
L'khah dodi likrat kallah. P'nei Shabbat n'kabe'lah.

לֹא תֵבוֹשִׁי וְלֹא תִכָּלְמִי, מַה תִּשְׁתּוֹחֲחִי וּמַה תֶּהֱמִי.
בָּךְ יֶחֱסוּ עֲנִיֵּי עַמִּי, וְנִבְנְתָה עִיר עַל תִּלָּהּ.
Lo teivoshi velo tikalmi, ma tishtoḥaḥi uma teh'heh'mi.
Bakh yeḥesu a'niyei a'mi, v'niv'netah ir al tillah.

לְכָה דוֹדִי לִקְרַאת כַּלָּה. פְּנֵי שַׁבָּת נְקַבְּלָה.
L'khah dodi likrat kallah. P'nei Shabbat n'kabe'lah.

וְהָיוּ לִמְשִׁסָּה שֹׁאסָיִךְ, וְרָחֲקוּ כָּל מְבַלְּעָיִךְ.
יָשִׂישׂ עָלַיִךְ אֱלֹהָיִךְ, כִּמְשׂוֹשׂ חָתָן עַל כַּלָּה.
Vehayu lim'shisah shosa'yikh, veraḥaku kol meval'ah'yikh.
Yasis ala'yikh eloha'yikh, kim'sos ḥatan al kallah.

לְכָה דוֹדִי לִקְרַאת כַּלָּה. פְּנֵי שַׁבָּת נְקַבְּלָה.
L'khah dodi likrat kallah. P'nei Shabbat n'kabe'lah.

יָמִין וּשְׂמֹאל תִּפְרוֹצִי, וְאֶת־יְיָ תַּעֲרִיצִי.
עַל יַד אִישׁ בֶּן פַּרְצִי, וְנִשְׂמְחָה וְנָגִילָה.
Yamin us'mol tif'rotsi, v'et Adonai ta'aritsi.
Al yad ish ben partsi, v'nis'meḥa v'nagila.

לְכָה דוֹדִי לִקְרַאת כַּלָּה. פְּנֵי שַׁבָּת נְקַבְּלָה.
L'khah dodi likrat kallah. P'nei Shabbat n'kabe'lah.

(Congregation rises and turns toward the door, as if welcoming the Shabbat as a guest)

בּוֹאִי בְשָׁלוֹם עֲטֶרֶת בַּעְלָהּ, גַּם בְּשִׂמְחָה וּבְצָהֳלָה.
תּוֹךְ אֱמוּנֵי עַם סְגֻלָּה, בּוֹאִי כַלָּה, בּוֹאִי כַלָּה.
Bo'i v'shalom ateret ba'lah, gam b'simḥah u'vetsahalah.
Tokh emunei am segulah, bo'i khallah, bo'i khallah.

לְכָה דוֹדִי לִקְרַאת כַּלָּה. פְּנֵי שַׁבָּת נְקַבְּלָה.
L'khah dodi likrat kallah. P'nei Shabbat n'kabe'lah.

Stir yourself; arouse yourself for your light has come.

Arise! Shine!

Arise! Arise! Utter a song!

The glory of the Lord has shone upon you.

Come my beloved to meet the bride; let us welcome the Shabbat!

Do not be ashamed or confused.

Why are you downcast and why are you mournful?

Even the poor amongst My people trust that the city

will be rebuilt upon its ancient site.

Come my beloved to meet the bride; let us welcome the Shabbat!

Those who despoiled you shall themselves be despoiled,

and those who devour you will be far away.

Your God will find joy in you,

just as a bridegroom joys over his bride.

Come my beloved to meet the bride; let us welcome the Shabbat!

You will spread out to the right and to the left

and show forth the Lord;

Through the hand of the son of Perets

and we will be glad and rejoice.

Come my beloved to meet the bride; let us welcome the Shabbat!

(Congregation rises and turns toward the door, as if welcoming the Shabbat as a guest)

Crown of your husband, come in peace,

with joy and good cheer,

into the midst of a faithful, chosen people.

Come, O bride! O bride, come!

Come my beloved to meet the bride; let us welcome the Shabbat!

Psalm 92

מִזְמוֹר שִׁיר לְיוֹם הַשַּׁבָּת. טוֹב לְהֹדוֹת לַייָ וּלְזַמֵּר לְשִׁמְךָ עֶלְיוֹן. לְהַגִּיד בַּבֹּקֶר חַסְדֶּךָ וֶאֱמוּנָתְךָ בַּלֵּילוֹת. עֲלֵי עָשׂוֹר וַעֲלֵי נָבֶל עֲלֵי הִגָּיוֹן בְּכִנּוֹר. כִּי שִׂמַּחְתַּנִי יְיָ בְּפָעֳלֶךָ בְּמַעֲשֵׂי יָדֶיךָ אֲרַנֵּן. מַה גָּדְלוּ מַעֲשֶׂיךָ יְיָ מְאֹד עָמְקוּ מַחְשְׁבֹתֶיךָ. אִישׁ בַּעַר לֹא יֵדָע וּכְסִיל לֹא יָבִין אֶת זֹאת. בִּפְרֹחַ רְשָׁעִים כְּמוֹ עֵשֶׂב וַיָּצִיצוּ כָּל פֹּעֲלֵי אָוֶן לְהִשָּׁמְדָם עֲדֵי עַד. וְאַתָּה מָרוֹם לְעֹלָם יְיָ. כִּי הִנֵּה אֹיְבֶיךָ יְיָ כִּי הִנֵּה אֹיְבֶיךָ יֹאבֵדוּ יִתְפָּרְדוּ כָּל פֹּעֲלֵי אָוֶן. וַתָּרֶם כִּרְאֵים קַרְנִי בַּלֹּתִי בְּשֶׁמֶן רַעֲנָן. וַתַּבֵּט עֵינִי בְּשׁוּרָי בַּקָּמִים עָלַי מְרֵעִים תִּשְׁמַעְנָה אָזְנָי. (Reader) צַדִּיק כַּתָּמָר יִפְרָח כְּאֶרֶז בַּלְּבָנוֹן יִשְׂגֶּה. שְׁתוּלִים בְּבֵית יְיָ בְּחַצְרוֹת אֱלֹהֵינוּ יַפְרִיחוּ. עוֹד יְנוּבוּן בְּשֵׂיבָה דְּשֵׁנִים וְרַעֲנַנִּים יִהְיוּ. לְהַגִּיד כִּי יָשָׁר יְיָ צוּרִי וְלֹא עַוְלָתָה בּוֹ.

Psalm 93

יְיָ מָלָךְ גֵּאוּת לָבֵשׁ, לָבֵשׁ יְיָ עֹז הִתְאַזָּר, אַף תִּכּוֹן תֵּבֵל בַּל תִּמּוֹט. נָכוֹן כִּסְאֲךָ מֵאָז, מֵעוֹלָם אָתָּה. נָשְׂאוּ נְהָרוֹת יְיָ נָשְׂאוּ נְהָרוֹת קוֹלָם יִשְׂאוּ נְהָרוֹת דָּכְיָם. (Reader) מִקֹּלוֹת מַיִם רַבִּים אַדִּירִים מִשְׁבְּרֵי יָם אַדִּיר בַּמָּרוֹם יְיָ. עֵדֹתֶיךָ נֶאֶמְנוּ מְאֹד לְבֵיתְךָ נָאֲוָה קֹדֶשׁ, יְיָ לְאֹרֶךְ יָמִים.

Revelation 15:2-4

וּכְיָם זְכוּכִית בָּלוּל בָּאֵשׁ נִרְאָה לְעֵינַי וְאֵלֶּה אֲשֶׁר גָּבְרוּ עַל הַחַיָּה וְעַל צַלְמָהּ וּמִסְפַּר שְׁמָהּ עֹמְדִים עַל יַם הַזְּכוּכִית וְכִנֹּרוֹת אֵל בְּיָדָם. אָז יָשִׁירוּ שִׁיר מֹשֶׁה עֶבֶד הָאֱלֹהִים וְשִׁיר הַשֶּׂה לֵאמֹר גְּדֹלִים וְנוֹרָאִים מַעֲשֶׂיךָ יְיָ אֱלֹהִים אֵל שַׁדַּי וּדְרָכֶיךָ אֶמֶת וָצֶדֶק מֶלֶךְ הַגּוֹיִם. מִי לֹא יִרָאֲךָ יְיָ מִי לֹא יִתֵּן כָּבוֹד לִשְׁמֶךָ קָדוֹשׁ אַתָּה לְבַדֶּךָ וְכָל הַגּוֹיִם יָבֹאוּ וְיִשְׁתַּחֲווּ לְפָנֶיךָ כִּי צִדְקָתְךָ נִגְלָתָה.

Revelation 5:11-13

אָז רָאִיתִי וְשָׁמַעְתִּי קוֹל מַלְאָכִים רַבִּים סָבִיב לַכִּסֵּא וְלַחַיּוֹת וְלַזְּקֵנִים וּמִסְפָּרָם רִבֹאוֹת רְבָבוֹת וְאַלְפֵי אֲלָפִים. וְהֵם עָנוּ בְּקוֹל רָם נָאֲוָה לַשֶּׂה הַטָּבוּחַ לָקַחַת עֹז וָעֹשֶׁר וְחָכְמָה וּגְבוּרָה וְהוֹד וְהָדָר וּבְרָכָה. וְכָל יְצוּר אֲשֶׁר בַּשָּׁמַיִם וּבָאָרֶץ וּמִתַּחַת לָאָרֶץ וַאֲשֶׁר עַל פְּנֵי הַיַּמִּים וְכֹל אֲשֶׁר בָּהֶם שָׁמַעְתִּי עֹנִים לֵאמֹר אֶל הַיֹּשֵׁב עַל הַכִּסֵּא וְאֶל הַשֶּׂה הַבְּרָכָה וְהַהוֹד וְהֶהָדָר וְהַמֶּמְשָׁלָה עַד עוֹלְמֵי עוֹלָמִים. וְאַרְבַּע הַחַיּוֹת עָנוּ אָמֵן וְהַזְּקֵנִים נָפְלוּ עַל פְּנֵיהֶם וַיִּשְׁתַּחֲווּ לְפָנָיו.

Psalm 92

A psalm, a song for the Shabbat day: It is good to give thanks to the Lord and to sing to Your Name, O Most High; to declare Your loving kindness in the morning and Your faithfulness at night, on the ten-stringed lyre and the lute, to the sound of the harp. Lord, You have made me glad through Your works; I joy in the work of Your hands. How great are Your works, O Lord! How deep Your designs! The stupid man cannot know and the fool cannot understand. When the wicked grow up like grass, and those who do evil flourish, it is that they may be destroyed forever. You are great forever. Behold Your enemies, O Lord. Behold, Your enemies will perish; all who work iniquity will be dispersed. You have exalted my strength as that of the wild ox. I have been anointed with fresh oil. My eye has seen my foes; my ear has heard my enemies. Those who are righteous flourish like the palm tree; they flourish like the cedars of Lebanon. Those who are planted in the house of the Lord shall flourish in the courts of our God. Even in their old age they will bear fruit. They will be vigorous and fresh. They will proclaim, "The Lord is just! He is my Rock; there is no wrong in Him!"

Psalm 93

The Lord is King; He is robed in majesty. The Lord is robed; He has girded Himself with strength. In this the world is firmly set; it cannot be moved. Your throne was established long ago; You are from eternity. Lord, the floods have lifted up - the floods have lifted up their voice; they have lifted up their waves. Above the sound of many waters, mighty breakers of the sea, the Lord on high is supreme. Your testimonies are very sure. Lord, Your house is adorned with holiness for all time.

Revelation 15:2-4

And I saw something like a sea of glass mingled with fire, and those who have the victory over the beast, over his image, over his mark, over the number of his name, standing on the sea of glass, having harps of God in their hands. They sing the song of Moses, the servant of God, and the song of the Lamb, saying: "Great and marvelous are Your works, Lord God Almighty! Just and true are Your ways; You are King of the ages. Who shall not fear and glorify Your Name, O Lord? For You alone are holy. All the nations shall come and worship You, for Your judgments have been made manifest."

Revelation 5:11-13

Then I looked again, and I heard the singing of thousands and tens of thousands of angels around the throne and the living beings and the elders. They sang in a mighty chorus: "The Lamb is worthy, the Lamb who was killed. He is worthy to receive power and riches and wisdom and strength and honor and glory and blessing." And then I heard every creature in heaven and on earth and under the earth and in the sea. They also sang: "Blessing and honor and glory and power belong to the One sitting on the throne and to the Lamb forever and ever."

מַעֲרִיב לְשַׁבָּת וְיוֹם טוֹב

בָּרְכוּ

(Recite standing, facing east or toward an open ark. Omit when praying without a minyan)
(Bow at בָּרְכוּ and straighten at יְיָ)

(Reader)

בָּרְכוּ אֶת יְיָ הַמְבֹרָךְ.

Bar'khu et Adonai ham'vorakh.

(Congregation then Reader)

בָּרוּךְ יְיָ הַמְבֹרָךְ לְעוֹלָם וָעֶד.

Barukh Adonai ham'vorakh l'olam va'ed.

(Silent Meditation)

יִתְבָּרַךְ וְיִשְׁתַּבַּח, וְיִתְפָּאַר וְיִתְרוֹמַם וְיִתְנַשֵּׂא שְׁמוֹ שֶׁל מֶלֶךְ מַלְכֵי הַמְּלָכִים, הַקָּדוֹשׁ בָּרוּךְ הוּא, שֶׁהוּא רִאשׁוֹן וְהוּא אַחֲרוֹן וּמִבַּלְעָדָיו אֵין אֱלֹהִים. סֹלּוּ לָרֹכֵב בָּעֲרָבוֹת, בְּיָהּ שְׁמוֹ, וְעִלְזוּ לְפָנָיו, וּשְׁמוֹ מְרוֹמָם עַל כָּל בְּרָכָה וּתְהִלָּה. בָּרוּךְ שֵׁם כְּבוֹד מַלְכוּתוֹ לְעוֹלָם וָעֶד. יְהִי שֵׁם יְיָ מְבֹרָךְ מֵעַתָּה וְעַד עוֹלָם.

בָּרוּךְ אַתָּה יְיָ, אֱלֹהֵינוּ מֶלֶךְ הָעוֹלָם, אֲשֶׁר בִּדְבָרוֹ מַעֲרִיב עֲרָבִים, בְּחָכְמָה פּוֹתֵחַ שְׁעָרִים, וּבִתְבוּנָה מְשַׁנֶּה עִתִּים, וּמַחֲלִיף אֶת הַזְּמַנִּים, וּמְסַדֵּר אֶת הַכּוֹכָבִים, בְּמִשְׁמְרוֹתֵיהֶם בָּרָקִיעַ כִּרְצוֹנוֹ. בּוֹרֵא יוֹם וָלַיְלָה, גּוֹלֵל אוֹר מִפְּנֵי חֹשֶׁךְ, וְחֹשֶׁךְ מִפְּנֵי אוֹר. וּמַעֲבִיר יוֹם וּמֵבִיא לַיְלָה, וּמַבְדִּיל בֵּין יוֹם וּבֵין לַיְלָה, יְיָ צְבָאוֹת שְׁמוֹ. אֵל חַי וְקַיָּם, תָּמִיד יִמְלוֹךְ עָלֵינוּ לְעוֹלָם וָעֶד. בָּרוּךְ אַתָּה יְיָ, הַמַּעֲרִיב עֲרָבִים.

אַהֲבַת עוֹלָם

אַהֲבַת עוֹלָם בֵּית יִשְׂרָאֵל עַמְּךָ אָהַבְתָּ, תּוֹרָה וּמִצְוֹת, חֻקִּים וּמִשְׁפָּטִים, אוֹתָנוּ לִמַּדְתָּ. עַל כֵּן יְיָ אֱלֹהֵינוּ, בְּשָׁכְבֵנוּ וּבְקוּמֵנוּ נָשִׂיחַ בְּחֻקֶּיךָ, וְנִשְׂמַח בְּדִבְרֵי תוֹרָתֶךָ וּבְמִצְוֹתֶיךָ לְעוֹלָם וָעֶד. כִּי הֵם חַיֵּינוּ וְאֹרֶךְ יָמֵינוּ, וּבָהֶם נֶהְגֶּה יוֹמָם וָלַיְלָה, וְאַהֲבָתְךָ אַל תָּסִיר מִמֶּנּוּ לְעוֹלָמִים. בָּרוּךְ אַתָּה יְיָ, אוֹהֵב עַמּוֹ יִשְׂרָאֵל.

Ahavat olam beit Yisraeil am'kha ahavtah, Torah umits'vot, ḥukim umish'patim, ohtanu lima'deta. Al kein Adonai Eloheinu, b'shakh'beinu uv'kumeinu nasi'aḥ b'ḥukeikha, v'nismaḥ b'divrei Torahtekha u'vemits'votekha l'olam va'ed. Ki heim ḥayeinu v'orekh yameinu, uvaḥem ne'geh yo'mam va'la'yla, v'ahavat'kha al tasir mimenu l'olamim. Barukh atah Adonai, oheiv amo Yisraeil.

Maariv Service for Shabbat and Festivals

Bar'khu

(Recite standing, facing east or toward an open ark. Omit when praying without a minyan)
*(Bow at **Bless** and Straighten at **Lord**)*

(Reader)
Bless the Lord, who is blessed!

(Congregation then Reader)
Blessed is the Lord, who is blessed forever and ever!

(Silent Meditation)
Blessed and praised, glorified, exalted and honored be the Name of the Supreme King of Kings, the Holy One, blessed be He. He is the first and the last, and there is no other god. Extol Him who abides in the heavens, and rejoice before the countenance of Him who is named Lord. His Name is exalted far beyond all blessings and psalms. His glorious Name and kingdom will be blessed forever and ever; let the Lord's Name be blessed both now and for all time.

Blessed are You, Lord our God, King of the universe, who at Your word brings on the evenings. With wisdom You open the gates of the heavens, and with understanding You change the times and vary the seasons. You arrange the stars in the places in the sky according to Your will. You create day and night; You roll away the light from before the darkness, and the darkness from before the light. You make the day to pass and the night to approach, and divide the day from the night. The Lord of hosts is Your Name. A God who lives and endures, may You reign over us for ever and ever. Blessed are You, Lord, who brings on the evening.

Ahavat Olam

You have loved Israel, Your people, with everlasting love. You have taught us Torah and precepts, statutes and judgments. Therefore, Lord our God, when we lie down and when we rise up, we will meditate upon Your statutes for all time and take joy in the words of Your Torah and in Your precepts, because they are our life and the length of our days. We will meditate upon them day and night, that Your love might not be removed from us through all the ages. Blessed are You, Lord, who loves Israel, Your people.

Mark 12:28-34

וְאֶחָד מִן הַסּוֹפְרִים בָּא וַיִּשְׁמַע אֹתָם נִדְבָּרִים יַחְדָּו וּבִרְאֹתוֹ כִּי הֵיטֵב עָנָה עַל דִּבְרֵיהֶם
וַיִּשְׁאָלֵהוּ מָה רֵאשִׁית כָּל הַמִּצְוֹת. וַיַּעַן יֵשׁוּעַ הָרִאשֹׁנָה הֲלֹא הִיא שְׁמַע יִשְׂרָאֵל
יְיָ אֱלֹהֵינוּ, יְיָ אֶחָד. וְאָהַבְתָּ אֵת יְיָ אֱלֹהֶיךָ, בְּכָל לְבָבְךָ, וּבְכָל נַפְשְׁךָ, וּבְכָל מְאֹדֶךָ.
וְהַשְּׁנִיָּה הֲלֹא הִיא וְאָהַבְתָּ לְרֵעֲךָ כָּמוֹךָ וְאֵין מִצְוָה גְדוֹלָה מִשְׁתַּיִם אֵלֶּה. וַיֹּאמֶר אֵלָיו
הַסּוֹפֵר אָמְנָם מוֹרִי אֱמֶת דִּבַּרְתָּ כִּי אֶחָד הוּא וְאֵין עוֹד מִלְבַדּוֹ. וּלְאַהֲבָה אֹתוֹ בְּכָל
לֵב וּבְכָל מַדָּע וּבְכָל מְאֹד וְלֶאֱהֹב אִישׁ אֶת רֵעֵהוּ כְּנַפְשׁוֹ הִיא גְדֹלָה מִכָּל עֹלָה וָזָבַח.
וַיַּרְא יֵשׁוּעַ כִּי הִשְׂכִּיל לַעֲנוֹת אֹתוֹ וַיֹּאמֶר אֵלָיו הִנְּךָ לֹא רָחוֹק מִמַּלְכוּת אֱלֹהִים וְלֹא
הֶעֱזוֹד אִישׁ לְהִתְוַכַּח עִמּוֹ בִּדְבָרִים מֵהַיּוֹם וָמָעְלָה.

שְׁמַע

(אֵל מֶלֶךְ נֶאֱמָן)
(When praying without a minyan begin by reciting:
(Recite loudly and slowly covering the eyes with the right hand)

שְׁמַע יִשְׂרָאֵל, יְיָ אֱלֹהֵינוּ, יְיָ אֶחָד.

Shema Yisraeil, Adonai Eloheinu, Adonai Eḥad.

(Recite softly and quickly without covering the eyes)

בָּרוּךְ שֵׁם כְּבוֹד מַלְכוּתוֹ לְעוֹלָם וָעֶד

Barukh shem k'vod mal'khuto l'olam va'ed.

וְאָהַבְתָּ אֵת יְיָ אֱלֹהֶיךָ, בְּכָל לְבָבְךָ, וּבְכָל נַפְשְׁךָ, וּבְכָל מְאֹדֶךָ. וְהָיוּ
הַדְּבָרִים הָאֵלֶּה, אֲשֶׁר אָנֹכִי מְצַוְּךָ הַיּוֹם, עַל לְבָבֶךָ. וְשִׁנַּנְתָּם לְבָנֶיךָ,
וְדִבַּרְתָּ בָּם בְּשִׁבְתְּךָ בְּבֵיתֶךָ, וּבְלֶכְתְּךָ בַדֶּרֶךְ וּבְשָׁכְבְּךָ, וּבְקוּמֶךָ.
וּקְשַׁרְתָּם לְאוֹת עַל יָדֶךָ, וְהָיוּ לְטֹטָפֹת בֵּין עֵינֶיךָ, וּכְתַבְתָּם עַל מְזֻזוֹת
בֵּיתֶךָ וּבִשְׁעָרֶיךָ.

V'ahav'ta eit Adonai Eloheikha, b'khol l'vavkha, uv'khol naf'shekha, uv'khol
me'odekha. V'hayu had'varim ha'eileh, asher anokhi m'tsav'kha hayom, al
l'vavekha. V'shinan'tam l'vanekha v'dibartah bam b'shiv'tekha b'veitekha,
uv'lekh'tekha vaderekh uv'shokh'bekha, uv'kumekha. Uk'shartam l'ot al
yadekha, v'hayu l'totafot bein einekha, ukh'tav'tam al mezuzot beitekha
u-visharekha.

Philippians 2:5-11

יְהֵא בָכֶם הַלֵּךְ רוּחַ זֶה אֲשֶׁר הָיָה בַּמָּשִׁיחַ יֵשׁוּעַ. הוּא אֲשֶׁר הָיָה קַיָּם בִּדְמוּת אֱלֹהִים
לֹא חָשַׁב לְשָׁלָל אֶת הֱיוֹתוֹ שָׁוֶה לֵאלֹהִים, אֶלָּא הֵרִיק אֶת עַצְמוֹ, נָטַל דְּמוּת עֶבֶד
וְנִהְיָה כִּבְנֵי אָדָם; וְכַאֲשֶׁר הָיָה בְּצוּרָתוֹ כְּאָדָם, הִשְׁפִּיל עַצְמוֹ וְצִיֵּת עַד מָוֶת, עַד מָוֶת
בַּצְּלָב. עַל כֵּן הִגְבִּיהוֹ אֱלֹהִים מְאֹד וְנָתַן לוֹ אֶת הַשֵּׁם הַנַּעֲלֶה עַל כָּל שֵׁם, לְמַעַן
תִּכְרַע בְּשֵׁם יֵשׁוּעַ כָּל בֶּרֶךְ, בַּשָּׁמַיִם וּבָאָרֶץ וּמִתַּחַת לָאָרֶץ, וְכָל לָשׁוֹן תּוֹדֶה כִּי יֵשׁוּעַ
הַמָּשִׁיחַ הוּא הָאָדוֹן, לְתִפְאֶרֶת אֱלֹהִים הָאָב.

Mark 12:28-34

Then one of the scribes came, and having heard them reasoning together, perceiving that He had answered them well, asked Him, "Which is the first commandment of all?" Yeshua answered him, "The first of all the commandments is: Hear, O Israel, the Lord our God, the Lord is one. And you shall love the Lord your God with all your heart, with all your soul, with all your mind, and with all your strength. This is the first commandment. And the second, like it, is this: You shall love your neighbor as yourself. And there is no other commandment greater than these two." So the scribe said to Him, "Well said, Rabbi. You have spoken the truth, for there is one God, and there is no other but He. And to love Him with all the heart, with all the understanding, with all the soul, and with all the strength, and to love one's neighbor as oneself, is more than all the whole burnt offerings and sacrifices." Now when Yeshua saw that the man answered Him wisely, He said to him, "You are not far from the kingdom of God." And no one ever dared to argue with Him any more in words from that day on.

Shema

(When praying without a minyan begin by reciting: **God, trustworthy King***)*

(Recite loudly and slowly covering the eyes with the right hand)

Hear, O Israel, the Lord our God, the Lord is One.

(Recite softly and quickly without covering the eyes)

Blessed is His glorious Name, whose kingdom is forever and ever.

And you shall love the Lord your God with all your heart and with all your soul and with all your strength. These words that I give to you today are to be upon your hearts. Teach them to your children. Speak of them when you sit at home and when you walk along the way, when you lie down and when you rise up. Bind them as a sign upon your hands and as frontlets between your eyes. Inscribe them on the doorposts of your house and on your gates.

Philippians 2:5-11

And let this be your true heart, as it was in Messiah Yeshua. He, who was found to be in all ways in the likeness of God, did not see being like God as a honor for Himself, so He put off His honor, and dressed Himself in the form of a servant, being in the likeness of man. And having been found in appearance as a man, He humbled Himself, and surrendered Himself up to death, to death upon the tree. Therefore, God has lifted Him up, and given to Him a name exalted above every name; that at the name Yeshua you shall bow: every knee of those in heaven, and of those in the earth, and of those under the earth. And every tongue shall swear that Yeshua the Messiah, He is the Lord, to the honor of God, the Father.

1 Corinthians 8:4-6

כִּי אֱלִיל כְּאַיִן הוּא בָּעוֹלָם וְכִי אֵין אֱלֹהִים זוּלָתִי אֶחָד. וְאַף כִּי יֵשׁ נִקְרָאִים אֱלֹהִים אִם בַּשָּׁמַיִם וְאִם בָּאָרֶץ כְּמוֹ הֵם אֱלֹהִים רַבִּים וַאֲדֹנִים רַבִּים. בְּכָל זֹאת לָנוּ רַק אֱלֹהִים אֶחָד הוּא אָבִי עַד אֲשֶׁר מִמֶּנּוּ הַכֹּל וְלוֹ אֲנַחְנוּ וְאָדוֹן אֶחָד יֵשׁוּעַ הַמָּשִׁיחַ אֲשֶׁר הַכֹּל עַל יָדוֹ וְעַל יָדוֹ גַּם אֲנַחְנוּ.

Deuteronomy 11:13-21

וְהָיָה אִם שָׁמֹעַ תִּשְׁמְעוּ אֶל מִצְוֹתַי, אֲשֶׁר אָנֹכִי מְצַוֶּה אֶתְכֶם הַיּוֹם, לְאַהֲבָה אֶת יְיָ אֱלֹהֵיכֶם, וּלְעָבְדוֹ בְּכָל לְבַבְכֶם וּבְכָל נַפְשְׁכֶם. וְנָתַתִּי מְטַר אַרְצְכֶם בְּעִתּוֹ, יוֹרֶה וּמַלְקוֹשׁ, וְאָסַפְתָּ דְגָנֶךָ וְתִירֹשְׁךָ וְיִצְהָרֶךָ. וְנָתַתִּי עֵשֶׂב בְּשָׂדְךָ לִבְהֶמְתֶּךָ, וְאָכַלְתָּ וְשָׂבָעְתָּ. הִשָּׁמְרוּ לָכֶם פֶּן יִפְתֶּה לְבַבְכֶם, וְסַרְתֶּם וַעֲבַדְתֶּם אֱלֹהִים אֲחֵרִים וְהִשְׁתַּחֲוִיתֶם לָהֶם. וְחָרָה אַף יְיָ בָּכֶם, וְעָצַר אֶת הַשָּׁמַיִם וְלֹא יִהְיֶה מָטָר, וְהָאֲדָמָה לֹא תִתֵּן אֶת יְבוּלָהּ וַאֲבַדְתֶּם מְהֵרָה מֵעַל הָאָרֶץ הַטֹּבָה אֲשֶׁר יְיָ נֹתֵן לָכֶם. וְשַׂמְתֶּם אֶת דְּבָרַי אֵלֶּה עַל לְבַבְכֶם וְעַל נַפְשְׁכֶם וּקְשַׁרְתֶּם אֹתָם לְאוֹת עַל יֶדְכֶם, וְהָיוּ לְטוֹטָפֹת בֵּין עֵינֵיכֶם. וְלִמַּדְתֶּם אֹתָם אֶת בְּנֵיכֶם, לְדַבֵּר בָּם, בְּשִׁבְתְּךָ בְּבֵיתֶךָ, וּבְלֶכְתְּךָ בַדֶּרֶךְ, וּבְשָׁכְבְּךָ וּבְקוּמֶךָ. וּכְתַבְתָּם עַל מְזוּזוֹת בֵּיתֶךָ וּבִשְׁעָרֶיךָ. לְמַעַן יִרְבּוּ יְמֵיכֶם וִימֵי בְנֵיכֶם עַל הָאֲדָמָה אֲשֶׁר נִשְׁבַּע יְיָ לַאֲבֹתֵיכֶם לָתֵת לָהֶם, כִּימֵי הַשָּׁמַיִם עַל הָאָרֶץ.

2 Timothy 2:8-13

זְכֹר אֶת יֵשׁוּעַ הַמָּשִׁיחַ שֶׁנֵּעוֹר מִן הַמֵּתִים, אֲשֶׁר הוּא מִזֶּרַע דָּוִד כִּדְבַר בְּשׂוֹרָתִי, הִיא הַבְּשׂוֹרָה שֶׁבַּעֲבוּרָהּ אֲנִי סוֹבֵל רָעוֹת עַד כְּדֵי שִׁכְתִּי בְּכְבָלִים כְּעוֹשֵׂה עָוֶל. אוּלָם דְּבַר הָאֱלֹהִים אֵינֶנּוּ אָסוּר בְּכְבָלִים. עַל כֵּן אֲנִי סוֹבֵל הַכֹּל לְמַעַן הַנִּבְחָרִים, כְּדֵי שֶׁגַּם הֵם יַשִּׂיגוּ תְשׁוּעָה בַּמָּשִׁיחַ יֵשׁוּעַ עִם כְּבוֹד עוֹלָמִים. מְהֵימָן הַדָּבָר: אִם מַתְנוּ אִתּוֹ, גַּם נִחְיֶה אִתּוֹ; אִם נַחֲזִיק מַעֲמָד, גַּם נִמְלֹךְ אִתּוֹ; אִם נִתְכַּחֵשׁ, גַּם הוּא יִתְכַּחֵשׁ לָנוּ; אִם אֵינֶנּוּ נֶאֱמָנִים, הוּא נִשְׁאָר נֶאֱמָן, כִּי לֹא יוּכַל לְהִתְכַּחֵשׁ לְעַצְמוֹ.

Numbers 15:37-41

וַיֹּאמֶר יְיָ אֶל מֹשֶׁה לֵּאמֹר: דַּבֵּר אֶל בְּנֵי יִשְׂרָאֵל וְאָמַרְתָּ אֲלֵהֶם. וְעָשׂוּ לָהֶם צִיצִת עַל כַּנְפֵי בִגְדֵיהֶם לְדֹרֹתָם, וְנָתְנוּ עַל צִיצִת הַכָּנָף פְּתִיל תְּכֵלֶת. וְהָיָה לָכֶם לְצִיצִת, וּרְאִיתֶם אֹתוֹ וּזְכַרְתֶּם אֶת כָּל מִצְוֹת יְיָ, וַעֲשִׂיתֶם אֹתָם, וְלֹא תָתוּרוּ אַחֲרֵי לְבַבְכֶם וְאַחֲרֵי עֵינֵיכֶם, אֲשֶׁר אַתֶּם זֹנִים אַחֲרֵיהֶם. לְמַעַן תִּזְכְּרוּ וַעֲשִׂיתֶם אֶת כָּל מִצְוֹתַי, וִהְיִיתֶם קְדֹשִׁים לֵאלֹהֵיכֶם. אֲנִי יְיָ אֱלֹהֵיכֶם, אֲשֶׁר הוֹצֵאתִי אֶתְכֶם מֵאֶרֶץ מִצְרַיִם, לִהְיוֹת לָכֶם לֵאלֹהִים, אֲנִי יְיָ אֱלֹהֵיכֶם.

1 Corinthians 8:4-6

For we know that an idol is nothing in the world, and that there is no other God but One. For even if there are so-called gods, whether in heaven or on earth (as there are many gods and many lords), yet for us there is only one God, the Father, from whom are all things, and we for Him; and one Lord, Yeshua the Messiah, through whom are all things, and through whom we live.

Deuteronomy 11:13-21

And if you will carefully listen to My commandments which I am commanding you today, to love the Lord your God and to serve Him with all your heart and with all your soul, then I will send rain for your land in its season, the early rain and the latter rain, that you may gather in your grain, your wine and your oil. And I will produce grass in your fields for your cattle, that you may eat and be satisfied. Take care, lest your heart be deceived, and you turn aside and serve other gods, so as to worship them. Then the Lord's anger will blaze against you; He will shut up the heavens so there will be no rain, and the land will not yield any produce, and you will perish from the good land which the Lord has given to you. Therefore, you shall put these words of mine in your heart and in your soul; you shall bind them as a sign upon your hand, and they shall be for frontlets between your eyes. Teach them to your children. Speak of them when you are sitting at home and when you walk along the way, when you lie down and when you rise up. Inscribe them on the doorposts of your house and on your gates, that your days and the days of your children may be prolonged in the land, which the Lord swore to give to your fathers, as the days of the heavens upon the earth.

2 Timothy 2:8-13

You remember that Yeshua the Messiah, who was raised from the dead, is of the seed of David. This is the Good News I have proclaimed. For, on your behalf, I have suffered trouble to overcome evil, even to the point of my being tortured in chains. But the Word of God cannot be bound by chains. For this reason I endure all the suffering, for the sake of the chosen, that they also may obtain their salvation through Yeshua the Messiah, and that they glory in the Glory of the age. This is a true saying: If we died with Him, we shall also live with Him. If we suffer with Him, we shall also reign with Him. If we deny Him, He also will deny us. If there is no faithfulness in us, He will remain faithful, for He cannot deny Himself.

Numbers 15:37-41

The Lord spoke to Moses, saying, "Speak to the children of Israel. Tell them to make for themselves tsitsit on the corners of their garments, throughout their generations, and to put a thread of blue on the tsitsit of each corner. When you look upon these tsitsit you shall remember to do all the commands of the Lord, and not to follow the desires of your heart and your eyes that lead you astray. They are a reminder to do all of My commandments, and to be holy to your God. I, the Lord your God, brought you out of the land of Egypt to be your God; I am the Lord your God."

(Reader) יְיָ אֱלֹהֵיכֶם אֱמֶת

אֱמֶת וֶאֱמוּנָה כָּל זֹאת, וְקַיָּם עָלֵינוּ, כִּי הוּא יְיָ אֱלֹהֵינוּ וְאֵין זוּלָתוֹ, וַאֲנַחְנוּ יִשְׂרָאֵל עַמּוֹ. הַפּוֹדֵנוּ מִיַּד מְלָכִים, מַלְכֵּנוּ הַגּוֹאֲלֵנוּ מִכַּף כָּל הֶעָרִיצִים. הָאֵל הַנִּפְרָע לָנוּ מִצָּרֵינוּ, וְהַמְשַׁלֵּם גְּמוּל לְכָל אֹיְבֵי נַפְשֵׁנוּ. הָעֹשֶׂה גְדֹלוֹת עַד אֵין חֵקֶר, וְנִפְלָאוֹת עַד אֵין מִסְפָּר. הַשָּׂם נַפְשֵׁנוּ בַּחַיִּים, וְלֹא נָתַן לַמּוֹט רַגְלֵנוּ. הַמַּדְרִיכֵנוּ עַל בָּמוֹת אוֹיְבֵינוּ, וַיָּרֶם קַרְנֵנוּ עַל כָּל שׂוֹנְאֵינוּ. הָעֹשֶׂה לָנוּ נִסִּים וּנְקָמָה בְּפַרְעֹה, אוֹתוֹת וּמוֹפְתִים בְּאַדְמַת בְּנֵי חָם. הַמַּכֶּה בְעֶבְרָתוֹ כָּל בְּכוֹרֵי מִצְרָיִם, וַיּוֹצֵא אֶת עַמּוֹ יִשְׂרָאֵל מִתּוֹכָם, לְחֵרוּת עוֹלָם. הַמַּעֲבִיר בָּנָיו בֵּין גִּזְרֵי יַם סוּף, אֶת רוֹדְפֵיהֶם וְאֶת שׂוֹנְאֵיהֶם, בִּתְהוֹמוֹת טִבַּע, וְרָאוּ בָנָיו גְּבוּרָתוֹ. שִׁבְּחוּ וְהוֹדוּ לִשְׁמוֹ. וּמַלְכוּתוֹ בְּרָצוֹן קִבְּלוּ עֲלֵיהֶם.

מִי כָמֹכָה

(Reader) מֹשֶׁה וּבְנֵי יִשְׂרָאֵל לְךָ עָנוּ שִׁירָה בְּשִׂמְחָה רַבָּה, וְאָמְרוּ כֻלָּם:
Moshe uv'nei Yisraeil l'kha anu shirah b'simhah rabah, v'amru khulam:

(All) מִי כָמֹכָה בָּאֵלִים יְיָ; מִי כָּמֹכָה נֶאְדָּר בַּקֹּדֶשׁ, נוֹרָא תְהִלֹּת, עֹשֵׂה פֶלֶא.
Mi khamokha ba'elim Adonai; mi khamokha nedar ba'kodesh, norah t'hilot, osei feleh.

(Reader) מַלְכוּתְךָ רָאוּ בָנֶיךָ, בּוֹקֵעַ יָם לִפְנֵי מֹשֶׁה; זֶה אֵלִי עָנוּ וְאָמְרוּ:
Mal'khutkha ra'u vanehkha, bokei'a yam lif'nei Moshe; zeh eili anu v'amru:

(All) יְיָ יִמְלֹךְ לְעוֹלָם וָעֶד.
Adonai yimlokh l'olam va'ed.

(Reader) וְנֶאֱמַר: כִּי פָדָה יְיָ אֶת יַעֲקֹב, וּגְאָלוֹ מִיַּד חָזָק מִמֶּנּוּ.
V'ne'emar: Ki fadah Adonai et Ya'akov, ug'alo miyad hazak mi'me-nu.

(All) בָּרוּךְ אַתָּה יְיָ, גָּאַל יִשְׂרָאֵל.
Barukh atah Adonai, ga'al Yisraeil.

(Reader) **The Lord your God is True**

True and trustworthy is all this. We are certain that He is the Lord our God, and no one else, and that we Israel are His people. It is He, our King, who redeemed us from the power of despots, delivered us from the grasp of all the tyrants, avenged us upon our oppressors, and requited all our mortal enemies. He did great, incomprehensible acts and countless wonders. He kept us alive, and did not let us slip. He made us tread upon the high places of our enemies, and raised our strength over all our foes. He performed for us miracles and vengeance upon Pharaoh, signs and wonders in the land of the Hamites, He smote in His wrath all the firstborn of Egypt, and brought His people Israel from their midst to enduring freedom. He made His children pass between the divided parts of the Red Sea, and engulfed their pursuers and their enemies in the depths. His children beheld His might; they gave praise and thanks to His Name, and willingly accepted His sovereignty.

Mi Khamokha

(Reader) Moses and the children of Israel sang a song to You, and with great joy they all said:

(All) "Who is like You, O Lord, among the gods? Who is like You, glorious in holiness, awesome in praise, doing wonders?"

(Reader) Your majesty was seen by Your children, as You parted the waters before Moses. They exclaimed, "This is my God" and they said:

(All) "The Lord will reign forever and ever."

(Reader) And it is said: "The Lord has set Jacob free, and has redeemed him from the hand of one who was stronger than he."

(All) Blessed are You, Lord, Redeemer of Israel!

הַשְׁכִּיבֵנוּ

הַשְׁכִּיבֵנוּ יְיָ אֱלֹהֵינוּ לְשָׁלוֹם, וְהַעֲמִידֵנוּ מַלְכֵּנוּ לְחַיִּים וּפְרוֹשׂ עָלֵינוּ סֻכַּת שְׁלוֹמֶךָ, וְתַקְּנֵנוּ בְּעֵצָה טוֹבָה מִלְּפָנֶיךָ, וְהוֹשִׁיעֵנוּ לְמַעַן שְׁמֶךָ, וְהָגֵן בַּעֲדֵנוּ, וְהָסֵר מֵעָלֵינוּ אוֹיֵב, דֶּבֶר, וְחֶרֶב, וְרָעָב, וְיָגוֹן, וְהָסֵר שָׂטָן מִלְּפָנֵינוּ וּמֵאַחֲרֵנוּ, וּבְצֵל כְּנָפֶיךָ תַּסְתִּירֵנוּ. כִּי אֵל שׁוֹמְרֵנוּ וּמַצִּילֵנוּ אָתָּה, כִּי אֵל מֶלֶךְ חַנּוּן וְרַחוּם אָתָּה, וּשְׁמוֹר צֵאתֵנוּ וּבוֹאֵנוּ, לְחַיִּים וּלְשָׁלוֹם, מֵעַתָּה וְעַד עוֹלָם. וּפְרוֹשׂ עָלֵינוּ סֻכַּת שְׁלוֹמֶךָ. בָּרוּךְ אַתָּה יְיָ, הַפּוֹרֵשׂ סֻכַּת שָׁלוֹם עָלֵינוּ וְעַל כָּל עַמּוֹ יִשְׂרָאֵל וְעַל יְרוּשָׁלָיִם.

וְשָׁמְרוּ

(All rise and remain standing through the conclusion of the עמידה)

וְשָׁמְרוּ בְנֵי יִשְׂרָאֵל אֶת הַשַּׁבָּת, לַעֲשׂוֹת אֶת הַשַּׁבָּת לְדֹרֹתָם בְּרִית עוֹלָם. בֵּינִי וּבֵין בְּנֵי יִשְׂרָאֵל אוֹת הִיא לְעוֹלָם, כִּי שֵׁשֶׁת יָמִים עָשָׂה יְיָ אֶת הַשָּׁמַיִם וְאֶת הָאָרֶץ, וּבַיּוֹם הַשְּׁבִיעִי שָׁבַת וַיִּנָּפַשׁ.

V'shamru v'nei Yisraeil et hashabbat, la'asot et hashabbat l'dorotam b'rit olam. Bei'nee u'vein b'nei Yisraeil ot hi l'olam, ki sheishet ya'mim asah Adonai et hashamayim v'et ha'arets, uvayom hash'vi'i sha'vat vayi'nafash.

(On Festivals but not Hol HaMoed add)

וַיְדַבֵּר מֹשֶׁה אֶת מֹעֲדֵי יְיָ אֶל בְּנֵי יִשְׂרָאֵל.
Va-yedabeir Moshe et mo'adei Adonai el Bnei Yisrael.

חֲצִי קַדִּישׁ

יִתְגַּדַּל וְיִתְקַדַּשׁ שְׁמֵהּ רַבָּא. (אָמֵן - Cong) בְּעָלְמָא דִּי בְרָא כִרְעוּתֵהּ, וְיַמְלִיךְ מַלְכוּתֵהּ בְּחַיֵּיכוֹן וּבְיוֹמֵיכוֹן וּבְחַיֵּי דְכָל בֵּית יִשְׂרָאֵל. בַּעֲגָלָא וּבִזְמַן קָרִיב, וְאִמְרוּ אָמֵן. (אָמֵן - Cong)

Yitgadal v'yitkadash sh'mei rabah. (Cong - Amein) B'almah di vera khir'utei, v'yamlikh mal'khutei b'hayeikhon uv'yomeikhon uv'hayei d'khal beit Yisraeil. Ba'agalah uviz'man kariv v'imru, Amein. (Cong - Amein)

(Together)

יְהֵא שְׁמֵהּ רַבָּא מְבָרַךְ לְעָלַם וּלְעָלְמֵי עָלְמַיָּא.
Y'hei sh'mei rabah m'varakh l'alam ul'al'mei al'mayah.

יִתְבָּרַךְ וְיִשְׁתַּבַּח, וְיִתְפָּאַר וְיִתְרוֹמַם וְיִתְנַשֵּׂא וְיִתְהַדָּר וְיִתְעַלֶּה וְיִתְהַלָּל שְׁמֵהּ דְּקֻדְשָׁא, בְּרִיךְ הוּא, (בְּרִיךְ הוּא - Cong)

Yit'barakh v'yish'tabah, v'yit'pa-ar v'yit'romam v'yit'nasei v'yit'hadar v'yit'aleh v'yit'halal sh'mei d'ku-deshah, b'rikh Hu, (Cong - b'rikh Hu)

**From Rosh Hashanah to Yom Kippur substitute:* *לְעֵלָּא וּלְעֵלָּא מִכָּל *l'eila u-l'eila mi-kal* — *לְעֵלָּא מִן כָּל *l'eila min kal*

בְּרְכָתָא וְשִׁירָתָא, תֻּשְׁבְּחָתָא וְנֶחֱמָתָא, דַּאֲמִירָן בְּעָלְמָא, וְאִמְרוּ אָמֵן. (אָמֵן - Cong)
bir'khatah v'shiratah, tush'bihatah v'nehematah, da'amiran b'almah, v'imru, Amein (Cong - Amein)

Hash'kivenu

Lord our God, cause us to lie down in peace; our King, make us rise up again to life. Spread over us the tabernacle of Your peace, and direct us with Your own good counsel. For Your Name's sake save us and protect us; keep every enemy, pestilence, sword, famine and sorrow far from us; remove the adversary from before us as well as from behind us, and shelter us in the shadow of Your wing. God, You are our Protector and our Deliverer; You are a gracious and compassionate God and King. Guard our going out and our coming in for life and for peace, both now and forever. Spread over us the shelter of Your peace. Blessed are You, Lord, who spreads the shelter of peace over us, over all Your people, Israel, and over Jerusalem.

V'shamru

(All rise and remain standing through the conclusion of the Amidah)

And the children of Israel will keep the Shabbat, observing the Shabbat to all generations as an everlasting covenant. It is a sign between Me and the children of Israel forever, for in six days the Lord made the heavens and the earth, and on the seventh day He ceased from work and He rested.

(On Festivals but not Hol HaMoed add)

Moses announced the Lord's festivals to the Children of Israel.

Ḥatsi Kaddish

Magnified and sanctified may God's great Name *(Cong - Amen)* be throughout the world which He has created according to His will. May He establish His kingdom in our lifetime, and during our days, and within the life of the entire house of Israel, speedily and soon; and say, *Amen. (Cong - Amen)*

(Together)

May the greatness of His Name be blessed forever and ever.

Let the Name of the Holy One, *blessed is He*, *(Cong - blessed is He)* be blessed and praised, glorified and exalted, extolled and honored, adored and lauded,

* beyond all

** From Rosh Hashanah to Yom Kippur substitute:*   **exceedingly* beyond all

of the blessings and songs, praises and consolations that are ever spoken in this world, and say, *Amen. (Cong - Amen)*

Ephesians 1:17-21

כִּי אֱלֹהֵי יֵשׁוּעַ הַמָּשִׁיחַ אֲדֹנֵנוּ אֲבִי הַכָּבוֹד יִתֵּן לָכֶם רוּחַ הַחָכְמָה וְהֶחָזוֹן לָדַעַת אֹתוֹ.
וּלְהָאִיר עֵינֵי שִׂכְלְכֶם לְהַשְׂכִּיל מָה הִיא תִּקְוַת קְרוּאָיו וּמָה חֹסֶן כְּבוֹד לִקְדֹשָׁיו בְּנַחֲלָתוֹ. וּמָה
עֹצֶם גֹּדֶל גְּבוּרָתוֹ אֲשֶׁר פָּעַל בָּנוּ הַמַּאֲמִינִים בּוֹ לְפִי תֹקֶף עֻזּוֹ. הוּא אֲשֶׁר פָּעַל בַּמָּשִׁיחַ
בַּאֲשֶׁר הֲקִימוֹ מִן הַמֵּתִים וַיּוֹשִׁיבֵהוּ לִימִינוּ בַּמָּרוֹם. גָּבוֹהַּ מִכָּל מִשְׂרָה וְשִׁלְטוֹן וּגְבוּרָה
וּמֶמְשָׁלָה וּמִכָּל אֲשֶׁר נִקְרָא בְּשֵׁם גַּם בָּעוֹלָם הַזֶּה וְגַם בָּעוֹלָם הַבָּא.

(Amidah for Weekday - see page 144; for Shabbat Shuva and Festivals - see page 166)

עמידה

(Recite standing, facing east or toward an open ark. Take three steps back, then three steps forward)

Adonai s'fatay tiftah u'fi yagid tehilatekha.   אֲדֹנָי שְׂפָתַי תִּפְתָּח וּפִי יַגִּיד תְּהִלָּתֶךָ:

אבות

(Bend the knees at בָּרוּךְ *Bow at* אַתָּה *Straighten at* יְיָ*)*

בָּרוּךְ אַתָּה יְיָ אֱלֹהֵינוּ וֵאלֹהֵי אֲבוֹתֵינוּ, אֱלֹהֵי אַבְרָהָם, אֱלֹהֵי יִצְחָק, וֵאלֹהֵי יַעֲקֹב.
הָאֵל הַגָּדוֹל הַגִּבּוֹר וְהַנּוֹרָא, אֵל עֶלְיוֹן, גּוֹמֵל חֲסָדִים טוֹבִים, וְקוֹנֵה הַכֹּל, וְזוֹכֵר
חַסְדֵי אָבוֹת אֲשֶׁר הֵבִיא, וּמֵבִיא, גּוֹאֵל לִבְנֵי בְנֵיהֶם לְמַעַן שְׁמוֹ בְּאַהֲבָה.

Barukh atah Adonai, Eloheinu veilohei avoteinu, Elohei Avraham, Elohei Yitshak,
veilohei Ya'akov. Ha'Eil hagadol hagibor v'hanorah, Eil Elyon, gomeil hasadim tovim,
v'konei hakol, v'zokheir has'dei avot, asher heivi, umeivi, go'eil liv'nei v'neihem,
l'ma'an sh'mo, b'ahavah.

(Bend the knees at בָּרוּךְ *Bow at* אַתָּה *Straighten at* יְיָ*)*

מֶלֶךְ עוֹזֵר וּמוֹשִׁיעַ וּמָגֵן. בָּרוּךְ אַתָּה יְיָ, מָגֵן אַבְרָהָם.

Melekh ozeir umoshia umagein. Barukh atah Adonai, magein Avraham.

גבורות

אַתָּה גִבּוֹר לְעוֹלָם אֲדֹנָי. מְחַיֵּה מֵתִים אַתָּה. רַב לְהוֹשִׁיעַ.

Atah gibor l'olam Adonai, m'hayei meitim atah, rav l'hoshia.

(Between Shemini Atseret and Pesah add)

Mashiv ha'ruah u'morid ha'geshem.   מַשִּׁיב הָרוּחַ וּמוֹרִיד הַגֶּשֶׁם.

מְכַלְכֵּל חַיִּים בְּחֶסֶד, מְחַיֵּה מֵתִים בְּרַחֲמִים רַבִּים, סוֹמֵךְ נוֹפְלִים, וְרוֹפֵא חוֹלִים,
וּמַתִּיר אֲסוּרִים, וּמְקַיֵּם אֱמוּנָתוֹ לִישֵׁנֵי עָפָר. מִי כָמוֹךָ בַּעַל גְּבוּרוֹת וּמִי דוֹמֶה
לָּךְ, מֶלֶךְ מֵמִית וּמְחַיֶּה וּמַצְמִיחַ יְשׁוּעָה. וְנֶאֱמָן אַתָּה לְהַחֲיוֹת מֵתִים. בָּרוּךְ אַתָּה
יְיָ, מְחַיֵּה הַמֵּתִים.

M'khalkeil hayim b'hesed, M'hayei meitim b'rahamim rabim. Someikh nof'lim, v'rofei
holim, umatir asurim, um'kayeim emunatoh lisheinei afar. Mi khamokha ba'al g'vurot,
umi do'meh lakh, melekh meimit um'hayeh umatsmiah yeshua. V'ne'eman atah
l'hahayot meitim. Barukh atah Adonai, m'hayei hameitim.

אַתָּה קָדוֹשׁ וְשִׁמְךָ קָדוֹשׁ וּקְדוֹשִׁים בְּכָל יוֹם יְהַלְלוּךָ, סֶּלָה. בָּרוּךְ אַתָּה יְיָ, הָאֵל
הַקָּדוֹשׁ.

Ephesians 1:17-21

I pray the God of our Lord Yeshua the Messiah, the Father of glory, may give to you the spirit of wisdom and revelation in the knowledge of Him. May the eyes of your understanding be enlightened that you may know what is the hope of His calling, what are the riches of the glory of His inheritance in the saints, and what is the exceeding greatness of His power toward us who believe, according to the working of His mighty power. He worked in the Messiah when He raised Him from the dead and seated Him at His right hand in the heavenly places, far above all principality and power and might and dominion, and every name that is named, not only in this age but also in that which is to come.

(עֲמִידָה *for Weekday - see page 145; for Shabbat Shuva and Festivals - see page 167)*

Amidah

(Recite standing, facing east or toward an open ark. Take three steps back, then three steps forward)

Lord, you will open my lips that my mouth may declare Your praise.

Avot

*(Bend the knees at **Blessed**, Bow at **Are You,** Straighten at **Lord**)*

Blessed are You, Lord our God and God of our fathers, God of Abraham, God of Isaac and God of Jacob. The great, mighty and awesome God, Most High God, who grants loving kindness and is Master of all, You remember the deeds of our fathers, and in Your love You have brought, and you bring, a Redeemer to their children's children for the sake of Your Name.

*(Bend the knees at **Blessed**, Bow at **Are You,** Straighten at **Lord**)*

King, Supporter, Savior and Shield. Blessed are You, Lord, Shield of Abraham.

G'vurot

Lord, You are mighty forever. You call the dead to life. You are mighty to save.

(Between Shemini Atseret and Pesah add)
You cause the wind to return and the rain to come down.

You sustain the living with loving kindness, and with great mercy You revive the dead. You uphold those who fall, heal the sick, set the captive free and keep faith with those who sleep in the dust. Lord of might, who is like You? King, who can be compared to You? You decree death and restore life, causing salvation to come forth. You are faithful to revive the dead. Blessed are You, Lord, who calls the dead to life.

You are holy, and Your Name is holy, and holy ones will proclaim Your praise daily. Blessed are You, Lord, holy God.

אַתָּה קִדַּשְׁתָּ אֶת־יוֹם הַשְּׁבִיעִי לִשְׁמֶךָ תַּכְלִית מַעֲשֵׂה שָׁמַיִם וָאָרֶץ, וּבֵרַכְתּוֹ מִכָּל־הַיָּמִים וְקִדַּשְׁתּוֹ מִכָּל־הַזְּמַנִּים, וְכֵן כָּתוּב בְּתוֹרָתֶךָ:

וַיְכֻלּוּ הַשָּׁמַיִם וְהָאָרֶץ וְכָל צְבָאָם. וַיְכַל אֱלֹהִים בַּיּוֹם הַשְּׁבִיעִי, מְלַאכְתּוֹ אֲשֶׁר עָשָׂה, וַיִּשְׁבֹּת בַּיּוֹם הַשְּׁבִיעִי, מִכָּל מְלַאכְתּוֹ אֲשֶׁר עָשָׂה. וַיְבָרֶךְ אֱלֹהִים אֶת יוֹם הַשְּׁבִיעִי וַיְקַדֵּשׁ אֹתוֹ, כִּי בוֹ שָׁבַת מִכָּל מְלַאכְתּוֹ, אֲשֶׁר בָּרָא אֱלֹהִים לַעֲשׂוֹת.

אֱלֹהֵינוּ וֵאלֹהֵי אֲבוֹתֵינוּ, רְצֵה בִמְנוּחָתֵנוּ. קַדְּשֵׁנוּ בְּמִצְוֺתֶיךָ וְתֵן חֶלְקֵנוּ בְּתוֹרָתֶךָ. שַׂבְּעֵנוּ מִטּוּבֶךָ, וְשַׂמְּחֵנוּ בִּישׁוּעָתֶךָ, וְטַהֵר לִבֵּנוּ לְעָבְדְּךָ בֶּאֱמֶת. וְהַנְחִילֵנוּ יְיָ אֱלֹהֵינוּ בְּאַהֲבָה וּבְרָצוֹן שַׁבַּת קָדְשֶׁךָ, וְיָנוּחוּ בָהּ יִשְׂרָאֵל מְקַדְּשֵׁי שְׁמֶךָ. בָּרוּךְ אַתָּה יְיָ, מְקַדֵּשׁ הַשַּׁבָּת.

אָבִינוּ

אָבִינוּ שֶׁבַּשָּׁמַיִם יִתְקַדֵּשׁ שְׁמֶךָ. תָּבֹא מַלְכוּתֶךָ יֵעָשֶׂה רְצוֹנְךָ בָּאָרֶץ כַּאֲשֶׁר נַעֲשָׂה בַּשָּׁמָיִם. תֶּן לָנוּ הַיּוֹם לֶחֶם חֻקֵּנוּ. וּסְלַח לָנוּ אֶת אַשְׁמָתֵנוּ כַּאֲשֶׁר סֹלְחִים אֲנַחְנוּ לַאֲשֶׁר אָשְׁמוּ לָנוּ. וְאַל תְּבִיאֵנוּ לִידֵי מַסָּה כִּי אִם הַצִּילֵנוּ מִן הָרָע. כִּי לְךָ הַמַּמְלָכָה וְהַגְּבוּרָה וְהַתִּפְאֶרֶת לְעוֹלְמֵי עוֹלָמִים.

רְצֵה, יְיָ אֱלֹהֵינוּ, בְּעַמְּךָ יִשְׂרָאֵל וּבִתְפִלָּתָם, וְהָשֵׁב אֶת הָעֲבוֹדָה לִדְבִיר בֵּיתֶךָ. וְאִשֵּׁי יִשְׂרָאֵל וּתְפִלָּתָם בְּאַהֲבָה תְקַבֵּל בְּרָצוֹן, וּתְהִי לְרָצוֹן תָּמִיד עֲבוֹדַת יִשְׂרָאֵל עַמֶּךָ.

(On Rosh Hodesh and Hol HaMoed Pesaḥ and Sukkot insert the appropriate blessing on page 156)

וְתֶחֱזֶינָה עֵינֵינוּ בְּשׁוּבְךָ לְצִיּוֹן בְּרַחֲמִים. בָּרוּךְ אַתָּה יְיָ, הַמַּחֲזִיר שְׁכִינָתוֹ לְצִיּוֹן.

מוֹדִים אֲנַחְנוּ

(Bend the knees at מוֹדִים אֲנַחְנוּ and straighten at יְיָ)

מוֹדִים אֲנַחְנוּ לָךְ שָׁאַתָּה הוּא יְיָ אֱלֹהֵינוּ וֵאלֹהֵי אֲבוֹתֵינוּ לְעוֹלָם וָעֶד. צוּר חַיֵּינוּ, מָגֵן יִשְׁעֵנוּ אַתָּה הוּא לְדוֹר וָדוֹר. נוֹדֶה לְּךָ וּנְסַפֵּר תְּהִלָּתֶךָ, עַל חַיֵּינוּ הַמְּסוּרִים בְּיָדֶךָ, וְעַל נִשְׁמוֹתֵינוּ הַפְּקוּדוֹת לָךְ, וְעַל נִסֶּיךָ שֶׁבְּכָל יוֹם עִמָּנוּ, וְעַל נִפְלְאוֹתֶיךָ וְטוֹבוֹתֶיךָ שֶׁבְּכָל עֵת, עֶרֶב וָבֹקֶר וְצָהֳרָיִם. הַטּוֹב כִּי לֹא כָלוּ רַחֲמֶיךָ, וְהַמְרַחֵם כִּי לֹא תַמּוּ חֲסָדֶיךָ, מֵעוֹלָם קִוִּינוּ לָךְ.

(On Ḥanukah and Purim insert the appropriate blessing on page 158)

וְעַל כֻּלָּם יִתְבָּרַךְ וְיִתְרוֹמַם שִׁמְךָ מַלְכֵּנוּ תָּמִיד לְעוֹלָם וָעֶד. וְכָל הַחַיִּים יוֹדוּךָ סֶּלָה, וִיהַלְלוּ אֶת שִׁמְךָ בֶּאֱמֶת, הָאֵל יְשׁוּעָתֵנוּ וְעֶזְרָתֵנוּ סֶלָה.

(Bend the knees at בָּרוּךְ Bow at אַתָּה Straighten at יְיָ)

בָּרוּךְ אַתָּה יְיָ, הַטּוֹב שִׁמְךָ וּלְךָ נָאֶה לְהוֹדוֹת.

שָׁלוֹם רָב

שָׁלוֹם רָב עַל יִשְׂרָאֵל עַמְּךָ תָּשִׂים לְעוֹלָם, כִּי אַתָּה הוּא מֶלֶךְ אָדוֹן לְכָל הַשָּׁלוֹם. וְטוֹב בְּעֵינֶיךָ לְבָרֵךְ אֶת עַמְּךָ יִשְׂרָאֵל בְּכָל עֵת וּבְכָל שָׁעָה בִּשְׁלוֹמֶךָ. בָּרוּךְ אַתָּה יְיָ, הַמְבָרֵךְ אֶת עַמּוֹ יִשְׂרָאֵל בַּשָּׁלוֹם.

*Shalom Rav al Yisraeil am'kha tasim l'olam,
ki atah hu Melekh Adon l'khol hashalom. V'tov b'ei-nekha l'vareikh et am'kha Yisraeil b'khol eit
uv'khal sha'ah bish'lomekha. Barukh atah Adonai, ham'vareikh et amo Yisraeil ba'shalom.*

You have sanctified to Yourself the seventh day, marking it as the end of the creation of heaven and earth; You have blessed it above all days and hallowed it above all festivals, as it is written:

Thus the heavens, and the earth, and all their hosts were finished. And on the seventh day God completed all the work in which He had been engaged, and on the seventh day He rested from all the work which He had made. And God blessed the seventh day calling it holy, for on it, He rested from all of the work which He had created.

Our God and God of our fathers, be pleased with our rest. Set us apart through Your commandments, and grant us a portion in Your Torah. Satisfy us with Your goodness, and make us glad in Your salvation. Purify our hearts to serve You in truth, and grant us, Lord our God, in love and in grace, that Your holy Shabbat remain an inheritance, and that Israel, who sanctifies Your Name, rests on it. Blessed are You, Lord, who makes the Shabbat holy.

Avinu

Our Father in Heaven, holy is Your name. Your kingdom will come; Your will shall be done, on the earth as it is in the heavens. Give us this day our daily bread. And forgive us our debts as we forgive our debtors. And lead us not into temptation, but deliver us from the evil one. For Yours is the kingdom, and the power, and the glory, forever.

Take pleasure, Lord our God, in Your people Israel, and in their prayer. Restore the service to Your most holy house, and receive Israel's offerings by fire, and their prayer with gracious love. May the worship of Your people Israel always be pleasing to You.

(On Rosh Ḥodesh and Ḥol HaMoed Pesaḥ and Sukkot insert the appropriate blessing on page 157)

May we see, with our own eyes, Your return to Tsiyon in compassion. Blessed are You, Lord, whose Presence is the restoration of Tsiyon.

Modim Anaḥnu
*(Bend the knees at **Lord, we are eternally grateful** and straighten at **Lord**)*

Lord, we are eternally grateful that You are the Lord our God and the God of our fathers. You are the strength of our life and the shield of our salvation. We will thank You from generation to generation, and we will recount Your praise; for our lives which are in Your hand; and for our souls which are in Your care; and for Your miracles which are seen every day; and for Your wondrous deeds and favors which are always with us evening, morning and noon. Beneficent One, Your compassion never fails; Merciful One, Your loving kindness never ends; You have always been our hope.

(On Ḥanukah and Purim insert the appropriate blessing on page 159)

For all these things we will bless and we will lift up Your Name, our King, always, to the end of the age, and until. All those living shall thank You and praise Your Name forever, God, for You are our salvation and help.

*(Bend the knees at **Blessed**, Bow at **Are You**, Straighten at **Lord**)*

Blessed are You, Lord, Your Name is good, and to You we are thankful.

Shalom Rav

Grant abundant peace to Israel, who will always be Your people, for You are He, King, who is Lord of all peace. May it be good in Your sight to bless Your people Israel at all times and in all hours with Your peace. Blessed are You, Lord, who is blessing His people Israel with peace.

(Add the following meditation after the עמידה)

אֱלֹהַי, נְצֹר לְשׁוֹנִי מֵרָע, וּשְׂפָתַי מִדַּבֵּר מִרְמָה, וְלִמְקַלְלַי נַפְשִׁי תִדֹּם, וְנַפְשִׁי כֶּעָפָר
לַכֹּל תִּהְיֶה. פְּתַח לִבִּי בְּתוֹרָתֶךָ, וּבְמִצְוֹתֶיךָ תִּרְדּוֹף נַפְשִׁי. וְכָל הַחוֹשְׁבִים עָלַי רָעָה,
מְהֵרָה הָפֵר עֲצָתָם וְקַלְקֵל מַחֲשַׁבְתָּם. עֲשֵׂה לְמַעַן שְׁמֶךָ, עֲשֵׂה לְמַעַן יְמִינֶךָ, עֲשֵׂה
לְמַעַן קְדֻשָּׁתֶךָ, עֲשֵׂה לְמַעַן תּוֹרָתֶךָ. לְמַעַן יֵחָלְצוּן יְדִידֶיךָ, הוֹשִׁיעָה יְמִינְךָ וַעֲנֵנִי. יִהְיוּ
לְרָצוֹן אִמְרֵי פִי וְהֶגְיוֹן לִבִּי לְפָנֶיךָ, יְיָ צוּרִי וְגוֹאֲלִי. עֹשֶׂה שָׁלוֹם בִּמְרוֹמָיו, הוּא יַעֲשֶׂה
שָׁלוֹם עָלֵינוּ, וְעַל כָּל יִשְׂרָאֵל. וְאִמְרוּ, אָמֵן.

(Remain standing)

ויכלו

וַיְכֻלּוּ הַשָּׁמַיִם וְהָאָרֶץ וְכָל צְבָאָם. וַיְכַל אֱלֹהִים בַּיּוֹם הַשְּׁבִיעִי מְלַאכְתּוֹ אֲשֶׁר עָשָׂה,
וַיִּשְׁבֹּת בַּיּוֹם הַשְּׁבִיעִי מִכָּל מְלַאכְתּוֹ אֲשֶׁר עָשָׂה. וַיְבָרֶךְ אֱלֹהִים אֶת יוֹם הַשְּׁבִיעִי,
וַיְקַדֵּשׁ אֹתוֹ, כִּי בוֹ שָׁבַת מִכָּל מְלַאכְתּוֹ, אֲשֶׁר בָּרָא אֱלֹהִים לַעֲשׂוֹת.

*Vay'khulu hashamayim v'ha'arets v'khol tseva'am. Vayikhal Elohim bayom ha'shvi'i
m'lakhto asher asah, vayish'bot, bayom hashvi'i mikal melakh'to asher asah.
Vayevarekh Elohim et yom hashvi'i vayekadeish otoh, ki vo shavat mikal m'lakhto,
asher barah Elohim la'asot.*

(Reader) בָּרוּךְ אַתָּה יְיָ, אֱלֹהֵינוּ וֵאלֹהֵי אֲבוֹתֵינוּ, אֱלֹהֵי אַבְרָהָם, אֱלֹהֵי יִצְחָק, וֵאלֹהֵי
יַעֲקֹב, הָאֵל הַגָּדוֹל הַגִּבּוֹר וְהַנּוֹרָא, אֵל עֶלְיוֹן, קוֹנֵה שָׁמַיִם וָאָרֶץ.

(Congregation then Reader) מָגֵן אָבוֹת בִּדְבָרוֹ, מְחַיֵּה מֵתִים בְּמַאֲמָרוֹ, הָאֵל הַקָּדוֹשׁ
שֶׁאֵין כָּמוֹהוּ, הַמֵּנִיחַ לְעַמּוֹ בְּיוֹם שַׁבַּת קָדְשׁוֹ, כִּי בָם רָצָה לְהָנִיחַ לָהֶם. לְפָנָיו נַעֲבוֹד
בְּיִרְאָה וָפַחַד, וְנוֹדֶה לִשְׁמוֹ בְּכָל יוֹם תָּמִיד מֵעֵין הַבְּרָכוֹת. אֵל הַהוֹדָאוֹת, אֲדוֹן
הַשָּׁלוֹם, מְקַדֵּשׁ הַשַּׁבָּת וּמְבָרֵךְ שְׁבִיעִי, וּמֵנִיחַ בִּקְדֻשָּׁה לְעַם מְדֻשְּׁנֵי עֹנֶג, זֵכֶר לְמַעֲשֵׂה
בְּרֵאשִׁית.

*Magein avot bid'varo, mihayei meitim bema'amaro, ha'eil hakadosh
sheh'ein ka'mohu, hameiniah l'amo b'yom shabbat kad'sho, ki vam ratsah l'hani'ah
la'hem. L'fanayv na'avod b'yirah vafa'had, v'nodeh lish'mo b'khol yom tamid mei'ein
ha'berakhot. Eil ha'hoda'ot, adon ha'shalom, mekadeish ha'shabbat u'mevareikh
shevi'i, u'meiniah bik'dushah l'am medush'nei oneg, zekher l'ma'asei ve'reishit.*

אלהינו ואלהי

אֱלֹהֵינוּ וֵאלֹהֵי אֲבוֹתֵינוּ רְצֵה בִמְנוּחָתֵנוּ. קַדְּשֵׁנוּ בְּמִצְוֹתֶיךָ וְתֵן חֶלְקֵנוּ בְּתוֹרָתֶךָ.
שַׂבְּעֵנוּ מִטּוּבֶךָ, וְשַׂמְּחֵנוּ בִּישׁוּעָתֶךָ, וְטַהֵר לִבֵּנוּ לְעָבְדְּךָ בֶּאֱמֶת. וְהַנְחִילֵנוּ יְיָ אֱלֹהֵינוּ
בְּאַהֲבָה וּבְרָצוֹן שַׁבַּת קָדְשֶׁךָ, וְיָנוּחוּ בָהּ יִשְׂרָאֵל מְקַדְּשֵׁי שְׁמֶךָ. בָּרוּךְ אַתָּה יְיָ, מְקַדֵּשׁ
הַשַּׁבָּת.

Eloheinu ve'lohei avoteinu r'tsei vim'nuhateinu.

*Kad'sheinu b'mits'vohtekha v'tein hehl'keinu b'toratekha. Sab'einu mituvekha,
v'sam'heinu bi'shuate'kha, v'taheir libeinu l'av'dekha be'emet. V'han'hileinu Adonai
Eloheinu b'ahavah uv'ratson shabbat kad'shekha, v'yanuhu va Yisraeil m'kad'shei
sh'mekha. Barukh atah Adonai, m'kadeish hashabbat.*

(The Full Kaddish is traditionally recited here - see page 202.
Between Pesah and Shavuot the omer is counted - see page 208. On Purim the Megillah is read - see page 208)

(Add the following meditation after the Amidah)

My God, guard my tongue from evil, and my lips from speaking falsehood. May my soul be silent to those who insult me, and may my soul be humble before all. Open my heart to Your Torah, that my soul might follow Your commands. As for all who plot evil against me, thwart their counsel and upset their plans. Do it for the sake of Your Name. Do it for the sake of Your Power. Do it for the sake of Your Holiness. Do it for the sake of Your Torah, that the one on whom You have set Your love might be rescued; save with Your right hand and answer us. May the words that proceed from my mouth and the secret thoughts that are in my heart be pleasing to You, O Lord, for You are my stronghold as well as my redeemer. May He who creates peace in His high heavens create peace for us and for all Israel, and say, "Amen."

(Remain standing)

Vay'khulu

Thus the heavens and the earth and all their hosts were finished. And on the seventh day God completed all the work in which He had been engaged, and on the seventh day He rested from all the work which He had made. And God blessed the seventh day, calling it holy, for on it He rested from all of the work which He had created.

(Reader) Blessed are You, Lord our God, and God of our fathers; God of Abraham, God of Isaac and God of Jacob, the great, the mighty and the awesome God, God Most High, Master of the heavens and earth.

(Congregation then Reader) By His word He was a shield to our fathers; at His bidding the dead are revived. The God, the Holy One, there is none to be compared to Him. The giver of rest was pleased to grant rest to His people on the holy Shabbat day. We will serve Him with awe and reverence, and every day we will give thanks to His Name for the blessings of that day. God of thanksgiving, Lord of peace, who sanctifies the Shabbat and gives blessing to the seventh day, in remembrance of the creation, grant holy, joyous rest to Your people.

Eloheinu Ve'lohei

Our God and God of our fathers, be pleased with our rest. Set us apart through Your commandments, and grant us a portion in Your Torah. Satisfy us with Your goodness, and make us glad in Your salvation. Purify our hearts to serve you in truth, and grant us, Lord our God, in love and in grace, that Your holy Shabbat remain an inheritance, and that Israel, who sanctifies Your Name, will rest on it. Blessed are You, Lord, who makes the Shabbat holy!

(The Full Kaddish is traditionally recited here - see page 203.
Between Pesah and Shavuot the omer is counted - see page 208. On Purim the Megillah is read - see page 208)

עָלֵינוּ

עָלֵינוּ לְשַׁבֵּחַ לַאֲדוֹן הַכֹּל, לָתֵת גְּדֻלָּה לְיוֹצֵר בְּרֵאשִׁית, שֶׁלֹּא עָשָׂנוּ כְּגוֹיֵי הָאֲרָצוֹת, וְלֹא שָׂמָנוּ כְּמִשְׁפְּחוֹת הָאֲדָמָה. שֶׁלֹּא שָׂם חֶלְקֵנוּ כָּהֶם, וְגֹרָלֵנוּ כְּכָל הֲמוֹנָם. (bow) וַאֲנַחְנוּ כּוֹרְעִים וּמִשְׁתַּחֲוִים וּמוֹדִים, (rise) לִפְנֵי מֶלֶךְ מַלְכֵי הַמְּלָכִים הַקָּדוֹשׁ בָּרוּךְ הוּא. שֶׁהוּא נוֹטֶה שָׁמַיִם וְיוֹסֵד אָרֶץ, וּמוֹשַׁב יְקָרוֹ בַּשָּׁמַיִם מִמַּעַל, וּשְׁכִינַת עֻזּוֹ בְּגָבְהֵי מְרוֹמִים. הוּא אֱלֹהֵינוּ אֵין עוֹד. אֱמֶת מַלְכֵּנוּ, אֶפֶס זוּלָתוֹ, כַּכָּתוּב בְּתוֹרָתוֹ: וְיָדַעְתָּ הַיּוֹם וַהֲשֵׁבֹתָ אֶל לְבָבֶךָ, כִּי יְיָ הוּא הָאֱלֹהִים בַּשָּׁמַיִם מִמַּעַל וְעַל הָאָרֶץ מִתָּחַת, אֵין עוֹד.

Aleinu l'shabeiaḥ l'adon ha'kol, lateit g'dulah l'yotser b'reishit, sheloh asanu k'goyei ha'aratsot, v'lo sa'manu k'mishp'hot ha'adamah. Sheloh sam hel'keinu kahem, v'goraleinu k'khol ha'monam. (bow) *Va'anaḥnu kor'im umish'taḥavim u'modim,* (rise) *lif'nei melekh, mal'khei ham'lakhim, hakadosh barukh hu. She'hu noteh shamayim v'yoseid arets, u'moshav y'karoh bashamayim mima'al, ush'khinat uzoh b'gav'hei m'romim. Hu Eloheinu ein od. Emet mal'keinu efes zulatoh, kakatuv b'torato: v'yada'tah ha'yom vahasheivota el l'vavekha, ki Adonai hu ha'Elohim bashamayim mima'al, v'al ha'arets mitaḥat, ein od.*

עַל כֵּן נְקַוֶּה לְּךָ יְיָ אֱלֹהֵינוּ לִרְאוֹת מְהֵרָה בְּתִפְאֶרֶת עֻזֶּךָ, לְהַעֲבִיר גִּלּוּלִים מִן הָאָרֶץ, וְהָאֱלִילִים כָּרוֹת יִכָּרֵתוּן, לְתַקֵּן עוֹלָם בְּמַלְכוּת שַׁדַּי. וְכָל בְּנֵי בָשָׂר יִקְרְאוּ בִשְׁמֶךָ, לְהַפְנוֹת אֵלֶיךָ כָּל רִשְׁעֵי אָרֶץ. יַכִּירוּ וְיֵדְעוּ כָּל יוֹשְׁבֵי תֵבֵל, כִּי לְךָ תִכְרַע כָּל בֶּרֶךְ, תִּשָּׁבַע כָּל לָשׁוֹן. לְפָנֶיךָ יְיָ אֱלֹהֵינוּ יִכְרְעוּ וְיִפֹּלוּ, וְלִכְבוֹד שִׁמְךָ יְקָר יִתֵּנוּ. וִיקַבְּלוּ כֻלָּם אֶת עֹל מַלְכוּתֶךָ. וְתִמְלוֹךְ עֲלֵיהֶם מְהֵרָה לְעוֹלָם וָעֶד. כִּי הַמַּלְכוּת שֶׁלְּךָ הִיא, וּלְעוֹלְמֵי עַד תִּמְלוֹךְ בְּכָבוֹד.

(Reader) כַּכָּתוּב בְּתוֹרָתֶךָ, יְיָ יִמְלֹךְ לְעוֹלָם וָעֶד.

(Congregation) וְנֶאֱמַר, וְהָיָה יְיָ לְמֶלֶךְ עַל כָּל הָאָרֶץ, בַּיּוֹם הַהוּא יִהְיֶה יְיָ אֶחָד, וּשְׁמוֹ אֶחָד.

(Reader) Kakatuv b'Toratekhah: Adonai yimlokh l'olam va'ed.

(Congregation) V'ne'emar v'hayah Adonai l'melekh al kal ha'arets, bayom hahu yih'yeh Adonai eḥad, ush'mo eḥad.

Philippians 2:9-11

עַל כֵּן הִגְבִּיהוּ אֱלֹהִים מְאֹד וְנָתַן לוֹ אֶת הַשֵּׁם הַנַּעֲלֶה עַל כָּל שֵׁם, לְמַעַן תִּכְרַע בְּשֵׁם יֵשׁוּעַ כָּל בֶּרֶךְ, בַּשָּׁמַיִם וּבָאָרֶץ וּמִתַּחַת לָאָרֶץ, וְכָל לָשׁוֹן תּוֹדֶה כִּי יֵשׁוּעַ הַמָּשִׁיחַ הוּא הָאָדוֹן, לְתִפְאֶרֶת אֱלֹהִים הָאָב.

Aleinu

It is our duty to give praise to the Lord of all, to ascribe greatness to Him who is the Creator from the beginning; for He has not made us like the nations of the other lands and He has not placed us like the families of the earth. He did not make our portion to be like theirs, nor our lot like that of all their multitudes. *(bow)* And therefore we bend the knee and bow, *(rise)* and acknowledge before the supreme King of kings, the Holy One, blessed be He, that He stretches forth the heavens and lays the foundations of the earth, and the seat of His glory is in the high heavens; the presence of His majesty is in the lofty heights. He is our God; there is no other. He is our King, truly, there is none beside Him, just as it is written in His Torah: "You shall know this day, and keep it in your heart, that the Lord, He is God in heaven above and on the earth beneath: There is none else."

Since we trust in You, Lord our God, may we soon behold the glory of Your might. When You remove the abominations from the earth and all idolatry is banished; when all the world will be made perfect under the reign of the Almighty, and all the children of men will call on Your Name, and all the wicked of the earth will be turned to You. May all the inhabitants of the world realize and know that every knee must bend and every tongue must swear allegiance to You. Lord our God, may they bend the knee and worship before You and give honor to the glory of Your Name. May they accept the yoke of Your kingdom, and may You establish Your reign over them quickly, forever and to eternity. The kingdom is Yours, and to all eternity You will reign in glory.

(Reader) As it is written in Your Torah: The Lord will reign forever and ever.

(Congregation) And it is said: And the Lord shall be King over all the earth; on that day the Lord will be One and His Name One.

Philippians 2:9-11

Therefore, God has lifted Him up, and given to Him a name exalted above every name; that at the name Yeshua you shall bow: every knee of those in heaven, and of those in the earth, and of those under the earth. And every tongue shall swear that Yeshua the Messiah, He is the Lord, to the honor of God, the Father.

קדיש יתום

(Mourners and those observing Yartseit)

יִתְגַּדַּל וְיִתְקַדַּשׁ שְׁמֵהּ רַבָּא. (אָמֵן - Cong) בְּעָלְמָא דִי בְרָא כִרְעוּתֵהּ,
וְיַמְלִיךְ מַלְכוּתֵהּ בְּחַיֵּיכוֹן וּבְיוֹמֵיכוֹן וּבְחַיֵּי דְכָל בֵּית יִשְׂרָאֵל. בַּעֲגָלָא וּבִזְמַן
קָרִיב, וְאִמְרוּ אָמֵן. (אָמֵן - Cong)

Yitgadal v'yitkadash sh'mei rabah. (Cong - Amein) B'almah di vera khir'utei,
v'yamlikh mal'khutei b'hayeikhon uv'yomeikhon uv'hayei d'khal beit Yisraeil.
Ba'agalah uviz'man kariv v'imru, Amein. (Cong - Amein)

(Congregation and Mourners together)

יְהֵא שְׁמֵהּ רַבָּא מְבָרַךְ לְעָלַם וּלְעָלְמֵי עָלְמַיָּא.

Y'hei sh'mei rabah m'varakh l'alam ul'al'mei al'mayah.

(Mourners)

יִתְבָּרַךְ וְיִשְׁתַּבַּח, וְיִתְפָּאַר וְיִתְרוֹמַם וְיִתְנַשֵּׂא וְיִתְהַדָּר וְיִתְעַלֶּה וְיִתְהַלָּל שְׁמֵהּ
דְּקֻדְשָׁא, בְּרִיךְ הוּא, (בְּרִיךְ הוּא - Cong)

Yit'barakh v'yish'tabah, v'yit'pa-ar v'yit'romam v'yit'nasei v'yit'hadar
v'yit'aleh v'yit'halal sh'mei d'ku-deshah, b'rikh Hu, (Cong - b'rikh Hu)

*לְעֵלָּא מִן כָּל   l'eila min kal

בִּרְכָתָא וְשִׁירָתָא, תֻּשְׁבְּחָתָא וְנֶחֱמָתָא, דַּאֲמִירָן בְּעָלְמָא,
וְאִמְרוּ אָמֵן. (אָמֵן - Cong)

bir'khatah v'shiratah, tush'behatah v'nehematah, da'amiran b'almah,
v'imru, Amein. (Cong - Amein)

יְהֵא שְׁלָמָא רַבָּא מִן שְׁמַיָּא וְחַיִּים עָלֵינוּ וְעַל כָּל יִשְׂרָאֵל,
וְאִמְרוּ אָמֵן. (אָמֵן - Cong)

Y'hei sh'lamah rabah min sh'mayah v'hayim aleinu v'al kal Yisraeil, v'imru,
Amein. (Cong - Amein)

עֹשֶׂה שָׁלוֹם בִּמְרוֹמָיו הוּא יַעֲשֶׂה שָׁלוֹם עָלֵינוּ וְעַל כָּל יִשְׂרָאֵל,
וְאִמְרוּ אָמֵן. (אָמֵן - Cong)

Oseh shalom bim'romav hu ya'aseh shalom aleinu v'al kal Yisraeil, v'imru,
Amein. (Cong - Amein)

אַל תִּירָא מִפַּחַד פִּתְאֹם, וּמִשֹּׁאַת רְשָׁעִים כִּי תָבֹא. עֻצוּ עֵצָה וְתֻפָר, דַּבְּרוּ
דָבָר וְלֹא יָקוּם, כִּי עִמָּנוּ אֵל. וְעַד זִקְנָה אֲנִי הוּא, וְעַד שֵׂיבָה אֲנִי אֶסְבֹּל,
אֲנִי עָשִׂיתִי וַאֲנִי אֶשָּׂא, וַאֲנִי אֶסְבֹּל וַאֲמַלֵּט.

Kaddish Yatom

(Mourners and those observing Yartseit)

Magnified and sanctified may God's great Name *(Cong - Amen)* be throughout the world which He has created according to His will. May He establish His kingdom in our lifetime, and during our days, and within the life of the entire house of Israel, speedily and soon; and say, *Amen. (Cong - Amen)*

(Congregation and Mourners together)

May the greatness of His Name be blessed forever and ever.

(Mourners)

Let the Name of the Holy One, *blessed is He*, *(Cong - blessed is He)* be blessed and praised, glorified and exalted, extolled and honored, adored and lauded,

* beyond all

**From Rosh Hashanah to Yom Kippur substitute:*   **exceedingly* beyond all

of the blessings and songs, praises and consolations that are ever spoken in this world, and say, *Amen. (Cong - Amen)*

May there be abundant peace from heaven, and life for us and for all Israel, and say, *Amen. (Cong - Amen)*

May He who creates peace in His high heavens create peace for us and for all Israel, and say, *Amen. (Cong - Amen)*

Do not fear sudden terror, or the storm that strikes the wicked. Form your plot, it will fail; lay your plan, it will not succeed; for God is with us. "When you are old I will be the same; I will sustain you even when your hair has turned gray. I have made you, and I will bear you! I will sustain you and save you!"

Ephesians 1:3-10

בָּרוּךְ הָאֱלֹהִים אֲבִי אֲדוֹנֵנוּ יֵשׁוּעַ הַמָּשִׁיחַ, אֲשֶׁר בֵּרַךְ אוֹתָנוּ בְּכָל בְּרָכָה
רוּחָנִית בַּשָּׁמַיִם, בַּמָּשִׁיחַ, כְּשֵׁם שֶׁבָּחַר אוֹתָנוּ בּוֹ בְּטֶרֶם הוּסַד תֵּבֵל, לִהְיוֹת
קְדוֹשִׁים וּבְלִי דֹפִי לְפָנָיו בְּאַהֲבָה. הוּא יָעַד אוֹתָנוּ לִהְיוֹת לוֹ לְבָנִים עַל־יְדֵי
יֵשׁוּעַ הַמָּשִׁיחַ, כְּחֶפֶץ רְצוֹנוֹ, לִתְהִלַּת כָּבוֹד עַל חַסְדּוֹ אֲשֶׁר הֶעֱנִיק לָנוּ
בָּאֲהוּבוֹ, שֶׁבְּדָמוֹ יֵשׁ לָנוּ הַפְּדוּת, סְלִיחַת הַחֲטָאִים כְּפִי עֹשֶׁר חֶסֶד הָאֱלֹהִים.
אֶת הַחֶסֶד הַזֶּה הוּא הִשְׁפִּיעַ עָלֵינוּ בִּמְלוֹא חָכְמָה וּבִינָה, וְהוֹדִיעַ לָנוּ אֶת
סוֹד רְצוֹנוֹ כְּפִי חֶפְצוֹ, אֶת הַתָּכְנִית שֶׁהִקְדִּים וְעָרַךְ בּוֹ הַתָּכְנִית לְקַבֵּץ אֶת
הַכֹּל בַּמָּשִׁיחַ בִּמְלֹאת הָעִתִּים, אֶת מַה שֶׁבַּשָּׁמַיִם וְאֶת מַה שֶׁבָּאָרֶץ.

אדון עולם

אֲדוֹן עוֹלָם אֲשֶׁר מָלַךְ, בְּטֶרֶם כָּל יְצִיר נִבְרָא.
לְעֵת נַעֲשָׂה בְחֶפְצוֹ כֹּל, אֲזַי מֶלֶךְ שְׁמוֹ נִקְרָא.

Adon olam, asher malakh, b'terem kal y'tsir niv'ra.
L'eit na'asah v'ḥeftso kol, azai melekh sh'mo nikra.

וְאַחֲרֵי כִּכְלוֹת הַכֹּל, לְבַדּוֹ יִמְלוֹךְ נוֹרָא.
וְהוּא הָיָה, וְהוּא הֹוֶה, וְהוּא יִהְיֶה, בְּתִפְאָרָה.

V'aḥarei kikhlot hakol, l'vado yimlokh nora.
V'hu hayah v'hu hove, v'hu yih'yeh, b'tifara.

וְהוּא אֶחָד וְאֵין שֵׁנִי, לְהַמְשִׁיל לוֹ לְהַחְבִּירָה.
בְּלִי רֵאשִׁית בְּלִי תַכְלִית, וְלוֹ הָעֹז וְהַמִּשְׂרָה.

V'hu eḥad v'ein sheini, l'hamshil lo l'haḥbirah.
B'li rei'shit b'li takhlit, v'lo ha'oz v'hamisrah.

וְהוּא אֵלִי וְחַי גֹּאֲלִי, וְצוּר חֶבְלִי בְּעֵת צָרָה.
וְהוּא נִסִּי וּמָנוֹס לִי, מְנָת כּוֹסִי בְּיוֹם אֶקְרָא.

V'hu Eli v'ḥai go'ali, v'tsur ḥevli b'eit tsarah.
V'hu nis'i u'manos li, m'nat kosi b'yom ekra.

בְּיָדוֹ אַפְקִיד רוּחִי, בְּעֵת אִישַׁן וְאָעִירָה.
וְעִם רוּחִי גְּוִיָּתִי, יְיָ לִי וְלֹא אִירָא.

B'yado af'kid ruḥi, b'eit ishan, v'a'irah.
V'im ruḥi g'vi'yati, Adonai li v'lo ira.

Ephesians 1:3-10

Blessed be the God and Father of our Lord Yeshua the Messiah,
who has blessed us in Messiah with every spiritual blessing in the heavenly places.

He chose us in Messiah before the foundation of the world
to be holy and blameless before Him in love.

He destined us for adoption as His children through Messiah Yeshua,
according to the good pleasure of His will.

To the praise of His glorious grace
which He has freely bestowed on us in the Beloved.

In Him we have redemption through His blood, the forgiveness of our trespasses,
according to the riches of His grace that He lavished on us.

With all wisdom and insight He has made known to us the mystery of His will,
according to His good pleasure that He set forth in Messiah.

A plan He has made for the fullness of time, to gather up all things in Him,
things in heaven and things on earth.

Adon Olam

Lord of the world, King supreme
Before anything was formed, He alone reigned.
When, by His will, all things were created,
His sovereign Name was made known.

And at the end, when all things cease to be
The exalted God alone will still be King.
He was, and He is,
and He will be forever glorious.

He is one, and there is no second
to compare Him to or to place next to Him.
He has no beginning and no end;
Power and dominion are His.

He is my living God who saves,
My rock when troubles and sorrows are mine;
My banner and my strong refuge,
My bounteous portion whenever I call.

I give my soul into His care,
For He is near when I sleep and when I wake.
With my soul, my body too;
God is with me, I shall not be afraid.

Erev Shabbat Blessings in the Home

Traditional Candle Lighting Blessing

בָּרוּךְ אַתָּה יְיָ אֱלֹהֵינוּ מֶלֶךְ הָעוֹלָם, אֲשֶׁר קִדְּשָׁנוּ בְּמִצְוֹתָיו, וְצִוָּנוּ לְהַדְלִיק נֵר שֶׁל שַׁבָּת.

Barukh atah Adonai Eloheinu Melekh Ha'Olam

asher kid'shanu b'mitsvotav v'tsivanu l'hadlik ner shel Shabbat.

Messianic Jewish Candle Lighting Blessing

בָּרוּךְ אַתָּה יְיָ אֱלֹהֵינוּ מֶלֶךְ הָעוֹלָם, אֲשֶׁר קִדְּשָׁנוּ בִּדְבָרוֹ, וְנָתַן לָנוּ אֶת יֵשׁוּעַ מְשִׁיחֵנוּ, וְצִוָּנוּ לִהְיוֹת אוֹר לָעוֹלָם.

Barukh atah Adonai Eloheinu Melekh Ha'Olam asher kid'shanu bidvaro, v'natan lanu et Yeshua Meshiḥeinu, v'tsivanu l'hiyot or l'olam.

שלום עליכם

שָׁלוֹם עֲלֵיכֶם, מַלְאֲכֵי הַשָּׁרֵת, מַלְאֲכֵי עֶלְיוֹן,

Shalom aleikhem mal'akhei hashareit,

מִמֶּלֶךְ מַלְכֵי הַמְּלָכִים, הַקָּדוֹשׁ בָּרוּךְ הוּא.

mal'akhei Elyon, mimelekh Malkhei ham'lakhim, Hakadosh barukh hu.

בּוֹאֲכֶם לְשָׁלוֹם, מַלְאֲכֵי הַשָּׁלוֹם, מַלְאֲכֵי עֶלְיוֹן,

Boakhem l'shalom, mal'akhei hashalom,

מִמֶּלֶךְ מַלְכֵי הַמְּלָכִים, הַקָּדוֹשׁ בָּרוּךְ הוּא.

mal'akhei Elyon, mimelekh Malkhei ham'lakhim, Hakadosh barukh hu.

בָּרְכוּנִי לְשָׁלוֹם, מַלְאֲכֵי הַשָּׁלוֹם, מַלְאֲכֵי עֶלְיוֹן,

Barkhuni l'shalom, mal'akhei hashalom,

מִמֶּלֶךְ מַלְכֵי הַמְּלָכִים, הַקָּדוֹשׁ בָּרוּךְ הוּא.

mal'akhei Elyon, mimelekh Malkhei ham'lakhim, Hakadosh barukh hu.

צֵאתְכֶם לְשָׁלוֹם, מַלְאֲכֵי הַשָּׁלוֹם, מַלְאֲכֵי עֶלְיוֹן,

Tseitkhem l'shalom, mal'akhei hashalom,

מִמֶּלֶךְ מַלְכֵי הַמְּלָכִים, הַקָּדוֹשׁ בָּרוּךְ הוּא.

mal'akhei Elyon, mimelekh Malkhei ham'lakhim, Hakadosh barukh hu.

אשת חיל

(Traditionally Proverbs 31 is read here by the husband to his wife - see page 216)

ברכת הבנים

For Boys: יְשִׂמְךָ אֱלֹהִים כְּאֶפְרַיִם וְכִמְנַשֶּׁה.

Y'simkha Elohim k'Efrayim v'khi Menashe.

For Girls: יְשִׂמֵךְ אֱלֹהִים כְּשָׂרָה רִבְקָה רָחֵל וְלֵאָה.

Y'simeikh Elohim k'Sara Rivka Raḥeil v'Leiah.

Y'varekh'kha Adonai v'yishm'rekha. יְבָרֶכְךָ יְיָ וְיִשְׁמְרֶךָ.

Ya-eir Adonai panav eilekha vihuneka. יָאֵר יְיָ פָּנָיו אֵלֶיךָ וִיחֻנֶּךָּ.

יִשָּׂא יְיָ פָּנָיו אֵלֶיךָ וְיָשֵׂם לְךָ שָׁלוֹם.

Yisa Adonai panav eilekha v'yaseim l'kha shalom.

Erev Shabbat Blessings in the Home

Traditional Candle Lighting Blessing

Blessed are You, Lord our God, King of the Universe, who has sanctified us with His commandments, and commanded us to light the Shabbat lights.

Messianic Jewish Candle Lighting Blessing

Blessed are You, Lord our God, King of the Universe, who has sanctified us with his word, and has given us Yeshua our Messiah, and commanded us to be light to the world.

Shalom Aleikhem

Peace be unto you, messengers who serve; messengers of the Almighty,
the sovereign King of kings, the Holy One, blessed is He.

Come in peace, you messengers of peace, messengers of the Almighty,
the sovereign King of kings, the Holy One, blessed is He.

Bless us with peace, you messengers of peace, messengers of the Almighty,
the sovereign King of kings, the Holy One, blessed is He.

Leave us in peace, you messengers of peace, messengers of the Almighty,
the sovereign King of kings, the Holy One, blessed is He.

Eishet Ḥayil

(Traditionally Proverbs 31 is read here by the husband to his wife - see page 217)

Blessing the Children

For Boys: May God make you like Ephraim and Manasseh.

For Girls: May God make you like Sarah, Rebekah, Rachel and Leah.

The Lord bless you and keep you!
The Lord make His face to shine upon you and be gracious unto you!
The Lord turn His face unto you, and give you peace!

קדוש לקבלת שבת

(Quietly : ‏וַיְהִי עֶרֶב וַיְהִי בֹקֶר) יוֹם הַשִּׁשִּׁי. וַיְכֻלּוּ הַשָּׁמַיִם וְהָאָרֶץ וְכָל צְבָאָם. וַיְכַל אֱלֹהִים בַּיּוֹם הַשְּׁבִיעִי מְלַאכְתּוֹ אֲשֶׁר עָשָׂה, וַיִּשְׁבֹּת בַּיּוֹם הַשְּׁבִיעִי מִכָּל מְלַאכְתּוֹ אֲשֶׁר עָשָׂה. וַיְבָרֶךְ אֱלֹהִים אֶת יוֹם הַשְּׁבִיעִי וַיְקַדֵּשׁ אֹתוֹ, כִּי בוֹ שָׁבַת מִכָּל מְלַאכְתּוֹ אֲשֶׁר בָּרָא אֱלֹהִים לַעֲשׂוֹת.

(Quietly: *Vay'hi erev vay'hi voker*) *yom hashishi. Vay'khulu hashamayim v'ha'arets v'khol ts'vaam. Vay'khal Elohim bayom hashvi'i m'lakhto asher asah, va'yishbot bayom hashvi'i mikal melakhto asher asah. Vaye'va-rekh Elohim et yom hashvi'i vay'kadeish otoh, ki vo shavat mikol melakh'to asher barah Elohim la'asot.*

בָּרוּךְ אַתָּה יְיָ אֱלֹהֵינוּ מֶלֶךְ הָעוֹלָם, בּוֹרֵא פְּרִי הַגָּפֶן.

Barukh atah Adonai Eloheinu Melekh Ha'Olam, borei p'ri hagafen.

בָּרוּךְ אַתָּה יְיָ אֱלֹהֵינוּ מֶלֶךְ הָעוֹלָם, אֲשֶׁר קִדְּשָׁנוּ בְּמִצְוֹתָיו וְרָצָה בָנוּ, וְשַׁבַּת קָדְשׁוֹ בְּאַהֲבָה וּבְרָצוֹן הִנְחִילָנוּ זִכָּרוֹן לְמַעֲשֵׂה בְרֵאשִׁית. כִּי הוּא יוֹם תְּחִלָּה לְמִקְרָאֵי קֹדֶשׁ, זֵכֶר לִיצִיאַת מִצְרָיִם. כִּי בָנוּ בָחַרְתָּ וְאוֹתָנוּ קִדַּשְׁתָּ, מִכָּל הָעַמִּים, וְשַׁבַּת קָדְשְׁךָ בְּאַהֲבָה וּבְרָצוֹן הִנְחַלְתָּנוּ. בָּרוּךְ אַתָּה יְיָ, מְקַדֵּשׁ הַשַּׁבָּת.

Barukh atah Adonai Eloheinu Melekh Ha'Olam, asher kid'shanu b'mitsvotav v'ratsah vanu, v'shabbat kadsho b'ahavah uv'ratson hin'hilanu zikaron lema'aseih v'reishit. Ki hu yom t'heelah l'mikra'ei kodesh, zeikher litsi'at mits'rayim. Ki vanu vaḥar'tah v'otanu kidash'ta mikal ha'amim, v'shabbat kad'shekha b'ahavah uv'ratson hin'ḥal-tanu. Baruch atah Adonai, m'kadeish ha'shabbat.

נטילת ידים

(It is an ancient Jewish tradition for a person to wash their hands before eating bread. Using a cup or traditional handwashing vessel, wash first the right hand, fully washing from the wrist down to the fingertips, then the left hand, alternating hands until both have been washed three times, then say the blessing, It is traditional not to speak after washing until one recites the Motsi)

בָּרוּךְ אַתָּה יְיָ אֱלֹהֵינוּ מֶלֶךְ הָעוֹלָם, אֲשֶׁר קִדְּשָׁנוּ בְּמִצְוֹתָיו, וְצִוָּנוּ עַל נְטִילַת יָדַיִם.

Barukh atah Adonai, Eloheinu Melekh Ha'Olam, asher kid'shanu b'mitsvotav, v'tsivanu al netilat yadayim

מוציא

בָּרוּךְ אַתָּה יְיָ אֱלֹהֵינוּ מֶלֶךְ הָעוֹלָם, הַמּוֹצִיא לֶחֶם מִן הָאָרֶץ.

Barukh atah Adonai Eloheinu Melekh Ha'Olam, hamotsi leḥem min ha'arets.

Kiddush for Erev Shabbat

(Quietly: And there was evening and there was morning) the sixth day. And thus the heavens, and the earth, and all their hosts were finished. And on the seventh day God completed all the work in which He had been engaged, and on the seventh day He rested from all the work which He had made. And God blessed the seventh day calling it holy, for on it He rested from all of the work which He had created.

Blessed are You, Lord our God, King of the Universe, who creates the fruit of the vine.

Blessed are You, Lord our God, King of the Universe, who was pleased with us, and who has set us apart with His commandments. In love and in favor He has given us His holy Shabbat as a part of our inheritance; a remembrance of the creation. The Shabbat is first among all the days of holy assembly to recall the exodus from Egypt. Surely You have chosen us; You have set us apart from all other peoples, and in love and favor You have given us Your holy Shabbat as an inheritance. Blessed are You, Lord, who has made the Shabbat holy.

Blessing for Washing Hands

(It is an ancient Jewish tradition for a person to wash their hands before eating bread. Using a cup or traditional handwashing vessel, wash first the right hand, fully washing from the wrist down to the fingertips, then the left hand, alternating hands until both have been washed three times, then say the blessing, It is traditional not to speak after washing until one recites the Motsi)

Blessed are You, Lord our God, King of the Universe, who has sanctified us with His commandments and has commanded us regarding washing our hands.

Motsi

Blessed are You, Lord our God, King of the Universe, who brings forth bread from the earth.

שחרית לשבת ויום טוב

(Preliminary blessings and prayers for the morning are found on page 128)

Psalm 30

מִזְמוֹר שִׁיר חֲנֻכַּת הַבַּיִת לְדָוִד. אֲרוֹמִמְךָ יְיָ כִּי דִלִּיתָנִי, וְלֹא שִׂמַּחְתָּ אֹיְבַי לִי. יְיָ
אֱלֹהָי, שִׁוַּעְתִּי אֵלֶיךָ וַתִּרְפָּאֵנִי. יְיָ הֶעֱלִיתָ מִן שְׁאוֹל נַפְשִׁי, חִיִּיתַנִי מִיָּרְדִי בוֹר. זַמְּרוּ
לַיְיָ חֲסִידָיו, וְהוֹדוּ לְזֵכֶר קָדְשׁוֹ. כִּי רֶגַע בְּאַפּוֹ, חַיִּים בִּרְצוֹנוֹ, בָּעֶרֶב יָלִין בֶּכִי וְלַבֹּקֶר
רִנָּה. וַאֲנִי אָמַרְתִּי בְשַׁלְוִי, בַּל אֶמּוֹט לְעוֹלָם. יְיָ בִּרְצוֹנְךָ הֶעֱמַדְתָּה לְהַרְרִי עֹז, הִסְתַּרְתָּ
פָנֶיךָ, הָיִיתִי נִבְהָל. אֵלֶיךָ יְיָ אֶקְרָא, וְאֶל אֲדֹנָי אֶתְחַנָּן. מַה בֶּצַע בְּדָמִי, בְּרִדְתִּי אֶל
שָׁחַת, הֲיוֹדְךָ עָפָר הֲיַגִּיד אֲמִתֶּךָ. שְׁמַע יְיָ וְחָנֵּנִי, יְיָ הֱיֵה עֹזֵר לִי.
(Reader) הָפַכְתָּ מִסְפְּדִי לְמָחוֹל לִי, פִּתַּחְתָּ שַׂקִּי וַתְּאַזְּרֵנִי שִׂמְחָה. לְמַעַן יְזַמֶּרְךָ כָבוֹד
וְלֹא יִדֹּם, יְיָ אֱלֹהַי לְעוֹלָם אוֹדֶךָּ.

קדיש יתום *(Sephardic Version)*

(Mourners and those observing Yartseit)

יִתְגַּדַּל וְיִתְקַדַּשׁ שְׁמֵהּ רַבָּא. (אָמֵן - Cong) בְּעָלְמָא דִּי בְרָא כִרְעוּתֵהּ, וְיַמְלִיךְ מַלְכוּתֵהּ
וְיַצְמַח פּוּרְקָנֵהּ וִיקָרֵב מְשִׁיחֵהּ. בְּחַיֵּיכוֹן וּבְיוֹמֵיכוֹן וּבְחַיֵּי דְכָל בֵּית יִשְׂרָאֵל. בַּעֲגָלָא
וּבִזְמַן קָרִיב, וְאִמְרוּ אָמֵן. (אָמֵן - Cong)

Yitgadal v'yitkadash sh'mei rabah. (Cong - Amein) B'almah di vera khir'utei, v'yamlikh
mal'khutei v'yats'mah pur'kanei vikareiv m'shiheih. B'hayeikhon uv'yomeikhon uv'hayei d'khal
beit Yisraeil. Ba'agala uviz'man kariv v'imru, Amein. (Cong - Amein)

(Congregation and Mourners together)

יְהֵא שְׁמֵהּ רַבָּא מְבָרַךְ לְעָלַם וּלְעָלְמֵי עָלְמַיָּא.

Y'hei sh'mei rabah m'varakh l'alam ul'al'mei al'mayah.

(Mourners)

יִתְבָּרַךְ וְיִשְׁתַּבַּח, וְיִתְפָּאַר וְיִתְרוֹמַם וְיִתְנַשֵּׂא וְיִתְהַדָּר וְיִתְעַלֶּה וְיִתְהַלָּל שְׁמֵהּ דְּקֻדְשָׁא,
בְּרִיךְ הוּא, (בְּרִיךְ הוּא - Cong)

Yit'barakh v'yish'tabah, v'yit'pa-ar v'yit'romam v'yit'nasei v'yit'hadar v'yit'aleh v'yit'halal
sh'mei d'ku-deshah, b'rikh Hu, (Cong - b'rikh Hu)

l'eila min kal לְעֵלָּא מִן כָּל*

*From Rosh Hashanah to Yom Kippur substitute: *l'eila u-l'eila mi-kal* לְעֵלָּא וּלְעֵלָּא מִכָּל*

בִּרְכָתָא וְשִׁירָתָא, תֻּשְׁבְּחָתָא וְנֶחֱמָתָא, דַּאֲמִירָן בְּעָלְמָא, וְאִמְרוּ אָמֵן. (אָמֵן - Cong)
bir'khatah v'shiratah, tush'behatah v'nehematah, da'amiran b'almah, v'imru, Amein.
(Cong - Amein)

יְהֵא שְׁלָמָא רַבָּא מִן שְׁמַיָּא וְחַיִּים עָלֵינוּ וְעַל כָּל יִשְׂרָאֵל, וְאִמְרוּ אָמֵן. (אָמֵן - Cong)
Y'hei sh'lamah rabah min sh'mayah v'hayim aleinu v'al kal Yisraeil, v'imru, Amein.
(Cong - Amein)

עֹשֶׂה שָׁלוֹם בִּמְרוֹמָיו הוּא יַעֲשֶׂה שָׁלוֹם עָלֵינוּ וְעַל כָּל יִשְׂרָאֵל,
וְאִמְרוּ אָמֵן. (אָמֵן - Cong)
Oseh shalom bim'romav hu ya'aseh shalom aleinu v'al kal Yisraeil, v'imru, amein.
(Cong - Amein)

Morning Service for Shabbat & Festivals

(Preliminary blessings and prayers for the morning are found on page 129)

Psalm 30

A psalm, a song by David for the dedication of the house: I will extol You, O Lord, for You have lifted me up; You have not allowed my enemies to rejoice over me. Lord God, I called to You and You healed me. Lord, You lifted my soul from Sheol; You kept me alive so that I would not go down to the pit. Sing to the Lord you righteous, and give thanks by remembering His holy Name. His anger is but for a moment; His favor lasts for a lifetime. There may be sorrow in the night, but rejoicing comes with the dawn. In my strength I thought, "I cannot be shaken." Lord, because of Your favor my mountain was established as a stronghold, but when You hid Your face from me I was troubled. Lord God, I will cry to You, and will say to my God, "What profit is there in my blood if I were to die? Will the dust give You thanks? Will it tell of Your faithfulness? Hear me, O Lord, and have mercy on me; Lord, You are my help." So You changed my mourning into dancing. You removed my sackcloth and have clothed me with joy. Therefore, my soul will praise You; it will not be silent. Lord God, I will thank You forever.

Kaddish Yatom *(Sephardic Version)*

(Mourners and those observing Yartseit)

Magnified and sanctified may God's great Name *(Cong - Amen)* be throughout the world which He has created according to His will. May He establish His kingdom, bring forth His redemption and hasten the coming of His Moshiach. May this be in our lifetime, and during our days, and within the life of the entire house of Israel, speedily and soon; and say, *Amen. (Cong - Amen)*

(Congregation and Mourners together)

May the greatness of His Name be blessed forever and ever.

(Mourners)

Let the Name of the Holy One, *blessed is He, (Cong - blessed is He)* be blessed and praised, glorified and exalted, extolled and honored, adored and lauded,

* beyond all

**From Rosh Hashanah to Yom Kippur substitute:*   **exceedingly* beyond all

of the blessings and songs, praises and consolations that are ever spoken in this world, and say, *Amen. (Cong - Amen)*

May there be abundant peace from heaven, and life for us and for all Israel, and say, *Amen. (Cong - Amen)*

May He who creates peace in His high heavens create peace for us and for all Israel, and say, *Amen. (Cong - Amen)*

פסוקי דזמרה

ברוך שאמר

בָּרוּךְ שֶׁאָמַר וְהָיָה הָעוֹלָם, בָּרוּךְ הוּא. בָּרוּךְ עֹשֶׂה בְרֵאשִׁית, בָּרוּךְ אוֹמֵר וְעֹשֶׂה, בָּרוּךְ גּוֹזֵר וּמְקַיֵּם, בָּרוּךְ מְרַחֵם עַל הָאָרֶץ, בָּרוּךְ מְרַחֵם עַל הַבְּרִיּוֹת, בָּרוּךְ מְשַׁלֵּם שָׂכָר טוֹב לִירֵאָיו, בָּרוּךְ חַי לָעַד וְקַיָּם לָנֶצַח, בָּרוּךְ פּוֹדֶה וּמַצִּיל, בָּרוּךְ שְׁמוֹ. בָּרוּךְ אַתָּה יְיָ אֱלֹהֵינוּ מֶלֶךְ הָעוֹלָם, הָאֵל הָאָב הָרַחֲמָן, הַמְהֻלָּל בְּפִי עַמּוֹ, מְשֻׁבָּח וּמְפֹאָר בִּלְשׁוֹן חֲסִידָיו וַעֲבָדָיו, וּבְשִׁירֵי דָוִד עַבְדֶּךָ. נְהַלֶּלְךָ יְיָ אֱלֹהֵינוּ בִּשְׁבָחוֹת וּבִזְמִרוֹת, וּנְגַדֶּלְךָ וּנְשַׁבֵּחֲךָ וּנְפָאֶרְךָ וְנַזְכִּיר שִׁמְךָ, וְנַמְלִיכְךָ, מַלְכֵּנוּ אֱלֹהֵינוּ,

(Reader) יָחִיד, חֵי הָעוֹלָמִים, מֶלֶךְ מְשֻׁבָּח וּמְפֹאָר עֲדֵי עַד שְׁמוֹ הַגָּדוֹל. בָּרוּךְ אַתָּה יְיָ, מֶלֶךְ מְהֻלָּל בַּתִּשְׁבָּחוֹת.

1 Chronicles 16:8-36

הוֹדוּ לַיְיָ קִרְאוּ בִשְׁמוֹ, הוֹדִיעוּ בָעַמִּים עֲלִילֹתָיו. שִׁירוּ לוֹ, זַמְּרוּ לוֹ, שִׂיחוּ בְּכָל נִפְלְאֹתָיו. הִתְהַלְלוּ בְּשֵׁם קָדְשׁוֹ, יִשְׂמַח לֵב מְבַקְשֵׁי יְיָ. דִּרְשׁוּ יְיָ וְעֻזּוֹ, בַּקְּשׁוּ פָנָיו תָּמִיד. זִכְרוּ נִפְלְאֹתָיו אֲשֶׁר עָשָׂה, מֹפְתָיו וּמִשְׁפְּטֵי פִיהוּ. זֶרַע יִשְׂרָאֵל עַבְדּוֹ, בְּנֵי יַעֲקֹב בְּחִירָיו. הוּא יְיָ אֱלֹהֵינוּ, בְּכָל הָאָרֶץ מִשְׁפָּטָיו.

זִכְרוּ לְעוֹלָם בְּרִיתוֹ, דָּבָר צִוָּה לְאֶלֶף דּוֹר. אֲשֶׁר כָּרַת אֶת אַבְרָהָם, וּשְׁבוּעָתוֹ לְיִצְחָק. וַיַּעֲמִידֶהָ לְיַעֲקֹב לְחֹק, לְיִשְׂרָאֵל בְּרִית עוֹלָם. לֵאמֹר לְךָ אֶתֵּן אֶרֶץ כְּנָעַן, חֶבֶל נַחֲלַתְכֶם. בִּהְיוֹתְכֶם מְתֵי מִסְפָּר, כִּמְעַט וְגָרִים בָּהּ. וַיִּתְהַלְּכוּ מִגּוֹי אֶל גּוֹי, וּמִמַּמְלָכָה אֶל עַם אַחֵר. לֹא הִנִּיחַ לְאִישׁ לְעָשְׁקָם, וַיּוֹכַח עֲלֵיהֶם מְלָכִים. אַל תִּגְּעוּ בִמְשִׁיחָי, וּבִנְבִיאַי אַל תָּרֵעוּ.

שִׁירוּ לַיְיָ כָּל הָאָרֶץ, בַּשְּׂרוּ מִיּוֹם אֶל יוֹם יְשׁוּעָתוֹ. סַפְּרוּ בַגּוֹיִם אֶת כְּבוֹדוֹ, בְּכָל הָעַמִּים נִפְלְאוֹתָיו. כִּי גָדוֹל יְיָ וּמְהֻלָּל מְאֹד, וְנוֹרָא הוּא עַל כָּל אֱלֹהִים.

(Reader) כִּי כָּל אֱלֹהֵי הָעַמִּים אֱלִילִים, וַיְיָ שָׁמַיִם עָשָׂה. הוֹד וְהָדָר לְפָנָיו, עֹז וְחֶדְוָה בִּמְקֹמוֹ. הָבוּ לַיְיָ מִשְׁפְּחוֹת עַמִּים, הָבוּ לַיְיָ כָּבוֹד וָעֹז. הָבוּ לַיְיָ כְּבוֹד שְׁמוֹ, שְׂאוּ מִנְחָה וּבֹאוּ לְפָנָיו, הִשְׁתַּחֲווּ לַיְיָ בְּהַדְרַת קֹדֶשׁ.

חִילוּ מִלְּפָנָיו כָּל הָאָרֶץ, אַף תִּכּוֹן תֵּבֵל בַּל תִּמּוֹט. יִשְׂמְחוּ הַשָּׁמַיִם וְתָגֵל הָאָרֶץ, וְיֹאמְרוּ בַגּוֹיִם יְיָ מָלָךְ. יִרְעַם הַיָּם וּמְלוֹאוֹ, יַעֲלֹץ הַשָּׂדֶה וְכָל אֲשֶׁר בּוֹ. אָז יְרַנְּנוּ עֲצֵי הַיָּעַר, מִלְּפְנֵי יְיָ, כִּי בָא לִשְׁפּוֹט אֶת הָאָרֶץ. הוֹדוּ לַיְיָ כִּי טוֹב, כִּי לְעוֹלָם חַסְדּוֹ. וְאִמְרוּ הוֹשִׁיעֵנוּ אֱלֹהֵי יִשְׁעֵנוּ, וְקַבְּצֵנוּ וְהַצִּילֵנוּ מִן הַגּוֹיִם, לְהֹדוֹת לְשֵׁם קָדְשֶׁךָ, לְהִשְׁתַּבֵּחַ בִּתְהִלָּתֶךָ. בָּרוּךְ יְיָ אֱלֹהֵי יִשְׂרָאֵל מִן הָעוֹלָם וְעַד הָעֹלָם, וַיֹּאמְרוּ כָל הָעָם, אָמֵן וְהַלֵּל לַיְיָ.

Pesukei DeZimrah
Barukh She'amar

Blessed is He who spoke the world into being, blessed is He. Blessed is He who was in the beginning. Blessed is He who spoke and it was. Blessed is He who decrees and is faithful. Blessed is He who shows mercy to the world. Blessed is He who shows mercy to all creatures. Blessed is He who rewards those who fear Him with good. Blessed is He who lives and has existed forever and to all eternity. Blessed is He who redeems and saves, bless His Name. Blessed are You, Lord our God, King of the universe, God, Father of mercy, who is praised by the mouth of Your people; extolled and glorified by the tongue of Your righteous servants. Lord our God, we give You praise through the songs of David, Your servant. Through his hymns and psalms we will exalt, and honor and glorify You. We will declare Your name; declaring You King, our King, our God. You alone, O King, are the life of the universe; the greatness of Your Name will be praised and glorified forever and ever. Blessed are You, Lord, King who is praised in song.

1 Chronicles 16:8-36

Give thanks to the Lord; call on His Name. Make His deeds known among the peoples. Sing to Him, praise Him, speak of His wondrous deeds. Glory in the Holy Name; let those who seek the Lord with their heart rejoice. Seek the Lord and His strength; seek His face always. Remember the wonders and the marvels He has done; the judgments of His mouth. O seed of Israel, His servant, children of Jacob, His chosen; He is the Lord our God. His judgments are in the whole earth.

Remember His covenant forever. The word He promised will last for a thousand generations; the oath which He declared to Abraham and to Isaac. He confirmed it as a statute to Jacob; to Israel as a covenant forever, saying, "I will give you the land of Canaan as a part of your inheritance." While you were very few in number and strangers in it; while you went about from nation to nation and from kingdom to kingdom He permitted no one to harm you. He warned kings concerning you: "Do not touch My anointed; do not cause harm to My prophets."

Let all the earth sing to the Lord; declare His salvation from day to day. Speak to the nations of His glory; to the peoples of His wonders. For great is the Lord who is worthy of praise; He is to be feared above all gods. For the gods of the peoples are mere idols, but the Lord made the heavens. Beauty and majesty are found in His countenance; in His place are found strength and joy. Ascribe to the Lord, O families of peoples, ascribe to the Lord glory and strength. Give honor to the Name of the Lord; bring an offering when you come before Him. Worship the Lord who is clothed in holiness.

Tremble before Him all the earth, for the world is firmly established. It shall not be moved. The heavens will rejoice and the earth will be glad, and they will say among the nations, "The Lord is King." The sea in all its fullness will roar; the field and all that is in it will rejoice; the trees of the forest will sing to the Lord who comes to rule the world. Give thanks to the Lord, who is good; His loving kindness is everlasting. Say, "Lord of our salvation, save us. Gather us together and deliver us from the nations, that we might give thanks to Your holy Name; that we might triumph in Your praise." Bless the Lord God of Israel, from eternity and to eternity. And all the people said, "Amen," and they praised the Lord.

(Reader) רוֹמְמוּ יְיָ אֱלֹהֵינוּ וְהִשְׁתַּחֲווּ לַהֲדֹם רַגְלָיו, קָדוֹשׁ הוּא. רוֹמְמוּ יְיָ אֱלֹהֵינוּ וְהִשְׁתַּחֲווּ לְהַר קָדְשׁוֹ, כִּי קָדוֹשׁ יְיָ אֱלֹהֵינוּ.

Rom'mu Adonai Eloheinu v'hishtaḥavu lahadom raglav kadosh hu. Rom'mu Adonai Eloheinu v'hish'taḥavu lehar kadsho, ki kadosh Adonai Eloheinu.

וְהוּא רַחוּם, יְכַפֵּר עָוֹן, וְלֹא יַשְׁחִית, וְהִרְבָּה לְהָשִׁיב אַפּוֹ, וְלֹא יָעִיר כָּל חֲמָתוֹ. אַתָּה יְיָ, לֹא תִכְלָא רַחֲמֶיךָ מִמֶּנִּי, חַסְדְּךָ וַאֲמִתְּךָ תָּמִיד יִצְּרוּנִי. זְכֹר רַחֲמֶיךָ יְיָ וַחֲסָדֶיךָ, כִּי מֵעוֹלָם הֵמָּה. תְּנוּ עֹז לֵאלֹהִים, עַל יִשְׂרָאֵל גַּאֲוָתוֹ, וְעֻזּוֹ בַּשְּׁחָקִים. נוֹרָא אֱלֹהִים מִמִּקְדָּשֶׁיךָ, אֵל יִשְׂרָאֵל, הוּא נֹתֵן עֹז וְתַעֲצֻמוֹת לָעָם, בָּרוּךְ אֱלֹהִים. אֵל נְקָמוֹת יְיָ, אֵל נְקָמוֹת הוֹפִיעַ. הִנָּשֵׂא שֹׁפֵט הָאָרֶץ, הָשֵׁב גְּמוּל עַל גֵּאִים. לַיְיָ הַיְשׁוּעָה, עַל עַמְּךָ בִרְכָתֶךָ פֶּלָה.

(Reader) יְיָ צְבָאוֹת עִמָּנוּ, מִשְׂגָּב לָנוּ, אֱלֹהֵי יַעֲקֹב סֶלָה. יְיָ צְבָאוֹת, אַשְׁרֵי אָדָם בֹּטֵחַ בָּךְ. יְיָ הוֹשִׁיעָה הַמֶּלֶךְ יַעֲנֵנוּ, בְיוֹם קָרְאֵנוּ.

הוֹשִׁיעָה אֶת עַמֶּךָ, וּבָרֵךְ אֶת נַחֲלָתֶךָ, וּרְעֵם וְנַשְּׂאֵם עַד הָעוֹלָם. נַפְשֵׁנוּ חִכְּתָה לַיְיָ, עֶזְרֵנוּ וּמָגִנֵּנוּ הוּא. כִּי בוֹ יִשְׂמַח לִבֵּנוּ, כִּי בְשֵׁם קָדְשׁוֹ בָטָחְנוּ. יְהִי חַסְדְּךָ יְיָ עָלֵינוּ, כַּאֲשֶׁר יִחַלְנוּ לָךְ. הַרְאֵנוּ יְיָ חַסְדֶּךָ, וְיֶשְׁעֲךָ תִּתֶּן לָנוּ. קוּמָה עֶזְרָתָה לָּנוּ, וּפְדֵנוּ לְמַעַן חַסְדֶּךָ. אָנֹכִי יְיָ אֱלֹהֶיךָ, הַמַּעַלְךָ מֵאֶרֶץ מִצְרָיִם, הַרְחֶב פִּיךָ וַאֲמַלְאֵהוּ. אַשְׁרֵי הָעָם שֶׁכָּכָה לּוֹ, אַשְׁרֵי הָעָם שֶׁיְיָ אֱלֹהָיו.

(Reader) וַאֲנִי בְּחַסְדְּךָ בָטַחְתִּי, יָגֵל לִבִּי בִּישׁוּעָתֶךָ, אָשִׁירָה לַיְיָ, כִּי גָמַל עָלָי.

Psalm 19

לַמְנַצֵּחַ מִזְמוֹר לְדָוִד: הַשָּׁמַיִם מְסַפְּרִים כְּבוֹד אֵל וּמַעֲשֵׂה יָדָיו מַגִּיד הָרָקִיעַ. יוֹם לְיוֹם יַבִּיעַ אֹמֶר וְלַיְלָה לְּלַיְלָה יְחַוֶּה דָּעַת. אֵין אֹמֶר וְאֵין דְּבָרִים בְּלִי נִשְׁמָע קוֹלָם. בְּכָל הָאָרֶץ יָצָא קַוָּם וּבִקְצֵה תֵבֵל מִלֵּיהֶם, לַשֶּׁמֶשׁ שָׂם אֹהֶל בָּהֶם. וְהוּא כְּחָתָן יֹצֵא מֵחֻפָּתוֹ יָשִׂישׂ כְּגִבּוֹר לָרוּץ אֹרַח. מִקְצֵה הַשָּׁמַיִם מוֹצָאוֹ וּתְקוּפָתוֹ עַל קְצוֹתָם וְאֵין נִסְתָּר מֵחַמָּתוֹ. תּוֹרַת יְיָ תְּמִימָה מְשִׁיבַת נָפֶשׁ עֵדוּת יְיָ נֶאֱמָנָה מַחְכִּימַת פֶּתִי. פִּקּוּדֵי יְיָ יְשָׁרִים מְשַׂמְּחֵי לֵב מִצְוַת יְיָ בָּרָה מְאִירַת עֵינָיִם. יִרְאַת יְיָ טְהוֹרָה עוֹמֶדֶת לָעַד מִשְׁפְּטֵי יְיָ אֱמֶת, צָדְקוּ יַחְדָּו. הַנֶּחֱמָדִים מִזָּהָב וּמִפַּז רָב וּמְתוּקִים מִדְּבַשׁ וְנֹפֶת צוּפִים. גַּם עַבְדְּךָ נִזְהָר בָּהֶם בְּשָׁמְרָם עֵקֶב רָב. שְׁגִיאוֹת מִי יָבִין מִנִּסְתָּרוֹת נַקֵּנִי. גַּם מִזֵּדִים חֲשֹׂךְ עַבְדֶּךָ אַל יִמְשְׁלוּ בִי, אָז אֵיתָם, וְנִקֵּיתִי מִפֶּשַׁע רָב.

(Reader) יִהְיוּ לְרָצוֹן אִמְרֵי פִי, וְהֶגְיוֹן לִבִּי לְפָנֶיךָ, יְיָ צוּרִי וְגֹאֲלִי.

Exalt the Lord our God, who is holy, and worship at His footstool. Exalt the Lord our God, and worship at his holy mountain, for the Lord our God is holy.

He is full of mercy and will forgive our trespasses, and will not destroy. Often He will turn His anger away, and He will not allow His wrath to break forth. Lord, You will not withhold Your mercy from me; Your loving kindness and faithfulness will always guard me. Lord, remember Your mercy and Your compassion which have always been Yours. Honor God, who rules over Israel; who is glorified in the heavens. Lord, You are revered in Your sanctuary, for the God of Israel gives strength and power to His people. Blessed be God; for salvation belongs to the Lord. Your blessings be upon Your people. The Lord of Hosts is with us; the God of Jacob is our stronghold. Lord of Hosts, happy is the man who trusts in You. Lord of salvation, may the King answer us in the day we call.

Save Your people and bless Your inheritance; always watch over them and sustain them. Our soul waited for the Lord; He is our strength and our shield. Our heart will find joy in Him, for our trust is in His holy Name. Lord, allow Your loving kindness to rest on us, for our trust is found in You. Lord, show us Your mercy, and grant us Your salvation. Because of Your loving kindness, come to our aid and set us free. "I am the Lord your God who took you out of the Land of Egypt; open your mouth wide and I will fill it." The people who are in this situation shall be glad, for happy are the people whose God is the Lord. I have put my trust in Your loving kindness; my heart shall rejoice in Your salvation. I will sing to the Lord, for He has treated me with kindness.

Psalm 19

A Psalm of David, for the song leader: The heavens declare the glory of God; the expanse of heaven speaks of the work of His hands. Day after day and night after night speech pours forth, revealing knowledge. We say, "There is no speech! There are no words!" for their voice is unheard. Yet their message has gone through all the earth; and it will be so till the end of the world. He set the heavens as the dwelling place for the sun, which is like a bridegroom coming out of his chamber; like an athlete who rejoices in the running of the course. It sets out from one end of heaven, and passes round to the other end; the Lord's testimony is able to be trusted; its wisdom is simple. The Lord's statutes are right; they make the heart glad. The Lord's commandment is clear, bringing light to the eyes. Fear of the Lord is pure; it endures for all time. The judgments of the Lord are completely true and righteous; they are more desirable than gold, even refined gold. They are sweeter than honey that has come from the honeycomb. In them Your servant is warned, for in keeping them there is great reward. Who will be able to know his own errors? Do not hold me guilty for unknown sins, and keep Your servant from sins of presumption. Do not allow them to rule over me. Only then will I be blameless; clear of all transgression. May the words that proceed from my mouth and the secret thoughts that are in my heart be pleasing to You, O Lord, for You are my stronghold as well as my redeemer.

Psalm 34

לְדָוִד בְּשַׁנּוֹתוֹ אֶת טַעְמוֹ לִפְנֵי אֲבִימֶלֶךְ, וַיְגָרְשֵׁהוּ וַיֵּלַךְ.   אֲבָרְכָה אֶת יְיָ
בְּכָל עֵת, תָּמִיד תְּהִלָּתוֹ בְּפִי.   בַּיְיָ תִּתְהַלֵּל נַפְשִׁי, יִשְׁמְעוּ עֲנָוִים וְיִשְׂמָחוּ.
גַּדְּלוּ לַיְיָ אִתִּי וּנְרוֹמְמָה שְׁמוֹ יַחְדָּו.   דָּרַשְׁתִּי אֶת יְיָ וְעָנָנִי וּמִכָּל מְגוּרוֹתַי
הִצִּילָנִי.   הִבִּיטוּ אֵלָיו וְנָהָרוּ, וּפְנֵיהֶם אַל יֶחְפָּרוּ.   זֶה עָנִי קָרָא וַיְיָ שָׁמֵעַ,
וּמִכָּל צָרוֹתָיו הוֹשִׁיעוֹ.   חֹנֶה מַלְאַךְ יְיָ סָבִיב לִירֵאָיו וַיְחַלְּצֵם.   טַעֲמוּ וּרְאוּ
כִּי טוֹב יְיָ, אַשְׁרֵי הַגֶּבֶר יֶחֱסֶה בּוֹ.   יְראוּ אֶת יְיָ קְדֹשָׁיו כִּי אֵין מַחְסוֹר
לִירֵאָיו.   כְּפִירִים רָשׁוּ וְרָעֵבוּ וְדֹרְשֵׁי יְיָ לֹא יַחְסְרוּ כָל טוֹב. לְכוּ בָנִים שִׁמְעוּ
לִי, יִרְאַת יְיָ אֲלַמֶּדְכֶם.   מִי הָאִישׁ הֶחָפֵץ חַיִּים, אֹהֵב יָמִים לִרְאוֹת טוֹב.
נְצֹר לְשׁוֹנְךָ מֵרָע וּשְׂפָתֶיךָ מִדַּבֵּר מִרְמָה.   סוּר מֵרָע וַעֲשֵׂה טוֹב, בַּקֵּשׁ
שָׁלוֹם וְרָדְפֵהוּ.   עֵינֵי יְיָ אֶל צַדִּיקִים, וְאָזְנָיו אֶל שַׁוְעָתָם: פְּנֵי יְיָ בְּעֹשֵׂי רָע,
לְהַכְרִית מֵאֶרֶץ זִכְרָם.   צָעֲקוּ וַיְיָ שָׁמֵעַ וּמִכָּל צָרוֹתָם הִצִּילָם.   קָרוֹב יְיָ
לְנִשְׁבְּרֵי לֵב, וְאֶת דַּכְּאֵי רוּחַ יוֹשִׁיעַ. רַבּוֹת רָעוֹת צַדִּיק וּמִכֻּלָּם יַצִּילֶנּוּ יְיָ.
שֹׁמֵר כָּל עַצְמוֹתָיו, אַחַת מֵהֵנָּה לֹא נִשְׁבָּרָה. תְּמוֹתֵת רָשָׁע רָעָה, וְשֹׂנְאֵי
צַדִּיק יֶאְשָׁמוּ.

(Reader)   פּוֹדֶה יְיָ נֶפֶשׁ עֲבָדָיו, וְלֹא יֶאְשְׁמוּ כָּל הַחֹסִים בּוֹ.

Psalm 90

תְּפִלָּה לְמֹשֶׁה אִישׁ הָאֱלֹהִים, אֲדֹנָי מָעוֹן אַתָּה הָיִיתָ לָּנוּ בְּדֹר וָדֹר.   בְּטֶרֶם
הָרִים יֻלָּדוּ וַתְּחוֹלֵל אֶרֶץ וְתֵבֵל, וּמֵעוֹלָם עַד עוֹלָם אַתָּה אֵל.   תָּשֵׁב אֱנוֹשׁ
עַד דַּכָּא, וַתֹּאמֶר שׁוּבוּ בְנֵי אָדָם.   כִּי אֶלֶף שָׁנִים בְּעֵינֶיךָ כְּיוֹם אֶתְמוֹל
כִּי יַעֲבֹר וְאַשְׁמוּרָה בַלָּיְלָה.   זְרַמְתָּם, שֵׁנָה יִהְיוּ, בַּבֹּקֶר כֶּחָצִיר יַחֲלֹף.
בַּבֹּקֶר יָצִיץ וְחָלָף לָעֶרֶב יְמוֹלֵל וְיָבֵשׁ.   כִּי כָלִינוּ בְאַפֶּךָ וּבַחֲמָתְךָ נִבְהָלְנוּ.
שַׁתָּ עֲוֹנֹתֵינוּ לְנֶגְדֶּךָ עֲלֻמֵנוּ לִמְאוֹר פָּנֶיךָ.   כִּי כָל יָמֵינוּ פָּנוּ בְעֶבְרָתֶךָ כִּלִּינוּ
שָׁנֵינוּ כְמוֹ הֶגֶה.   יְמֵי שְׁנוֹתֵינוּ בָהֶם שִׁבְעִים שָׁנָה, וְאִם בִּגְבוּרֹת שְׁמוֹנִים
שָׁנָה, וְרָהְבָּם עָמָל וָאָוֶן, כִּי גָז חִישׁ וַנָּעֻפָה.   מִי יוֹדֵעַ עֹז אַפֶּךָ, וּכְיִרְאָתְךָ
עֶבְרָתֶךָ.   לִמְנוֹת יָמֵינוּ כֵּן הוֹדַע וְנָבִא לְבַב חָכְמָה.   שׁוּבָה יְיָ עַד מָתַי
וְהִנָּחֵם עַל עֲבָדֶיךָ.   שַׂבְּעֵנוּ בַבֹּקֶר חַסְדֶּךָ, וּנְרַנְּנָה וְנִשְׂמְחָה בְּכָל יָמֵינוּ
שַׂמְּחֵנוּ כִּימוֹת עִנִּיתָנוּ שְׁנוֹת רָאִינוּ רָעָה.

(Reader)   יֵרָאֶה אֶל עֲבָדֶיךָ פָעֳלֶךָ וַהֲדָרְךָ עַל בְּנֵיהֶם.   וִיהִי נֹעַם אֲדֹנָי אֱלֹהֵינוּ
עָלֵינוּ, וּמַעֲשֵׂה יָדֵינוּ כּוֹנְנָה עָלֵינוּ, וּמַעֲשֵׂה יָדֵינוּ כּוֹנְנֵהוּ.

Psalm 34

A song of David, when he feigned madness before Avimelech, who then drove him out, and he departed: I will bless the Lord at all times; His song is always in my mouth. My soul makes its boast in the Lord; those who are humble hear and are glad. Exalt the Lord with me; let us tell of His Name together. I called to the Lord and He answered me; He delivered me from all my fears. Those who looked to Him are glad; they will never be put to shame. In poverty the poor cried out, and the Lord heard; He saved him from all of his troubles. The Angel of the Lord is around those who fear Him, and He rescues them. Look, see the goodness of the Lord; happy is the one who trusts Him. Fear the Lord, you righteous; those who fear Him want for nothing. Young lions may suffer want and hunger, but those who seek the Lord shall want for no good thing. Come children, come listen to me; I will teach you the fear of the Lord. Who is the man that desires to live and longs for a life filled with good? Just keep your tongue from evil, and your lips from lies. Run from evil and do what is right. Seek peace; indeed, pursue it. The eyes of the Lord are on the righteous; His ears hear their cry. The Lord has set His anger against the wicked; their trace shall be cut off from the earth. When the righteous cry, He listens and delivers them from all their troubles. The Lord comes near to those who have a broken heart; He saves those whose spirit is bruised. The righteous may experience many troubles, but the Lord delivers him from them all. All of his bones are guarded; not even one shall be broken. Evil shall destroy the wicked, and those who hate the righteous are condemned. The Lord redeems the soul of His servants; those who trust in Him are never left desolate.

Psalm 90

A prayer of Moses, the man of God: Lord, You have been our shelter generation after generation. Before the mountains were made, before the earth and the world were formed; from eternity to eternity You are God. You turn men to dust, saying, "Return, O children of men." A thousand years in Your sight are like a day which has past; it is but a watch in the night. You sweep them away and they sleep; they are like the grass that grows in the morning. In the morning it will flourish and grow; in the evening it will wither and fade. We have been consumed by Your anger; by Your wrath we are filled with terror. You have set our sins before You; all of our secret sins have been laid bare in the light of Your countenance. All of our days have passed away because of Your anger. Suddenly our years are over; they are like the sound of a sigh. Our length of days is seventy years - perhaps, if we are strong, eighty. Their only boast is their labors and their sorrows; they speed by and we are gone. Who understands the power of Your wrath? For if we knew Your anger, we would fear You all the more. Teach us to number our days, that we might gain a heart of wisdom. Lord, how long will it be before You return, and have compassion on Your servants? Satisfy us in the morning with Your loving kindness, then we will sing and be glad all of our days. Gladden us according to the number of days in which we were afflicted; the years in which we have seen evil. May Your works be revealed to Your servants; Your glory to their children. Lord our God, may Your good will rest on us, and may You establish the work of our hands, establish the work of our hands.

Psalm 91

יֹשֵׁב בְּסֵתֶר עֶלְיוֹן, בְּצֵל שַׁדַּי יִתְלוֹנָן. אֹמַר לַיְיָ מַחְסִי וּמְצוּדָתִי, אֱלֹהַי אֶבְטַח בּוֹ. כִּי הוּא יַצִּילְךָ מִפַּח יָקוּשׁ מִדֶּבֶר הַוּוֹת. בְּאֶבְרָתוֹ יָסֶךְ לָךְ, וְתַחַת כְּנָפָיו תֶּחְסֶה, צִנָּה וְסֹחֵרָה אֲמִתּוֹ. לֹא תִירָא מִפַּחַד לָיְלָה, מֵחֵץ יָעוּף יוֹמָם. מִדֶּבֶר בָּאֹפֶל יַהֲלֹךְ מִקֶּטֶב יָשׁוּד צָהֳרָיִם. יִפֹּל מִצִּדְּךָ אֶלֶף וּרְבָבָה מִימִינֶךָ אֵלֶיךָ לֹא יִגָּשׁ. רַק בְּעֵינֶיךָ תַבִּיט, וְשִׁלֻּמַת רְשָׁעִים תִּרְאֶה. כִּי אַתָּה יְיָ מַחְסִי, עֶלְיוֹן שַׂמְתָּ מְעוֹנֶךָ. לֹא תְאֻנֶּה אֵלֶיךָ רָעָה, וְנֶגַע לֹא יִקְרַב בְּאָהֳלֶךָ. כִּי מַלְאָכָיו יְצַוֶּה לָּךְ, לִשְׁמָרְךָ בְּכָל דְּרָכֶיךָ. עַל כַּפַּיִם יִשָּׂאוּנְךָ פֶּן תִּגֹּף בָּאֶבֶן רַגְלֶךָ. עַל שַׁחַל וָפֶתֶן תִּדְרֹךְ תִּרְמֹס כְּפִיר וְתַנִּין. כִּי בִי חָשַׁק וַאֲפַלְּטֵהוּ אֲשַׂגְּבֵהוּ כִּי יָדַע שְׁמִי. יִקְרָאֵנִי וְאֶעֱנֵהוּ, עִמּוֹ אָנֹכִי בְצָרָה, אֲחַלְּצֵהוּ וַאֲכַבְּדֵהוּ.

(Reader) אֹרֶךְ יָמִים אַשְׂבִּיעֵהוּ, וְאַרְאֵהוּ בִּישׁוּעָתִי. אֹרֶךְ יָמִים אַשְׂבִּיעֵהוּ, וְאַרְאֵהוּ בִּישׁוּעָתִי.

Luke 1:46-55

וַתַּעַן מִרְיָם וַתֹּאמַר, תְּגַדֵּל נַפְשִׁי אֶת יְיָ. וַתָּגֵל רוּחִי בֵּאלֹהֵי יִשְׁעִי. כִּי רָאָה בְּעֳנִי שִׁפְחָתוֹ מֵהַיּוֹם הַזֶּה וָמַעְלָה יְאַשְּׁרוּנִי כָּל הַדֹּרוֹת. גְּדֹלוֹת עָשָׂה עִמָּדִי אַדִּיר הוּא וְקָדוֹשׁ שְׁמוֹ. וְחַסְדּוֹ עַל יְרֵאָיו בְּכָל דּוֹר וָדוֹר. בִּזְרֹעוֹ עָשָׂה נִפְלָאוֹת הֵפִיץ גֵּאִים בִּמְזִמַּת לִבָּם. שַׁלִּיטִים הָדַף מִכִּסְאוֹתָם וַיָּשֶׂם שְׁפָלִים לַמָּרוֹם. רְעֵבִים מִלֵּא טוֹב וַעֲשִׁירִים שָׁלַח רֵיקָם.

(Reader) הֶחֱזִיק בְּיִשְׂרָאֵל עַבְדּוֹ וַיִּזְכֹּר לוֹ אֶת רַחֲמָיו. כַּאֲשֶׁר דִּבֶּר לַאֲבֹתֵינוּ לְאַבְרָהָם וּלְזַרְעֲהֶם עַד עוֹלָם.

Psalm 135

הַלְלוּיָהּ הַלְלוּ אֶת שֵׁם יְיָ, הַלְלוּ עַבְדֵי יְיָ. שֶׁעֹמְדִים בְּבֵית יְיָ, בְּחַצְרוֹת בֵּית אֱלֹהֵינוּ. הַלְלוּיָהּ כִּי טוֹב יְיָ, זַמְּרוּ לִשְׁמוֹ כִּי נָעִים. כִּי יַעֲקֹב בָּחַר לוֹ יָהּ יִשְׂרָאֵל לִסְגֻלָּתוֹ. כִּי אֲנִי יָדַעְתִּי כִּי גָדוֹל יְיָ, וַאֲדֹנֵינוּ מִכָּל אֱלֹהִים. כֹּל אֲשֶׁר חָפֵץ יְיָ עָשָׂה, בַּשָּׁמַיִם וּבָאָרֶץ בַּיַּמִּים וְכָל תְּהֹמוֹת. מַעֲלֶה נְשִׂאִים מִקְצֵה הָאָרֶץ, בְּרָקִים לַמָּטָר עָשָׂה, מוֹצֵא רוּחַ מֵאוֹצְרוֹתָיו. שֶׁהִכָּה בְּכוֹרֵי מִצְרָיִם, מֵאָדָם עַד בְּהֵמָה. שָׁלַח אוֹתֹת וּמֹפְתִים בְּתוֹכֵכִי מִצְרָיִם, בְּפַרְעֹה וּבְכָל עֲבָדָיו. שֶׁהִכָּה גּוֹיִם רַבִּים, וְהָרַג מְלָכִים עֲצוּמִים. לְסִיחוֹן מֶלֶךְ הָאֱמֹרִי, וּלְעוֹג מֶלֶךְ הַבָּשָׁן, וּלְכֹל מַמְלְכוֹת כְּנָעַן. וְנָתַן אַרְצָם נַחֲלָה, נַחֲלָה לְיִשְׂרָאֵל עַמּוֹ. יְיָ שִׁמְךָ לְעוֹלָם, יְיָ זִכְרְךָ לְדֹר וָדֹר. כִּי יָדִין יְיָ עַמּוֹ וְעַל עֲבָדָיו יִתְנֶחָם. עֲצַבֵּי הַגּוֹיִם כֶּסֶף וְזָהָב, מַעֲשֵׂה יְדֵי אָדָם. פֶּה לָהֶם וְלֹא יְדַבֵּרוּ, עֵינַיִם לָהֶם וְלֹא יִרְאוּ. אָזְנַיִם לָהֶם וְלֹא יַאֲזִינוּ, אַף אֵין יֶשׁ רוּחַ בְּפִיהֶם. כְּמוֹהֶם יִהְיוּ עֹשֵׂיהֶם, כֹּל אֲשֶׁר בֹּטֵחַ בָּהֶם.

(Reader) בֵּית יִשְׂרָאֵל בָּרְכוּ אֶת יְיָ, בֵּית אַהֲרֹן בָּרְכוּ אֶת יְיָ. בֵּית הַלֵּוִי בָּרְכוּ אֶת יְיָ, יִרְאֵי יְיָ בָּרְכוּ אֶת יְיָ. בָּרוּךְ יְיָ מִצִּיּוֹן שֹׁכֵן יְרוּשָׁלָיִם, הַלְלוּיָהּ.

Psalm 91

He who dwells in the shelter of the Most High shall abide in the shadow of the Almighty.
I will say of the Lord that He is my refuge and my fortress; my God in whom I put my trust.
Surely He will deliver you from the trap of the hunter and from the deadly plague. He will
cover you with His feathers, and you will find refuge under His wings; His faithfulness is
your shield and protection. Do not be afraid; not of terror in the night, the flight of arrows
in the day, the pestilence that walks in the darkness, or the destruction that lays waste in the
noon. Though a thousand fall at your side, and ten thousand at your right hand, nothing
shall come near to you. Only with your eyes will you look and see the rewards of the
wicked. Lord, You are my refuge. Because you have made the Most High your shelter, no
evil will befall you; no plague will come near your dwelling place. He will give His angels
a charge concerning you, to keep you in all your ways. They will bear you up with their
hands lest you dash your foot on a stone. You can tread on the lion and the serpent. The
young lion and the serpent you will trample underfoot. "Because he has set his love on Me,
I will deliver him; I will lift him up because he knows My Name. When he calls on Me,
I will answer him; I will be with him in times of trouble, I will rescue him and I will honor
him. I will satisfy him with long life, and I will show him the power of My salvation."

Luke 1:46-55

Miryam responded and said, "My soul will magnify the Lord, and my spirit will rejoice in
God, my Savior. Because He has taken notice of the humble state of His maidservant,
behold, from this time on, all generations will call me blessed. He who is mighty has done
great things for me; Holy is His Name. His mercy is on those who fear Him, from
generation to generation. He has shown the strength of His arm; He has scattered the proud
in the imagination of their hearts. He has pulled the mighty from their thrones, and He has
exalted the lowly. He has satisfied the hungry with good things, but the rich He has sent
away empty. He remembered His loving kindness, and He has helped Israel, His servant,
just as He spoke to our fathers; to Abraham and to his seed forever."

Psalm 135

Praise the Lord! Praise the Name of the Lord; praise Him, you servants of the Lord, who
stand in the house of the Lord - in the courts of our God. Praise the Lord, for the Lord is
good; it is pleasant to sing to His Name. The Lord has chosen Jacob as His own; Israel as
His peculiar treasure. I know the greatness of the Lord; our Lord is over all gods. The
Lord does what He chooses to do in heaven, and in the earth, in the seas and in all their
depths. He makes the clouds rise from the ends of the earth. He makes the lightning for the
rainstorm. He calls forth the wind from His storehouse. He struck down the firstborn of
Egypt, both man and beast. He sent signs and wonders upon Pharaoh and his servants, in
the very midst of you, O Egypt. He struck down many nations, and slew mighty kings:
Sihon, king of the Amorites, Og, king of Bashan, and all the kingdoms of Canaan. He gave
their land to His people, Israel, as a possession and an inheritance. Lord, Your Name is
from eternity; Your fame to all generations. The Lord is the judge of Israel, His people,
and He will have compassion on His servants. The gods of the nations are silver and gold,
the work of men's hands. They have a mouth, but they cannot speak. They have eyes, but
they cannot see. They have ears, but they cannot hear. Is there any breath in their mouths?
Those who make them are like them, as is everyone who trusts in them. House of Israel,
bless the Lord! House of Aaron, bless the Lord! House of Levi, bless the Lord! You who
revere the Lord, bless the Lord! Blessed is the Lord out of Tsiyon, you who dwell in
Jerusalem! Praise the Lord!

Psalm 136

Ki l'olam ḥasdo

הוֹדוּ לַיְיָ כִּי טוֹב,   כִּי לְעוֹלָם חַסְדּוֹ.

הוֹדוּ לֵאלֹהֵי הָאֱלֹהִים,   כִּי לְעוֹלָם חַסְדּוֹ.

הוֹדוּ לַאֲדֹנֵי הָאֲדֹנִים,   כִּי לְעוֹלָם חַסְדּוֹ.

לְעֹשֵׂה נִפְלָאוֹת גְּדֹלוֹת לְבַדּוֹ,   כִּי לְעוֹלָם חַסְדּוֹ.

לְעֹשֵׂה הַשָּׁמַיִם בִּתְבוּנָה,   כִּי לְעוֹלָם חַסְדּוֹ.

לְרוֹקַע הָאָרֶץ עַל הַמָּיִם,   כִּי לְעוֹלָם חַסְדּוֹ.

לְעֹשֵׂה אוֹרִים גְּדֹלִים,   כִּי לְעוֹלָם חַסְדּוֹ.

אֶת הַשֶּׁמֶשׁ לְמֶמְשֶׁלֶת בַּיּוֹם,   כִּי לְעוֹלָם חַסְדּוֹ

אֶת הַיָּרֵחַ וְכוֹכָבִים לְמֶמְשְׁלוֹת בַּלָּיְלָה, כִּי לְעוֹלָם חַסְדּוֹ.

לְמַכֵּה מִצְרַיִם בִּבְכוֹרֵיהֶם,   כִּי לְעוֹלָם חַסְדּוֹ.

וַיּוֹצֵא יִשְׂרָאֵל מִתּוֹכָם,   כִּי לְעוֹלָם חַסְדּוֹ.

בְּיָד חֲזָקָה וּבִזְרוֹעַ נְטוּיָה,   כִּי לְעוֹלָם חַסְדּוֹ.

לְגֹזֵר יַם סוּף לִגְזָרִים,   כִּי לְעוֹלָם חַסְדּוֹ.

וְהֶעֱבִיר יִשְׂרָאֵל בְּתוֹכוֹ,   כִּי לְעוֹלָם חַסְדּוֹ.

וְנִעֵר פַּרְעֹה וְחֵילוֹ בְיַם סוּף,   כִּי לְעוֹלָם חַסְדּוֹ.

לְמוֹלִיךְ עַמּוֹ בַּמִּדְבָּר,   כִּי לְעוֹלָם חַסְדּוֹ.

לְמַכֵּה מְלָכִים גְּדֹלִים,   כִּי לְעוֹלָם חַסְדּוֹ.

וַיַּהֲרֹג מְלָכִים אַדִּירִים,   כִּי לְעוֹלָם חַסְדּוֹ.

לְסִיחוֹן מֶלֶךְ הָאֱמֹרִי,   כִּי לְעוֹלָם חַסְדּוֹ.

וּלְעוֹג מֶלֶךְ הַבָּשָׁן,   כִּי לְעוֹלָם חַסְדּוֹ.

וְנָתַן אַרְצָם לְנַחֲלָה,   כִּי לְעוֹלָם חַסְדּוֹ.

נַחֲלָה לְיִשְׂרָאֵל עַבְדּוֹ,   כִּי לְעוֹלָם חַסְדּוֹ.

שֶׁבְּשִׁפְלֵנוּ זָכַר לָנוּ,   כִּי לְעוֹלָם חַסְדּוֹ

וַיִּפְרְקֵנוּ מִצָּרֵינוּ,   כִּי לְעוֹלָם חַסְדּוֹ.

(Reader) נוֹתֵן לֶחֶם לְכָל בָּשָׂר,   כִּי לְעוֹלָם חַסְדּוֹ.

הוֹדוּ לְאֵל הַשָּׁמָיִם,   כִּי לְעוֹלָם חַסְדּוֹ.

Psalm 136

Give thanks to the Lord, for He is good;	His mercy endures forever.
Give thanks to the God of gods;	**His mercy endures forever.**
Give thanks to the Lord of lords;	His mercy endures forever.
To Him who alone does great things;	**His mercy endures forever.**
To Him who made the heavens with wisdom;	His mercy endures forever.
To Him who put the earth upon the waters;	**His mercy endures forever.**
To Him who made the great lights;	His mercy endures forever.
The sun to rule by day;	**His mercy endures forever.**
The moon and the stars to rule by night;	His mercy endures forever.
To Him who struck the firstborn of Egypt;	**His mercy endures forever.**
And brought Israel from their midst;	His mercy endures forever.
With a strong hand and an outstretched arm;	**His mercy endures forever.**
To Him who divided the Red Sea;	His mercy endures forever.
And made Israel pass through its midst;	**His mercy endures forever.**
And drowned Pharaoh's army in it;	His mercy endures forever.
To Him who led His people through the wilderness;	**His mercy endures forever.**
To Him who struck down great kings;	His mercy endures forever.
And slew kings of renown;	**His mercy endures forever.**
Sihon, king of the Amorites;	His mercy endures forever.
And Og, king of Bashan;	**His mercy endures forever.**
He gave their land as an inheritance;	His mercy endures forever.
An inheritance to Israel, His servant;	**His mercy endures forever.**
Who remembered us in our low estate;	His mercy endures forever.
And rescued us from our enemies;	**His mercy endures forever.**
Who gives food to all creatures;	His mercy endures forever.
Give thanks to the God of heaven;	**His mercy endures forever.**

Psalm 33

רַנְּנוּ צַדִּיקִים בַּיְיָ, לַיְשָׁרִים נָאוָה תְהִלָּה. הוֹדוּ לַיְיָ בְּכִנּוֹר, בְּנֵבֶל עָשׂוֹר זַמְּרוּ לוֹ. שִׁירוּ לוֹ שִׁיר חָדָשׁ הֵיטִיבוּ נַגֵּן בִּתְרוּעָה. כִּי יָשָׁר דְּבַר יְיָ, וְכָל מַעֲשֵׂהוּ בֶּאֱמוּנָה. אֹהֵב צְדָקָה וּמִשְׁפָּט, חֶסֶד יְיָ מָלְאָה הָאָרֶץ. בִּדְבַר יְיָ שָׁמַיִם נַעֲשׂוּ, וּבְרוּחַ פִּיו כָּל צְבָאָם. כּוֹנֵס כַּנֵּד מֵי הַיָּם, נֹתֵן בְּאוֹצָרוֹת תְּהוֹמוֹת. יִירְאוּ מֵיְיָ כָּל הָאָרֶץ, מִמֶּנּוּ יָגוּרוּ כָּל יֹשְׁבֵי תֵבֵל. כִּי הוּא אָמַר וַיֶּהִי הוּא צִוָּה וַיַּעֲמֹד. יְיָ הֵפִיר עֲצַת גּוֹיִם, הֵנִיא מַחְשְׁבוֹת עַמִּים. עֲצַת יְיָ לְעוֹלָם תַּעֲמֹד מַחְשְׁבוֹת לִבּוֹ לְדֹר וָדֹר. אַשְׁרֵי הַגּוֹי אֲשֶׁר יְיָ אֱלֹהָיו, הָעָם בָּחַר לְנַחֲלָה לוֹ. מִשָּׁמַיִם הִבִּיט יְיָ, רָאָה אֶת כָּל בְּנֵי הָאָדָם. מִמְּכוֹן שִׁבְתּוֹ הִשְׁגִּיחַ, אֶל כָּל יֹשְׁבֵי הָאָרֶץ. הַיֹּצֵר יַחַד לִבָּם, הַמֵּבִין אֶל כָּל מַעֲשֵׂיהֶם. אֵין הַמֶּלֶךְ נוֹשָׁע בְּרָב חָיִל, גִּבּוֹר לֹא יִנָּצֵל בְּרָב כֹּחַ. שֶׁקֶר הַסּוּס לִתְשׁוּעָה, וּבְרֹב חֵילוֹ לֹא יְמַלֵּט. הִנֵּה עֵין יְיָ אֶל יְרֵאָיו, לַמְיַחֲלִים לְחַסְדּוֹ. לְהַצִּיל מִמָּוֶת נַפְשָׁם, וּלְחַיּוֹתָם בָּרָעָב.

(Reader) נַפְשֵׁנוּ חִכְּתָה לַיְיָ, עֶזְרֵנוּ וּמָגִנֵּנוּ הוּא. כִּי בוֹ יִשְׂמַח לִבֵּנוּ, כִּי בְשֵׁם קָדְשׁוֹ בָטָחְנוּ. יְהִי חַסְדְּךָ יְיָ עָלֵינוּ, כַּאֲשֶׁר יִחַלְנוּ לָךְ.

Psalm 92

מִזְמוֹר שִׁיר לְיוֹם הַשַּׁבָּת: טוֹב לְהֹדוֹת לַיְיָ, וּלְזַמֵּר לְשִׁמְךָ עֶלְיוֹן. לְהַגִּיד בַּבֹּקֶר חַסְדֶּךָ וֶאֱמוּנָתְךָ בַּלֵּילוֹת. עֲלֵי עָשׂוֹר וַעֲלֵי נָבֶל, עֲלֵי הִגָּיוֹן בְּכִנּוֹר. כִּי שִׂמַּחְתַּנִי יְיָ בְּפָעֳלֶךָ בְּמַעֲשֵׂי יָדֶיךָ אֲרַנֵּן. מַה גָּדְלוּ מַעֲשֶׂיךָ יְיָ, מְאֹד עָמְקוּ מַחְשְׁבֹתֶיךָ. אִישׁ בַּעַר לֹא יֵדָע, וּכְסִיל לֹא יָבִין אֶת זֹאת. בִּפְרֹחַ רְשָׁעִים כְּמוֹ עֵשֶׂב וַיָּצִיצוּ כָּל פֹּעֲלֵי אָוֶן, לְהִשָּׁמְדָם עֲדֵי עַד. וְאַתָּה מָרוֹם לְעֹלָם יְיָ. כִּי הִנֵּה אֹיְבֶיךָ יְיָ, כִּי הִנֵּה אֹיְבֶיךָ יֹאבֵדוּ יִתְפָּרְדוּ כָּל פֹּעֲלֵי אָוֶן. וַתָּרֶם כִּרְאֵים קַרְנִי, בַּלֹּתִי בְּשֶׁמֶן רַעֲנָן. וַתַּבֵּט עֵינִי בְּשׁוּרָי, בַּקָּמִים עָלַי מְרֵעִים, תִּשְׁמַעְנָה אָזְנָי.

(Reader) צַדִּיק כַּתָּמָר יִפְרָח, כְּאֶרֶז בַּלְּבָנוֹן יִשְׂגֶּה. שְׁתוּלִים בְּבֵית יְיָ, בְּחַצְרוֹת אֱלֹהֵינוּ יַפְרִיחוּ. עוֹד יְנוּבוּן בְּשֵׂיבָה, דְּשֵׁנִים וְרַעֲנַנִּים יִהְיוּ. לְהַגִּיד כִּי יָשָׁר יְיָ, צוּרִי וְלֹא עַוְלָתָה בּוֹ.

Psalm 93

יְיָ מָלָךְ גֵּאוּת לָבֵשׁ, לָבֵשׁ יְיָ עֹז הִתְאַזָּר, אַף תִּכּוֹן תֵּבֵל בַּל תִּמּוֹט. נָכוֹן כִּסְאֲךָ מֵאָז, מֵעוֹלָם אָתָּה. נָשְׂאוּ נְהָרוֹת יְיָ, נָשְׂאוּ נְהָרוֹת קוֹלָם, יִשְׂאוּ נְהָרוֹת דָּכְיָם.

(Reader) מִקֹּלוֹת מַיִם רַבִּים, אַדִּירִים מִשְׁבְּרֵי יָם, אַדִּיר בַּמָּרוֹם יְיָ. עֵדֹתֶיךָ נֶאֶמְנוּ מְאֹד לְבֵיתְךָ נָאֲוָה קֹדֶשׁ, יְיָ לְאֹרֶךְ יָמִים.

Psalm 33

You who are righteous, rejoice in the Lord; it is fitting to sing His praises. Give thanks to the Lord on the harp; make a melody to Him with the ten stringed lute. Sing a new song to Him; play skillfully amid joyful shouting. The word of the Lord is right; all His doings are faithful. He loves charity and justice; the Lord's mercy fills the earth. The heavens came into being by the word of the Lord; all their host by the breath of His mouth. He, like a vessel, gathers the seas; he lays up the deep in storehouses. The whole earth will fear the Lord; all its inhabitants will hold Him in awe. Because He spoke, and it was; He commanded, and it stood firm. The Lord brought the counsel of the nations to naught; He foiled the plans of the peoples. The Lord's counsel stands forever; the desire of His heart from generation to generation. Blessed is the nation whose God is the Lord; the people He has chosen as His own. The Lord looked from the heavens upon all the sons of men; from His dwelling place He looked on all the inhabitants of the world. He fashioned all their hearts; He knows all their deeds. The king is not saved by his armies; nor the warrior by great strength. Horses bring false hope; for all its strength it cannot deliver. But the eye of the Lord is on those who fear Him, who trust in His loving kindness: to deliver their soul from death and to keep them alive in times of famine. Our soul waited for the Lord; He is our help and our shield. Our heart will rejoice in Him; our trust is in the Holy Name. Lord, may Your mercies be on us, as our hope is in You.

Psalm 92

A psalm, a song for the Shabbat day: It is good to give thanks to the Lord and to sing to Your Name, O Most High; to declare Your loving kindness in the morning and Your faithfulness at night, on the ten-stringed lyre and the lute, to the sound of the harp. Lord, You have made me glad through Your works; I joy in the work of Your hands. How great are Your works, O Lord! How deep Your designs! The stupid man will not know and the fool will not understand; when the wicked grow up like grass, and those who do evil flourish, it is that they may be destroyed forever. Lord, You are great forever. Behold Your enemies, O Lord. Behold, Your enemies will perish; all who work iniquity will be dispersed. You have exalted my strength as that of the wild ox. I have been anointed with fresh oil. My eye has seen my foes; my ear has heard my enemies. Those who are righteous will flourish like the palm tree; they will flourish like the cedars of Lebanon. Those who are planted in the house of the Lord shall flourish in the courts of our God. Even in their old age they will bear fruit. They will be vigorous and fresh. They will proclaim, "The Lord is just! He is my Rock; there is no wrong in Him!"

Psalm 93

The Lord is King; He is robed in majesty. The Lord is robed; He has girded Himself with strength. In this, the world is firmly set; it cannot be moved. Your throne was established long ago; You are from eternity. Lord, the floods have lifted up - the floods have lifted up their voice; they have lifted up their waves. Above the sound of many waters, mighty breakers of the sea, the Lord on high is supreme. Your testimonies are very sure. Lord, Your house is adorned with holiness for all time.

Revelation 4:2-11

וְהִנֵּה כִסֵּא נִצָּב בַּשָּׁמַיִם וְאֶחָד יֹשֵׁב עַל הַכִּסֵּא. וְהַיֹּשֵׁב הַהוּא כְּמַרְאֵה אֶבֶן יָשְׁפֵה כְּאֶבֶן אֹדֶם וְקֶשֶׁת סָבִיב לַכִּסֵּא כְּעֵין בָּרָקֶת. וְעֶשְׂרִים וְאַרְבָּעָה כִסְאוֹת עֹמְדִים אֶל הַכִּסֵּא מִסָּבִיב וְאֶל הַכִּסְאוֹת רָאִיתִי עֶשְׂרִים וְאַרְבָּעָה זְקֵנִים יֹשְׁבִים מְלֻבָּשִׁים בְּגָדִים לְבָנִים וְעֲטָרוֹת זָהָב בְּרָאשֵׁיהֶם. וּמִתּוֹךְ הַכִּסֵּא יֹצֵא בָרָק רַעַם וָרַעַשׁ וְשִׁבְעָה לַפִּידִים בֹּעֲרִים לִפְנֵי הַכִּסֵּא אֲשֶׁר הֵם שִׁבְעָא רוּחוֹת הָאֱלֹהִים. וְלִפְנֵי הַכִּסֵּא יָם זְכוֹכִית כְּעֵין הַקָּרַח וּבְתוֹךְ הַכִּסֵּא וְסָבִיב לוֹ אַרְבַּע חַיּוֹת מְלֵאוֹת עֵינַיִם מִפָּנִים וּמֵאָחוֹר. דְּמוּת הַחַיָּה הָרִאשׁוֹנָה כְּאַרְיֵה וְהַחַיָּה הַשֵּׁנִית כְּעֵגֶל וְהַחַיָּה הַשְּׁלִישִׁית פָּנִים לָהּ כִּפְנֵי אָדָם וּדְמוּת הַחַיָּה הָרְבִיעִית כְּנֶשֶׁר מְעוֹפֵף. וְאַרְבַּע הַחַיּוֹת שֵׁשׁ כְּנָפַיִם שֵׁשׁ כְּנָפַיִם לְאֶחָת וְהֵן מְלֵאוֹת עֵינַיִם מִסָּבִיב וּמִלְפָנִים וְהַשְׁקֵט אֵין לָהֶן יוֹמָם לַיְלָה כִּי קֹרְאוֹת קָדוֹשׁ קָדוֹשׁ קָדוֹשׁ יְיָ אֱלֹהִים אֵל שַׁדַּי אֲשֶׁר הוּא הָיָה הֹוֶה וְעָתִיד לָבֹא. וּלְעֵת הַחַיּוֹת נֹתְנוֹת הוֹד וְהָדָר וְשֶׁבַח לַיֹּשֵׁב עַל הַכִּסֵּא אֲשֶׁר הוּא חַי עַד עוֹלְמֵי עוֹלָמִים. כֵּן יִפְּלוּ הָעֶשְׂרִים וְאַרְבָּעָה הַזְּקֵנִים עַל פְּנֵיהֶם וּמִשְׁתַּחֲוִים לִפְנֵי הַיֹּשֵׁב עַל הַכִּסֵּה אֲשֶׁר הוּא חַי עַד עוֹלְמֵי עוֹלָמִים לֵאמֹר.

(Reader) לְךָ יְיָ אֱלֹהֵינוּ יָאֲתָה לָקַחַת הוֹד וְהָדָר וָעֹז כִּי אַתָּה בָרָאתָ כָּל אֵלֶּה וּבִרְצוֹנְךָ נִהְיוּ וְנִבְרָאוּ.

יְהִי כְבוֹד יְיָ לְעוֹלָם, יִשְׂמַח יְיָ בְּמַעֲשָׂיו. יְהִי שֵׁם יְיָ מְבֹרָךְ, מֵעַתָּה וְעַד עוֹלָם. מִמִּזְרַח שֶׁמֶשׁ עַד מְבוֹאוֹ, מְהֻלָּל שֵׁם יְיָ. רָם עַל כָּל גּוֹיִם יְיָ, עַל הַשָּׁמַיִם כְּבוֹדוֹ. יְיָ שִׁמְךָ לְעוֹלָם, יְיָ זִכְרְךָ לְדֹר וָדֹר. יְיָ בַּשָּׁמַיִם הֵכִין כִּסְאוֹ, וּמַלְכוּתוֹ בַּכֹּל מָשָׁלָה. יִשְׂמְחוּ הַשָּׁמַיִם וְתָגֵל הָאָרֶץ, וְיֹאמְרוּ בַגּוֹיִם יְיָ מָלָךְ. יְיָ מֶלֶךְ, יְיָ מָלָךְ, יְיָ יִמְלֹךְ לְעֹלָם וָעֶד. יְיָ מֶלֶךְ עוֹלָם וָעֶד, אָבְדוּ גוֹיִם מֵאַרְצוֹ. יְיָ הֵפִיר עֲצַת גּוֹיִם, הֵנִיא מַחְשְׁבוֹת עַמִּים. רַבּוֹת מַחֲשָׁבוֹת בְּלֶב אִישׁ, וַעֲצַת יְיָ הִיא תָקוּם. עֲצַת יְיָ לְעוֹלָם תַּעֲמֹד, מַחְשְׁבוֹת לִבּוֹ לְדֹר וָדֹר. כִּי הוּא אָמַר וַיֶּהִי, הוּא צִוָּה וַיַּעֲמֹד. כִּי בָחַר יְיָ בְּצִיּוֹן, אִוָּה לְמוֹשָׁב לוֹ. כִּי יַעֲקֹב בָּחַר לוֹ יָהּ, יִשְׂרָאֵל לִסְגֻלָּתוֹ. כִּי לֹא יִטֹּשׁ יְיָ עַמּוֹ, וְנַחֲלָתוֹ לֹא יַעֲזֹב. **(Reader)** וְהוּא רַחוּם יְכַפֵּר עָוֹן וְלֹא יַשְׁחִית, וְהִרְבָּה לְהָשִׁיב אַפּוֹ, וְלֹא יָעִיר כָּל חֲמָתוֹ. יְיָ הוֹשִׁיעָה, הַמֶּלֶךְ יַעֲנֵנוּ בְיוֹם קָרְאֵנוּ.

Revelation 4:2-11

A throne was set in heaven, and One sat on the throne. And He who sat there was like a jasper and a sardius stone in appearance; and there was a rainbow around the throne, in appearance like an emerald. Twenty-four thrones were around the throne, and sitting on the thrones I saw twenty-four elders who were clothed in robes of white and on their heads they had crowns of gold. Lightning and thunder and voices came out from the throne; and before the throne, seven lamp stands were burning, which are the seven Spirits of God. There was a sea of glass, like crystal, that was before the throne, and all around the throne were four living creatures, full of eyes, in front and in back. The first living creature was like a lion, the second was like an ox. The face of the third living creature was in the likeness of a man, and the fourth living creature was like an eagle in flight. Each of these creatures had six wings, and they were full of eyes, around and within. Day and night, without rest, they kept saying, "Holy, holy, holy, Lord God Almighty, Who was and Who is and Who is to come!" And whenever the living creatures give glory to Him who sits on the throne, to Him who lives forever and ever, the twenty-four elders fall down before Him who sits on the throne, and they worship Him who lives forever and ever. They cast their crowns before the throne, saying, "Lord, You are worthy to receive glory and honor and power; for You have created all things, and by Your will they existed and were created."

The glory of the Lord is everlasting; may the Lord take joy in all He has done. Lord, may Your Name be blessed now and forever. From the rising of the sun to the setting of the same, the Name of the Lord is to be praised. The Lord is over all the nations; His glory is above the heavens. Lord, Your Name is forever; Your renown is to every generation. The Lord's throne is set in the heavens; His kingdom is over all. The heavens rejoice and the earth exalts; let them say to the nations, "The Lord is King, the Lord was King, the Lord shall be King forever and to eternity." The Lord is King forever and ever; the nations have vanished from His land. He brings the counsel of the nations to nothing; He ruins the plans of the peoples. There are many plans in the heart of man, but only what the Lord purposes will succeed. The Lord's counsel stands forever; His plans are from generation to generation. He spoke and it was; He commanded and it stood firm. The Lord has chosen Tsiyon; He has desired it as His dwelling place. The Lord has chosen Jacob for Himself, Israel as His peculiar treasure. The Lord will not abandon His people; He will not forsake His inheritance. And He, being full of mercy, forgave their iniquity and did not destroy. Indeed, He frequently turns His anger aside and does not stir up His wrath. Lord, save us! May the King answer us in the day that we call.

(A transliterated version of the Ashrei-Psalm 145 can be found starting on page 132)

אַשְׁרֵי יוֹשְׁבֵי בֵיתֶךָ, עוֹד יְהַלְלוּךָ, פֶּלָה.

אַשְׁרֵי הָעָם שֶׁכָּכָה לּוֹ, אַשְׁרֵי הָעָם שֶׁיְיָ אֱלֹהָיו.

Psalm 145   תְּהִלָּה לְדָוִד:

אֲרוֹמִמְךָ אֱלוֹהַי הַמֶּלֶךְ, וַאֲבָרְכָה שִׁמְךָ לְעוֹלָם וָעֶד.

בְּכָל יוֹם אֲבָרְכֶךָּ, וַאֲהַלְלָה שִׁמְךָ לְעוֹלָם וָעֶד.

גָּדוֹל יְיָ וּמְהֻלָּל מְאֹד, וְלִגְדֻלָּתוֹ אֵין חֵקֶר.

דּוֹר לְדוֹר יְשַׁבַּח מַעֲשֶׂיךָ, וּגְבוּרֹתֶיךָ יַגִּידוּ.

הֲדַר כְּבוֹד הוֹדֶךָ, וְדִבְרֵי נִפְלְאֹתֶיךָ אָשִׂיחָה.

וֶעֱזוּז נוֹרְאוֹתֶיךָ יֹאמֵרוּ וּגְדוּלָּתְךָ אֲסַפְּרֶנָּה.

זֵכֶר רַב טוּבְךָ יַבִּיעוּ, וְצִדְקָתְךָ יְרַנֵּנוּ.

חַנּוּן וְרַחוּם יְיָ, אֶרֶךְ אַפַּיִם וּגְדָל חָסֶד.

טוֹב יְיָ לַכֹּל, וְרַחֲמָיו עַל כָּל מַעֲשָׂיו.

יוֹדוּךָ יְיָ כָּל מַעֲשֶׂיךָ, וַחֲסִידֶיךָ יְבָרְכוּכָה.

כְּבוֹד מַלְכוּתְךָ יֹאמֵרוּ, וּגְבוּרָתְךָ יְדַבֵּרוּ.

לְהוֹדִיעַ לִבְנֵי הָאָדָם גְּבוּרֹתָיו, וּכְבוֹד הֲדַר מַלְכוּתוֹ.

מַלְכוּתְךָ מַלְכוּת כָּל עֹלָמִים, וּמֶמְשַׁלְתְּךָ בְּכָל דּוֹר וָדֹר.

סוֹמֵךְ יְיָ לְכָל הַנֹּפְלִים, וְזוֹקֵף לְכָל הַכְּפוּפִים.

עֵינֵי כֹל אֵלֶיךָ יְשַׂבֵּרוּ, וְאַתָּה נוֹתֵן לָהֶם אֶת אָכְלָם בְּעִתּוֹ.

פּוֹתֵחַ אֶת יָדֶךָ, וּמַשְׂבִּיעַ לְכָל חַי רָצוֹן.

צַדִּיק יְיָ בְּכָל דְּרָכָיו, וְחָסִיד בְּכָל מַעֲשָׂיו.

קָרוֹב יְיָ לְכָל קֹרְאָיו, לְכֹל אֲשֶׁר יִקְרָאֻהוּ בֶאֱמֶת.

רְצוֹן יְרֵאָיו יַעֲשֶׂה, וְאֶת שַׁוְעָתָם יִשְׁמַע וְיוֹשִׁיעֵם.

שׁוֹמֵר יְיָ אֶת כָּל אֹהֲבָיו, וְאֵת כָּל הָרְשָׁעִים יַשְׁמִיד.

(Reader) תְּהִלַּת יְיָ יְדַבֶּר פִּי, וִיבָרֵךְ כָּל בָּשָׂר שֵׁם קָדְשׁוֹ, לְעוֹלָם וָעֶד.

וַאֲנַחְנוּ נְבָרֵךְ יָהּ, מֵעַתָּה וְעַד עוֹלָם, הַלְלוּיָהּ.

Psalm 146

הַלְלוּיָהּ, הַלְלִי נַפְשִׁי אֶת יְיָ. אֲהַלְלָה יְיָ בְּחַיָּי, אֲזַמְּרָה לֵאלֹהַי בְּעוֹדִי. אַל תִּבְטְחוּ בִנְדִיבִים, בְּבֶן אָדָם, שֶׁאֵין לוֹ תְשׁוּעָה. תֵּצֵא רוּחוֹ יָשֻׁב לְאַדְמָתוֹ, בַּיּוֹם הַהוּא אָבְדוּ עֶשְׁתֹּנֹתָיו. אַשְׁרֵי שֶׁאֵל יַעֲקֹב בְּעֶזְרוֹ, שִׂבְרוֹ עַל יְיָ אֱלֹהָיו. עֹשֶׂה שָׁמַיִם וָאָרֶץ, אֶת הַיָּם וְאֶת כָּל אֲשֶׁר בָּם הַשֹּׁמֵר אֱמֶת לְעוֹלָם. עֹשֶׂה מִשְׁפָּט לַעֲשׁוּקִים, נֹתֵן לֶחֶם לָרְעֵבִים, יְיָ מַתִּיר אֲסוּרִים. יְיָ פֹּקֵחַ עִוְרִים, יְיָ זֹקֵף כְּפוּפִים, יְיָ אֹהֵב צַדִּיקִים. יְיָ שֹׁמֵר אֶת גֵּרִים, יָתוֹם וְאַלְמָנָה יְעוֹדֵד, וְדֶרֶךְ רְשָׁעִים יְעַוֵּת.

(Reader) יִמְלֹךְ יְיָ לְעוֹלָם, אֱלֹהַיִךְ צִיּוֹן לְדֹר וָדֹר הַלְלוּיָהּ.

(A transliterated version of the Ashrei-Psalm 145 can be found starting on page 132)

Happy are they who abide in Your house; they are always praising You. Happy are the people who are so situated. Happy are the people whose God is the Lord.

Psalm 145 A psalm of David:

My God, the King, I will exalt You, and I will bless Your Name forever and ever.
> ***Each day I will bless You, and I will praise Your Name forever and ever.***

The Lord is great and most worthy to be praised; His greatness is beyond understanding.
> ***One generation shall praise Your works to the next and they will tell of Your mighty deeds.***

I will meditate on the splendor of Your majesty and on Your wonders.
> ***They will speak of Your awesome might; I will tell of Your greatness.***

The remembrances of Your great goodness will bubble forth, they will sing of Your righteousness.
> ***The Lord is gracious and full of compassion, slow to anger, and great in mercy.***

The Lord is good to all, and His compassion is over all His works.
> ***Lord, all Your works will give You praise, and Your righteous ones will bless You.***

They will speak of Your might, and of the splendor of Your kingdom;
> ***To let men know of Your glorious deeds, and the majesty of Your kingdom.***

Your kingdom is an everlasting kingdom; Your dominion is over all generations.
> ***The Lord upholds all who fall, and lifts up all who are bowed down.***

All eyes will look to You with hope, and You give them food in due season.
> ***You open Your hand, and satisfy the needs of every living thing.***

The Lord is righteous in all His ways, and gracious in all His deeds.
> ***The Lord is near to all who call on Him; to all who truly will call on Him.***

He will fulfill the desire of those who fear Him; He will hear their cry and save them.
> ***The Lord will keep all who love Him, but the wicked will be destroyed.***

My mouth will declare the praise of the Lord, and His Holy Name will forever be blessed by all flesh.
> ***We will bless the Lord both now and forever. Praise the Lord.***

Psalm 146

Praise the Lord! Praise the Lord, O my soul! I will praise the Lord as long as I live; as long as I exist I will sing to my God. Do not put your trust in princes, or in the sons of men who can give you no help. On the day his spirit departs, he returns to dust and his plans come to nothing. Happy are those whose help is the God of Jacob; whose hope is in the Lord his God, the maker of heaven and earth, the sea and all that is in them; Who preserves the truth forever, renders justice to the oppressed, and feeds those who hunger. The Lord sets the captive free. The Lord opens the eyes of the blind. The Lord raises those who are bowed down. The Lord loves the righteous. The Lord guards those who are strangers; He upholds the fatherless and the widow, but He makes the way of the wicked crooked. The Lord will reign forever; your God, O Tsiyon, from generation to generation. Praise the Lord!

Psalm 147

הַלְלוּיָהּ, כִּי טוֹב זַמְּרָה אֱלֹהֵינוּ, כִּי נָעִים נָאוָה תְהִלָּה. בּוֹנֵה יְרוּשָׁלַיִם יְיָ, נִדְחֵי יִשְׂרָאֵל יְכַנֵּס. הָרוֹפֵא לִשְׁבוּרֵי לֵב, וּמְחַבֵּשׁ לְעַצְּבוֹתָם. מוֹנֶה מִסְפָּר לַכּוֹכָבִים לְכֻלָּם שֵׁמוֹת יִקְרָא. גָּדוֹל אֲדוֹנֵינוּ וְרַב כֹּחַ, לִתְבוּנָתוֹ אֵין מִסְפָּר. מְעוֹדֵד עֲנָוִים יְיָ, מַשְׁפִּיל רְשָׁעִים עֲדֵי אָרֶץ. עֱנוּ לַיְיָ בְּתוֹדָה, זַמְּרוּ לֵאלֹהֵינוּ בְכִנּוֹר. הַמְכַסֶּה שָׁמַיִם בְּעָבִים, הַמֵּכִין לָאָרֶץ מָטָר הַמַּצְמִיחַ הָרִים חָצִיר. נוֹתֵן לִבְהֵמָה לַחְמָהּ, לִבְנֵי עֹרֵב אֲשֶׁר יִקְרָאוּ: לֹא בִגְבוּרַת הַסּוּס יֶחְפָּץ, לֹא בְשׁוֹקֵי הָאִישׁ יִרְצֶה. רוֹצֶה יְיָ אֶת יְרֵאָיו, אֶת הַמְיַחֲלִים לְחַסְדּוֹ. שַׁבְּחִי יְרוּשָׁלַיִם אֶת יְיָ, הַלְלִי אֱלֹהַיִךְ צִיּוֹן. כִּי חִזַּק בְּרִיחֵי שְׁעָרָיִךְ, בֵּרַךְ בָּנַיִךְ בְּקִרְבֵּךְ. הַשָּׂם גְּבוּלֵךְ שָׁלוֹם, חֵלֶב חִטִּים יַשְׂבִּיעֵךְ. הַשֹּׁלֵחַ אִמְרָתוֹ אָרֶץ, עַד מְהֵרָה יָרוּץ דְּבָרוֹ. הַנֹּתֵן שֶׁלֶג כַּצָּמֶר, כְּפוֹר כָּאֵפֶר יְפַזֵּר. מַשְׁלִיךְ קַרְחוֹ כְפִתִּים, לִפְנֵי קָרָתוֹ מִי יַעֲמֹד. יִשְׁלַח דְּבָרוֹ וְיַמְסֵם, יַשֵּׁב רוּחוֹ יִזְּלוּ מָיִם.

(Reader) מַגִּיד דְּבָרָיו לְיַעֲקֹב, חֻקָּיו וּמִשְׁפָּטָיו לְיִשְׂרָאֵל. לֹא עָשָׂה כֵן לְכָל גּוֹי, וּמִשְׁפָּטִים בַּל יְדָעוּם, הַלְלוּיָהּ.

Psalm 148

הַלְלוּיָהּ, הַלְלוּ אֶת יְיָ מִן הַשָּׁמַיִם הַלְלוּהוּ בַּמְּרוֹמִים. הַלְלוּהוּ כָל מַלְאָכָיו, הַלְלוּהוּ כָּל צְבָאָיו. הַלְלוּהוּ שֶׁמֶשׁ וְיָרֵחַ, הַלְלוּהוּ כָּל כּוֹכְבֵי אוֹר. הַלְלוּהוּ שְׁמֵי הַשָּׁמַיִם, וְהַמַּיִם אֲשֶׁר מֵעַל הַשָּׁמָיִם. יְהַלְלוּ אֶת שֵׁם יְיָ, כִּי הוּא צִוָּה וְנִבְרָאוּ. וַיַּעֲמִידֵם לָעַד לְעוֹלָם, חָק נָתַן וְלֹא יַעֲבוֹר. הַלְלוּ אֶת יְיָ מִן הָאָרֶץ, תַּנִּינִים וְכָל תְּהֹמוֹת. אֵשׁ וּבָרָד שֶׁלֶג וְקִיטוֹר, רוּחַ סְעָרָה עֹשָׂה דְבָרוֹ. הֶהָרִים וְכָל גְּבָעוֹת, עֵץ פְּרִי וְכָל אֲרָזִים. הַחַיָּה וְכָל בְּהֵמָה, רֶמֶשׂ וְצִפּוֹר כָּנָף. מַלְכֵי אֶרֶץ וְכָל לְאֻמִּים שָׂרִים וְכָל שֹׁפְטֵי אָרֶץ. בַּחוּרִים וְגַם בְּתוּלוֹת, זְקֵנִים עִם נְעָרִים.

(Reader) יְהַלְלוּ אֶת שֵׁם יְיָ, כִּי נִשְׂגָּב שְׁמוֹ לְבַדּוֹ, הוֹדוֹ עַל אֶרֶץ וְשָׁמָיִם. וַיָּרֶם קֶרֶן לְעַמּוֹ, תְּהִלָּה לְכָל חֲסִידָיו, לִבְנֵי יִשְׂרָאֵל עַם קְרֹבוֹ, הַלְלוּיָהּ.

Psalm 149

הַלְלוּיָהּ, שִׁירוּ לַיְיָ שִׁיר חָדָשׁ, תְּהִלָּתוֹ בִּקְהַל חֲסִידִים. יִשְׂמַח יִשְׂרָאֵל בְּעֹשָׂיו, בְּנֵי צִיּוֹן יָגִילוּ בְמַלְכָּם. יְהַלְלוּ שְׁמוֹ בְמָחוֹל, בְּתֹף וְכִנּוֹר יְזַמְּרוּ לוֹ. כִּי רוֹצֶה יְיָ בְּעַמּוֹ, יְפָאֵר עֲנָוִים בִּישׁוּעָה. יַעְלְזוּ חֲסִידִים בְּכָבוֹד, יְרַנְּנוּ עַל מִשְׁכְּבוֹתָם. רוֹמְמוֹת אֵל בִּגְרוֹנָם, וְחֶרֶב פִּיפִיּוֹת בְּיָדָם. לַעֲשׂוֹת נְקָמָה בַּגּוֹיִם, תּוֹכֵחֹת בַּלְאֻמִּים.

(Reader) לֶאְסֹר מַלְכֵיהֶם בְּזִקִּים, וְנִכְבְּדֵיהֶם בְּכַבְלֵי בַרְזֶל. לַעֲשׂוֹת בָּהֶם מִשְׁפָּט כָּתוּב, הָדָר הוּא לְכָל חֲסִידָיו, הַלְלוּיָהּ.

Psalm 147

Praise the Lord, because it is good to sing praise to our God; because it is pleasant and fitting. The Lord rebuilds Jerusalem; He will gather together the outcasts of Israel. He heals the brokenhearted and binds up their sorrows. He counts the number of the stars, and will call each by its name. Great is our Lord whose power is without end; His wisdom is unsearchable. The humble are lifted up by the Lord, but He casts the wicked down to the ground. Sing to the Lord with thanksgiving; sing to our God, to the sound of the harp. It is He who covers the heavens with clouds, who brings rain upon the earth and who causes the grass to grow upon the hills. He feeds the beasts of the field and gives food to the young raven when it calls. He is not impressed by the strength of the horse, nor does He delight in the strength of a man. The Lord is pleased with those who fear Him; who trust in His loving kindness. Praise to the Lord, O Jerusalem; praise to your God, O Tsiyon! He has fortified the bars of your gates, He has blessed the children in the midst of you. He establishes peace within your borders, and satisfies you with the finest of wheat. His word runs swiftly as He sends forth His command to the earth. He sends snow like fine wool, scattering frost like ashes, casting forth His hail as if they were crumbs. Who can stand before His cold? Again, He sends forth His word, and they melt; He causes His wind to blow, and the waters flow again. He has declared His word to Jacob, His statutes and ordinances to Israel. He has not done this with any other nation. They have not known His judgments. Praise the Lord!

Psalm 148

Praise the Lord! Praise the Lord from the heavens! Praise Him in the heights! Praise Him, all His angels! Praise Him, all His hosts! Praise Him, sun and moon! Praise Him, all you stars of light! Let the waters above the heavens, and the highest heavens, praise Him! They will praise the Name of the Lord, for He commanded and they were. He made a decree, establishing them forever and ever; it shall not pass away. Praise the Lord from the earth, you sea monsters and all the deep; fire and hail, snow and cloud, stormy wind, making His word full. Mountains as well as hills, fruit trees as well as cedars, wild beasts as well as cattle, creeping things as well as birds of the air, kings of the earth and all of their nations, princes and all who rule upon the earth, young men and young women, old men and children: let them praise the Name of the Lord. His Name alone is to be exalted! His majesty is over earth and heaven, and He has exalted the horn of His people, the praise of all His righteous ones, the children of Israel, a people near to Him. Praise the Lord!

Psalm 149

Praise the Lord! Sing a new song to the Lord, His praise in the righteous assembly. Rejoice in your Maker, O Israel. O children of Tsiyon, be joyful in your King. They will praise His Name with dance! They will make music with the timbrel and harp, for the Lord is pleased with His people, adorning the meek with salvation. The righteous ones will joy in His glory; sing aloud on your beds. The praises of God are in their mouth, a double-edged sword in their hand. Execute vengeance upon the nations, and judgment on the peoples. Bind their kings with chains and their rulers with bands of iron. Execute upon them the judgment that is written. He is the honor of His people. Praise the Lord.

Psalm 150

הַלְלוּיָהּ, הַלְלוּ אֵל בְּקָדְשׁוֹ, הַלְלוּהוּ בִּרְקִיעַ עֻזּוֹ. הַלְלוּהוּ בִגְבוּרֹתָיו, הַלְלוּהוּ כְּרֹב גֻּדְלוֹ. הַלְלוּהוּ בְּתֵקַע שׁוֹפָר, הַלְלוּהוּ בְּנֵבֶל וְכִנּוֹר. הַלְלוּהוּ בְתֹף וּמָחוֹל, הַלְלוּהוּ בְּמִנִּים וְעֻגָב. הַלְלוּהוּ בְצִלְצְלֵי שָׁמַע, הַלְלוּהוּ בְּצִלְצְלֵי תְרוּעָה.

(Reader) *Kol ha-neshama t'halleil ya, halleluyah.* כֹּל הַנְּשָׁמָה תְּהַלֵּל יָהּ, הַלְלוּיָהּ.

Revelation 15:2-4

וָכֵים זְכוּכִית בָּלוּל בָּאֵשׁ נִרְאָה לְעֵינַי וְאֵלֶּה אֲשֶׁר גָּבְרוּ עַל הַחַיָּה וְעַל צַלְמָהּ וּמִסְפַּר שְׁמָהּ עֹמְדִים עַל יַם הַזְּכוּכִית וְכִנֹּרוֹת אֵל בְּיָדָם. אָז יָשִׁירוּ שִׁיר מֹשֶׁה עֶבֶד הָאֱלֹהִים וְשִׁיר הַשֶּׂה לֵאמֹר גְּדֹלִים וְנוֹרָאִים מַעֲשֶׂיךָ יְיָ אֱלֹהִים אֵל שַׁדַּי וּדְרָכֶיךָ אֱמֶת וָצֶדֶק מֶלֶךְ הַגּוֹיִם. מִי לֹא יִרָאֲךָ יְיָ מִי לֹא יִתֵּן כָּבוֹד לִשְׁמֶךָ קָדוֹשׁ אַתָּה לְבַדְּךָ וְכָל הַגּוֹיִם יָבֹאוּ וְיִשְׁתַּחֲווּ לְפָנֶיךָ כִּי צִדְקָתְךָ נִגְלָתָה.

בָּרוּךְ יְיָ לְעוֹלָם, אָמֵן וְאָמֵן. בָּרוּךְ יְיָ מִצִּיּוֹן, שֹׁכֵן יְרוּשָׁלָיִם, הַלְלוּיָהּ. בָּרוּךְ יְיָ אֱלֹהִים אֱלֹהֵי יִשְׂרָאֵל, עֹשֵׂה נִפְלָאוֹת לְבַדּוֹ.

(Reader) וּבָרוּךְ שֵׁם כְּבוֹדוֹ לְעוֹלָם, וְיִמָּלֵא כְבוֹדוֹ אֶת כָּל הָאָרֶץ, אָמֵן וְאָמֵן.

נשמת

נִשְׁמַת כָּל חַי, תְּבָרֵךְ אֶת שִׁמְךָ יְיָ אֱלֹהֵינוּ. וְרוּחַ כָּל בָּשָׂר, תְּפָאֵר וּתְרוֹמֵם זִכְרְךָ מַלְכֵּנוּ תָּמִיד, מִן הָעוֹלָם וְעַד הָעוֹלָם אַתָּה אֵל. וּמִבַּלְעָדֶיךָ אֵין לָנוּ מֶלֶךְ גּוֹאֵל וּמוֹשִׁיעַ, פּוֹדֶה וּמַצִּיל וּמְפַרְנֵס וּמְרַחֵם, בְּכָל עֵת צָרָה וְצוּקָה. אֵין לָנוּ מֶלֶךְ אֶלָּא אָתָּה.

אֱלֹהֵי הָרִאשׁוֹנִים וְהָאַחֲרוֹנִים, אֱלוֹהַּ כָּל בְּרִיּוֹת, אֲדוֹן כָּל תּוֹלָדוֹת, הַמְהֻלָּל בְּרֹב הַתִּשְׁבָּחוֹת, הַמְנַהֵג עוֹלָמוֹ בְּחֶסֶד, וּבְרִיּוֹתָיו בְּרַחֲמִים. וַיְיָ לֹא יָנוּם וְלֹא יִישָׁן, הַמְעוֹרֵר יְשֵׁנִים וְהַמֵּקִיץ נִרְדָּמִים, וְהַמֵּשִׂיחַ אִלְּמִים, וְהַמַּתִּיר אֲסוּרִים, וְהַסּוֹמֵךְ נוֹפְלִים, וְהַזּוֹקֵף כְּפוּפִים. לְךָ לְבַדְּךָ אֲנַחְנוּ מוֹדִים.

אִלּוּ פִינוּ מָלֵא שִׁירָה כַיָּם, וּלְשׁוֹנֵנוּ רִנָּה כַּהֲמוֹן גַּלָּיו, וְשִׂפְתוֹתֵינוּ שֶׁבַח כְּמֶרְחֲבֵי רָקִיעַ, וְעֵינֵינוּ מְאִירוֹת כַּשֶּׁמֶשׁ וְכַיָּרֵחַ, וְיָדֵינוּ פְרוּשׂוֹת כְּנִשְׁרֵי שָׁמַיִם, וְרַגְלֵינוּ קַלּוֹת כָּאַיָּלוֹת, אֵין אֲנַחְנוּ מַסְפִּיקִים, לְהוֹדוֹת לְךָ יְיָ אֱלֹהֵינוּ וֵאלֹהֵי אֲבוֹתֵינוּ, וּלְבָרֵךְ אֶת שְׁמֶךָ עַל אַחַת מֵאֶלֶף אֶלֶף אַלְפֵי אֲלָפִים וְרִבֵּי רְבָבוֹת פְּעָמִים, הַטּוֹבוֹת שֶׁעָשִׂיתָ עִם אֲבוֹתֵינוּ וְעִמָּנוּ. מִמִּצְרַיִם גְּאַלְתָּנוּ יְיָ אֱלֹהֵינוּ, וּמִבֵּית עֲבָדִים פְּדִיתָנוּ, בְּרָעָב זַנְתָּנוּ, וּבְשָׂבָע כִּלְכַּלְתָּנוּ, מֵחֶרֶב הִצַּלְתָּנוּ, וּמִדֶּבֶר מִלַּטְתָּנוּ, וּמֵחֳלָיִם רָעִים וְנֶאֱמָנִים דִּלִּיתָנוּ. עַד הֵנָּה עֲזָרוּנוּ רַחֲמֶיךָ, וְלֹא עֲזָבוּנוּ חֲסָדֶיךָ וְאַל תִּטְּשֵׁנוּ יְיָ אֱלֹהֵינוּ לָנֶצַח.

Psalm 150

Praise the Lord! Praise God in His sanctuary! Praise Him in the expanse of heaven! Praise Him for His mighty works! Praise Him for His abundant greatness! Praise Him with the sound of the shofar! Praise Him with the harp and the lyre! Praise Him with the timbrel and dance! Praise Him with strings and with the flute! Praise Him with cymbals, with loud clashing cymbals! Everything that has breath will praise the Lord! Praise the Lord!

Revelation 15:2-4

And I saw something like a sea of glass mingled with fire, and those who have the victory over the beast, over his image and over his mark and over the number of his name, standing on the sea of glass, having harps of God. They sing the song of Moses, the servant of God, and the song of the Lamb, saying: "Great and marvelous are Your works, Lord God Almighty! Just and true are Your ways; You are King of the nations. Who shall not fear and glorify Your name, O Lord? For You alone are holy. All the nations shall come and worship You, for Your judgments have been made manifest."

The Lord is to be blessed forever. Amen and amen! May the Lord who dwells in Jerusalem be blessed from Tsiyon. Praise the Lord! Blessed be the Lord God, the God of Israel, who alone does wondrous things, and may the glory of His Name be blessed forever. Indeed, the whole earth will be filled with His glory. Amen and amen!

Nishmat

Lord our God, the soul of every living being will bless Your Name, and the spirit of all flesh will always glorify and exalt Your fame, our King. From eternity and to eternity You are God, and aside from You, we have no King who redeems and saves, ransoms and rescues, sustains and has compassion in times of trouble and distress. We have no King but You.

God of the beginning and of the end, God of all creation, Lord of all that is born; He who guides His world with loving kindness and His creation with compassion will be endlessly praised. The Lord does not slumber or sleep; it is He who wakens the sleeper and rouses the one who slumbers. He gives words to the one who is silent, and He sets the captive free. He supports those who fall and raises up those who are bowed down. To You alone we offer thanks.

If our mouth was filled with song as the sea is and our tongue able to shout as do the waves; if our lips poured forth adoration as the heavens do and if our eyes were as bright as the sun and moon; if our hands were outstretched as the eagles in the sky and if our feet were as swift as the deer, we would never be able to thank You for even one thousandth of the countless millions of blessings which You bestowed on our fathers and on us. Lord, You are our God and God of our fathers. Lord our God, You redeemed us from Egypt and brought us out of slavery. In times of famine, You nourished and satisfied us with plenty. You delivered us from the sword and made us escape the plagues. You give us relief from severe and lasting diseases. Out of compassion You have always helped us, and in Your loving kindness You have not forsaken us. May the Lord our God never forsake us.

עַל כֵּן אֵבָרִים שֶׁפִּלַּגְתָּ בָּנוּ, וְרוּחַ וּנְשָׁמָה שֶׁנָּפַחְתָּ בְּאַפֵּינוּ, וְלָשׁוֹן אֲשֶׁר שַׂמְתָּ בְּפִינוּ.   הֵן הֵם יוֹדוּ וִיבָרְכוּ וִישַׁבְּחוּ וִיפָאֲרוּ וִירוֹמְמוּ וְיַעֲרִיצוּ וְיַקְדִּישׁוּ וְיַמְלִיכוּ אֶת שִׁמְךָ מַלְכֵּנוּ, כִּי כָל פֶּה לְךָ יוֹדֶה, וְכָל לָשׁוֹן לְךָ תִשָּׁבַע, וְכָל בֶּרֶךְ לְךָ תִכְרַע, וְכָל קוֹמָה לְפָנֶיךָ תִשְׁתַּחֲוֶה, וְכָל לְבָבוֹת יִירָאוּךָ, וְכָל קֶרֶב וּכְלָיוֹת יְזַמְּרוּ לִשְׁמֶךָ.   כַּדָּבָר שֶׁכָּתוּב, כָּל עַצְמוֹתַי תֹּאמַרְנָה יְיָ מִי כָמוֹךָ. מַצִּיל עָנִי מֵחָזָק מִמֶּנּוּ, וְעָנִי וְאֶבְיוֹן מִגֹּזְלוֹ: מִי יִדְמֶה לָּךְ, וּמִי יִשְׁוֶה לָּךְ וּמִי יַעֲרָךְ לָךְ.   הָאֵל הַגָּדוֹל הַגִּבּוֹר וְהַנּוֹרָא, אֵל עֶלְיוֹן קֹנֵה שָׁמַיִם וָאָרֶץ.

(Reader) נְהַלֶּלְךָ וּנְשַׁבֵּחֲךָ וּנְפָאֶרְךָ וּנְבָרֵךְ אֶת־שֵׁם קָדְשֶׁךָ.   כָּאָמוּר, לְדָוִד, בָּרְכִי נַפְשִׁי אֶת יְיָ, וְכָל קְרָבַי אֶת שֵׁם קָדְשׁוֹ.

Bar'khi naf'shi et Adonai, v'khol k'ravai et sheim kadsho.

(On Festivals the Reader begins here)

הָאֵל בְּתַעֲצֻמוֹת עֻזֶּךָ. הַגָּדוֹל בִּכְבוֹד שְׁמֶךָ, הַגִּבּוֹר לָנֶצַח וְהַנּוֹרָא בְּנוֹרְאוֹתֶיךָ, הַמֶּלֶךְ הַיּוֹשֵׁב עַל כִּסֵּא רָם וְנִשָּׂא:

(On Shabbat the Reader begins here)

שׁוֹכֵן עַד

שׁוֹכֵן עַד, מָרוֹם וְקָדוֹשׁ שְׁמוֹ.   וְכָתוּב, רַנְּנוּ צַדִּיקִים בַּיְיָ, לַיְשָׁרִים נָאוָה תְהִלָּה.   בְּפִי יְשָׁרִים תִּתְהַלָּל.   וּבְדִבְרֵי צַדִּיקִים תִּתְבָּרַךְ.   וּבִלְשׁוֹן חֲסִידִים תִּתְרוֹמָם. וּבְקֶרֶב קְדוֹשִׁים תִּתְקַדָּשׁ.

Shokhein ahd marom v'kadosh sh'mo. V'khatuv ran'nu tsadikim, ba'Adonai la-yesharim na'va t'hillah. B'fi y'sharim tit'hallal, uv'divrei tsadikim tit'barakh. Uvil'shon ḥasidim tit'romam uv'kerev k'doshim tit'kadash.

וּבְמַקְהֲלוֹת רִבְבוֹת עַמְּךָ בֵּית יִשְׂרָאֵל, בְּרִנָּה יִתְפָּאֵר שִׁמְךָ מַלְכֵּנוּ, בְּכָל דּוֹר וָדוֹר, שֶׁכֵּן חוֹבַת כָּל הַיְצוּרִים, לְפָנֶיךָ יְיָ אֱלֹהֵינוּ, וֵאלֹהֵי אֲבוֹתֵינוּ,

(Reader) לְהוֹדוֹת לְהַלֵּל לְשַׁבֵּחַ לְפָאֵר לְרוֹמֵם לְהַדֵּר לְבָרֵךְ לְעַלֵּה וּלְקַלֵּס, עַל כָּל דִּבְרֵי שִׁירוֹת וְתִשְׁבְּחוֹת דָּוִד בֶּן יִשַׁי עַבְדְּךָ מְשִׁיחֶךָ.

(Rise and remain standing until after ברכו if a minyan is present)

יִשְׁתַּבַּח שִׁמְךָ לָעַד מַלְכֵּנוּ, הָאֵל הַמֶּלֶךְ הַגָּדוֹל וְהַקָּדוֹשׁ בַּשָּׁמַיִם וּבָאָרֶץ. כִּי לְךָ נָאֶה, יְיָ אֱלֹהֵינוּ וֵאלֹהֵי אֲבוֹתֵינוּ. שִׁיר וּשְׁבָחָה, הַלֵּל וְזִמְרָה, עֹז וּמֶמְשָׁלָה, נֶצַח, גְּדֻלָּה וּגְבוּרָה, תְּהִלָּה וְתִפְאֶרֶת, קְדֻשָּׁה וּמַלְכוּת. בְּרָכוֹת וְהוֹדָאוֹת מֵעַתָּה וְעַד עוֹלָם.

(Reader) בָּרוּךְ אַתָּה יְיָ, אֵל מֶלֶךְ גָּדוֹל בַּתִּשְׁבָּחוֹת, אֵל הַהוֹדָאוֹת, אֲדוֹן הַנִּפְלָאוֹת, הַבּוֹחֵר בְּשִׁירֵי זִמְרָה, מֶלֶךְ, אֵל חֵי הָעוֹלָמִים.

Therefore, the limbs which You have apportioned in us, and the spirit and soul which You breathed into our nostrils, and the tongue which You put in our mouth, will thank and bless, praise and glorify, extol and honor, sanctify and revere Your Name, our King. Indeed, every mouth will give You praise, every tongue will swear allegiance to You, every person will bend the knee and bow down before You, every heart will fear You, and a person's innermost being will sing to Your Name, as it is written: All my being will say, "Who is like You, O Lord? You deliver the poor from one who is too strong for him, and the one who is poor and defenseless from one who would rob him." Who is like You? Who is equal to You? Who can be compared to You? You are the great, mighty and awesome God; the Almighty God; the Master of heaven and earth. We will praise and laud and glorify and bless Your holy Name, as it was said by David, "May my soul bless the Lord, and my whole being honor His holy Name."

(On Festivals the Reader begins here)

O God, mighty in Your power, great in Your glorious Name; You are magnificent forever and revered because of Your awesome works. You, O King, are seated upon a high and lofty throne.

(On Shabbat the Reader begins here)

Shokhein Ahd

Abiding forever, His Name is exalted and holy! It is written, "Be joyful in the Lord, you righteous ones; it is fitting that the upright sing." The mouth of the upright will sing praise, and by the speech of the righteous You will be blessed. You will be extolled by the tongue of the faithful and in the midst of the holy, You will be sanctified.

In the assemblies of the tens of thousands of Your people, the house of Israel, Your Name, our King, will be glorified in every generation with ringing song. This is the duty of all creatures, Lord our God, and God of our fathers, to thank, praise, laud, glorify, extol, honor, bless, exalt and proclaim You through the words of the songs of praise by David, the son of Jesse, Your anointed servant!

(Rise and remain standing until after Bar'khu if a minyan is present)

Your Name will be praised forever, Our King, in heaven and in earth, for You are the great and holy God and King. To You, Lord our God, and God of our fathers, belongs song and honor, praise and hymn, power and dominion, victory, greatness and might, renown and glory, holiness and kingship, blessings and thanks, from now and forever.

Blessed are You, Lord God, King most high, God of thanksgiving, Lord of wonders, Who is pleased with songs and hymns. King, God, the life of all generations.

Revelation 5:11-13

אָז רָאִיתִי וְשָׁמַעְתִּי קוֹל מַלְאָכִים רַבִּים סָבִיב לַכִּסֵּא וְלַחַיּוֹת וְלַזְּקֵנִים וּמִסְפָּרָם רִבּאוֹת רְבָבוֹת וְאַלְפֵי אֲלָפִים. וְהֵם עָנוּ בְּקוֹל רָם נָאוֶה לַשֶּׂה הַטָּבוּחַ לָקַחַת עֹז וְעֹשֶׁר וְחָכְמָה וּגְבוּרָה וְהוֹד וְהָדָר וּבְרָכָה. וְכָל יָצוּר אֲשֶׁר בַּשָּׁמַיִם וּבָאָרֶץ וּמִתַּחַת לָאָרֶץ וַאֲשֶׁר עַל פְּנֵי הַיָּמִּים וְכָל אֲשֶׁר בָּהֶם שָׁמַעְתִּי עָנִים לֵאמֹר אֶל הַיּוֹשֵׁב עַל הַכִּסֵּא וְאֶל הַשֶּׂה הַבְּרָכָה וְהֶהָדָר וְהֶהוֹד וְהַמֶּמְשָׁלָה עַד עוֹלְמֵי עוֹלָמִים. וְאַרְבַּע הַחַיּוֹת עָנוּ אָמֵן וְהַזְּקֵנִים נָפְלוּ עַל פְּנֵיהֶם וַיִּשְׁתַּחֲווּ לְפָנָיו.

חֲצִי קַדִּישׁ

יִתְגַּדַּל וְיִתְקַדַּשׁ שְׁמֵהּ רַבָּא. (אָמֵן - *Cong*) בְּעָלְמָא דִי בְרָא כִרְעוּתֵהּ, וְיַמְלִיךְ מַלְכוּתֵהּ בְּחַיֵּיכוֹן וּבְיוֹמֵיכוֹן וּבְחַיֵּי דְכָל בֵּית יִשְׂרָאֵל. בַּעֲגָלָא וּבִזְמַן קָרִיב, וְאִמְרוּ אָמֵן.

(אָמֵן - *Cong*)

*Yitgadal v'yitkadash sh'mei rabah. (Cong - Amein) B'almah di vera khir'utei, v'yamlikh
mal'khutei b'hayeikhon uv'yomeikhon uv'hayei d'khal beit Yisraeil. Ba'agalah
uviz'man kariv v'imru, Amein. (Cong - Amein)*

(*Together*)

יְהֵא שְׁמֵהּ רַבָּא מְבָרַךְ לְעָלַם וּלְעָלְמֵי עָלְמַיָּא.

Y'hei sh'mei rabah m'varakh l'alam ul'al'mei al'mayah.

יִתְבָּרַךְ וְיִשְׁתַּבַּח, וְיִתְפָּאַר וְיִתְרוֹמַם וְיִתְנַשֵּׂא וְיִתְהַדָּר וְיִתְעַלֶּה וְיִתְהַלָּל שְׁמֵהּ דְּקֻדְשָׁא, בְּרִיךְ הוּא, (בְּרִיךְ הוּא - *Cong*)

*Yit'barakh v'yish'tabah, v'yit'pa-ar v'yit'romam v'yit'nasei v'yit'hadar v'yit'aleh
v'yit'halal sh'mei d'ku-deshah, b'rikh Hu, (Cong - b'rikh Hu)*

*לְעֵלָּא מִן כָּל   *l'eila min kal*

בִּרְכָתָא וְשִׁירָתָא, תֻּשְׁבְּחָתָא וְנֶחֱמָתָא, דַּאֲמִירָן בְּעָלְמָא, וְאִמְרוּ אָמֵן. (אָמֵן - *Cong*)
*bir'khatah v'shiratah, tush'behatah v'nehematah, da'amiran b'almah, v'imru, Amein.
(Cong - Amein)*

בָּרְכוּ

(*Recite standing, facing east or toward an open ark. Omit when praying without a minyan*)
(*Bow at* בָּרְכוּ *and straighten at* יְיָ)

(*Reader*)

בָּרְכוּ אֶת יְיָ הַמְבֹרָךְ.

Bar'khu et Adonai ham'vorakh.

(*Congregation then Reader*)

בָּרוּךְ יְיָ הַמְבֹרָךְ לְעוֹלָם וָעֶד.

Barukh Adonai ham'vorakh l'olam va'ed.

(*Silent Meditation*)

יִתְבָּרַךְ וְיִשְׁתַּבַּח, וְיִתְפָּאַר וְיִתְרוֹמַם וְיִתְנַשֵּׂא שְׁמוֹ שֶׁל מֶלֶךְ מַלְכֵי הַמְּלָכִים, הַקָּדוֹשׁ בָּרוּךְ הוּא, שֶׁהוּא רִאשׁוֹן וְהוּא אַחֲרוֹן וּמִבַּלְעָדָיו אֵין אֱלֹהִים. סֹלּוּ לָרֹכֵב בָּעֲרָבוֹת, בְּיָהּ שְׁמוֹ, וְעָלְזוּ לְפָנָיו, וּשְׁמוֹ מְרוֹמָם עַל כָּל בְּרָכָה וּתְהִלָּה. בָּרוּךְ שֵׁם כְּבוֹד מַלְכוּתוֹ לְעוֹלָם וָעֶד. יְהִי שֵׁם יְיָ מְבֹרָךְ מֵעַתָּה וְעַד עוֹלָם.

בָּרוּךְ אַתָּה יְיָ, אֱלֹהֵינוּ מֶלֶךְ הָעוֹלָם, יוֹצֵר אוֹר, וּבוֹרֵא חְשֶׁךְ, עֹשֶׂה שָׁלוֹם וּבוֹרֵא אֶת הַכֹּל.

Revelation 5:11-13

Then I looked again, and I heard the singing of thousands and tens of thousands of angels around the throne and the living beings and the elders. And they sang in a mighty chorus: "The Lamb is worthy, the Lamb who was slain. He is worthy to receive power and riches and wisdom and strength and honor and glory and blessing."

And then I heard every creature in heaven and on earth and under the earth and in the sea. They also sang: "Blessing and honor and glory and power belong to the One sitting on the throne and to the Lamb forever and ever."

Ḥatsi Kaddish

Magnified and sanctified may God's great Name *(Cong - Amen)* be throughout the world which He has created according to His will. May He establish His kingdom in our lifetime, and during our days, and within the life of the entire house of Israel, speedily and soon; and say, *Amen. (Cong - Amen)*

(Together)

May the greatness of His Name be blessed forever and ever.

Let the Name of the Holy One, *blessed is He*, *(Cong - blessed is He)* be blessed and praised, glorified and exalted, extolled and honored, adored and lauded,

* beyond all

**From Rosh Hashanah to Yom Kippur substitute:*   **exceedingly* beyond all

of the blessings and songs, praises and consolations that are ever spoken in this world, and say, *Amen. (Cong - Amen)*

Bar'khu
(Recite standing, facing east or toward an open ark. Omit when praying without a minyan)
*(Bow at **Bless** and Straighten at **Lord**)*

(Reader)
Bless the Lord, who is blessed!

(Congregation then Reader)
Blessed is the Lord, who is blessed forever and ever!

(Silent Meditation)
Blessed and praised, glorified, exalted and honored be the Name of the Supreme King of Kings, the Holy One, blessed be He. He is the first and the last, and there is no other god. Extol Him who abides in the heavens, and rejoice before the countenance of Him who is named Lord. His Name is exalted far beyond all blessings and psalms. His glorious Name and kingdom will be blessed forever and ever; let the Lord's Name be blessed both now and for all time.

Blessed are You, Lord our God, King of the universe, who created both light and darkness; who makes peace and brings forth all things.

(On Shabbat recite)

הַכֹּל יוֹדוּךָ, וְהַכֹּל יְשַׁבְּחוּךָ, וְהַכֹּל יֹאמְרוּ אֵין קָדוֹשׁ כַּיְיָ. הַכֹּל יְרוֹמְמוּךָ סֶּלָה, יוֹצֵר הַכֹּל. הָאֵל הַפּוֹתֵחַ בְּכָל יוֹם דַּלְתוֹת שַׁעֲרֵי מִזְרָח, וּבוֹקֵעַ חַלּוֹנֵי רָקִיעַ מוֹצִיא חַמָּה מִמְּקוֹמָהּ, וּלְבָנָה מִמְּכוֹן שִׁבְתָּהּ, וּמֵאִיר לָעוֹלָם כֻּלּוֹ וּלְיוֹשְׁבָיו, שֶׁבָּרָא בְּמִדַּת הָרַחֲמִים. הַמֵּאִיר לָאָרֶץ וְלַדָּרִים עָלֶיהָ בְּרַחֲמִים. וּבְטוּבוֹ מְחַדֵּשׁ בְּכָל יוֹם תָּמִיד מַעֲשֵׂה בְרֵאשִׁית. הַמֶּלֶךְ הַמְרוֹמָם לְבַדּוֹ מֵאָז. הַמְשֻׁבָּח וְהַמְפֹאָר וְהַמִּתְנַשֵּׂא מִימוֹת עוֹלָם. אֱלֹהֵי עוֹלָם, בְּרַחֲמֶיךָ הָרַבִּים רַחֵם עָלֵינוּ. אֲדוֹן עֻזֵּנוּ צוּר מִשְׂגַּבֵּנוּ, מָגֵן יִשְׁעֵנוּ, מִשְׂגָּב בַּעֲדֵנוּ. אֵין כְּעֶרְכֶּךָ וְאֵין זוּלָתֶךָ, אֶפֶס בִּלְתֶּךָ, וּמִי דּוֹמֶה לָּךְ.

(Reader) אֵין כְּעֶרְכְּךָ יְיָ אֱלֹהֵינוּ, בָּעוֹלָם הַזֶּה, וְאֵין זוּלָתְךָ מַלְכֵּנוּ לְחַיֵּי הָעוֹלָם הַבָּא. אֶפֶס בִּלְתְּךָ גּוֹאֲלֵנוּ לִימוֹת הַמָּשִׁיחַ יֵשׁוּעַ. וְאֵין דּוֹמֶה לְךָ מוֹשִׁיעֵנוּ לִתְחִיַּת הַמֵּתִים.

(A transliterated version of El Adon can be found on page 218)

אל אדון

אֵל אָדוֹן עַל כָּל הַמַּעֲשִׂים. בָּרוּךְ וּמְבֹרָךְ בְּפִי כָּל נְשָׁמָה, גָּדְלוֹ וְטוּבוֹ מָלֵא עוֹלָם, דַּעַת וּתְבוּנָה סֹבְבִים אֹתוֹ.

הַמִּתְגָּאֶה עַל חַיּוֹת הַקֹּדֶשׁ וְנֶהְדָּר בְּכָבוֹד עַל הַמֶּרְכָּבָה, זְכוּת וּמִישׁוֹר לִפְנֵי כִסְאוֹ, חֶסֶד וְרַחֲמִים לִפְנֵי כְבוֹדוֹ.

טוֹבִים מְאוֹרוֹת שֶׁבָּרָא אֱלֹהֵינוּ, יְצָרָם בְּדַעַת בְּבִינָה וּבְהַשְׂכֵּל, כֹּחַ וּגְבוּרָה נָתַן בָּהֶם, לִהְיוֹת מוֹשְׁלִים בְּקֶרֶב תֵּבֵל.

מְלֵאִים זִיו וּמְפִיקִים נֹגַהּ, נָאֶה זִיוָם בְּכָל הָעוֹלָם, שְׂמֵחִים בְּצֵאתָם וְשָׂשִׂים בְּבוֹאָם, עֹשִׂים בְּאֵימָה רְצוֹן קוֹנָם.

פְּאֵר וְכָבוֹד נוֹתְנִים לִשְׁמוֹ, צָהֳלָה וְרִנָּה לְזֵכֶר מַלְכוּתוֹ, קָרָא לַשֶּׁמֶשׁ וַיִּזְרַח אוֹר, רָאָה, וְהִתְקִין צוּרַת הַלְּבָנָה.

שֶׁבַח נוֹתְנִים לוֹ כָּל צְבָא מָרוֹם, תִּפְאֶרֶת וּגְדֻלָּה, שְׂרָפִים וְאוֹפַנִּים וְחַיּוֹת הַקֹּדֶשׁ.

לָאֵל אֲשֶׁר שָׁבַת מִכָּל הַמַּעֲשִׂים, בַּיּוֹם הַשְּׁבִיעִי הִתְעַלָּה, וְיָשַׁב עַל כִּסֵּא כְבוֹדוֹ, תִּפְאֶרֶת עָטָה לְיוֹם הַמְּנוּחָה, עֹנֶג קָרָא לְיוֹם הַשַּׁבָּת. זֶה שֶׁבַח שֶׁל יוֹם הַשְּׁבִיעִי, שֶׁבּוֹ שָׁבַת אֵל מִכָּל מְלַאכְתּוֹ, וְיוֹם הַשְּׁבִיעִי מְשַׁבֵּחַ וְאוֹמֵר, מִזְמוֹר שִׁיר לְיוֹם הַשַּׁבָּת, טוֹב לְהוֹדוֹת לַיְיָ, לְפִיכָךְ יְפָאֲרוּ וִיבָרְכוּ לָאֵל כָּל יְצוּרָיו, שֶׁבַח יְקָר וּגְדֻלָּה וְכָבוֹד יִתְּנוּ לָאֵל מֶלֶךְ יוֹצֵר כֹּל, הַמַּנְחִיל מְנוּחָה לְעַמּוֹ יִשְׂרָאֵל בִּקְדֻשָּׁתוֹ, בְּיוֹם שַׁבַּת קֹדֶשׁ, שִׁמְךָ יְיָ אֱלֹהֵינוּ יִתְקַדָּשׁ, וְזִכְרְךָ מַלְכֵּנוּ יִתְפָּאַר, בַּשָּׁמַיִם מִמַּעַל וְעַל הָאָרֶץ מִתָּחַת.

(On Shabbat recite)

All shall thank You; all shall praise You; all shall proclaim: There is none holy like the Lord! You will forever be extolled as the Creator of all. Each day, O God, You open the eastern gates, the windows of the sky, and You bring the sun from its place, the moon from its abode. You give light to the whole world and its inhabitants, whom You have created with compassion.

You give light to the earth and to those who, in Your mercy, dwell on it. Each day, out of Your goodness, the creation is renewed. The King alone is ever exalted; You are praised and glorified and extolled from eternity. God of eternity, in Your compassion You have shown us Your mercy. Lord, You are our strength, our secure stronghold, the shield of our salvation, our refuge.

There is none like You and none beside You; there is nothing without You. Who can be compared to You? Lord our God, there is none to be compared to You in this world, and there is none besides You, our King, in the life of the world to come. Our Redeemer, there is none but You in the days of the Messiah Yeshua. There is none like You, our Deliverer, in the revival of the dead.

(A transliterated version of El Adon can be found on page 218)

El Adon

God is Lord of all creation. He is, and will be, blessed by the mouth of every soul. His great goodness fills the universe; knowledge and understanding surround Him.

He is exalted above the holy beings and adorned with majestic glory. Purity and uprightness are before His throne, and in His presence are compassion and mercy.

Good are the luminaries which our God has created; they were made with knowledge, wisdom and insight. Strength and power were given them that they might rule over the world.

Full of splendor and radiating brightness, their light brings beauty to all the world. Rejoice in their rising and be exultant in their setting, performing with reverence the will of the Creator.

They give glory and honor to His Name, singing joyously at the fame of His kingdom. He spoke to the sun, and it began to shine; He looked to regulate the form of the moon.

Give Him praise all you hosts on high; Seraphim and Ophanim and all the holy beings, render glory and grandeur...

... to God who, on the seventh day, ascended to sit upon His throne of glory, and rested from all the work of creation. He gave the day of rest beauty, and He called the Shabbat a delight. Such is the distinction of the seventh day, that on it, God rested from all His work. And so, the seventh day offers praise, saying, "A song for the Shabbat day. It is good to give thanks to the Lord." Therefore, let all God's creatures glorify and bless Him, and render honor, glory and grandeur to God, the King and the Creator of all things. He has, in His holiness, given rest to His people Israel, on the holy Shabbat day. Lord our God, Your Name will be sanctified, and Your fame, our King, will be glorified in the heavens above and on the earth beneath.

(On Shabbat and Weekdays recite)
Matthew 5:14-16

אַתֶּם אוֹר הָעוֹלָם. עִיר שׁוֹכֶנֶת עַל הַר אֵינָהּ יְכוֹלָה לְהִסָּתֵר. גַּם אֵין מַדְלִיקִים מְנוֹרָה וְשָׂמִים אוֹתָהּ תַּחַת כְּלִי, אֶלָּא עַל כֵּן שָׂמִים אוֹתָהּ וְאָז תָּאִיר לְכָל בָּאֵי הַבָּיִת. כָּךְ יָאֵר נָא אוֹרְכֶם לִפְנֵי בְּנֵי אָדָם, לְמַעַן יִרְאוּ אֶת מַעֲשֵׂיכֶם הַטּוֹבִים וִיכַבְּדוּ אֶת אֲבִיכֶם שֶׁבַּשָּׁמָיִם.

לָאֵל בָּרוּךְ נְעִימוֹת יִתֵּנוּ. לְמֶלֶךְ אֵל חַי וְקַיָּם זְמִרוֹת יֹאמֵרוּ וְתִשְׁבָּחוֹת יַשְׁמִיעוּ. כִּי הוּא לְבַדּוֹ פּוֹעֵל גְּבוּרוֹת, עוֹשֶׂה חֲדָשׁוֹת, בַּעַל מִלְחָמוֹת, זוֹרֵעַ צְדָקוֹת, מַצְמִיחַ יְשׁוּעוֹת, בּוֹרֵא רְפוּאוֹת, נוֹרָא תְהִלּוֹת, אֲדוֹן הַנִּפְלָאוֹת. הַמְחַדֵּשׁ בְּטוּבוֹ בְּכָל יוֹם תָּמִיד מַעֲשֵׂה בְרֵאשִׁית. כָּאָמוּר לְעֹשֵׂה אוֹרִים גְּדוֹלִים, כִּי לְעוֹלָם חַסְדּוֹ.

אור חדש

אוֹר חָדָשׁ עַל צִיּוֹן תָּאִיר וְנִזְכֶּה כֻלָּנוּ מְהֵרָה לְאוֹרוֹ. בָּרוּךְ אַתָּה יְיָ יוֹצֵר הַמְּאוֹרוֹת.

Or ḥadash al Tsiyon ta-ir v'niz'ke khulanu m'heira l'oroh.
Barukh atah Adonai yotseir ham'orot.

John 8:12

הַמָּשִׁיחַ יֵשׁוּעַ הוֹסִיף לְדַבֵּר אֲלֵיהֶם וְאָמַר: אֲנִי אוֹר הָעוֹלָם. אִישׁ הַהוֹלֵךְ אַחֲרַי לֹא יִתְהַלֵּךְ בַּחֹשֶׁךְ, אֶלָּא אוֹר הַחַיִּים יִהְיֶה לוֹ.

אַהֲבָה רַבָּה אֲהַבְתָּנוּ, יְיָ אֱלֹהֵינוּ, חֶמְלָה גְדוֹלָה וִיתֵרָה חָמַלְתָּ עָלֵינוּ. אָבִינוּ מַלְכֵּנוּ, בַּעֲבוּר אֲבוֹתֵינוּ שֶׁבָּטְחוּ בְךָ, וַתְּלַמְּדֵם חֻקֵּי חַיִּים, כֵּן תְּחָנֵּנוּ וּתְלַמְּדֵנוּ. אָבִינוּ, הָאָב הָרַחֲמָן, הַמְרַחֵם, רַחֵם עָלֵינוּ, וְתֵן בְּלִבֵּנוּ לְהָבִין וּלְהַשְׂכִּיל, לִשְׁמֹעַ, לִלְמֹד וּלְלַמֵּד, לִשְׁמֹר וְלַעֲשׂוֹת וּלְקַיֵּם אֶת כָּל דִּבְרֵי תַלְמוּד תּוֹרָתֶךָ בְּאַהֲבָה.

Ahavah rabbah ahavtanu, Adonai Eloheinu, ḥemlah gedolah viteirah ḥamalta
aleinu. Avinu Malkenu ba'avur avoteinu shebat'hu v'kha, vat'lamdeim ḥukei
ḥayim, kein t'ḥaneinu ut'lamdeinu. Avinu ha'Av ha'raḥaman, ham'raḥeim,
raḥeim aleinu, v'tein b'libeinu l'havin ul'haskil, lishmo'a, lilmod u-l'lameid,
lishmor v'la-asot, ul'kayeim et kal divrei talmud Toratekha b'ahavah.

וְהָאֵר עֵינֵינוּ בְּתוֹרָתֶךָ, וְדַבֵּק לִבֵּנוּ בְּמִצְוֹתֶיךָ, וְיַחֵד לְבָבֵנוּ לְאַהֲבָה וּלְיִרְאָה אֶת שְׁמֶךָ, וְלֹא נֵבוֹשׁ לְעוֹלָם וָעֶד. כִּי בְשֵׁם קָדְשְׁךָ הַגָּדוֹל וְהַנּוֹרָא בָּטָחְנוּ, נָגִילָה וְנִשְׂמְחָה בִּישׁוּעָתֶךָ.

V'ha-eir eineinu b'Toratekha, v'dabeik libeinu bemits'voteikha, v'yaḥeid
liva'veinu, l'ahavah u-l'yirah et sh'mekha. V'lo neivosh l'olam va'ed. Ki v'sheim
kad'shekha hagadol v'hanora ba'tah'nu na'gilah venis'mehah bi'shua'tekha.

וַהֲבִיאֵנוּ לְשָׁלוֹם מֵאַרְבַּע כַּנְפוֹת הָאָרֶץ, וְתוֹלִיכֵנוּ קוֹמְמִיּוּת לְאַרְצֵנוּ, כִּי אֵל פּוֹעֵל יְשׁוּעוֹת אָתָּה, וּבָנוּ בָחַרְתָּ מִכָּל עַם וְלָשׁוֹן. וְקֵרַבְתָּנוּ לְשִׁמְךָ הַגָּדוֹל סֶלָה בֶּאֱמֶת לְהוֹדוֹת לְךָ וּלְיַחֶדְךָ בְּאַהֲבָה. בָּרוּךְ אַתָּה יְיָ, הַבּוֹחֵר בְּעַמּוֹ יִשְׂרָאֵל בְּאַהֲבָה.

(On Shabbat and Weekdays recite)
Matthew 5:14-16

You are the light of the world. A city set on a hill cannot be hid. Neither do people light a lamp, and put it under a basket, but on a lampstand and let it shine for all that are in the house. Even so, let your light shine before others that they may see your good actions, and glorify your Father who is in heaven.

To God, the blessed One, they will offer melodies; to the King, God of life eternal, they will utter hymns and praises. He alone performs mighty acts: He creates all things new, He wars to bring justice, He brings forth salvation and creates healing; great is His renown. He is the Lord of Wonders. In His goodness He renews the creation each day, as it is said: He makes the great lights; His loving kindness endures forever.

Or Ḥadash

Cause a new light to shine upon Tsiyon, and may it be soon that we all enjoy its brightness. Blessed are You, Lord, Creator of the Light.

John 8:12

Messiah Yeshua spoke unto them, saying: I am the light of the world. A person that follows after me shall not walk in the darkness, but shall have the light of life.

Lord our God, You have loved us with a great love, and You have shown us great and abundant mercy. Our Father, our King, for the sake of our fathers who placed their trust in You and to whom You taught the laws of life, be gracious to us and teach us as well. Our Father, merciful Father, You who are always compassionate, have mercy on us and inspire us to discern and to understand, to listen, to learn and to teach, to observe, to do and to fulfill with love all the words of Your instruction.

Enlighten our eyes in Your instruction; cause our heart to cleave to Your commandments, and unify our heart to love and to fear Your Name, so we will never be put to shame. In Your holy, great and awesome Name we trusted, that we might thrill with joy in Your salvation.

Bring us home in peace from the four corners of the earth, and lead us upright into our land, for You are the God who brings salvation. You have chosen us from among all peoples and tongues. You have forever brought us near Your great Name in truth, so that we might praise You and, out of love, declare Your oneness. Blessed are You, Lord, who has lovingly chosen Israel as Your people.

Mark 12:28-34

וְאֶחָד מִן הַסּוֹפְרִים בָּא וַיִּשְׁמַע אֹתָם נִדְבָּרִים יַחְדָּו וּבִרְאֹתוֹ כִּי הֵיטֵב עָנָה עַל דִּבְרֵיהֶם וַיִּשְׁאָלֵהוּ מָה רֵאשִׁית כָּל הַמִּצְוֹת. וַיַּעַן יֵשׁוּעַ הָרִאשֹׁנָה הֲלֹא הִיא שְׁמַע יִשְׂרָאֵל יְיָ אֱלֹהֵינוּ, יְיָ אֶחָד. וְאָהַבְתָּ אֵת יְיָ אֱלֹהֶיךָ, בְּכָל לְבָבְךָ, וּבְכָל נַפְשְׁךָ, וּבְכָל מְאֹדֶךָ. וְהַשְּׁנִיָּה הֲלֹא הִיא וְאָהַבְתָּ לְרֵעֲךָ כָּמוֹךָ וְאֵין מִצְוָה גְדוֹלָה מִשְׁתַּיִם אֵלֶּה. וַיֹּאמֶר אֵלָיו הַסּוֹפֵר אָמְנָם מוֹרִי אֱמֶת דִּבַּרְתָּ כִּי אֶחָד הוּא וְאֵין עוֹד מִלְבַדּוֹ. וּלְאַהֲבָה אֹתוֹ בְּכָל לֵב וּבְכָל מַדָּע וּבְכָל מְאֹד וְלֶאֱהֹב אִישׁ אֶת רֵעֵהוּ כְּנַפְשׁוֹ הִיא גְדֹלָה מִכָּל עֹלָה וָזָבַח. וַיַּרְא יֵשׁוּעַ כִּי הִשְׂכִּיל לַעֲנוֹת אֹתוֹ וַיֹּאמֶר אֵלָיו הִנְּךָ לֹא רָחוֹק מִמַּלְכוּת אֱלֹהִים וְלֹא הֶעֱזוֹד אִישׁ לְהִתְוַכַּח עִמּוֹ בִּדְבָרִים מֵהַיּוֹם וָמָעְלָה.

שְׁמַע

(When praying without a minyan begin by reciting: אֵל מֶלֶךְ נֶאֱמָן *)*

(Recite loudly and slowly covering the eyes with the right hand)

שְׁמַע יִשְׂרָאֵל, יְיָ אֱלֹהֵינוּ, יְיָ אֶחָד

Shema Yisraeil, Adonai Eloheinu, Adonai Eḥad.

(Recite softly and quickly without covering the eyes)

בָּרוּךְ שֵׁם כְּבוֹד מַלְכוּתוֹ לְעוֹלָם וָעֶד

Barukh sheim k'vod mal'khuto l'olam va'ed.

וְאָהַבְתָּ אֵת יְיָ אֱלֹהֶיךָ, בְּכָל לְבָבְךָ, וּבְכָל נַפְשְׁךָ, וּבְכָל מְאֹדֶךָ. וְהָיוּ הַדְּבָרִים הָאֵלֶּה, אֲשֶׁר אָנֹכִי מְצַוְּךָ הַיּוֹם, עַל לְבָבֶךָ. וְשִׁנַּנְתָּם לְבָנֶיךָ, וְדִבַּרְתָּ בָּם בְּשִׁבְתְּךָ בְּבֵיתֶךָ, וּבְלֶכְתְּךָ בַדֶּרֶךְ וּבְשָׁכְבְּךָ, וּבְקוּמֶךָ. וּקְשַׁרְתָּם לְאוֹת עַל יָדֶךָ, וְהָיוּ לְטֹטָפֹת בֵּין עֵינֶיךָ, וּכְתַבְתָּם עַל מְזֻזוֹת בֵּיתֶךָ וּבִשְׁעָרֶיךָ.

V'ahav'ta eit Adonai Eloheikha, b'khal l'vavkha, uv'khal naf'shekha, uv'khal m'odekha. V'hayu ha-d'varim ha-eileh, asher anokhi metsav'kha hayom, al l'vavekha. V'shinan'tam l'vanekha v'dibarta bam beshiv'tekha bevei'tekhha, uv'lekhtekha vaderekh u-veshakh'bekha, u-v'kumekha. U-k'shartam l'ot al yadekha, v'hayu l'totafot bein einekha, u-kh'tavtam al m'zuzot beitekha u'visharekha.

1 Corinthians 8:4-6

כִּי אֱלִיל כְּאַיִן הוּא בָּעוֹלָם וְכִי אֵין אֱלֹהִים זוּלָתִי אֶחָד. וְאַף כִּי יֵשׁ נִקְרָאִים אֱלֹהִים אִם בַּשָּׁמַיִם וְאִם בָּאָרֶץ כְּמוֹ הֵם אֱלֹהִים רַבִּים וַאֲדֹנִים רַבִּים. בְּכָל זֹאת לָנוּ רַק אֱלֹהִים אֶחָד הוּא אָבִי עַד אֲשֶׁר מִמֶּנּוּ הַכֹּל וְלוֹ אֲנַחְנוּ וְאָדוֹן אֶחָד יֵשׁוּעַ הַמָּשִׁיחַ אֲשֶׁר הַכֹּל עַל יָדוֹ וְעַל יָדוֹ גַּם אֲנַחְנוּ.

Mark 12:28-34

Then one of the scribes came, and having heard them reasoning together, perceiving that He had answered them well, asked Him, "Which is the first commandment of all?" Yeshua answered him, "The first of all the commandments is: Hear, O Israel, the Lord our God, the Lord is one. And you shall love the Lord your God with all your heart, with all your soul, with all your mind, and with all your strength. This is the first commandment. And the second, like it, is this: You shall love your neighbor as yourself. And there is no other commandment greater than these two." So the scribe said to Him, "Well said, Rabbi. You have spoken the truth, for there is one God, and there is no other but He. And to love Him with all the heart, with all the understanding, with all the soul, and with all the strength, and to love one's neighbor as oneself, is more than all the whole burnt offerings and sacrifices." Now when Yeshua saw that the man answered Him wisely, He said to him, "You are not far from the kingdom of God." And no one ever dared to argue with Him any more in words from that day on.

Shema

(When praying without a minyan begin by reciting: **God, trustworthy King***)*

(Recite loudly and slowly covering the eyes with the right hand)

Hear, O Israel, the Lord our God, the Lord is One!

(Recite softly and quickly without covering the eyes)
Blessed is His glorious Name, whose kingdom is forever and ever.

And you shall love the Lord your God with all your heart and with all your soul and with all your strength. These words that I give to you today are to be upon your hearts. Teach them to your children. Speak of them when you sit at home and when you walk along the way, when you lie down and when you rise up. Bind them as a sign upon your hands and as frontlets between your eyes. Inscribe them on the doorposts of your house and on your gates.

1 Corinthians 8:4-6

For we know that an idol is nothing in the world, and that there is no other God but One. For even if there are so-called gods, whether in heaven or on earth (as there are many gods and many lords), yet for us there is only one God, the Father, from whom are all things, and we for Him; and one Lord, Yeshua the Messiah, through whom are all things, and through whom we live.

Deuteronomy 11:13-21

וְהָיָה אִם שָׁמֹעַ תִּשְׁמְעוּ אֶל מִצְוֹתַי, אֲשֶׁר אָנֹכִי מְצַוֶּה אֶתְכֶם הַיּוֹם, לְאַהֲבָה אֶת יְיָ אֱלֹהֵיכֶם, וּלְעָבְדוֹ בְּכָל לְבַבְכֶם וּבְכָל נַפְשְׁכֶם. וְנָתַתִּי מְטַר אַרְצְכֶם בְּעִתּוֹ, יוֹרֶה וּמַלְקוֹשׁ, וְאָסַפְתָּ דְגָנֶךָ וְתִירֹשְׁךָ וְיִצְהָרֶךָ. וְנָתַתִּי עֵשֶׂב בְּשָׂדְךָ לִבְהֶמְתֶּךָ, וְאָכַלְתָּ וְשָׂבָעְתָּ. הִשָּׁמְרוּ לָכֶם פֶּן יִפְתֶּה לְבַבְכֶם, וְסַרְתֶּם וַעֲבַדְתֶּם אֱלֹהִים אֲחֵרִים וְהִשְׁתַּחֲוִיתֶם לָהֶם. וְחָרָה אַף יְיָ בָּכֶם, וְעָצַר אֶת הַשָּׁמַיִם וְלֹא יִהְיֶה מָטָר, וְהָאֲדָמָה לֹא תִתֵּן אֶת יְבוּלָהּ, וַאֲבַדְתֶּם מְהֵרָה מֵעַל הָאָרֶץ הַטֹּבָה אֲשֶׁר יְיָ נֹתֵן לָכֶם. וְשַׂמְתֶּם אֶת דְּבָרַי אֵלֶּה עַל לְבַבְכֶם וְעַל נַפְשְׁכֶם וּקְשַׁרְתֶּם אֹתָם לְאוֹת עַל יֶדְכֶם, וְהָיוּ לְטוֹטָפֹת בֵּין עֵינֵיכֶם. וְלִמַּדְתֶּם אֹתָם אֶת בְּנֵיכֶם, לְדַבֵּר בָּם, בְּשִׁבְתְּךָ בְּבֵיתֶךָ, וּבְלֶכְתְּךָ בַדֶּרֶךְ, וּבְשָׁכְבְּךָ וּבְקוּמֶךָ. וּכְתַבְתָּם עַל מְזוּזוֹת בֵּיתֶךָ וּבִשְׁעָרֶיךָ. לְמַעַן יִרְבּוּ יְמֵיכֶם וִימֵי בְנֵיכֶם עַל הָאֲדָמָה אֲשֶׁר נִשְׁבַּע יְיָ לַאֲבֹתֵיכֶם לָתֵת לָהֶם, כִּימֵי הַשָּׁמַיִם עַל הָאָרֶץ.

2 Timothy 2:8-13

זְכֹר אֶת יֵשׁוּעַ הַמָּשִׁיחַ שֶׁנֵּעוֹר מִן הַמֵּתִים, אֲשֶׁר הוּא מִזֶּרַע דָּוִד כְּדִבַר בְּשׂוֹרָתִי, הִיא הַבְּשׂוֹרָה שֶׁבַּעֲבוּרָהּ אֲנִי סוֹבֵל רָעוֹת עַד כְּדֵי שִׁבְתִּי בִכְבָלִים כְּעוֹשֵׂה עָוֶל. אוּלָם דְּבַר הָאֱלֹהִים אֵינֶנּוּ אָסוּר בִּכְבָלִים. עַל כֵּן אֲנִי סוֹבֵל הַכֹּל לְמַעַן הַנִּבְחָרִים, כְּדֵי שֶׁגַּם הֵם יַשִּׂיגוּ תְּשׁוּעָה בַּמָּשִׁיחַ יֵשׁוּעַ עִם כְּבוֹד עוֹלָמִים. מְהֵימָן הַדָּבָר: אִם מַתְנוּ אִתּוֹ, גַּם נִחְיֶה אִתּוֹ; אִם נַחֲזִיק מַעֲמָד, גַּם נִמְלֹךְ אִתּוֹ; אִם נִתְכַּחֵשׁ, גַּם הוּא יִתְכַּחֵשׁ לָנוּ; אִם אֵינֶנּוּ נֶאֱמָנִים, הוּא נִשְׁאָר נֶאֱמָן, כִּי לֹא יוּכַל לְהִתְכַּחֵשׁ לְעַצְמוֹ.

Numbers 15:37-41

וַיֹּאמֶר יְיָ אֶל מֹשֶׁה לֵּאמֹר: דַּבֵּר אֶל בְּנֵי יִשְׂרָאֵל וְאָמַרְתָּ אֲלֵהֶם. וְעָשׂוּ לָהֶם צִיצִת עַל כַּנְפֵי בִגְדֵיהֶם לְדֹרֹתָם, וְנָתְנוּ עַל צִיצִת הַכָּנָף פְּתִיל תְּכֵלֶת. וְהָיָה לָכֶם לְצִיצִת, וּרְאִיתֶם אֹתוֹ וּזְכַרְתֶּם אֶת כָּל מִצְוֹת יְיָ, וַעֲשִׂיתֶם אֹתָם, וְלֹא תָתוּרוּ אַחֲרֵי לְבַבְכֶם וְאַחֲרֵי עֵינֵיכֶם, אֲשֶׁר אַתֶּם זֹנִים אַחֲרֵיהֶם. לְמַעַן תִּזְכְּרוּ וַעֲשִׂיתֶם אֶת כָּל מִצְוֹתַי, וִהְיִיתֶם קְדֹשִׁים לֵאלֹהֵיכֶם. אֲנִי יְיָ אֱלֹהֵיכֶם, אֲשֶׁר הוֹצֵאתִי אֶתְכֶם מֵאֶרֶץ מִצְרַיִם, לִהְיוֹת לָכֶם לֵאלֹהִים, אֲנִי יְיָ אֱלֹהֵיכֶם.

(Reader) יְיָ אֱלֹהֵיכֶם אֱמֶת

אֱמֶת וְיַצִּיב וְנָכוֹן וְקַיָּם וְיָשָׁר וְנֶאֱמָן וְאָהוּב וְחָבִיב וְנֶחְמָד וְנָעִים וְנוֹרָא וְאַדִּיר וּמְתֻקָּן וּמְקֻבָּל וְטוֹב וְיָפֶה הַדָּבָר הַזֶּה עָלֵינוּ לְעוֹלָם וָעֶד. אֱמֶת אֱלֹהֵי עוֹלָם מַלְכֵּנוּ צוּר יַעֲקֹב, מָגֵן יִשְׁעֵנוּ. **(Reader)** לְדֹר וָדֹר הוּא קַיָּם, וּשְׁמוֹ קַיָּם, וְכִסְאוֹ נָכוֹן, וּמַלְכוּתוֹ וֶאֱמוּנָתוֹ לָעַד קַיָּמֶת. וּדְבָרָיו חָיִים וְקַיָּמִים, נֶאֱמָנִים וְנֶחֱמָדִים לָעַד וּלְעוֹלְמֵי עוֹלָמִים. עַל אֲבוֹתֵינוּ וְעָלֵינוּ, עַל בָּנֵינוּ וְעַל דּוֹרוֹתֵינוּ, וְעַל כָּל דּוֹרוֹת זֶרַע יִשְׂרָאֵל עֲבָדֶיךָ.

עַל הָרִאשׁוֹנִים וְעַל הָאַחֲרוֹנִים, דָּבָר טוֹב וְקַיָּם לְעוֹלָם וָעֶד, אֱמֶת וֶאֱמוּנָה חֹק וְלֹא יַעֲבֹר. **(Reader)** אֱמֶת שָׁאַתָּה הוּא יְיָ אֱלֹהֵינוּ וֵאלֹהֵי אֲבוֹתֵינוּ, מַלְכֵּנוּ מֶלֶךְ אֲבוֹתֵינוּ, גֹּאֲלֵנוּ גֹּאֵל אֲבוֹתֵינוּ, יוֹצְרֵנוּ צוּר יְשׁוּעָתֵנוּ, פּוֹדֵנוּ וּמַצִּילֵנוּ מֵעוֹלָם שְׁמֶךָ, אֵין אֱלֹהִים זוּלָתֶךָ.

Deuteronomy 11:13-21

And if you will carefully listen to My commandments which I am commanding you today, to love the Lord your God and to serve Him with all your heart and with all your soul, then I will send rain for your land in its season, the early rain and the latter rain, that you may gather in your grain, your wine and your oil. And I will produce grass in your fields for your cattle, that you may eat and be satisfied. Take care, lest your heart be deceived, and you turn aside and serve other gods, so as to worship them. Then the Lord's anger will blaze against you; He will shut up the heavens so there will be no rain, and the land will not yield any produce, and you will perish from the good land which the Lord has given to you. Therefore, you shall put these words of mine in your heart and in your soul; you shall bind them as a sign upon your hand, and they shall be for frontlets between your eyes. Teach them to your children. Speak of them when you are sitting at home and when you walk along the way, when you lie down and when you rise up. Inscribe them on the doorposts of your house and on your gates, that your days and the days of your children may be prolonged in the land, which the Lord swore to give to your fathers, as the days of the heavens upon the earth.

2 Timothy 2:8-13

You remember that Yeshua the Messiah, who was raised from the dead, is of the seed of David. This is the Good News I have proclaimed. For, on your behalf, I have suffered trouble to overcome evil, even to the point of my being tortured in chains. But the Word of God cannot be bound by chains. For this reason I endure all the suffering, for the sake of the chosen, that they also may obtain their salvation through Yeshua the Messiah, and that they glory in the Glory of the age. This is a true saying: If we died with Him, we shall also live with Him. If we suffer with Him, we shall also reign with Him. If we deny Him, He also will deny us. If there is no faithfulness in us, He will remain faithful, for He cannot deny Himself.

Numbers 15:37-41

The Lord spoke to Moses, saying, "Speak to the children of Israel. Tell them to make for themselves tsitsit on the corners of their garments, throughout their generations, and to put a thread of blue on the tsitsit of each corner. When you look upon these tsitsit you shall remember to do all the commands of the Lord, and not to follow the desires of your heart and your eyes that lead you astray. They are a reminder to do all of My commandments, and to be holy to your God. I, the Lord your God, brought you out of the land of Egypt to be your God; I am the Lord your God."

(Reader) **The Lord your God is True**

True and certain, established and enduring, right and faithful, beloved and precious, desirable and pleasant, revered and mighty, well ordered and acceptable, good and beautiful is Your teaching to us, forever and ever. It is true, the God of the universe is our King; the Rock of Jacob is our saving Shield. From generation to generation He endures and His Name endures; His throne is established, and His kingdom and faithfulness will endure forever. His words live and endure, faithful and desirable, forever and to all eternity, for our fathers and for us, for our generation and for our children, and for all the descendants of the seed of Israel.

Alike to the first and last generation, Your word is good; it endures forever and ever. True and trustworthy, it is a law that will not pass away. True, You are the Lord our God and the God of our fathers, our King and the King of our fathers, our Redeemer and the Redeemer of our fathers, our Maker, the Rock of our Salvation, our Deliverer and our Rescuer. Your Name is from time immemorial; there is no God but You.

עֶזְרַת אֲבוֹתֵינוּ אַתָּה הוּא מֵעוֹלָם, מָגֵן וּמוֹשִׁיעַ לִבְנֵיהֶם אַחֲרֵיהֶם בְּכָל דּוֹר וָדוֹר. בְּרוּם עוֹלָם מוֹשָׁבֶךָ, וּמִשְׁפָּטֶיךָ וְצִדְקָתְךָ עַד אַפְסֵי אָרֶץ. אַשְׁרֵי אִישׁ שֶׁיִּשְׁמַע לְמִצְוֹתֶיךָ, וְתוֹרָתְךָ וּדְבָרְךָ יָשִׂים עַל לִבּוֹ. אֱמֶת, אַתָּה הוּא אָדוֹן לְעַמֶּךָ, וּמֶלֶךְ גִּבּוֹר לָרִיב רִיבָם. אֱמֶת, אַתָּה הוּא רִאשׁוֹן וְאַתָּה הוּא אַחֲרוֹן, וּמִבַּלְעָדֶיךָ אֵין לָנוּ מֶלֶךְ גּוֹאֵל וּמוֹשִׁיעַ. מִמִּצְרַיִם גְּאַלְתָּנוּ, יְיָ אֱלֹהֵינוּ, וּמִבֵּית עֲבָדִים פְּדִיתָנוּ. כָּל בְּכוֹרֵיהֶם הָרָגְתָּ, וּבְכוֹרְךָ גָּאָלְתָּ, וְיַם סוּף בָּקַעְתָּ, וְזֵדִים טִבַּעְתָּ, וִידִידִים הֶעֱבַרְתָּ. וַיְכַסּוּ מַיִם צָרֵיהֶם, אֶחָד מֵהֶם לֹא נוֹתָר.

עַל זֹאת שִׁבְּחוּ אֲהוּבִים וְרוֹמְמוּ אֵל, וְנָתְנוּ יְדִידִים זְמִירוֹת, שִׁירוֹת וְתִשְׁבָּחוֹת, בְּרָכוֹת וְהוֹדָאוֹת לַמֶּלֶךְ, אֵל חַי וְקַיָּם. רָם וְנִשָּׂא, גָּדוֹל וְנוֹרָא, מַשְׁפִּיל גֵּאִים וּמַגְבִּיהַּ שְׁפָלִים, מוֹצִיא אֲסִירִים וּפוֹדֶה עֲנָוִים, וְעוֹזֵר דַּלִּים, וְעוֹנֶה לְעַמּוֹ בְּעֵת שַׁוְּעָם אֵלָיו. תְּהִלּוֹת לְאֵל עֶלְיוֹן, בָּרוּךְ הוּא וּמְבֹרָךְ.

Ephesians 1:17-21

כִּי אֱלֹהֵי יֵשׁוּעַ הַמָּשִׁיחַ אֲדוֹנֵינוּ אֲבִי הַכָּבוֹד יִתֵּן לָכֶם רוּחַ הַחָכְמָה וְהֶחָזוֹן לָדַעַת אֹתוֹ. וּלְהָאִיר עֵינֵי שִׂכְלְכֶם לְהַשְׂכִּיל מָה הִיא תִּקְוַת קְרוּאָיו וּמָה חֹסֶן כְּבוֹד לְקָדְשָׁיו בְּנַחֲלָתוֹ. וּמָה עֶצֶם גֹּדֶל גְּבוּרָתוֹ אֲשֶׁר פָּעַל בָּנוּ הַמַּאֲמִינִים בּוֹ לְפִי תֹקֶף עֻזּוֹ. הוּא אֲשֶׁר פָּעַל בַּמָּשִׁיחַ בַּאֲשֶׁר הֱקִימוֹ מִן הַמֵּתִים וַיּוֹשִׁיבֵהוּ לִימִינוֹ בַּמָּרוֹם. גָּבוֹהַ מִכָּל מִשְׂרָה וְשִׁלְטוֹן וּמֶמְשָׁלָה וּמִכָּל אֲשֶׁר נִקְרָא בְּשֵׁם גַּם בָּעוֹלָם הַזֶּה וְגַם בָּעוֹלָם הַבָּא.

מִי כָמְכָה

(Reader) מֹשֶׁה וּבְנֵי יִשְׂרָאֵל לְךָ עָנוּ שִׁירָה בְּשִׂמְחָה רַבָּה, וְאָמְרוּ כֻלָּם:

Moshe uv'nei Yisraeil l'kha anu shirah b'simḥah rabah, v'amru khulam.

(All) מִי כָמְכָה בָּאֵלִים יְיָ, מִי כָּמְכָה נֶאְדָּר בַּקֹּדֶשׁ, נוֹרָא תְהִלֹּת, עֹשֵׂה פֶלֶא.

Mi khamokhah ba'eilim Adonai, mi kamokhah ne'dar ba'kodesh, norah t'hillot, osei feleh.

(Reader) שִׁירָה חֲדָשָׁה שִׁבְּחוּ גְאוּלִים לְשִׁמְךָ עַל שְׂפַת הַיָּם, יַחַד כֻּלָּם הוֹדוּ וְהִמְלִיכוּ וְאָמְרוּ:

Shirah ḥadashah shib'ḥu ge'ulim l'shim'khah al s'fat hayam, yaḥad kulam hodu v'himlikhu v'amru.

(All) יְיָ יִמְלֹךְ לְעוֹלָם וָעֶד.

Adonai yim-lokh l'olam vah'ed.

(Reader) צוּר יִשְׂרָאֵל, קוּמָה בְּעֶזְרַת יִשְׂרָאֵל, וּפְדֵה כִנְאֻמֶךָ יְהוּדָה וְיִשְׂרָאֵל. גְּאָלֵנוּ יְיָ צְבָאוֹת שְׁמוֹ, קְדוֹשׁ יִשְׂרָאֵל. בָּרוּךְ אַתָּה יְיָ גָּאַל יִשְׂרָאֵל.

Tsur Yisraeil kumah be'ezrat Yisraeil, uf'dei khin'umekha Yehudah v'Yisraeil. Go'aleinu Adonai Tseva'ot shemo, kedosh Yisraeil. Barukh atah Adonai ga'al Yisraeil.

You helped our fathers from ages past, and have been a shield and savior to their children in every generation. You inhabit the heights above and Your justice and righteousness reach to the farthest ends of the earth. Happy is the one who obeys Your commands and takes Your instructions and words to heart. It is true that You are the Lord of Your people and a mighty king who champions their cause. It is true that You are the first and that You are the last; besides You we have no king who redeems and saves. From Egypt You redeemed us, Lord our God, and from the house of slavery You delivered us. All of their first born You killed, but our first born You saved. You divided the Red Sea and drowned their prideful ones, but Your beloved people You took through the water safely. The water covered them; not one of them was left.

Therefore, the beloved ones praised and exalted God. They offered hymns of praise, songs, blessings and thanksgiving to the King, the living and eternal God. High and exalted, great and awesome; He brings the arrogant down and raises the lowly up. He sets the captive free, delivers the humble, helps the poor and answers His people when they call to Him. The Most High God is to be praised. Blessed is He who is blessed.

Ephesians 1:17-21

I pray the God of our Lord Yeshua the Messiah, the Father of glory, may give to you the spirit of wisdom and revelation in the knowledge of Him. That the eyes of your understanding may be enlightened. That you may know what is the hope of His calling, what are the riches of the glory of His inheritance in the saints, and what is the exceeding greatness of His power toward us who believe, according to the working of His mighty power which He worked in the Messiah when He raised Him from the dead and seated Him at His right hand in the heavenly places, far above all principality and power and might and dominion, and every name that is named, not only in this age but also in that which is to come.

Mi Khamokha

(Reader) Moses and the children of Israel sang a song to You. With great joy they all said:

(All) Who is like You, O Lord, among the gods? Who is like You, glorious in holiness, awesome in praise, doing wonders?

(Reader) At the seashore, the people You redeemed sang a new song of praise to Your Name. With one voice they gave thanks and proclaimed You King, saying:

(All) The Lord shall reign forever and ever!

(Reader) O Rock of Israel, arise to the help of Israel; deliver Judah and Israel, as You have promised. He is called Our Redeemer, Lord of Hosts, the Holy One of Israel. Blessed are You, Lord, who has redeemed Israel.

(עמידה for Weekday - see page 144; for Shabbat Shuva and Festivals - see page 166)

עמידה

(All rise and face east or toward an open ark - take three steps back, then three steps forward)

Adonai s'fatay tiftaḥ ufi yagid tehilatekha.　　אֲדֹנָי שְׂפָתַי תִּפְתָּח וּפִי יַגִּיד תְּהִלָּתֶךָ.

אבות

(Bend the knees at בָּרוּךְ Bow at אַתָּה Straighten at יְיָ)

בָּרוּךְ אַתָּה יְיָ אֱלֹהֵינוּ וֵאלֹהֵי אֲבוֹתֵינוּ, אֱלֹהֵי אַבְרָהָם, אֱלֹהֵי יִצְחָק, וֵאלֹהֵי יַעֲקֹב, הָאֵל הַגָּדוֹל הַגִּבּוֹר וְהַנּוֹרָא, אֵל עֶלְיוֹן, גּוֹמֵל חֲסָדִים טוֹבִים, וְקוֹנֵה הַכֹּל, וְזוֹכֵר חַסְדֵי אָבוֹת אֲשֶׁר הֵבִיא, וּמֵבִיא, גּוֹאֵל לִבְנֵי בְנֵיהֶם לְמַעַן שְׁמוֹ בְּאַהֲבָה.

Barukh atah Adonai, Eloheinu vailohei avoteinu, Elohei Avraham, Elohei Yitzḥak, vei-Elohei Ya'akov. Ha-El hagadol hagibor v'hanorah, El Elyon, gomeil ḥasadim tovim, v'konei hakol, v'zokheir ḥas'dei avot, asher heivi, u-meivi, go'eil liv'nei v'neihem l'ma-an sh'mo b'ahavah.

(Bend the knees at בָּרוּךְ Bow at אַתָּה Straighten at יְיָ)

מֶלֶךְ עוֹזֵר וּמוֹשִׁיעַ וּמָגֵן.　　בָּרוּךְ אַתָּה יְיָ, מָגֵן אַבְרָהָם.

Melekh ozer umoshia umagein. Barukh atah Adonai, magein Avraham.

גבורות

אַתָּה גִבּוֹר לְעוֹלָם אֲדֹנָי, מְחַיֵּה מֵתִים אַתָּה, רַב לְהוֹשִׁיעַ.

Atah gibor l'olam, Adonai, meḥayei meitim atah, rav l'hoshia.

(Between Shemini Atseret and Pesaḥ add)

Mashiv ha'ruaḥ u'morid ha'geshem.　　מַשִּׁיב הָרוּחַ וּמוֹרִיד הַגָּשֶׁם.

מְכַלְכֵּל חַיִּים בְּחֶסֶד, מְחַיֵּה מֵתִים בְּרַחֲמִים רַבִּים, סוֹמֵךְ נוֹפְלִים, וְרוֹפֵא חוֹלִים, וּמַתִּיר אֲסוּרִים, וּמְקַיֵּם אֱמוּנָתוֹ לִישֵׁנֵי עָפָר, מִי כָמוֹךָ בַּעַל גְּבוּרוֹת וּמִי דּוֹמֶה לָּךְ, מֶלֶךְ מֵמִית וּמְחַיֶּה וּמַצְמִיחַ יְשׁוּעָה. וְנֶאֱמָן אַתָּה לְהַחֲיוֹת מֵתִים. בָּרוּךְ אַתָּה יְיָ, מְחַיֵּה הַמֵּתִים.

M'khalkeil ḥayim b'ḥesed, M'ḥayei meitim b'raḥamim rabim. Someikh nof'lim, v'rofei ḥolim, umatir asurim, um'kayeim emunatoh lisheinei afar. Mi khamokha ba'al g'vurot, umi do'meh lakh, melekh meimit um'ḥayeh u'matsmiaḥ yeshua. V'ne'eman atah l'haḥayot meitim. Barukh atah Adonai, m'ḥayei hameitim.

(During the silent Amidah continue with אַתָּה קָדוֹשׁ on page 88.

During the Reader's repetition continue here. Rise on your toes at קָדוֹשׁ, קָדוֹשׁ, בָּרוּךְ and (יִמְלֹךְ)

קדושה

(All) נְקַדֵּשׁ אֶת שִׁמְךָ בָּעוֹלָם, כְּשֵׁם שֶׁמַּקְדִּישִׁים אוֹתוֹ בִּשְׁמֵי מָרוֹם, כַּכָּתוּב עַל יַד
N'kadeish et shim'kha ba'olam, k'sheim　　נְבִיאֶךָ, וְקָרָא זֶה אֶל זֶה וְאָמַר:
shemak'dishim oto bish'mei marom, kakatuv al yad n'vi'ekha, v'kara ze el ze v'amar:

קָדוֹשׁ, קָדוֹשׁ, קָדוֹשׁ, יְיָ צְבָאוֹת, מְלֹא כָל הָאָרֶץ כְּבוֹדוֹ.
Kadosh, kadosh, kadosh, Adonai Ts'vaot, m'lo khal ha'arets k'vodo.

(Reader) אָז בְּקוֹל רַעַשׁ גָּדוֹל אַדִּיר וְחָזָק מַשְׁמִיעִים קוֹל, מִתְנַשְּׂאִים לְעֻמַּת שְׂרָפִים, לְעֻמָּתָם בָּרוּךְ יֹאמֵרוּ.

(All) בָּרוּךְ כְּבוֹד יְיָ, מִמְּקוֹמוֹ.
Barukh k'vod Adonai mim'komo

(Amidah for Weekday - see page 145; for Shabbat Shuva and Festivals - see page 167)

Amidah

(All rise and face east or toward an open ark - take three steps back, then three steps forward)

Lord, you will open my lips that my mouth may declare Your praise.

Avot

*(Bend the knees at **Blessed**, Bow at **Are You**, Straighten at **Lord**)*

Blessed are You, Lord our God and God of our fathers, God of Abraham, God of Isaac and God of Jacob. The great, mighty and awesome God, Most High God, who grants loving kindness and is Master of all. You remember the deeds of our fathers, and in Your love You have brought, and you bring, a Redeemer to their children's children for the sake of Your Name.

*(Bend the knees at **Blessed**, Bow at **Are You**, Straighten at **Lord**)*

King, Supporter, Savior and Shield, blessed are You, Lord, Shield of Abraham.

G'vurot

Lord, You are mighty forever. You call the dead to life. You are mighty to save.

(Between Shemini Atseret and Pesah add)
You cause the wind to return and the rain to come down.

You sustain the living with loving kindness, and with great mercy You revive the dead. You uphold those who fall, heal the sick, set the captive free and keep faith with those who sleep in the dust. Lord of might, who is like You? King, who can be compared to You? You decree death and restore life, causing salvation to come forth. You are faithful to revive the dead. Blessed are You, Lord, who calls the dead to life.

*(During the silent Amidah continue with **You are Holy** on page 89.*
During the Reader's repetition begin here.
*Rise on your toes at **Holy, Holy, Holy**, **Blessed** and **The Lord will Reign**)*

Kedushah

(All) We will sanctify Your Name in this world, even as they sanctify it in the heavens above, as it is written by Your prophet, They continuously call to one another:

Holy, holy, holy is the Lord of Hosts; the whole earth is filled with His glory.

(Reader) Then with a loud sound, mighty and strong, they make their voices heard, raising themselves toward the Seraphim, they respond by saying:

(All) Blessed. . . Blessed is the glory of the Lord from His abode.

מִמְּקוֹמְךָ מַלְכֵּנוּ תוֹפִיעַ, וְתִמְלֹךְ עָלֵינוּ, כִּי מְחַכִּים אֲנַחְנוּ לָךְ.   מָתַי תִּמְלֹךְ בְּצִיּוֹן, בְּקָרוֹב בְּיָמֵינוּ, לְעוֹלָם וָעֶד תִּשְׁכּוֹן.   תִּתְגַּדַּל וְתִתְקַדַּשׁ בְּתוֹךְ יְרוּשָׁלַיִם עִירְךָ, לְדוֹר וָדוֹר וּלְנֵצַח נְצָחִים.   וְעֵינֵינוּ תִרְאֶינָה מַלְכוּתֶךָ, כַּדָּבָר הָאָמוּר בְּשִׁירֵי עֻזֶּךָ, עַל יְדֵי דָוִד מְשִׁיחַ צִדְקֶךָ.

(All)   יִמְלֹךְ יְיָ לְעוֹלָם, אֱלֹהַיִךְ צִיּוֹן לְדֹר וָדֹר, הַלְלוּיָהּ.

Yim'lokh Adonai l'olam Elohayikh Tsiyon, l'dor vador, halleluyah

(Reader)   לְדוֹר וָדוֹר נַגִּיד גָּדְלֶךָ וּלְנֵצַח נְצָחִים קְדֻשָּׁתְךָ נַקְדִּישׁ, וְשִׁבְחֲךָ אֱלֹהֵינוּ מִפִּינוּ לֹא יָמוּשׁ לְעוֹלָם וָעֶד, כִּי אֵל מֶלֶךְ גָּדוֹל וְקָדוֹשׁ אָתָּה.   בָּרוּךְ אַתָּה יְיָ, הָאֵל הַקָּדוֹשׁ.

(During the silent Amidah continue here)

אַתָּה קָדוֹשׁ וְשִׁמְךָ קָדוֹשׁ, וּקְדוֹשִׁים בְּכָל יוֹם יְהַלְלוּךָ, סֶּלָה.   בָּרוּךְ אַתָּה יְיָ, הָאֵל הַקָּדוֹשׁ.

וְשָׁמְרוּ

וְשָׁמְרוּ בְנֵי יִשְׂרָאֵל אֶת הַשַּׁבָּת, לַעֲשׂוֹת אֶת הַשַּׁבָּת לְדֹרֹתָם בְּרִית עוֹלָם.   בֵּינִי וּבֵין בְּנֵי יִשְׂרָאֵל אוֹת הִיא לְעֹלָם, כִּי שֵׁשֶׁת יָמִים עָשָׂה יְיָ אֶת הַשָּׁמַיִם וְאֶת הָאָרֶץ, וּבַיּוֹם הַשְּׁבִיעִי שָׁבַת וַיִּנָּפַשׁ.

V'shamru v'nei Yisraeil et ha'shabbat, la'asot et ha'shabbat l'dorotam b'rit olam. Beini uvein b'nei Yisraeil ot hi l'olam, ki sheishet yamim asah Adonai et hashamayim v'et ha'arets, uvayom hash'vi-i shavat vayinafash.

עַם מְקַדְּשֵׁי שְׁבִיעִי, כֻּלָּם יִשְׂבְּעוּ וְיִתְעַנְּגוּ מִטּוּבֶךָ, וּבַשְּׁבִיעִי רָצִיתָ בּוֹ וְקִדַּשְׁתּוֹ, חֶמְדַּת יָמִים אוֹתוֹ קָרָאתָ, זֵכֶר לְמַעֲשֵׂה בְרֵאשִׁית.

אֱלֹהֵינוּ וֵאלֹהֵי

אֱלֹהֵינוּ וֵאלֹהֵי אֲבוֹתֵינוּ, רְצֵה בִמְנוּחָתֵנוּ.   קַדְּשֵׁנוּ בְּמִצְוֹתֶיךָ וְתֵן חֶלְקֵנוּ בְּתוֹרָתֶךָ, שַׂבְּעֵנוּ מִטּוּבֶךָ, וְשַׂמְּחֵנוּ בִּישׁוּעָתֶךָ, וְטַהֵר לִבֵּנוּ לְעָבְדְּךָ בֶּאֱמֶת, וְהַנְחִילֵנוּ יְיָ אֱלֹהֵינוּ בְּאַהֲבָה וּבְרָצוֹן שַׁבַּת קָדְשֶׁךָ, וְיָנוּחוּ בָהּ יִשְׂרָאֵל, מְקַדְּשֵׁי שְׁמֶךָ.   בָּרוּךְ אַתָּה יְיָ, מְקַדֵּשׁ הַשַּׁבָּת.

Eloheinu veilohei avoteinu, r'tsei bim'nuhateinu. Kad'sheinu b'mits'votekha v'tein hel'keinu b'toratekha, sab'einu mituvekha v'sam'heinu bishu'ateka, v'taheir libeinu l'avdekha be'emet, v'han'hileinu Adonai Eloheinu b'ahava uv'ratson shabbat kad'shekha, v'yanuhu va Yisraeil m'kad'shei sh'mekha. Barukh atah Adonai, m'kadesh ha'shabbat.

רְצֵה, יְיָ אֱלֹהֵינוּ, בְּעַמְּךָ יִשְׂרָאֵל וּבִתְפִלָּתָם, וְהָשֵׁב אֶת הָעֲבוֹדָה לִדְבִיר בֵּיתֶךָ, וְאִשֵּׁי יִשְׂרָאֵל, וּתְפִלָּתָם בְּאַהֲבָה תְקַבֵּל בְּרָצוֹן, וּתְהִי לְרָצוֹן תָּמִיד עֲבוֹדַת יִשְׂרָאֵל עַמֶּךָ.

(On Rosh Hodesh, Hol HaMoed Pesah and Sukkot insert the appropriate blessing here from page 156)

וְתֶחֱזֶינָה עֵינֵינוּ בְּשׁוּבְךָ לְצִיּוֹן בְּרַחֲמִים. בָּרוּךְ אַתָּה יְיָ, הַמַּחֲזִיר שְׁכִינָתוֹ לְצִיּוֹן.

V'teheze-na ei'neinu b'shuvkha l'Tsiyon b'rahamim. Barukh atah Adonai, hamahazir sh'khinato l'Tsiyon.

Our King, You will come forth from Your abode and You will reign over us, for we wait for You. When will You reign in Tsiyon? Quickly, indeed, in our days, dwell there forever. May Your greatness and Your holiness be seen in Your city, Jerusalem, through all generations and to all eternity. May our eyes behold your Kingdom, as it is said by your righteous anointed one David, in Your songs of glory:

> *(All)* The Lord will reign forever; your God, O Tsiyon,
> from generation to generation. Halleluyah!

(Reader) We will declare Your greatness from generation to generation. We will proclaim Your holiness to all eternity. Your praise, our God, will never depart from our mouth, for You, God, are a great and mighty King. Blessed are You, Lord, holy God.

(During the silent Amidah continue here)

You are holy, and Your Name is holy, and holy ones proclaim Your praise daily. Blessed are You, Lord, holy God.

V'shamru

And the children of Israel will keep the Shabbat, observing the Shabbat to all generations as an everlasting covenant. It is a sign between Me and the children of Israel forever, for in six days the Lord made the heavens and the earth, and on the seventh day He ceased from work and He rested.

The people who set apart the seventh day shall all be satisfied and will delight in Your goodness. You took pleasure in the seventh day and made it holy, proclaiming it the most desirable of days; a remembrance of the beginning.

Eloheinu Ve'lohei

Our God, and God of our fathers, be pleased with our rest. Set us apart through Your commandments, and grant us a portion in Your Torah. Satisfy us with Your goodness, and make us glad in Your salvation. Purify our hearts to serve You in truth, and grant us, Lord our God, in love and in grace, that Your holy Shabbat remain an inheritance, and that Israel, who sanctifies Your Name, will rest on it. Blessed are You, Lord, who makes the Shabbat holy!

Take pleasure, Lord our God, in Your people Israel, and in their prayer. Restore the service to Your most holy house, and receive Israel's offerings by fire, and their prayer with gracious love. May the worship of Your people Israel always be pleasing to You.

(On Rosh Ḥodesh, Ḥol HaMoed Pesaḥ and Sukkot insert the appropriate blessing here from page 157)

May we see, with our own eyes, Your return to Tsiyon in compassion. Blessed are You, Lord, whose Presence is the restoration of Tsiyon.

מודים אנחנו

(While the Reader recites out loud the מוֹדִים אֲנַחְנוּ*, the Congregation recites* מוֹדִים דְּרַבָּנָן *softly.*
Bend the knees at מוֹדִים אֲנַחְנוּ *and straighten at* יְיָ*)*

מוֹדִים אֲנַחְנוּ לָךְ שָׁאַתָּה הוּא יְיָ אֱלֹהֵינוּ
וֵאלֹהֵי אֲבוֹתֵינוּ לְעוֹלָם וָעֶד. צוּר חַיֵּינוּ, מָגֵן
יִשְׁעֵנוּ, אַתָּה הוּא לְדוֹר וָדוֹר, נוֹדֶה לְּךָ
וּנְסַפֵּר תְּהִלָּתֶךָ, עַל חַיֵּינוּ הַמְּסוּרִים בְּיָדֶךָ,
וְעַל נִשְׁמוֹתֵינוּ הַפְּקוּדוֹת לָךְ, וְעַל נִסֶּיךָ
שֶׁבְּכָל יוֹם עִמָּנוּ, וְעַל נִפְלְאוֹתֶיךָ וְטוֹבוֹתֶיךָ
שֶׁבְּכָל עֵת, עֶרֶב וָבֹקֶר וְצָהֳרָיִם, הַטּוֹב, כִּי
לֹא כָלוּ רַחֲמֶיךָ, וְהַמְרַחֵם, כִּי לֹא תַמּוּ
חֲסָדֶיךָ, מֵעוֹלָם קִוִּינוּ לָךְ.

מודים דרבנן

מוֹדִים אֲנַחְנוּ לָךְ, שָׁאַתָּה הוּא יְיָ אֱלֹהֵינוּ
וֵאלֹהֵי אֲבוֹתֵינוּ, אֱלֹהֵי כָל בָּשָׂר, יוֹצְרֵנוּ,
יוֹצֵר בְּרֵאשִׁית. בְּרָכוֹת וְהוֹדָאוֹת לְשִׁמְךָ
הַגָּדוֹל וְהַקָּדוֹשׁ, עַל שֶׁהֶחֱיִיתָנוּ וְקִיַּמְתָּנוּ. כֵּן
תְּחַיֵּנוּ וּתְקַיְּמֵנוּ, וְתֶאֱסוֹף גָּלֻיּוֹתֵינוּ לְחַצְרוֹת
קָדְשֶׁךָ, לִשְׁמֹר חֻקֶּיךָ וְלַעֲשׂוֹת רְצוֹנֶךָ,
וּלְעָבְדְּךָ בְּלֵבָב שָׁלֵם, עַל שֶׁאֲנַחְנוּ מוֹדִים
לָךְ. בָּרוּךְ אֵל הַהוֹדָאוֹת.

(On Hanukah and Purim insert the appropriate blessing here from page 158)

וְעַל כֻּלָּם יִתְבָּרַךְ וְיִתְרוֹמַם שִׁמְךָ מַלְכֵּנוּ תָּמִיד לְעוֹלָם וָעֶד. וְכֹל הַחַיִּים יוֹדוּךָ סֶּלָה,
וִיהַלְלוּ אֶת שִׁמְךָ בֶּאֱמֶת, הָאֵל יְשׁוּעָתֵנוּ וְעֶזְרָתֵנוּ, סֶלָה.

(Bend the knees at בָּרוּךְ *Bow at* אַתָּה *Straighten at* יְיָ*)*

בָּרוּךְ אַתָּה יְיָ, הַטּוֹב שִׁמְךָ וּלְךָ נָאֶה לְהוֹדוֹת.

(The Reader recites the Aaronic Blessing during his repetition)

אֱלֹהֵינוּ וֵאלֹהֵי אֲבוֹתֵינוּ, בָּרְכֵנוּ בַבְּרָכָה הַמְשֻׁלֶּשֶׁת בַּתּוֹרָה הַכְּתוּבָה עַל יְדֵי מֹשֶׁה
עַבְדֶּךָ, הָאֲמוּרָה מִפִּי אַהֲרֹן וּבָנָיו כֹּהֲנִים, עַם קְדוֹשֶׁךָ, כָּאָמוּר.

Cong - *Kein yehi ratson* (קהל-כֵּן יְהִי רָצוֹן) יְבָרֶכְךָ יְיָ וְיִשְׁמְרֶךָ.

Cong - *Kein yehi ratson* (קהל-כֵּן יְהִי רָצוֹן) יָאֵר יְיָ פָּנָיו אֵלֶיךָ וִיחֻנֶּךָּ.

Cong - *Kein yehi ratson* (קהל-כֵּן יְהִי רָצוֹן) יִשָּׂא יְיָ פָּנָיו אֵלֶיךָ וְיָשֵׂם לְךָ שָׁלוֹם.

שים שלום

שִׂים שָׁלוֹם טוֹבָה וּבְרָכָה, חֵן וָחֶסֶד וְרַחֲמִים, עָלֵינוּ וְעַל כָּל יִשְׂרָאֵל עַמֶּךָ. בָּרְכֵנוּ,
אָבִינוּ, כֻּלָּנוּ כְּאֶחָד בְּאוֹר פָּנֶיךָ, כִּי בְאוֹר פָּנֶיךָ נָתַתָּ לָּנוּ, יְיָ אֱלֹהֵינוּ, תּוֹרַת חַיִּים
וְאַהֲבַת חֶסֶד, וּצְדָקָה וּבְרָכָה וְרַחֲמִים וְחַיִּים וְשָׁלוֹם, וְטוֹב בְּעֵינֶיךָ לְבָרֵךְ אֶת עַמְּךָ
יִשְׂרָאֵל בְּכָל עֵת וּבְכָל שָׁעָה בִּשְׁלוֹמֶךָ. בָּרוּךְ אַתָּה יְיָ, הַמְבָרֵךְ אֶת עַמּוֹ יִשְׂרָאֵל
בַּשָּׁלוֹם.

Sim Shalom tovah uvrakha ḥein vaḥesed v'raḥamim aleinu v'al kal Yisraeil amekha.
Barkheinu avinu kulanu ke'eḥad b'or panekha, ki v'or panekha natahta lanu, Adonai
Eloheinu, Torat ḥayim v'ahavat ḥesed, uts'daka uv'rakha v'raḥamim v'ḥayim v'shalom,
v'tov b'eineikha l'vareikh et am'kha Yisraeil b'khal eit uv'khal sha'ah bish'lomekha.
Barukh atah Adonai, ham'vareikh et amo Yisraeil ba'shalom.

(After the Amidah the following meditation is added)

אֱלֹהַי, נְצוֹר לְשׁוֹנִי מֵרָע. וּשְׂפָתַי מִדַּבֵּר מִרְמָה. וְלִמְקַלְלַי נַפְשִׁי תִדּוֹם. וְנַפְשִׁי כֶּעָפָר לַכֹּל תִּהְיֶה. פְּתַח לִבִּי בְּתוֹרָתֶךָ.
וּבְמִצְוֹתֶיךָ תִּרְדּוֹף נַפְשִׁי. וְכָל הַחוֹשְׁבִים עָלַי רָעָה, מְהֵרָה הָפֵר עֲצָתָם וְקַלְקֵל מַחֲשַׁבְתָּם. עֲשֵׂה לְמַעַן שְׁמֶךָ, עֲשֵׂה לְמַעַן
יְמִינֶךָ, עֲשֵׂה לְמַעַן קְדֻשָּׁתֶךָ. עֲשֵׂה לְמַעַן תּוֹרָתֶךָ. לְמַעַן יֵחָלְצוּן יְדִידֶיךָ, הוֹשִׁיעָה יְמִינְךָ וַעֲנֵנִי. יִהְיוּ לְרָצוֹן אִמְרֵי פִי וְהֶגְיוֹן
לִבִּי לְפָנֶיךָ. יְיָ צוּרִי וְגוֹאֲלִי. עֹשֶׂה שָׁלוֹם בִּמְרוֹמָיו, הוּא יַעֲשֶׂה שָׁלוֹם עָלֵינוּ, וְעַל כָּל יִשְׂרָאֵל, וְאִמְרוּ, אָמֵן.

(At Shaharit only on Rosh Hodesh, Hol HaMoed and Hanukah continue with Hallel on page 180)

Modim Anaḥnu

(While the Reader recites out loud **Modim Anaḥnu**, *the Congregation recites* **Modim of the Rabbis** *softly.*
Bend the knees at **Lord, we are eternally grateful** *and straighten at* **Lord**)

Modim of the Rabbis

Lord, we are eternally grateful that You are the Lord our God and the God of our fathers. God of all flesh, our Creator and Creator in the beginning; blessings and thanks are due Your great and holy Name, for You have kept us alive and You sustained us. May You continue to grant us life and to sustain us. Bring our dispersed to Your courts, that in holiness they would observe Your laws, do Your will and serve You with all their heart; for these things we give You thanks. Blessed is the God of thanksgiving.

Lord, we are eternally grateful that You are the Lord our God and the God of our fathers. You are the strength of our life and the Shield of our Salvation. We thank You from generation to generation, and recount Your praise; for our lives which are in Your hand; and for our souls which are in Your care; and for Your miracles which are seen every day; and for Your wondrous deeds and favors which are always with us - evening, morning and noon. Beneficent One, Your compassion never fails; Merciful One, Your loving kindness never ends; You have always been our hope.

(On Ḥanukah and Purim insert the appropriate blessing here from page 159)

For all these things we will bless and we will lift up Your Name, our King, always, to the end of the age, and until. And all the living will thank You, and in truth they will praise Your Name; the God of our Salvation and our Help at all times.

(Bend the knees at **Blessed**, *Bow at* **Are You**, *Straighten at* **Lord**)

Blessed are You, Lord; it is right to give thanks to You, for Your Name is good.

(The Reader recites the Aaronic Blessing during his repetition)

Our God and God of our fathers, bless us with the threefold blessing written in Torah by Moses, Your servant, and spoken through the mouth of Aaron; and his sons, the priests, Your holy people, as it is said:

May the Lord bless you and keep you!
(Congregation: *May it be Your will!*)
May the Lord lift up His countenance to you, and be gracious to you!
(Congregation: *May it be Your will!*)
May the Lord turn His countenance toward you, and establish peace for you!
(Congregation: *May it be Your will!*)

Sim Shalom

Grant peace, happiness, blessing, grace, kindness and mercy to us and all Israel, Your people. Our Father, bless us all alike with the light of Your countenance. Lord our God, by the light of Your countenance You have given us a Torah of life, loving kindness, charity, blessing, mercy, life and peace. May it be good in Your sight to bless Your people Israel with peace at all times and at every hour. Blessed are You, Lord, the one who blessed His nation Israel with peace.

(After the Amidah the following meditation is added)

My God, guard my tongue from evil, and my lips from speaking falsehood. May my soul be silent to those who insult me, and may my soul be humble before all. Open my heart to Your Torah, that my soul might follow Your commands. As for all who plot evil against me, thwart their counsel and upset their plans. Do it for the sake of Your Name. Do it for the sake of Your power. Do it for the sake of Your holiness. Do it for the sake of Your Torah, that the one on whom You have set Your love might be rescued; save with Your right hand and answer us. May the words that proceed from my mouth and the secret thoughts that are in my heart be pleasing to You, O Lord, for You are my Stronghold as well as my Redeemer. May He who creates peace in His high heavens create peace for us and for all Israel, and say, "Amen."

(At Shaḥarit only on Rosh Hodesh, Hol HaMoed and Ḥanukah continue with Hallel on page 181)

קריאת התורה

Matthew 5:17-19

וַיֹּאמֶר יֵשׁוּעַ: אַל תַּחְשְׁבוּ שֶׁבָּאתִי לְבַטֵּל אֶת הַתּוֹרָה אוֹ אֶת הַנְּבִיאִים; לֹא בָאתִי לְבַטֵּל כִּי אִם לְקַיֵּם. אָמֵן. אוֹמֵר אֲנִי לָכֶם, עַד אֲשֶׁר יַעַבְרוּ הַשָּׁמַיִם וְהָאָרֶץ אַף יוֹד אַחַת אוֹ תָג אֶחָד לֹא יַעַבְרוּ מִן הַתּוֹרָה בְּטֶרֶם יִתְקַיֵּם הַכֹּל. לָכֵן כָּל הַמֵּפֵר אַחַת מִן הַמִּצְוֹת הַקְּטַנּוֹת הָאֵלֶּה וּמְלַמֵּד כָּךְ אֶת הַבְּרִיּוֹת, קָטוֹן יִקָּרֵא בְּמַלְכוּת הַשָּׁמַיִם. אֲבָל כָּל הָעוֹשֶׂה וּמְלַמֵּד, הוּא גָּדוֹל יִקָּרֵא בְּמַלְכוּת הַשָּׁמַיִם.

אין כמוך

אֵין כָּמוֹךָ בָאֱלֹהִים, יְיָ, וְאֵין כְּמַעֲשֶׂיךָ. מַלְכוּתְךָ מַלְכוּת כָּל עֹלָמִים, וּמֶמְשַׁלְתְּךָ בְּכָל דֹר וָדֹר. יְיָ מֶלֶךְ, יְיָ מָלָךְ, יְיָ יִמְלֹךְ לְעֹלָם וָעֶד. יְיָ עֹז לְעַמּוֹ יִתֵּן, יְיָ יְבָרֵךְ אֶת עַמּוֹ בַשָּׁלוֹם. אַב הָרַחֲמִים, הֵיטִיבָה בִרְצוֹנְךָ אֶת צִיּוֹן תִּבְנֶה חוֹמוֹת יְרוּשָׁלָיִם. כִּי בְךָ לְבַד בָּטַחְנוּ, מֶלֶךְ אֵל רָם וְנִשָּׂא, אֲדוֹן עוֹלָמִים.

Ein kamokha vaElohim Adonai, v'ein kema'asekha, malkhut'kha, malkhut kal olamim umem'shal'tekha b'khal dor vador. Adonai Melekh, Adonai Malakh, Adonai Yimlokh l'olam va'ed. Adonai oz l'amo yitein, Adonai y'vareikh et amo ba'shalom. Av harahamim heitiva bir'tson'kha et Tsiyon. Tiv'neh homot Y'rushalayim. Ki v'kha l'vad batah'nu Melekh El ram v'nisah Adon Olamim.

(The ark is opened - all rise)

John 1:1-3, 14

בְּרֵאשִׁית הָיָה הַדָּבָר, וְהַדָּבָר הָיָה עִם הָאֱלֹהִים, וֵאלֹהִים הָיָה הַדָּבָר. הוּא הָיָה בְּרֵאשִׁית עִם הָאֱלֹהִים. הַכֹּל נִהְיָה עַל־יָדָיו, וּמִבַּלְעָדָיו לֹא נִהְיָה כָּל אֲשֶׁר נִהְיָה. הַדָּבָר נִהְיָה בָּשָׂר וְשָׁכַן בְּתוֹכֵנוּ, וַאֲנַחְנוּ רָאִינוּ אֶת כְּבוֹדוֹ, כְּבוֹד בֵּן יָחִיד מִלִּפְנֵי אָבִיו, מָלֵא חֶסֶד וֶאֱמֶת

ויהי בנסע

וַיְהִי בִּנְסֹעַ הָאָרֹן וַיֹּאמֶר מֹשֶׁה, קוּמָה יְיָ, וְיָפֻצוּ אֹיְבֶיךָ, וְיָנֻסוּ מְשַׂנְאֶיךָ מִפָּנֶיךָ. כִּי מִצִּיּוֹן תֵּצֵא תוֹרָה, וּדְבַר יְיָ מִירוּשָׁלָיִם. בָּרוּךְ שֶׁנָּתַן תּוֹרָה לְעַמּוֹ יִשְׂרָאֵל בִּקְדֻשָּׁתוֹ.

Vay'hi binso'a ha'aron vayomer Moshe, kumah Adonai, v'yafutsu o'yevekha v'yanusu m'sanekha mipanekha. Ki miTsiyon teitsei Torah, u-devar Adonai miYrushalayim. Barukh shenatan Torah l'amo Yisraeil bik'dushato.

(On Festivals but not on a Shabbat recite the following statement three times)

יְיָ, יְיָ, אֵל רַחוּם וְחַנּוּן, אֶרֶךְ אַפַּיִם, וְרַב חֶסֶד וֶאֱמֶת. נֹצֵר חֶסֶד לָאֲלָפִים, נֹשֵׂא עָוֹן וָפֶשַׁע וְחַטָּאָה, וְנַקֵּה.

Adonai, Adonai, Eil rahum v'hanun, erekh a-pa-yim, v'rav hesed v'emet. Notseir hesed la-alafim, nosei avohn vafe-sha v'hata'ah, v'nakeih.

Kriat HaTorah

Matthew 5:17-19

And Yeshua said, "Don't misunderstand why I have come. I did not come to abolish the law of Moses or the writings of the prophets. No, I came to fulfill them. I assure you, until heaven and earth disappear, even the smallest detail of God's law will remain until its purpose is achieved. So if you break the smallest commandment and, in so doing, teach others to do the same, you will be the least in the Kingdom of Heaven. But anyone who obeys God's laws and, in so doing, teaches them, will be great in the Kingdom of Heaven."

Ein Kamokha

Lord, there is no God like You, and no deeds like Yours. Your kingdom is a kingdom for all eternity, and Your dominion is from generation to generation. The Lord is King, the Lord was King, the Lord will be King forever and ever. The Lord will give strength to His people; Lord, give Your blessing of peace to Your people. Compassionate Father, may it please You to favor Tsiyon with Your goodness; rebuild the walls of Jerusalem. We trust only in You, King, God, high and exalted Lord of Eternity.

(The ark is opened - all rise)

John 1:1-3, 14

In the beginning was the Word, and the Word was with God, and the Word was God. The Word was in the beginning with God. All things were made through Him, and without Him was not anything made that has been made. And the Word became flesh, and lived among us, and we saw His glory, glory as of the only begotten from the Father, full of grace and truth.

Vay'hi Binso'ah

And it came to pass, whenever the Ark went forth, Moses would say, "Rise up, Lord, and scatter Your enemies, and may those who hate You run from Your countenance." Instruction will go forth out of Tsiyon and the Lord's Word from Jerusalem. Blessed is He who, in holiness, gave Torah to His people Israel.

(On Festivals but not on a Shabbat recite the following statement three times)

The Lord, the Lord God is compassionate and merciful, slow to anger, and abundant in loving kindness. He keeps loving kindness to the thousands of generations, forgiving and acquitting sin and iniquity and transgression.

בֵּהּ אֲנָא רָחֵץ, וְלִשְׁמֵהּ קַדִּישָׁא יַקִּירָא אֲנָא אֵימַר תֻּשְׁבְּחָן. יְהֵא רַעֲוָא
קֳדָמָךְ דְּתִפְתַּח לִבָּאי בְּאוֹרַיְתָא, וְתַשְׁלִים מִשְׁאֲלִין דְּלִבָּאי, וְלִבָּא דְכָל
עַמָּךְ יִשְׂרָאֵל, לְטָב וּלְחַיִּין וְלִשְׁלָם.

Bei ana raheits, v'lish-meih kadisha yakira ana eimar tush-b'han. Y'hei ra'ava
ka'damakh d'tif'tah liba'i b'oray'tah v'tash'leim mish'alin d'liba'i, v'liba
d'khal amakh Yisraeil, l'tav ul'hayin v'lish'lam.

(The Torah is taken from the ark. On the morning of Shemini Atseret-Simhat Torah, process the Torah scrolls
seven times around the reading table reciting the Hakafot from page 188)

(Reader then Congregation)

שְׁמַע יִשְׂרָאֵל, יְיָ אֱלֹהֵינוּ, יְיָ אֶחָד.

Sh'ma Yisraeil, Adonai Eloheinu, Adonai Ehad.

(Reader then Congregation)

אֶחָד אֱלֹהֵינוּ, גָּדוֹל אֲדוֹנֵנוּ, קָדוֹשׁ שְׁמוֹ.

Ehad Eloheinu, gadol Adoneinu, kadosh sh'mo.

(Reader)

גַּדְּלוּ לַיְיָ אִתִּי, וּנְרוֹמְמָה שְׁמוֹ יַחְדָּו.

Gad'lu la'Adonai i'ti, u'neromema sh'mo yahdav.

לְךָ יְיָ הַגְּדֻלָּה וְהַגְּבוּרָה וְהַתִּפְאֶרֶת וְהַנֵּצַח וְהַהוֹד, כִּי כֹל בַּשָּׁמַיִם וּבָאָרֶץ,
לְךָ יְיָ הַמַּמְלָכָה וְהַמִּתְנַשֵּׂא לְכֹל לְרֹאשׁ.

L'kha Adonai hag'dulah v'hag'vurah v'hatif'eret v'hanei'tsah v'hahod, ki khol
bashama'yim uva-ar'ets. L'kha Adonai hamam'lakhah v'hamit'nasei l'khol
l'rosh.

רוֹמְמוּ יְיָ אֱלֹהֵינוּ, וְהִשְׁתַּחֲווּ לַהֲדֹם רַגְלָיו, קָדוֹשׁ הוּא.
רוֹמְמוּ יְיָ אֱלֹהֵינוּ, וְהִשְׁתַּחֲווּ לְהַר קָדְשׁוֹ, כִּי קָדוֹשׁ יְיָ אֱלֹהֵינוּ.

Rom'mu Adonai Eloheinu, v'hish'taha-vu laha'rom rag'layv kadosh hu.
Rom'mu Adonai Eloheinu, v'hish'taha-vu l'har kad'sho, Ki kadosh Adonai
Eloheinu.

(Torah is placed on the reading table)

(The Reader or Gabbai uses the following to call a Kohen to the Torah. The Oleh is called up
by his Hebrew name and his father's Hebrew name)

וְיַעֲזֹר וְיָגֵן וְיוֹשִׁיעַ לְכָל הַחוֹסִים בּוֹ, וְנֹאמַר אָמֵן. הַכֹּל הָבוּ גֹדֶל לֵאלֹהֵינוּ,
וּתְנוּ כָבוֹד לַתּוֹרָה. כֹּהֵן, קְרָב; יַעֲמֹד (פְּלוֹנִי בֶּן פְּלוֹנִי) הַכֹּהֵן:

(If there is no Kohen, then he calls for a Levi, no Levi, than Israel)

אֵין כָּאן כֹּהֵן, יַעֲמֹד לֵוִי-יִשְׂרָאֵל (פְּלוֹנִי בֶּן פְּלוֹנִי)

(Reader then Congregation)

וְאַתֶּם הַדְּבֵקִים בַּיְיָ אֱלֹהֵיכֶם, חַיִּים כֻּלְּכֶם הַיּוֹם.
V'atem had'veikim baAdonai Elohei'khem, hayim kulkhem hayom.

In Him I put my trust, and I utter praise to His Name, which is holy and full of glory. Show me Your will. Open my heart to Your command, and fulfill the desires of my heart and the heart of Israel, Your people, for goodness and for life and for peace.

(The Torah is taken from the ark. On the morning of Shemini Atseret-Simhat Torah, process the Torah scrolls seven times around the reading table reciting the Hakafot from page 189)

(Reader then Congregation)
Hear, O Israel, the Lord our God, the Lord is One!

(Reader then Congregation)
One is our God; great is our Lord, holy is His Name.

(Reader)
Exalt the Lord with me, and let us exalt His Name together.

Lord, everything in heaven and in earth is Yours; the greatness, and the power, and the glory, and the victory and the majesty. Lord, Yours is the kingdom, and You are the sovereign head over all.

Exalt the Lord our God, and bow down at His footstool, for He is holy. Exalt the Lord our God, and bow down at His holy mountain,for holy is the Lord our God.

(Torah is placed on the reading table)

(The Reader or Gabbai uses the following to call a Kohen to the Torah. The Oleh is called up by his Hebrew name and his father's Hebrew name)

May He help, shield and save all who trust in Him; and let us say, Amen. Let us all ascribe greatness to our God, and give honor to the Torah. Kohen come forward:
___________________ ben ___________________ .

(If there is no Kohen, then he calls for a Levi, no Levi, than Israel)

There is no Kohen. Levy come forward / Israel come forward...

(Reader then Congregation)
You who cling to the Lord our God are all alive today.

(Blessing before reading Torah)

(Oleh) בָּרְכוּ אֶת יְיָ הַמְבֹרָךְ.

Bar'khu et Adonai ham'vorakh.

(Congregation then Oleh)

בָּרוּךְ יְיָ הַמְבֹרָךְ לְעוֹלָם וָעֶד.

Barukh Adonai ham'vorakh l'olam va'ed.

(Oleh) בָּרוּךְ אַתָּה יְיָ אֱלֹהֵינוּ מֶלֶךְ הָעוֹלָם, אֲשֶׁר בָּחַר בָּנוּ מִכָּל הָעַמִּים וְנָתַן לָנוּ אֶת תּוֹרָתוֹ. בָּרוּךְ אַתָּה יְיָ, נוֹתֵן הַתּוֹרָה.

Barukh atah Adonai Eloheinu Melekh Ha'Olam, asher baḥar banu mikal ha'amim v'natan lanu et toratoh. Barukh atah Adonai, notein haTorah.

(Blessing after reading Torah)

(Oleh) בָּרוּךְ אַתָּה יְיָ אֱלֹהֵינוּ מֶלֶךְ הָעוֹלָם, אֲשֶׁר נָתַן לָנוּ תּוֹרַת אֱמֶת, וְחַיֵּי עוֹלָם נָטַע בְּתוֹכֵנוּ. בָּרוּךְ אַתָּה יְיָ, נוֹתֵן הַתּוֹרָה.

Barukh atah Adonai Eloheinu Melekh Ha'Olam, asher natan lanu torat emet, v'ḥayei olam natah b'tokheinu. Barukh atah Adonai, notein haTorah.

(Mishebeirakh Blessings for Oleh, Thanksgiving, Birth of a Child, Bar\Bat Mitzvah are on pages 198 and 200)

(A traditional prayer for healing is on page 200)

(The Reader recites חצי קדיש before hagbah)

יִתְגַּדַּל וְיִתְקַדַּשׁ שְׁמֵהּ רַבָּא. (אָמֵן - *Cong*) בְּעָלְמָא דִי בְרָא כִרְעוּתֵהּ, וְיַמְלִיךְ מַלְכוּתֵהּ בְּחַיֵּיכוֹן וּבְיוֹמֵיכוֹן וּבְחַיֵּי דְכָל בֵּית יִשְׂרָאֵל. בַּעֲגָלָא וּבִזְמַן קָרִיב, וְאִמְרוּ אָמֵן.

Yitgadal v'yitkadash sh'mei rabah. (Cong - Amein)

(Cong - אָמֵן)

B'almah di vera khir'utei, v'yamlikh mal'khutei b'ḥayeikhon uv'yomeikhon uv'ḥayei d'khal beit Yisraeil. Ba'agalah uviz'man kariv v'imru, Amein. (Cong - Amein)

(Together) יְהֵא שְׁמֵהּ רַבָּא מְבָרַךְ לְעָלַם וּלְעָלְמֵי עָלְמַיָּא.

Y'hei sh'mei rabah m'varakh l'alam ul'al'mei al'mayah.

יִתְבָּרַךְ וְיִשְׁתַּבַּח, וְיִתְפָּאַר וְיִתְרוֹמַם וְיִתְנַשֵּׂא וְיִתְהַדָּר וְיִתְעַלֶּה וְיִתְהַלָּל שְׁמֵהּ דְּקֻדְשָׁא, בְּרִיךְ הוּא. (בְּרִיךְ הוּא - *Cong*)

Yit'barakh v'yish'tabaḥ, v'yit'pa-ar v'yit'romam v'yit'nasei v'yit'hadar v'yit'aleh v'yit'halal sh'mei d'ku-deshah, b'rikh Hu, (Cong - b'rikh Hu)

l'eila min kal *לְעֵלָּא מִן כָּל

בִּרְכָתָא וְשִׁירָתָא, תֻּשְׁבְּחָתָא וְנֶחֱמָתָא, דַּאֲמִירָן בְּעָלְמָא, וְאִמְרוּ אָמֵן. (אָמֵן - *Cong*)

bir'khatah v'shiratah, tush'beḥatah v'neḥematah, da'amiran b'almah, v'imru, Amein. (Cong - Amein)

Matthew 7:24-29

לָכֵן כָּל הַשֹּׁמֵעַ לִדְבָרַי אֵלֶּה וְעֹשֶׂה אֹתָם אֲעָרְכֶנּוּ לְחָכָם לֵב אֲשֶׁר בָּנָה בֵיתוֹ עַל הַסָּלַע. הַגֶּשֶׁם נִתַּךְ אַרְצָה נַחֲלֵי מַיִם יִשְׁטֹפוּ וְרוּחַ גְּדוֹלָה בָּאָה וַיִּפְגְּעוּ בַּבַּיִת הַהוּא וְלֹא נָפַל כִּי יֻסַּד בַּסָּלַע. וְכָל הַשֹּׁמֵעַ לִדְבָרַי אֵלֶּה וְלֹא יַעֲשֶׂה אֹתָם נִמְשַׁל לַחֲסַר לֵב אֲשֶׁר בָּנָה בֵיתוֹ עַל הַחוֹל. הַגֶּשֶׁם נִתַּךְ אַרְצָה נַחֲלֵי מַיִם יִשְׁטֹפוּ וְרוּחַ גְּדוֹלָה בָּאָה וַיִּפְגְּעוּ בַּבַּיִת הַהוּא וַיִּפֹּל וַיְהִי לְמַפֵּלָה גְדוֹלָה. וַיְהִי כְּכַלּוֹת יֵשׁוּעַ אֶת הַדְּבָרִים הָאֵלֶּה וַיִּתְמְהוּ הֲמוֹן הָעָם עַל תּוֹרָתוֹ. כִּי הָיָה מוֹרֶה אֹתָם כְּהוֹרֹת אִישׁ שִׁלְטוֹן וְלֹא כַסּוֹפְרִים.

(Blessing before reading Torah)

(Oleh)

Bless the Lord who is blessed.

(Congregation then Oleh)

Blessed is the Lord who is blessed forever and ever.

(Oleh) Blessed are You, Lord our God, King of the Universe, who has chosen us from all peoples, and has given us Your Instruction. Blessed are You, Lord, giver of the Torah.

(Blessing after reading Torah)

(Oleh) Blessed are You, Lord our God, King of the universe, who has given us true instruction, and has planted everlasting life in the midst of us. Blessed are You, Lord, giver of the Torah.

(Mishebeirakh Blessings for Oleh, Thanksgiving, Birth of a Child, Bar\Bat Mitzvah are on pages 199 and 201)

(A traditional prayer for healing is on page 201)

*(The Reader recites **Half-Kaddish** before hagbah)*

Magnified and sanctified may God's great Name **(Cong - Amen)** be throughout the world which He has created according to His will. May He establish His kingdom in our lifetime, and during our days, and within the life of the entire house of Israel, speedily and soon; and say, **Amen. (Cong - Amen)**

(Together)

May the greatness of His Name be blessed forever and ever.

Let the Name of the Holy One, **blessed is He**, **(Cong - blessed is He)** be blessed and praised, glorified and exalted, extolled and honored, adored and lauded,

* beyond all

**From Rosh Hashanah to Yom Kippur substitute:*   **exceedingly* beyond all

of the blessings and songs, praises and consolations that are ever spoken in this world, and say, **Amen. (Cong - Amen)**

Matthew 7:24-29

"Anyone who listens to My teaching and obeys Me is wise, like a person who builds a house on solid rock. Though the rain comes in torrents and the floodwaters rise and the winds beat against that house, it won't collapse, because it is built on rock. But anyone who hears My teaching and ignores it is foolish, like a person who builds a house on sand. When the rains and floods come and the winds beat against that house, it will fall with a mighty crash." After Yeshua finished speaking, the crowds were amazed at His teaching, for He taught as one who had real authority, quite unlike the scribes.

(All rise)

(The Torah is raised and the following is said)

וְזֹאת הַתּוֹרָה אֲשֶׁר שָׂם מֹשֶׁה לִפְנֵי בְּנֵי יִשְׂרָאֵל עַל פִּי יְיָ בְּיַד מֹשֶׁה.

V'zot ha'Torah asher sam Moshe lif'nei b'nei Yisraeil al pi Adonai b'yad Moshe.

עֵץ חַיִּים

עֵץ חַיִּים הִיא לַמַּחֲזִיקִים בָּהּ, וְתֹמְכֶיהָ מְאֻשָּׁר. דְּרָכֶיהָ דַרְכֵי נֹעַם, וְכָל נְתִיבוֹתֶיהָ שָׁלוֹם. אֹרֶךְ יָמִים בִּימִינָהּ, בִּשְׂמֹאלָהּ עֹשֶׁר וְכָבוֹד. יְיָ חָפֵץ לְמַעַן צִדְקוֹ, יַגְדִּיל תּוֹרָה וְיַאְדִּיר.

Eits ḥayim hi lama'ḥazikim bah, v'tom'kheha m'ushar. D'rakheha dar'khei no'am, v'khal n'tivoteha shalom.

(Blessing before reading Haftarah)

בָּרוּךְ אַתָּה יְיָ אֱלֹהֵינוּ מֶלֶךְ הָעוֹלָם, אֲשֶׁר בָּחַר בִּנְבִיאִים טוֹבִים, וְרָצָה בְדִבְרֵיהֶם הַנֶּאֱמָרִים בֶּאֱמֶת, בָּרוּךְ אַתָּה יְיָ, הַבּוֹחֵר בַּתּוֹרָה וּבְמֹשֶׁה עַבְדּוֹ, וּבְיִשְׂרָאֵל עַמּוֹ וּבִנְבִיאֵי הָאֱמֶת וָצֶדֶק.

Barukh atah Adonai Eloheinu Melekh Ha'Olam,

asher baḥar bin'vi'im tovim, v'ratsa v'divrehem hane'emarim be'emet. Barukh atah Adonai, haboḥeir ba'Torah, uv'Moshe av'do, uv'Yisraeil amo, u-vin'vi-ei ha-emet va-tsedek.

(Blessings after reading Haftarah)

בָּרוּךְ אַתָּה יְיָ אֱלֹהֵינוּ מֶלֶךְ הָעוֹלָם, צוּר כָּל הָעוֹלָמִים, צַדִּיק בְּכָל הַדּוֹרוֹת, הָאֵל הַנֶּאֱמָן הָאוֹמֵר וְעֹשֶׂה, הַמְדַבֵּר וּמְקַיֵּם, שֶׁכָּל דְּבָרָיו אֱמֶת וָצֶדֶק.

Barukh atah Adonai Eloheinu Melekh Ha'Olam, tsur kal ha-olamim, tsaddik bekhal ha-dorot, ha'Eil ha-ne'eman ha-omeir v'oseh, ha-medabeir u-mekayeim, shekal d'varayv emet vatsedek.

נֶאֱמָן אַתָּה הוּא יְיָ אֱלֹהֵינוּ, וְנֶאֱמָנִים דְּבָרֶיךָ, וְדָבָר אֶחָד מִדְּבָרֶיךָ אָחוֹר לֹא יָשׁוּב רֵיקָם, כִּי אֵל מֶלֶךְ נֶאֱמָן וְרַחֲמָן אָתָּה. בָּרוּךְ אַתָּה יְיָ, הָאֵל הַנֶּאֱמָן בְּכָל דְּבָרָיו.

Ne'eman atah hu Adonai Eloheinu, vene'manim d'varekha,

v'davar eḥad mid'varekha aḥor lo yashuv reikam, ki Eil Melekh ne'eman v'raḥaman atah. Barukh atah, Adonai, ha'Eil ha-ne'eman bekhal d'varayv.

רַחֵם עַל צִיּוֹן כִּי הִיא בֵּית חַיֵּינוּ, וְלַעֲלוּבַת נֶפֶשׁ תּוֹשִׁיעַ בִּמְהֵרָה בְיָמֵינוּ. בָּרוּךְ אַתָּה יְיָ, מְשַׂמֵּחַ צִיּוֹן בְּבָנֶיהָ.

שַׂמְּחֵנוּ יְיָ אֱלֹהֵינוּ בְּאֵלִיָּהוּ הַנָּבִיא עַבְדֶּךָ, וּבְמַלְכוּת בֵּית דָּוִד יְשׁוּעַ מְשִׁיחֶךָ, בִּמְהֵרָה יָבֹא וְיָגֵל לִבֵּנוּ, עַל כִּסְאוֹ לֹא יֵשֵׁב זָר וְלֹא יִנְחֲלוּ עוֹד אֲחֵרִים אֶת כְּבוֹדוֹ, כִּי בְשֵׁם קָדְשְׁךָ נִשְׁבַּעְתָּ לּוֹ, שֶׁלֹּא יִכְבֶּה נֵרוֹ לְעוֹלָם וָעֶד. בָּרוּךְ אַתָּה יְיָ, מָגֵן דָּוִד.

(All rise)

(The Torah is raised and the following is said)

And this is the Torah that Moses placed before the children of Israel. It is given by the hand of Moses; it is from the mouth of God.

Eits Ḥaim

It is a tree of life to those who take hold of it, and happy are those who support it. Its ways are ways of pleasantness, and all its paths are peace. Long life is in its right hand, and in its left hand are riches and honor. The Lord is pleased for the sake of His righteousness to make the Torah great and glorious.

(Blessing before reading Haftarah)

Blessed are You, Lord our God, King of the universe, who has chosen good prophets and has taken pleasure in the words they have spoken in truth. Blessed are You, Lord, the chooser of Torah, and of Moses, Your servant, and of Israel, Your people, and of the true and righteous prophets.

(Blessings after reading Haftarah)

Blessed are You, Lord our God, King of the universe, Creator of all the worlds, righteous through all generations; faithful God, who says and who does, who speaks and who fulfills. All Your words are true and just.

You are faithful, Lord our God, and Your words are faithful. No word of Yours shall return unfulfilled, for You are a faithful and merciful God and King! Blessed are You, Lord God, whose every word is faithful.

Have compassion on Tsiyon; it is the dwelling place of our life. Quickly save, with Your Right Hand, she whose soul is poor! Blessed are You, Lord, who makes Tsiyon rejoice in her children.

Lord our God, cause us to rejoice in Your servant, Elijah the prophet, and in the reign of the House of David, Your Messiah Yeshua. Bring Him quickly and gladden our hearts. Do not allow a stranger to sit on David's throne. And do not allow another to inherit His glory any longer, for in Your Holy Name You did swear to Him, that His lamp would never be put out! Blessed are You, Lord, the Shield of David.

עַל הַתּוֹרָה, וְעַל הָעֲבוֹדָה, וְעַל הַנְּבִיאִים, וְעַל יוֹם הַשַּׁבָּת הַזֶּה, שֶׁנָּתַתָּ לָּנוּ יְיָ אֱלֹהֵינוּ, לִקְדֻשָּׁה וְלִמְנוּחָה, לְכָבוֹד וּלְתִפְאָרֶת. עַל הַכֹּל יְיָ אֱלֹהֵינוּ, אֲנַחְנוּ מוֹדִים לָךְ, וּמְבָרְכִים אוֹתָךְ, יִתְבָּרַךְ שִׁמְךָ בְּפִי כָּל חַי תָּמִיד לְעוֹלָם וָעֶד. בָּרוּךְ אַתָּה יְיָ, מְקַדֵּשׁ הַשַּׁבָּת.

John 5:39; 45-47

וַיֹּאמֶר יֵשׁוּעַ: אַתֶּם דֹּרְשִׁים מֵעַל כִּתְבֵי הַקֹּדֶשׁ כִּי בָהֶם אַתֶּם אֹמְרִים חַיֵּי עוֹלָם לָכֶם וְהֵם הֵמָּה הַמְּעִידִים עָלָי. . . .אַל תַּחְשְׁבוּ כִּי אֲנִי אָבִיא שִׂטְנָה עֲלֵיכֶם לִפְנֵי הָאָב יֵשׁ אֶחָד מֵבִיא שִׂטְנָה עֲלֵיכֶם מֹשֶׁה אֲשֶׁר בְּטַחְתֶּם בּוֹ. כִּי לוּ הֶאֱמַנְתֶּם בְּמֹשֶׁה הֶאֱמַנְתֶּם גַּם בִּי כִּי עָלַי הוּא כָתַב. אַךְ אִם בִּכְתָבָיו לֹא תַאֲמִינוּ אֵיךְ תַּאֲמִינוּ בִּדְבָרָי.

Jeremiah 31:30, 32; Ezekiel 36:27, 37:14

הִנֵּה יָמִים בָּאִים נְאֻם־יְיָ וְכָרַתִּי אֶת־בֵּית יִשְׂרָאֵל וְאֶת־בֵּית יְהוּדָה בְּרִית חֲדָשָׁה. נָתַתִּי אֶת־תּוֹרָתִי בְּקִרְבָּם וְעַל־לִבָּם אֶכְתֲּבֶנָּה. וְאֶת־רוּחִי אֶתֵּן בְּקִרְבְּכֶם וְעָשִׂיתִי אֵת אֲשֶׁר־בְּחֻקַּי תֵּלֵכוּ וּמִשְׁפָּטַי תִּשְׁמְרוּ וַעֲשִׂיתֶם. וִידַעְתֶּם כִּי־אֲנִי יְיָ דִּבַּרְתִּי וְעָשִׂיתִי נְאֻם־יְיָ.

(Blessing before reading B'rit Hadashah)

בָּרוּךְ אַתָּה יְיָ אֱלֹהֵינוּ מֶלֶךְ הָעוֹלָם, אֲשֶׁר בָּחַר בָּנוּ מִכָּל הָעַמִּים וְנָתַן לָנוּ בְּרִית חֲדָשָׁה. בָּרוּךְ אַתָּה יְיָ, נוֹתֵן הַדָּבָר.

Barukh atah Adonai Eloheinu Melekh Ha'Olam, asher baḥar banu mikal ha'amim, v'natan lanu B'rit Ḥadashah. Barukh atah Adonai, notein haDavar.

(Blessing after reading B'rit Hadashah)

בָּרוּךְ אַתָּה יְיָ אֱלֹהֵינוּ מֶלֶךְ הָעוֹלָם, אֲשֶׁר נָתַן לָנוּ דְּבַר אֱמֶת, וְחַיֵּי עוֹלָם נָטַע בְּתוֹכֵנוּ. בָּרוּךְ אַתָּה יְיָ, נוֹתֵן בְּרִית חֲדָשָׁה.

Barukh atah Adonai Eloheinu Melekh Ha'Olam, asher natan lanu Devar Emet, vehayei olam natah betokheinu. Barukh atah Adonai, notein B'rit Ḥadashah.

(A prayer for the congregation, only recited on Shabbat)

יְקוּם פּוּרְקָן

יְקוּם פּוּרְקָן מִן שְׁמַיָּא חִנָּא וְחִסְדָּא וְרַחֲמֵי וְחַיֵּי אֲרִיכֵי וּמְזוֹנֵי רְוִיחֵי וְסִיַּעְתָּא דִשְׁמַיָּא וּבַרְיוּת גּוּפָא וּנְהוֹרָא מַעַלְיָא. זַרְעָא חַיָּא וְקַיָּמָא זַרְעָא דִי לָא יִפְסוֹק וְדִי לָא יִבְטוֹל מִפִּתְגָּמֵי אוֹרַיְתָא. לְכָל קְהָלָא קַדִּישָׁא הָדֵין בְּשֵׁם יֵשׁוּעַ מְשִׁיחֵנוּ, רַבְרְבַיָּא עִם זְעֵרַיָּא טַפְלָא וּנְשַׁיָּא. מַלְכָּא דְעָלְמָא יְבָרֵךְ יַתְכוֹן יַפִּישׁ חַיֵּיכוֹן וְיַסְגֵּי יוֹמֵיכוֹן וְיִתֵּן אַרְכָא לִשְׁנֵיכוֹן וְתִתְפָּרְקוּן וְתִשְׁתֵּזְבוּן מִן כָּל עָקָא וּמִן כָּל מַרְעִין בִּישִׁין. מָרַן דִּי בִשְׁמַיָּא יְהֵא בְּסַעְדְּכוֹן כָּל זְמַן וְעִדָּן וְנֹאמַר, אָמֵן.

(Traditionally, a prayer for Israel and the nation one is residing in is offered here. Suggested prayers on behalf of Israel and the Israeli Defense Forces are on pages 134, 198 & 209. A prayer for the United States is on page 209)

For the Torah, and for the service of worship, and for the prophets and for this Shabbat day which You, Lord our God, have given to us for sanctity and for rest, for glory and for honor: for all these things, blessings are Yours. Lord our God, we are ever grateful to You. May Your Name be blessed by every living thing, forever and to eternity. Blessed are You, Lord, who sanctifies the Shabbat.

John 5:39; 45-47

Yeshua said, "You search the Scriptures because you believe they give you eternal life. But the Scriptures point to Me!. . . I will not accuse you before the Father. Moses will accuse you! Yes, Moses, on whom you set your trust. If you had believed Moses, you would have believed Me because he wrote about Me. But, since you don't believe what he wrote, how will you believe what I say?"

Jeremiah 31:30, 32; Ezekiel 36:27, 37:14

Behold, days are coming when I will make a new covenant with the House of Israel and the House of Judah. I will put My Torah within them and write it on their heart ... "I will put My Ruach within you and you will live. Then I will cause you to walk in My laws, so you will keep My rulings and do them. Then you will know that I the Lord have spoken this and done this," declares the Lord.

(Blessing before reading B'rit Ḥadashah)

Blessed are You, Lord our God, King of the universe, who has chosen us from among all people and has given us the New Covenant. Blessed are You, Lord, Giver of the Word.

(Blessing after reading B'rit Ḥadashah)

Blessed are You, Lord our God, King of the universe, who has given us the Word of truth and planted everlasting life in our midst. Blessed are You, Lord, Giver of the New Covenant.

(A prayer for the congregation, only recited on Shabbat)

Yekum Purkan

May salvation arise from heaven. May grace, kindness and mercy - long life, ample provision and divine aid; physical health, perfect vision and healthy children who will never neglect the study of God's Instruction - be granted to this entire congregation in the name of Messiah Yeshua, great and small, women and children. May the King of the Universe bless you, prolong your lives, increase your days and add to your years; may you be saved and delivered from all distress and disease. May our Master in Heaven be your help at all times, and let us say, Amen.

(Traditionally, a prayer for Israel and the nation one is residing in is offered here. Suggested prayers on behalf of Israel and the Israeli Defense Forces are on pages 135, 199 & 209. A prayer for the United States is on page 209)

ברכת החדש

(Recited on the Shabbat before Rosh Hodesh. Congregation stands)

יְהִי רָצוֹן מִלְּפָנֶיךָ יְיָ אֱלֹהֵינוּ וֵאלֹהֵי אֲבוֹתֵינוּ, שֶׁתְּחַדֵּשׁ עָלֵינוּ אֶת הַחֹדֶשׁ הַזֶּה לְטוֹבָה וְלִבְרָכָה.

Yehi ratson mil'fanekha, Adonai Eloheinu, vEilohei Avoteinu, shet'hadesh aleinu et hahodesh hazeh l'tova v'livrakha.

(The Reader recites the following while holding a Torah scroll before the ark)

מִי שֶׁעָשָׂה נִסִּים לַאֲבוֹתֵינוּ וְגָאַל אוֹתָם מֵעַבְדוּת לְחֵרוּת, הוּא יִגְאַל אוֹתָנוּ בְּקָרוֹב, וִיקַבֵּץ נִדְחֵינוּ מֵאַרְבַּע כַּנְפוֹת הָאָרֶץ, חֲבֵרִים כָּל יִשְׂרָאֵל וְנֹאמַר אָמֵן.

Rosh Ḥodesh _________________   _________ רֹאשׁ חֹדֶשׁ

Y'hiyeh b'yom _________________   _________ יִהְיֶה בְּיוֹם

For Sunday, insert **רִאשׁוֹן** *(rishon); Monday,* **שֵׁנִי** *(shaini);*

Tuesday, **שְׁלִישִׁי** *(sh'lishi); Wednesday,* **רְבִיעִי** *(revi'i); Thursday,* **חֲמִישִׁי** *(hamishi);*

Friday, **שִׁשִּׁי** *(shishi); Saturday,* **שַׁבַּת קֹדֶשׁ** *(Shabbat Kodesh).*

Haba aleinu v'al kal Yisraeil l'tovah.   הַבָּא עָלֵינוּ וְעַל כָּל יִשְׂרָאֵל לְטוֹבָה.

יְחַדְּשֵׁהוּ הַקָּדוֹשׁ בָּרוּךְ הוּא, עָלֵינוּ וְעַל כָּל עַמּוֹ בֵּית יִשְׂרָאֵל, לְחַיִּים וּלְשָׁלוֹם. לְשָׂשׂוֹן וּלְשִׂמְחָה. לִישׁוּעָה וּלְנֶחָמָה. וְנֹאמַר אָמֵן. (אָמֵן - Cong)

(The Reader recites the following holding a Torah scroll in his right arm)

(Reader)   יְהַלְלוּ אֶת שֵׁם יְיָ כִּי נִשְׂגָּב שְׁמוֹ לְבַדּוֹ.

Y'hallelu et shem Adonai ki nis'gav sh'moh l'vadoh.

(Congregation)   הוֹדוֹ עַל אֶרֶץ וְשָׁמָיִם, וַיָּרֶם קֶרֶן לְעַמּוֹ תְּהִלָּה לְכָל חֲסִידָיו לִבְנֵי יִשְׂרָאֵל עַם קְרֹבוֹ, הַלְלוּיָהּ.

Hodoh al erets v'shamayim, vayarem keren l'amo t'hillah l'khal ḥasidayv liv'nei Yisraeil am k'rovo, halleluyah.

עֵץ חַיִּים

(Reader)   כִּי לֶקַח טוֹב נָתַתִּי לָכֶם, תּוֹרָתִי אַל תַּעֲזֹבוּ.

Ki lekah tov natati lakhem, Torati al ta'az'vo.

(All)   עֵץ חַיִּים הִיא לַמַּחֲזִיקִים בָּהּ, וְתֹמְכֶיהָ מְאֻשָּׁר. דְּרָכֶיהָ דַרְכֵי נֹעַם, וְכָל נְתִיבוֹתֶיהָ שָׁלוֹם. הֲשִׁיבֵנוּ יְיָ, אֵלֶיךָ וְנָשׁוּבָה, חַדֵּשׁ יָמֵינוּ כְּקֶדֶם.

Eits ḥayim hi lama'ḥazikim ba, v'tom'kheha m'ushar. D'rakheha dar'khei no'am, v'khal n'tivoteyha shalom. Hashiveinu Adonai, eilekha v'nashuvah, hadeish yameinu k'kedem.

Birkhat HaKodesh

(Recited on the Shabbat before Rosh Ḥodesh. Congregation stands)

May it be Your will, Lord our God and God of our Fathers, to make this new month for us a time of happiness and blessing.

(The Reader recites the following while holding a Torah scroll before the ark)
May He who performed miracles for our fathers and freed them from slavery, speedily redeem us and gather our dispersed people from the four corners of the earth so that all Israel will be together, and let us say, ***Amen. (Cong - Amen)***

The new month of ______________________

will begin on ______________________

For Sunday, insert **first day;** *Monday,* **second day;**
Tuesday, **third day;** *Wednesday,* **fourth day;** *Thursday,* **fifth day;**
Friday, **sixth day;** *Saturday,* **Holy Shabbat.**

May it bring happiness to us and to all Israel.

May the Holy One, blessed be He, grant that the new month bring to us and to all His people, the House of Israel, life and peace, joy and gladness, salvation and comfort. And let us say, ***Amen. (Cong - Amen)***

(The Reader recites the following holding a Torah scroll in his right arm)

(Reader) Let them praise the name of the Lord, for His Name alone is to be exalted.

(Congregation) His praise is over earth and heaven; for He has lifted up the power of His people, to the honor of His loving ones, the children of Israel, the people near to Him. Praise the Lord.

Eits Ḥaim

(Reader) I have given good instruction to you. Do not forsake My Torah!

(All) It is a tree of life to those who take hold of it, and happy are those who support it. Its ways are ways of pleasantness, and all its paths are peace. Lord, turn us to You and we will return. Renew our days as of old.

(When closing the ark say)

נֶאֱמָן אַתָּה הוּא יְיָ אֱלֹהֵינוּ, וְנֶאֱמָנִים דְּבָרֶיךָ, וְדָבָר אֶחָד מִדְּבָרֶיךָ אָחוֹר לֹא
יָשׁוּב רֵיקָם, כִּי אֵל מֶלֶךְ נֶאֱמָן וְרַחֲמָן אָתָּה. בָּרוּךְ אַתָּה יְיָ, הָאֵל הַנֶּאֱמָן
בְּכָל דְּבָרָיו.

Ne'eman atah hu Adonai Eloheinu, vene'emanim devarekha,
vedavar eḥad mid'varekha aḥor lo yashuv reikam, ki El Melekh ne'eman
v'raḥaman atah. Barukh atah Adonai, ha'El hane'eman bekhol d'varayv.

(מוסף), *or additional service, is recited here after the Torah service on Shabbat and Festivals to commemorate the*
additional sacrifices on those special days. A Musaf service for Shabbat can be found on page 136)

(Traditionally קדיש שלם *is recited here - see page 202)*

ברכת המשיח

בָּרוּךְ אַתָּה, יְיָ אֱלֹהֵינוּ, מֶלֶךְ הָעוֹלָם, אֲשֶׁר נָתַן לָנוּ דְּבַר הַחַיִּים, מָשִׁיחַ
יֵשׁוּעַ.

Barukh atah Adonai Eloheinu Melekh Ha'Olam, asher natan lanu d'var haḥayim,
Mashiaḥ Yeshua.

אין כאלהינו

אֵין כֵּאלֹהֵינוּ, אֵין כַּאדוֹנֵינוּ, אֵין כְּמַלְכֵּנוּ, אֵין כְּמוֹשִׁיעֵנוּ.

Ein Keloheinu, Ein Kadoneinu,
Ein K'malkeinu, Ein K'moshieinu.

מִי כֵאלֹהֵינוּ, מִי כַאדוֹנֵינוּ, מִי כְמַלְכֵּנוּ, מִי כְמוֹשִׁיעֵנוּ.

Mi Kheloheinu, Mi Khadoneinu,
Mi Kh'malkeinu Mi Kh'moshienu.

נוֹדֶה לֵאלֹהֵינוּ, נוֹדֶה לַאדוֹנֵינוּ, נוֹדֶה לְמַלְכֵּנוּ, נוֹדֶה לְמוֹשִׁיעֵנוּ.

Nodeh Leloheinu, Nodeh Ladoneinu,
Nodeh L'malkeinu, Nodeh L'moshieinu

בָּרוּךְ אֱלֹהֵינוּ, בָּרוּךְ אֲדוֹנֵינוּ, בָּרוּךְ מַלְכֵּנוּ, בָּרוּךְ מוֹשִׁיעֵנוּ.

Barukh Eloheinu, Barukh Adoneinu,
Barukh Malkeinu, Barukh Moshieinu.

אַתָּה הוּא אֱלֹהֵינוּ, אַתָּה הוּא אֲדוֹנֵינוּ, אַתָּה הוּא מַלְכֵּנוּ, אַתָּה הוּא
מוֹשִׁיעֵנוּ.

Atah hu Eloheinu, Atah hu Adoneinu,
Atah hu Malkeinu, Atah hu Moshienu.

אַתָּה הוּא שֶׁהִקְטִירוּ אֲבוֹתֵינוּ לְפָנֶיךָ אֶת קְטֹרֶת הַסַּמִּים.

Atah hu she'hiktiru avoteinu l'fanekha et k'toret hasamim.

(When closing the ark say)

You are faithful, Lord our God, and Your words are faithful, for no word of Yours shall remain unfulfilled. You are a faithful God and King. Blessed are You, Lord our God, who is faithful in fulfilling Your words.

*(**Musaf**, or additional service, is recited here after the Torah service on Shabbat and Festivals to commemorate the additional sacrifices on those special days. A Musaf service for Shabbat can be found on page 137)*

(Traditionally the Full Kaddish is recited here - see page 203)

Birkhat HaMashiaḥ

Blessed are You, Lord our God, King of the Universe, who has given us the Word of Life, Messiah Yeshua.

Ein Keloheynu

There is none like our God; there is none like our Lord;
there is none like our King; there is none like our Savior.

Who is like our God? Who is like our Lord?
Who is like our King? Who is like our Savior?

We give thanks to our God; We give thanks to our Lord;
We give thanks to our King; We give thanks to our Savior.

Blessed is our God; Blessed is our Lord;
Blessed is our King; Blessed is our Savior.

You are our God; You are our Lord;
You are our King; You are our Savior.

You are He before whose countenance our fathers offered the spices of incense.

עָלֵינוּ

עָלֵינוּ לְשַׁבֵּחַ לַאֲדוֹן הַכֹּל, לָתֵת גְּדֻלָּה לְיוֹצֵר בְּרֵאשִׁית, שֶׁלֹּא עָשָׂנוּ כְּגוֹיֵי הָאֲרָצוֹת, וְלֹא שָׂמָנוּ כְּמִשְׁפְּחוֹת הָאֲדָמָה. שֶׁלֹּא שָׂם חֶלְקֵנוּ כָּהֶם, וְגוֹרָלֵנוּ כְּכָל הֲמוֹנָם. (bow) וַאֲנַחְנוּ כּוֹרְעִים וּמִשְׁתַּחֲוִים וּמוֹדִים, (rise) לִפְנֵי מֶלֶךְ מַלְכֵי הַמְּלָכִים הַקָּדוֹשׁ בָּרוּךְ הוּא. שֶׁהוּא נוֹטֶה שָׁמַיִם וְיֹסֵד אָרֶץ, וּמוֹשַׁב יְקָרוֹ בַּשָּׁמַיִם מִמַּעַל, וּשְׁכִינַת עֻזּוֹ בְּגָבְהֵי מְרוֹמִים. הוּא אֱלֹהֵינוּ אֵין עוֹד. אֱמֶת מַלְכֵּנוּ, אֶפֶס זוּלָתוֹ, כַּכָּתוּב בְּתוֹרָתוֹ: וְיָדַעְתָּ הַיּוֹם וַהֲשֵׁבֹתָ אֶל לְבָבֶךָ, כִּי יְיָ הוּא הָאֱלֹהִים בַּשָּׁמַיִם מִמַּעַל וְעַל הָאָרֶץ מִתָּחַת, אֵין עוֹד.

Aleinu l'shabei'aḥ l'adon ha'kol, lateit g'dulah l'yotser b'reishit, sheloh asanu k'goyei ha'aratsot, v'lo sa'manu k'mishp'hot ha'adamah. Sheloh sam ḥel'keinu kahem, v'goraleinu k'khol ha'monam. (bow) *Va'anaḥnu kor'im umish'taḥavim u'modim,* (rise) *lif'nei melekh, mal'khei ham'lakhim, hakadosh barukh hu. She'hu noteh shamayim v'yoseid arets, u'moshav y'karoh bashamayim mima'al, ush'khinat uzoh b'gav'hei m'romim. Hu Eloheinu ein od. Emet mal'keinu efes zulatoh, kakatuv b'torato: v'yada'tah ha'yom vahasheivota el l'vavekha, ki Adonai hu ha'Elohim bashamayim mima'al, v'al ha'arets mitaḥat, ein od.*

עַל כֵּן נְקַוֶּה לְּךָ יְיָ אֱלֹהֵינוּ לִרְאוֹת מְהֵרָה בְּתִפְאֶרֶת עֻזֶּךָ, לְהַעֲבִיר גִּלּוּלִים מִן הָאָרֶץ, וְהָאֱלִילִים כָּרוֹת יִכָּרֵתוּן, לְתַקֵּן עוֹלָם בְּמַלְכוּת שַׁדַּי. וְכָל בְּנֵי בָשָׂר יִקְרְאוּ בִשְׁמֶךָ, לְהַפְנוֹת אֵלֶיךָ כָּל רִשְׁעֵי אָרֶץ. יַכִּירוּ וְיֵדְעוּ כָּל יוֹשְׁבֵי תֵבֵל, כִּי לְךָ תִּכְרַע כָּל בֶּרֶךְ, תִּשָּׁבַע כָּל לָשׁוֹן. לְפָנֶיךָ יְיָ אֱלֹהֵינוּ יִכְרְעוּ וְיִפֹּלוּ, וְלִכְבוֹד שִׁמְךָ יְקָר יִתֵּנוּ. וִיקַבְּלוּ כֻלָּם אֶת עוֹל מַלְכוּתֶךָ. וְתִמְלֹךְ עֲלֵיהֶם מְהֵרָה לְעוֹלָם וָעֶד. כִּי הַמַּלְכוּת שֶׁלְּךָ הִיא, וּלְעוֹלְמֵי עַד תִּמְלוֹךְ בְּכָבוֹד.

(Reader) כַּכָּתוּב בְּתוֹרָתֶךָ, יְיָ יִמְלֹךְ לְעוֹלָם וָעֶד.

(Congregation) וְנֶאֱמַר, וְהָיָה יְיָ לְמֶלֶךְ עַל כָּל הָאָרֶץ, בַּיּוֹם הַהוּא יִהְיֶה יְיָ אֶחָד, וּשְׁמוֹ אֶחָד.

(Reader) Kakatuv b'Toratekhah: Adonai yimlokh l'olam va'ed.
(Congregation) V'ne'emar v'hayah Adonai l'Melekh al kal ha'arets, bayom hahu yih'yeh Adonai eḥad, ush'mo eḥad.

Philippians 2:9-11

עַל כֵּן הִגְבִּיהוּ אֱלֹהִים מְאֹד וְנָתַן לוֹ אֶת הַשֵּׁם הַנַּעֲלֶה עַל כָּל שֵׁם, לְמַעַן תִּכְרַע בְּשֵׁם יֵשׁוּעַ כָּל בֶּרֶךְ, בַּשָּׁמַיִם וּבָאָרֶץ וּמִתַּחַת לָאָרֶץ, וְכָל לָשׁוֹן תּוֹדֶה כִּי יֵשׁוּעַ הַמָּשִׁיחַ הוּא הָאָדוֹן, לְתִפְאֶרֶת אֱלֹהִים הָאָב.

Aleinu

It is our duty to give praise to the Lord of all, to ascribe greatness to Him who is the Creator from the beginning; for He has not made us like the nations of the other lands and He has not placed us like the families of the earth. He did not make our portion to be like theirs, nor our lot like that of all their multitudes. *(bow)* And therefore we bend the knee and bow, *(rise)* and acknowledge before the supreme King of kings, the Holy One, blessed be He, that He stretches forth the heavens and lays the foundations of the earth, and the seat of His glory is in the high heavens; the presence of His majesty is in the lofty heights. He is our God; there is no other. He is our King, truly, there is none beside Him, just as it is written in His Torah: "You shall know this day, and keep it in your heart, that the Lord, He is God in heaven above and on the earth beneath: There is none else."

Since we trust in You, Lord our God, may we soon behold the glory of Your might. When You remove the abominations from the earth and all idolatry is banished; when all the world will be made perfect under the reign of the Almighty, and all the children of men will call on Your Name, and all the wicked of the earth will be turned to You. May all the inhabitants of the world realize and know that every knee must bend and every tongue must swear allegiance to You. Lord our God, may they bend the knee and worship before You and give honor to the glory of Your Name. May they accept the yoke of Your kingdom, and may You establish Your reign over them quickly, forever and to eternity. The kingdom is Yours, and to all eternity You will reign in glory.

(Reader) As it is written in Your Torah: "The Lord will reign forever and ever."

(Congregation) And it is said, "And the Lord shall be King over all the earth; on that day the Lord will be One and His Name One."

Philippians 2:9-11

Therefore, God has lifted Him up, and given to Him a name exalted above every name; that at the name Yeshua you shall bow: every knee of those in heaven, and of those in the earth, and of those under the earth. And every tongue shall swear that Yeshua the Messiah, He is the Lord, to the honor of God, the Father.

קדיש יתום

(Mourners and those observing Yartseit)

יִתְגַּדַּל וְיִתְקַדַּשׁ שְׁמֵהּ רַבָּא. (אָמֵן - Cong) בְּעָלְמָא דִּי בְרָא כִרְעוּתֵהּ,
וְיַמְלִיךְ מַלְכוּתֵהּ בְּחַיֵּיכוֹן וּבְיוֹמֵיכוֹן וּבְחַיֵּי דְכָל בֵּית יִשְׂרָאֵל. בַּעֲגָלָא וּבִזְמַן
קָרִיב, וְאִמְרוּ אָמֵן. (אָמֵן - Cong)

Yitgadal v'yitkadash sh'mei rabah. (Cong - Amein) B'almah di vera khir'utei,
v'yamlikh mal'khutei b'hayeikhon uv'yomeikhon uv'hayei d'khal beit Yisraeil.
Ba'agalah uviz'man kariv v'imru, Amein. (Cong - Amein)

(Congregation and Mourners together)

יְהֵא שְׁמֵהּ רַבָּא מְבָרַךְ לְעָלַם וּלְעָלְמֵי עָלְמַיָּא.

Y'hei sh'mei rabah m'varakh l'alam ul'al'mei al'mayah.

(Mourners)

יִתְבָּרַךְ וְיִשְׁתַּבַּח, וְיִתְפָּאַר וְיִתְרוֹמַם וְיִתְנַשֵּׂא וְיִתְהַדָּר וְיִתְעַלֶּה וְיִתְהַלָּל שְׁמֵהּ
דְּקֻדְשָׁא, בְּרִיךְ הוּא, (בְּרִיךְ הוּא - Cong)

Yit'barakh v'yish'tabah, v'yit'pa-ar v'yit'romam v'yit'nasei v'yit'hadar
v'yit'aleh v'yit'halal sh'mei d'ku-deshah, b'rikh Hu, (Cong - b'rikh Hu)

*לְעֵלָּא מִן כָּל *l'eila min kal*

From Rosh Hashanah to Yom Kippur substitute: *l'eila u-l'eila mi-kal* *לְעֵלָּא וּלְעֵלָּא מִכָּל

בִּרְכָתָא וְשִׁירָתָא, תֻּשְׁבְּחָתָא וְנֶחֱמָתָא, דַּאֲמִירָן בְּעָלְמָא,
וְאִמְרוּ אָמֵן. (אָמֵן - Cong)

bir'khatah v'shiratah, tush'behatah v'nehematah, da'amiran b'almah,
v'imru, Amein. (Cong - Amein)

יְהֵא שְׁלָמָא רַבָּא מִן שְׁמַיָּא וְחַיִּים עָלֵינוּ וְעַל כָּל יִשְׂרָאֵל,
וְאִמְרוּ אָמֵן. (אָמֵן - Cong)

Y'hei sh'lamah rabah min sh'mayah v'hayim aleinu v'al kal Yisraeil, v'imru,
Amein. (Cong - Amein)

עֹשֶׂה שָׁלוֹם בִּמְרוֹמָיו הוּא יַעֲשֶׂה שָׁלוֹם עָלֵינוּ וְעַל כָּל יִשְׂרָאֵל,
וְאִמְרוּ אָמֵן. (אָמֵן - Cong)

Oseh shalom bim'romav hu ya'aseh shalom aleinu v'al kal Yisraeil, v'imru,
Amein. (Cong - Amein)

אַל תִּירָא מִפַּחַד פִּתְאֹם, וּמִשֹּׁאַת רְשָׁעִים כִּי תָבֹא. עֻצוּ עֵצָה וְתֻפָר, דַּבְּרוּ
דָבָר וְלֹא יָקוּם, כִּי עִמָּנוּ אֵל. וְעַד זִקְנָה אֲנִי הוּא, וְעַד שֵׂיבָה אֲנִי אֶסְבֹּל,
אֲנִי עָשִׂיתִי וַאֲנִי אֶשָּׂא, וַאֲנִי אֶסְבֹּל וַאֲמַלֵּט.

Kaddish Yatom

(Mourners and those observing Yartseit)

Magnified and sanctified may God's great Name *(Cong - Amen)* be throughout the world which He has created according to His will. May He establish His kingdom in our lifetime, and during our days, and within the life of the entire house of Israel, speedily and soon; and say, *Amen. (Cong - Amen)*

(Congregation and Mourners together)

May the greatness of His Name be blessed forever and ever.

(Mourners)

Let the Name of the Holy One, ***blessed is He***, *(Cong - blessed is he)* be blessed and praised, glorified and exalted, extolled and honored, adored and lauded,

* beyond all

** From Rosh Hashanah to Yom Kippur substitute:*   **exceedingly* beyond all

of the blessings and songs, praises and consolations that are ever spoken in this world, and say, *Amen. (Cong - Amen)*

May there be abundant peace from heaven, and life for us and for all Israel, and say, *Amen. (Cong - Amen)*

May He who creates peace in His high heavens create peace for us and for all Israel, and say, *Amen. (Cong - Amen)*

Do not fear sudden terror, or the storm that strikes the wicked. Form your plot, it will fail; lay your plan, it will not succeed; for God is with us. "When you are old I will be the same; I will sustain you even when your hair has turned grey. I have made you, and I will bear you! I will sustain you and save you!"

שיר הכבוד

אַנְעִים זְמִירוֹת וְשִׁירִים אֶאֱרוֹג, כִּי אֵלֶיךָ נַפְשִׁי תַעֲרוֹג. נַפְשִׁי חִמְּדָה בְּצֵל יָדֶךָ, לָדַעַת כָּל רָז סוֹדֶךָ.

מִדֵּי דַבְּרִי בִּכְבוֹדֶךָ, הוֹמֶה לִבִּי אֶל דּוֹדֶיךָ. עַל כֵּן אֲדַבֵּר בְּךָ נִכְבָּדוֹת, וְשִׁמְךָ אֲכַבֵּד בְּשִׁירֵי יְדִידוֹת. אֲסַפְּרָה כְבוֹדְךָ וְלֹא רְאִיתִיךָ, אֲדַמְּךָ אֲכַנְּךָ וְלֹא יְדַעְתִּיךָ. בְּיַד נְבִיאֶךָ בְּסוֹד עֲבָדֶיךָ, דִּמִּיתָ הֲדַר כְּבוֹד הוֹדֶךָ. גְּדֻלָּתְךָ וּגְבוּרָתֶךָ, כִּנּוּ לְתֹקֶף פְּעֻלָּתֶךָ.

דִּמּוּ אוֹתְךָ וְלֹא כְּפִי יֶשְׁךָ, וַיְשַׁוּוּךָ לְפִי מַעֲשֶׂיךָ. הִמְשִׁילוּךָ בְּרֹב חֶזְיוֹנוֹת, הִנְּךָ אֶחָד בְּכָל דִּמְיוֹנוֹת.

לְךָ יְיָ הַגְּדֻלָּה וְהַגְּבוּרָה וְהַתִּפְאֶרֶת וְהַנֵּצַח וְהַהוֹד, כִּי כֹל בַּשָּׁמַיִם וּבָאָרֶץ. לְךָ יְיָ הַמַּמְלָכָה וְהַמִּתְנַשֵּׂא לְכֹל לְרֹאשׁ. מִי יְמַלֵּל גְּבוּרוֹת יְיָ, יַשְׁמִיעַ כָּל תְּהִלָּתוֹ.

(Traditionally Psalm 92 is recited on Shabbat here - see page 62)

אדון עולם

אֲדוֹן עוֹלָם אֲשֶׁר מָלַךְ, בְּטֶרֶם כָּל יְצִיר נִבְרָא.
לְעֵת נַעֲשָׂה בְחֶפְצוֹ כֹּל, אֲזַי מֶלֶךְ שְׁמוֹ נִקְרָא.

Adon olam, asher malakh, b'terem kol y'tsir niv'ra.
L'et na'asah v'heftso kol, azai melekh sh'mo nikra.

וְאַחֲרֵי כִּכְלוֹת הַכֹּל, לְבַדּוֹ יִמְלוֹךְ נוֹרָא.

וְהוּא הָיָה, וְהוּא הֹוֶה, וְהוּא יִהְיֶה, בְּתִפְאָרָה.

V'aharei kikhlot hakol, l'vado yimlokh nora.
V'hu hayah v'hu hove, v'hu yih'yeh, b'tifara.

וְהוּא אֶחָד וְאֵין שֵׁנִי, לְהַמְשִׁיל לוֹ לְהַחְבִּירָה.

בְּלִי רֵאשִׁית בְּלִי תַכְלִית, וְלוֹ הָעֹז וְהַמִּשְׂרָה.

V'hu ehad v'ein sheini, l'hamshil lo l'hahbirah.
B'li rei'shit b'li takhlit, v'lo ha'oz v'hamisrah.

וְהוּא אֵלִי וְחַי גֹּאֲלִי, וְצוּר חֶבְלִי בְּעֵת צָרָה.

וְהוּא נִסִּי וּמָנוֹס לִי, מְנָת כּוֹסִי בְּיוֹם אֶקְרָא.

V'hu Eli v'hai go'ali, v'tsur hevli b'eit tsarah.
V'hu nis'i u'manos li, m'nat kosi b'yom ekra.

בְּיָדוֹ אַפְקִיד רוּחִי, בְּעֵת אִישַׁן וְאָעִירָה.

וְעִם רוּחִי גְּוִיָּתִי, יְיָ לִי וְלֹא אִירָא.

B'yado af'kid ruhi, b'eit ishan, v'a'irah.
V'im ruhi g'vi'yati, Adonai li v'lo ira.

Shir HaKavod

I will sing hymns and compose songs, for my soul will long for You. My soul desires to be hidden in the shadow of Your hand; to know all of Your mysteries.

When I speak about Your glory, my heart seeks after Your love. Hence, I will continually declare Your glories, and I will offer songs of love to You. Though I have not seen You, I will utter Your praise; though I have not known You, I will seek to describe You.

Through Your prophets, in the midst of those who worship You, You have shown Your majesty and praise. Your greatness and Your power are written in Your mighty works.

They did not describe You as You are; they described You only by Your acts. They have seen You in many visions, but despite all these visions You are One.

Lord, everything in heaven and in earth is Yours; the greatness, and the power, and the glory, and the victory and the majesty. Lord, Yours is the kingdom, and You are the Sovereign Head over all. Who can declare the power of the Lord, or utter all of His praise?

(Traditionally Psalm 92 is recited on Shabbat here - see page 63)

Adon Olam

Lord of the world, King supreme
Before anything was formed, He alone reigned.
When, by His will, all things were created,
His sovereign Name was made known.

And at the end, when all things cease to be
The exalted God alone will still be King.
He was, and He is,
and He will be forever glorious.

He is one, and there is no second
to compare Him to or to place next to Him.
He has no beginning and no end;
Power and dominion are His.

He is my living God who saves,
My rock when troubles and sorrows are mine;
My banner and my strong refuge,
My bounteous portion whenever I call.

I give my soul into His care,
For He is near when I sleep and when I wake.
With my soul, my body too;
God is with me, I shall not be afraid.

קדוש לשבת שחרית

Isaiah 58:13-14

אִם־תָּשִׁיב מִשַּׁבָּת רַגְלֶךָ עֲשׂוֹת חֲפָצֶיךָ בְּיוֹם קָדְשִׁי וְקָרָאתָ לַשַּׁבָּת עֹנֶג לִקְדוֹשׁ יְיָ מְכֻבָּד וְכִבַּדְתּוֹ מֵעֲשׂוֹת דְּרָכֶיךָ מִמְּצוֹא חֶפְצְךָ וְדַבֵּר דָּבָר. אָז תִּתְעַנַּג עַל־יְיָ וְהִרְכַּבְתִּיךָ עַל־בָּמֳתֵי אָרֶץ וְהַאֲכַלְתִּיךָ נַחֲלַת יַעֲקֹב אָבִיךָ כִּי פִּי יְיָ דִּבֵּר.

ושמרו

Exodus 31:16-17

וְשָׁמְרוּ בְנֵי יִשְׂרָאֵל אֶת הַשַּׁבָּת, לַעֲשׂוֹת אֶת הַשַּׁבָּת לְדֹרֹתָם בְּרִית עוֹלָם. בֵּינִי וּבֵין בְּנֵי יִשְׂרָאֵל אוֹת הִיא לְעֹלָם, כִּי שֵׁשֶׁת יָמִים עָשָׂה יְיָ אֶת הַשָּׁמַיִם וְאֶת הָאָרֶץ, וּבַיּוֹם הַשְּׁבִיעִי שָׁבַת וַיִּנָּפַשׁ.

V'shamru v'nei Yisraeil et ha'shabbat, la'asot et ha'shabbat l'dorotam b'rit olam. Beini uvein b'nei Yisraeil ot hi l'olam, ki sheishet yamim asah Adonai et hashamayim v'et ha'arets, uvayom hash'vi-i shavat vayinafash.

Exodus 20:8-11

זָכוֹר אֶת יוֹם הַשַּׁבָּת לְקַדְּשׁוֹ. שֵׁשֶׁת יָמִים תַּעֲבֹד וְעָשִׂיתָ כָּל מְלַאכְתֶּךָ. וְיוֹם הַשְּׁבִיעִי שַׁבָּת לַיְיָ אֱלֹהֶיךָ, לֹא תַעֲשֶׂה כָל מְלָאכָה, אַתָּה וּבִנְךָ וּבִתֶּךָ עַבְדְּךָ וַאֲמָתְךָ וּבְהֶמְתֶּךָ, וְגֵרְךָ אֲשֶׁר בִּשְׁעָרֶיךָ. כִּי שֵׁשֶׁת יָמִים עָשָׂה יְיָ אֶת הַשָּׁמַיִם וְאֶת הָאָרֶץ אֶת הַיָּם וְאֶת כָּל אֲשֶׁר בָּם, וַיָּנַח בַּיּוֹם הַשְּׁבִיעִי, עַל כֵּן בֵּרַךְ יְיָ אֶת יוֹם הַשַּׁבָּת וַיְקַדְּשֵׁהוּ.

בָּרוּךְ אַתָּה יְיָ אֱלֹהֵינוּ מֶלֶךְ הָעוֹלָם, בּוֹרֵא פְּרִי הַגָּפֶן.
Barukh atah Adonai Eloheinu Melekh Ha'Olam, borei p'ri hagafen.

Kiddush for Shabbat Morning

Isaiah 58:13-14

If you keep your foot from breaking the Shabbat, from pursuing your own pleasure on my holy day, and if you call the Shabbat a delight and the holy day of the Lord honorable, and honor it by not pursuing your own interests or pleasure, nor speaking your own words, then you will delight yourself in the Lord, and I will make you to ride upon the high places of the earth. I will feed you with the inheritance of Jacob your father, for the mouth of the Lord has spoken.

V'shamru
Exodus 31:16-17

And the children of Israel will keep the Shabbat, observing the Shabbat to all generations as an everlasting covenant. It is a sign between Me and the children of Israel forever, for in six days the Lord made the heavens and the earth, and on the seventh day He ceased from work and He rested.

Exodus 20:8-11

Remember the Shabbat day, so that you keep it holy. For six days you will labor and do all your work, but the seventh day is the Shabbat of the Lord your God. You shall do no work on it; neither you, nor your son, nor your daughter, nor your male servant, nor your female servant, nor your cattle, nor the stranger who dwells within your gates. For in six days the Lord made the heavens and the earth, the sea, and all that is in them, and He rested on the seventh day. Therefore, the Lord blessed the Shabbat day and made it holy.

Blessed are You, Lord our God, King of the Universe, who creates the fruit of the vine.

הַבְדָלָה

(The Havdalah candle is lit and the following is recited)

הִנֵּה אֵל יְשׁוּעָתִי, אֶבְטַח וְלֹא אֶפְחָד, כִּי עָזִּי וְזִמְרָת יָהּ יְיָ, וַיְהִי לִי לִישׁוּעָה. וּשְׁאַבְתֶּם מַיִם בְּשָׂשׂוֹן מִמַּעַיְנֵי הַיְשׁוּעָה. לַיְיָ הַיְשׁוּעָה עַל עַמְּךָ בִרְכָתֶךָ. יְיָ צְבָאוֹת עִמָּנוּ מִשְׂגָּב לָנוּ אֱלֹהֵי יַעֲקֹב. יְיָ צְבָאוֹת אַשְׁרֵי אָדָם בֹּטֵחַ בָּךְ. יְיָ הוֹשִׁיעָה הַמֶּלֶךְ יַעֲנֵנוּ בְיוֹם קָרְאֵנוּ. לַיְּהוּדִים הָיְתָה אוֹרָה וְשִׂמְחָה וְשָׂשׂוֹן וִיקָר. כֵּן תִּהְיֶה לָּנוּ, כּוֹס יְשׁוּעוֹת אֶשָּׂא. וּבְשֵׁם יְיָ אֶקְרָא.

(Recite the following over an overflowing cup of wine or grape juice and a lit havdalah candle)

בָּרוּךְ אַתָּה יְיָ, אֱלֹהֵינוּ מֶלֶךְ הָעוֹלָם, בּוֹרֵא פְּרִי הַגָּפֶן.

Barukh atah Adonai Eloheinu Melekh Ha'Olam, borei p'ri ha'gafen.

(Recite the following over spices which are then passed to each person)

בָּרוּךְ אַתָּה יְיָ, אֱלֹהֵינוּ מֶלֶךְ הָעוֹלָם, בּוֹרֵא מִינֵי בְשָׂמִים.

Barukh atah Adonai Eloheinu Melekh Ha'Olam, bohrei minei v'samim.

(Recite the following over the havdalah candle)

בָּרוּךְ אַתָּה יְיָ, אֱלֹהֵינוּ מֶלֶךְ הָעוֹלָם, בּוֹרֵא מְאוֹרֵי הָאֵשׁ.

Barukh atah Adonai Eloheinu Melekh Ha'Olam, borei me'orei ha'eish.

בָּרוּךְ אַתָּה יְיָ, אֱלֹהֵינוּ מֶלֶךְ הָעוֹלָם, הַמַּבְדִּיל בֵּין קֹדֶשׁ לְחוֹל, בֵּין אוֹר לְחֹשֶׁךְ, בֵּין יִשְׂרָאֵל לָעַמִּים, בֵּין יוֹם הַשְּׁבִיעִי, לְשֵׁשֶׁת יְמֵי הַמַּעֲשֶׂה.

Barukh atah Adonai Eloheinu Melekh Ha'Olam, hamav'dil bein kodesh l'hol, bein ohr l'hoshekh, bein Yisraeil la'amim, bein yom hashvi'i, l'sheshet y'mei hama'aseh.

בָּרוּךְ אַתָּה יְיָ, הַמַּבְדִּיל בֵּין קֹדֶשׁ לְחוֹל.

Barukh atah Adonai, ha'mavdil bein kodesh l'hol.

אֵלִיָּהוּ הַנָּבִיא, אֵלִיָּהוּ הַתִּשְׁבִּי, אֵלִיָּהוּ הַגִּלְעָדִי. בִּמְהֵרָה בְיָמֵינוּ, יָבֹא אֵלֵינוּ, עִם מָשִׁיחַ יֵשׁוּעַ בֶּן דָּוִד.

Eliyahu haNavi, Eliyahu haTishbi, Eliyahu haGiladi. Bim'hera ve'yameinu yavo eileinu, im Mashiaḥ Yeshua ben David.

הַמַּבְדִּיל בֵּין קֹדֶשׁ

הַמַּבְדִּיל בֵּין קֹדֶשׁ לְחֹל חַטֹּאתֵינוּ הוּא יִמְחֹל, זַרְעֵנוּ וְכַסְפֵּנוּ יַרְבֶּה כַחוֹל וְכַכּוֹכָבִים בַּלָּיְלָה. שָׁבֻעַ טוֹב...

Havdalah

(The Havdalah candle is lit and the following is recited)

Behold, God is my salvation; I will trust and will not be afraid; for God is my strength and my song; indeed, He has saved me. You will drink with joy from the waters of salvation; the salvation of the Lord. Your blessing be upon Your people. The Lord of Hosts is with us; the God of Jacob is our stronghold. To the Jews were given light and joy, gladness and honor; so may it be for us. I will raise up the cup of salvation, and call on the Name of the Lord.

(Recite the following over an overflowing cup of wine or grape juice and a lit havdalah candle)

Blessed are You, Lord our God, King of the Universe, who creates the fruit of the vine.

(Recite the following over spices which are then passed to each person)

Blessed are You, Lord our God, King of the Universe, who creates fragrant spices.

(Recite the following over the havdalah candle)

Blessed are You, Lord our God, King of the Universe, who creates the light of the fire.

Blessed are You, Lord our God, You have made a distinction between that which is holy and that which is common; between light and darkness; between Israel and the other nations; between the seventh day and the six days of work.

Blessed are You, Lord, who has made a distinction between the holy and the profane.

May Elijah the Prophet, Elijah of the Tishbi, Elijah of the Giladi: come to us in our days proclaiming redemption, and with him Messiah Yeshua son of David.

Ha'Mavdil bain Kodesh

May He who distinguishes between the holy and the profane forgive our sin;
may our offspring and our means be as the sand and as the stars in the night.
May it be a good week!

Shavua Tov...

שָׁבֻעַ טוֹב...

יוֹם פָּנָה כְּצֵל תֹּמֶר אֶקְרָא לָאֵל עָלַי גֹּמֵר;
אָמַר שׁוֹמֵר אָתָא בֹקֶר וְגַם לָיְלָה.

שָׁבֻעַ טוֹב...

צִדְקָתְךָ כְּהַר תָּבוֹר עַל חֲטָאַי עָבֹר תַּעֲבֹר;
כְּיוֹם אֶתְמוֹל כִּי יַעֲבֹר וְאַשְׁמוּרָה בַלָּיְלָה.

שָׁבֻעַ טוֹב...

חָלְפָה עוֹנַת מִנְחָתִי מִי יִתֵּן מְנוּחָתִי?
יָגַעְתִּי בְאַנְחָתִי אַשְׂחֶה בְכָל לָיְלָה.

שָׁבֻעַ טוֹב...

קוֹלִי בַּל יֻטַּל פְּתַח לִי שַׁעַר הַמְנֻטָּל;
שֶׁרֹּאשִׁי נִמְלָא טָל קְוֻצּוֹתַי רְסִיסֵי לָיְלָה.

שָׁבֻעַ טוֹב...

הֵעָתֵר נוֹרָא וְאָיֹם אֲשַׁוֵּעַ תְּנָה פִּדְיוֹם;
בְּנֶשֶׁף בְּעֶרֶב יוֹם בְּאִישׁוֹן לָיְלָה.

שָׁבֻעַ טוֹב...

קְרָאתִיךָ יָהּ הוֹשִׁיעֵנִי אֹרַח חַיִּים תּוֹדִיעֵנִי;
מִדַּלָּה תְבַצְּעֵנִי מִיּוֹם עַד לָיְלָה.

שָׁבֻעַ טוֹב...

טַהֵר טִנּוּף מַעֲשַׂי פֶּן יֹאמְרוּ מַכְעִיסַי;
אַיֵּה אֱלוֹהַּ עֹשַׂי נֹתֵן זְמִרוֹת בַּלָּיְלָה.

שָׁבֻעַ טוֹב...

נַחְנוּ בְיָדְךָ כַּחֹמֶר סְלַח נָא עַל קַל וָחֹמֶר;
יוֹם לְיוֹם יַבִּיעַ אֹמֶר וְלַיְלָה לְלָיְלָה.

שָׁבֻעַ טוֹב...

הַמַּבְדִּיל בֵּין קֹדֶשׁ לְחֹל חַטֹּאתֵינוּ הוּא יִמְחֹל;
זַרְעֵנוּ וְכַסְפֵּנוּ יַרְבֶּה כַּחוֹל וְכַכּוֹכָבִים בַּלָּיְלָה.

שָׁבֻעַ טוֹב...

Shavua Tov...

The day has turned as the shadow of the date palm, I shall call upon God to fulfill
His promise to me; the Watchman has said, "Morning has come with the night."

Shavua tov...

Your justice is as the heights of Mount Tabor.   Pardon my transgressions and
overlook them as yesterday and today pass on; as a watch in the night.

Shavua tov...

The time of my offering is gone, who will grant me my rest again?
I grow weary in my groaning and tears every night.

Shavua tov...

May my voice not be as the dew. Open to me the gates that were closed;
my head is covered with dew, my hair is wet as I stand waiting in the night.

Shavua tov...

You who are Awesome and Terrible, when I cry out to You, grant redemption
at the end of the day, in the evening and in the dark of the night.

Shavua tov...

God, I called upon You and You rescued me. Declare to me the way of life.
Quickly bring to an end my poverty, as from the day to the night.

Shavua tov...

May the impurity of my deeds be changed, lest those who torment me say,
"Where is the God who made you; who gave you songs in the night?"

Shavua tov...

We are like clay in Your hand. Please forgive us, we are but clay, both great and
small. Day after day and night after night this word shall be poured forth.

Shavua tov...

May He who distinguishes between the holy and the profane forgive our sin;
may our offspring and our means be as the sand and as the stars in the night.

Shavua tov...

בִּרְכַּת הַמָּזוֹן

(On weekdays recite Psalm 137)

עַל נַהֲרוֹת בָּבֶל שָׁם יָשַׁבְנוּ גַּם בָּכִינוּ בְּזָכְרֵנוּ אֶת צִיּוֹן. עַל עֲרָבִים בְּתוֹכָהּ תָּלִינוּ כִּנֹּרוֹתֵינוּ. כִּי שָׁם שְׁאֵלוּנוּ שׁוֹבֵינוּ דִּבְרֵי שִׁיר, וְתוֹלָלֵינוּ שִׂמְחָה; שִׁירוּ לָנוּ מִשִּׁיר צִיּוֹן. אֵיךְ נָשִׁיר אֶת שִׁיר יְיָ עַל אַדְמַת נֵכָר. אִם אֶשְׁכָּחֵךְ יְרוּשָׁלַיִם, תִּשְׁכַּח יְמִינִי. תִּדְבַּק לְשׁוֹנִי לְחִכִּי, אִם לֹא אֶזְכְּרֵכִי, אִם לֹא אַעֲלֶה אֶת יְרוּשָׁלַיִם עַל רֹאשׁ שִׂמְחָתִי. זְכֹר יְיָ לִבְנֵי אֱדוֹם אֵת יוֹם יְרוּשָׁלַיִם; הָאֹמְרִים עָרוּ עָרוּ, עַד הַיְסוֹד בָּהּ. בַּת בָּבֶל הַשְּׁדוּדָה, אַשְׁרֵי שֶׁיְשַׁלֶּם לָךְ אֶת גְּמוּלֵךְ שֶׁגָּמַלְתְּ לָנוּ. אַשְׁרֵי שֶׁיֹּאחֵז וְנִפֵּץ אֶת עֹלָלַיִךְ אֶל הַסָּלַע.

(On Shabbat and Yom Tov recite Psalm 126 - a transliteration can be found on page 210)

שִׁיר הַמַּעֲלוֹת, בְּשׁוּב יְיָ אֶת שִׁיבַת צִיּוֹן הָיִינוּ כְּחֹלְמִים. אָז יִמָּלֵא שְׂחוֹק פִּינוּ, וּלְשׁוֹנֵנוּ רִנָּה; אָז יֹאמְרוּ בַגּוֹיִם, הִגְדִּיל יְיָ לַעֲשׂוֹת עִם אֵלֶּה. הִגְדִּיל יְיָ לַעֲשׂוֹת עִמָּנוּ, הָיִינוּ שְׂמֵחִים. שׁוּבָה יְיָ אֶת שְׁבִיתֵנוּ, כַּאֲפִיקִים בַּנֶּגֶב. הַזֹּרְעִים בְּדִמְעָה, בְּרִנָּה יִקְצֹרוּ. הָלוֹךְ יֵלֵךְ וּבָכֹה נֹשֵׂא מֶשֶׁךְ הַזָּרַע; בֹּא יָבֹא בְרִנָּה נֹשֵׂא אֲלֻמֹּתָיו.

(Recite the zimmun if three or more have eaten together, include words in parentheses when a minyan is present)

(The Leader selected by the group begins the zimmun)

Haveiray n'vareikh!

חֲבֵרַי נְבָרֵךְ.

(Those around the table respond)

Y'hi shem Adonai m'vorakh mei-atah v'ad olam.

יְהִי שֵׁם יְיָ מְבֹרָךְ מֵעַתָּה וְעַד עוֹלָם.

(The Leader says)

יְהִי שֵׁם יְיָ מְבֹרָךְ מֵעַתָּה וְעַד עוֹלָם. בִּרְשׁוּת חֲבֵרַי, נְבָרֵךְ (אֱלֹהֵינוּ) שֶׁאָכַלְנוּ מִשֶּׁלוֹ.

Y'hi shem Adonai m'vorakh mei-atah v'ad olam.
Birshut ḥaveiray, n'vareikh (Eloheinu) shea-kha'lenu mishelo.

(Those around the table respond and then the Leader repeats)

בָּרוּךְ (אֱלֹהֵינוּ) שֶׁאָכַלְנוּ מִשֶּׁלוֹ וּבְטוּבוֹ חָיִינוּ.

Barukh (Eloheinu) shea-kha'lenu mishelo uv'tuvo ḥayinu.

(Together)

Barukh hu uvarukh sh'mo   בָּרוּךְ הוּא וּבָרוּךְ שְׁמוֹ.

בָּרוּךְ אַתָּה יְיָ, אֱלֹהֵינוּ מֶלֶךְ הָעוֹלָם, הַזָּן אֶת הָעוֹלָם כֻּלּוֹ בְּטוּבוֹ בְּחֵן בְּחֶסֶד וּבְרַחֲמִים. הוּא נוֹתֵן לֶחֶם לְכָל בָּשָׂר כִּי לְעוֹלָם חַסְדּוֹ. וּבְטוּבוֹ הַגָּדוֹל תָּמִיד לֹא חָסַר לָנוּ, וְאַל יֶחְסַר לָנוּ מָזוֹן לְעוֹלָם וָעֶד, בַּעֲבוּר שְׁמוֹ הַגָּדוֹל. כִּי הוּא אֵל זָן וּמְפַרְנֵס לַכֹּל וּמֵטִיב לַכֹּל, וּמֵכִין מָזוֹן לְכָל בְּרִיּוֹתָיו אֲשֶׁר בָּרָא. בָּרוּךְ אַתָּה יְיָ, הַזָּן אֶת הַכֹּל.

Barukh atah Adonai, Eloheinu Melekh haolam, hazan et ha-olam kulo b'tuvo, b'hein b'hesed uv'raḥamim. Hu notein leḥem l'khol basar ki l'olam ḥasdo. Uv'tuvo hagadol tamid lo ḥasar lanu, v'al yeḥsar lanu, mazon l'olam va-ed, baavur sh'mo hagadol. Ki hu El zan um'farneis lakol umeitiv lakol, umeikhin mazon l'khol b'riyotav asher bara. Barukh atah Adonai, hazan et hakol.

(An Abridged Version can be followed from here on page 126.
A very brief version of Birkat HaMazon that contains just the traditional minimal requirement to mention the Food, the Land of Israel, Jerusalem's sanctity and God's Goodness after eating can be found on page 224)

Birkat HaMazon

(On weekdays recite Psalm 137)

By the waters of Babylon, there we sat down and wept, when we remembered Zion. On the willows there we hung up our harps. For there our captors required of us songs, and our tormentors, mirth, saying, "Sing us one of the songs of Tsion!" How can we sing the Lord's song in a foreign land? If I forget you, O Jerusalem, let my right hand wither! Let my tongue cleave to the roof of my mouth, if I do not remember you, if I do not set Jerusalem above my highest joy! Remember, O Lord, against the Edomites the day of Jerusalem, how they said, "Raze it, raze it! Down to its foundations!" O daughter of Babylon, you devastator! Happy shall he be who repays you with what you have done to us! Happy shall he be who takes your little ones and dashes them against the rock!

(On Shabbat and Yom Tov recite Psalm 126 - a transliteration can be found on page 210)

When the Lord restored the fortunes of Zion, we were like those who dream. Then our mouth was filled with laughter, and our tongue with shouts of joy; then they said among the nations, "The Lord has done great things for them." The Lord has done great things for us; we are glad. Restore our fortunes, O Lord, like the watercourses in the Negeb! May those who sow in tears reap with shouts of joy! He that goes forth weeping, bearing the seed for sowing, shall come home with shouts of joy, bringing his sheaves with him.

(Recite the zimmun if three or more have eaten together, include words in parentheses when a minyan is present)

(The Leader selected by the group begins the zimmun)
Friends, let us give blessing!

(Those around the table respond)
May the Name of the Lord be blessed both now and forever!

(The Leader says)
May the Name of the Lord be blessed both now and forever! With your permission friends, let us shout with joy, (blessing God) for the bounty we have shared.

(Those around the table respond and then the Leader repeats)
Blessed (is our God), for the bounty we have shared, and whose goodness is upon our life.

(Together)
Blessed is He and blessed is His Name!

Blessed are You, Lord our God, King of the universe, who, through His goodness, nourishes the whole world with grace, loving kindness and compassion. Indeed, "He gives bread to all flesh because His loving kindness endures forever." His great goodness, with which we are sustained, has never diminished toward us; nor will it ever, for the sake of His great Name. He is God who provides nourishment for all, and who does good to all. He provides food for all His creation. Blessed are You, Lord, who provides food for all.

(An Abridged Version can be followed from here on page 127.
A very brief version of Birkat HaMazon that contains just the traditional minimal requirement to mention the Food, the Land of Israel, Jerusalem's sanctity and God's Goodness after eating can be found on page 224)

נוֹדֶה לְךָ יְיָ אֱלֹהֵינוּ עַל שֶׁהִנְחַלְתָּ לַאֲבוֹתֵינוּ, אֶרֶץ חֶמְדָּה טוֹבָה וּרְחָבָה. וְעַל שֶׁהוֹצֵאתָנוּ יְיָ אֱלֹהֵינוּ מֵאֶרֶץ מִצְרַיִם, וּפְדִיתָנוּ מִבֵּית עֲבָדִים. וְעַל בְּרִיתְךָ שֶׁחָתַמְתָּ בִּבְשָׂרֵנוּ. וְעַל תּוֹרָתְךָ שֶׁלִּמַּדְתָּנוּ. וְעַל חֻקֶּיךָ שֶׁהוֹדַעְתָּנוּ וְעַל חַיִּים חֵן וָחֶסֶד שֶׁחוֹנַנְתָּנוּ. וְעַל אֲכִילַת מָזוֹן שָׁאַתָּה זָן וּמְפַרְנֵס אוֹתָנוּ תָּמִיד, בְּכָל יוֹם וּבְכָל עֵת וּבְכָל שָׁעָה.

Nodeh l'ka, Adonai Eloheinu, al shehin'ha'leta laavoteinu, erets ḥemdah tovah ur'havah; v'al shehotseitanu, Adonai Eloheinu mei-erets Mitsrayim; uf'ditanu mibeit avadim; v'al b'rit'ka sheḥatamta biv'sareinu. V'al Torat'ka she-limad'tanu. V'al ḥukeka shehodatanu, v'al ḥayim ḥein vaḥesed shehonantanu, v'al akhilat mazon shaatah zan um'farneis otanu tamid, b'khol yom uv'khol eit uv'khol shaah.

(On Ḥanukah and Purim insert the appropriate blessing on page 158)

וְעַל הַכֹּל יְיָ אֱלֹהֵינוּ אֲנַחְנוּ מוֹדִים לָךְ, וּמְבָרְכִים אוֹתָךְ. יִתְבָּרַךְ שִׁמְךָ בְּפִי כָּל חַי תָּמִיד לְעוֹלָם וָעֶד. כַּכָּתוּב, וְאָכַלְתָּ וְשָׂבָעְתָּ, וּבֵרַכְתָּ אֶת יְיָ אֱלֹהֶיךָ עַל הָאָרֶץ הַטֹּבָה אֲשֶׁר נָתַן לָךְ. בָּרוּךְ אַתָּה יְיָ, עַל הָאָרֶץ וְעַל הַמָּזוֹן.

V'al hakol, Adonai Eloheinu, anaḥnu modim lakh, u'mevar'khim otakh. Yit'barakh shim'ka b'fi kol ḥai tamid l'olam va-ed. Kakatuv, v'akhal'ta v'sava'ta, uveirakhta et Adonai Eloheka al haarets hatovah asher natan lakh. Barukh atah Adonai, al haarets v'al hamazon.

רַחֵם יְיָ אֱלֹהֵינוּ, עַל יִשְׂרָאֵל עַמֶּךָ, וְעַל יְרוּשָׁלַיִם עִירֶךָ, וְעַל צִיּוֹן מִשְׁכַּן כְּבוֹדֶךָ, וְעַל מַלְכוּת בֵּית דָּוִד מְשִׁיחֶךָ, וְעַל הַבַּיִת הַגָּדוֹל וְהַקָּדוֹשׁ שֶׁנִּקְרָא שִׁמְךָ עָלָיו. אֱלֹהֵינוּ, אָבִינוּ, רְעֵנוּ, זוּנֵנוּ, פַּרְנְסֵנוּ, וְכַלְכְּלֵנוּ, וְהַרְוִיחֵנוּ, וְהַרְוַח לָנוּ יְיָ אֱלֹהֵינוּ מְהֵרָה מִכָּל צָרוֹתֵינוּ. וְנָא, אַל תַּצְרִיכֵנוּ. יְיָ אֱלֹהֵינוּ, לֹא לִידֵי מַתְּנַת בָּשָׂר וָדָם, וְלֹא לִידֵי הַלְוָאָתָם. כִּי אִם לְיָדְךָ הַמְּלֵאָה, הַפְּתוּחָה, הַקְּדוֹשָׁה וְהָרְחָבָה. שֶׁלֹּא נֵבוֹשׁ וְלֹא נִכָּלֵם לְעוֹלָם וָעֶד.

Raḥeim, Adonai Eloheinu, al Yisraeil ameka, v'al Y'rushalayim ireka, v'al Tsiyon mishkan k'vodeka, v'al malkhut beit David M'shiḥeka. V'al habayit hagaol v'hakadosh shenikra shimka alayv. Eloheinu Avinu, r'einu zuneinu, par'neseinu v'khal'keleinu v'harviḥeinu, v'har'vaḥ lanu, Adonai Eloheinu, m'heirah mikol tzaroteinu. V'na al tatsrikheinu, Adonai Eloheinu, lo lidei mat'nat basar vadam, v'lo lidei hal'vaatam, ki im l'yad'ka ham'lei-ah, hap'tuḥah hak'doshah v'har'ḥavah, shelo neivosh v'lo nikaleim l'olam va-ed.

(On Shabbat add)

רְצֵה וְהַחֲלִיצֵנוּ יְיָ אֱלֹהֵינוּ בְּמִצְוֹתֶיךָ וּבְמִצְוַת יוֹם הַשְּׁבִיעִי הַשַּׁבָּת הַגָּדוֹל וְהַקָּדוֹשׁ הַזֶּה. כִּי יוֹם זֶה גָּדוֹל וְקָדוֹשׁ הוּא לְפָנֶיךָ. לִשְׁבָּת בּוֹ וְלָנוּחַ בּוֹ בְּאַהֲבָה כְּמִצְוַת רְצוֹנֶךָ וּבִרְצוֹנְךָ הָנִיחַ לָנוּ יְיָ אֱלֹהֵינוּ, שֶׁלֹּא תְהֵא צָרָה וְיָגוֹן וַאֲנָחָה בְּיוֹם מְנוּחָתֵנוּ. וְהַרְאֵנוּ יְיָ אֱלֹהֵינוּ בְּנֶחָמַת צִיּוֹן עִירֶךָ, וּבְבִנְיַן יְרוּשָׁלַיִם עִיר קָדְשֶׁךָ, כִּי אַתָּה הוּא בַּעַל הַיְשׁוּעוֹת וּבַעַל הַנֶּחָמוֹת.

Lord our God, we thank You that besides this, You have given as an inheritance to our fathers a desirable, good, and abundant land. And besides this, Lord our God, You have brought us out of the land of Egypt, ransoming us from the house of slavery. And besides this, You have given us the sign of the covenant upon our flesh. And besides this, You have given us Your instruction that we might study. And besides this, You have made Your precepts known to us. And besides this, You have pardoned us, giving us a life of grace and loving kindness. And besides this, You have given us food to eat; food which nourishes us always: every day, and every season, and every hour.

(On Ḥanukah and Purim insert the appropriate blessing on page 159)

And besides all these things, Lord our God, we give You thanks and bless You for Your miracles. Your Name will be magnified by the mouth of all who live, forever and to all eternity. As it is written, "You shall eat and be satisfied, and give blessing to the Lord your God for the good land He has given to you." Blessed are You, Lord, for the land and for its produce.

Lord our God, in time, have compassion upon Israel Your people, and upon Jerusalem Your city, and upon Tsiyon the dwelling place of Your glory, and upon the kingdom of the House of David Your Anointed, and upon the great and holy House on which Your Name has been named. Our God, our Father, our Shepherd, our Sustainer, our Supporter, and our Provider ...provide for us, Lord our God, bringing relief from all our present troubles. Lord our God, may we never depend on gifts or loans from the hand of flesh and blood, but only from Your hand ...overflowing, open, holy, and bountiful; that we may never be shamed by others nor ashamed of ourselves.

(On Shabbat add)

Lord our God, may You take pleasure in strengthening us through all Your commandments and in the command concerning the seventh day, this great and holy Shabbat. For before Your countenance, this day is great and holy; that we might dwell in Your rest and in Your love, in keeping with the desire of Your command. And may it be Your will, Lord our God, to grant us such rest; that there be no misfortune, or grief, or sighing on the day of our rest. Lord our God, may we behold Tsiyon Your city being comforted, and our descendents in Jerusalem Your holy city, for You are the Master of all salvation, and the Master of all consolation.

(On Rosh Hodesh and Festivals add)

אֱלֹהֵינוּ וֵאלֹהֵי אֲבוֹתֵינוּ, יַעֲלֶה וְיָבֹא וְיַגִּיעַ, וְיֵרָאֶה וְיֵרָצֶה, וְיִשָּׁמַע, וְיִפָּקֵד, וְיִזָּכֵר זִכְרוֹנֵנוּ וּפִקְדוֹנֵנוּ, וְזִכְרוֹן אֲבוֹתֵינוּ, וְזִכְרוֹן מָשִׁיחַ יֵשׁוּעַ בֶּן דָּוִד עַבְדֶּךָ, וְזִכְרוֹן יְרוּשָׁלַיִם עִיר קָדְשֶׁךָ, וְזִכְרוֹן כָּל עַמְּךָ בֵּית יִשְׂרָאֵל לְפָנֶיךָ, לִפְלֵיטָה לְטוֹבָה לְחֵן וּלְחֶסֶד וּלְרַחֲמִים, לְחַיִּים וּלְשָׁלוֹם בְּיוֹם

לְרֹאשׁ הַחֹדֶשׁ: רֹאשׁ הַחֹדֶשׁ

לְפֶסַח: חַג הַמַּצּוֹת

לְשָׁבוּעוֹת: חַג הַשָּׁבוּעוֹת

לְרֹאשׁ הַשָּׁנָה: הַזִּכָּרוֹן

לְסֻכּוֹת: חַג הַסֻּכּוֹת

לִשְׁמִינִי עֲצֶרֶת: הַשְּׁמִינִי חַג הָעֲצֶרֶת

הַזֶּה. זָכְרֵנוּ יְיָ אֱלֹהֵינוּ בּוֹ לְטוֹבָה. וּפָקְדֵנוּ בּוֹ לִבְרָכָה, וְהוֹשִׁיעֵנוּ בּוֹ לְחַיִּים. וּבִדְבַר יְשׁוּעָה וְרַחֲמִים, חוּס וְחָנֵּנוּ, וְרַחֵם עָלֵינוּ וְהוֹשִׁיעֵנוּ. כִּי אֵלֶיךָ עֵינֵינוּ, כִּי אֵל מֶלֶךְ חַנּוּן וְרַחוּם אָתָּה.

(On other days continue here)

וּבְנֵה יְרוּשָׁלַיִם עִיר הַקֹּדֶשׁ בִּמְהֵרָה בְיָמֵינוּ. בָּרוּךְ אַתָּה יְיָ, בּוֹנֶה בְרַחֲמָיו יְרוּשָׁלָיִם. אָמֵן.

Uv'neih Y'rushalayim ir hakodesh bimheirah v'yameinu.
Barukh atah Adonai, boneh v'raḥamav Y'rushalayim. Amen

בָּרוּךְ אַתָּה יְיָ אֱלֹהֵינוּ מֶלֶךְ הָעוֹלָם, הָאֵל אָבִינוּ, מַלְכֵּנוּ, אַדִּירֵנוּ בּוֹרְאֵנוּ, גּוֹאֲלֵנוּ, יוֹצְרֵנוּ, קְדוֹשֵׁנוּ קְדוֹשׁ יַעֲקֹב, רוֹעֵנוּ רוֹעֵה יִשְׂרָאֵל. הַמֶּלֶךְ הַטּוֹב, וְהַמֵּטִיב לַכֹּל, שֶׁבְּכָל יוֹם וָיוֹם הוּא הֵטִיב, הוּא מֵטִיב, הוּא יֵיטִיב לָנוּ. הוּא גְמָלָנוּ, הוּא גוֹמְלֵנוּ, הוּא יִגְמְלֵנוּ לָעַד לְחֵן וּלְחֶסֶד וּלְרַחֲמִים וּלְרֶוַח הַצָּלָה וְהַצְלָחָה בְּרָכָה וִישׁוּעָה, נֶחָמָה, פַּרְנָסָה וְכַלְכָּלָה, וְרַחֲמִים, וְחַיִּים וְשָׁלוֹם, וְכָל טוֹב, וּמִכָּל טוֹב לְעוֹלָם אַל יְחַסְּרֵנוּ.

Barukh atah Adonai, Eloheinu Melekh haolam, ha-El Avinu Malkeinu Adireinu,
Bor'einu, Goaleinu, Yots'reinu, K'dosheinu, K'dosh Yaakov, Ro-einu Ro-eih Yisraeil,
HaMelekh hatov v'hameitiv lakol, sheb'khol yom vayom hu heitiv, hu meitiv, hu yeitiv
lanu. Hu g'malanu, hu gom'leinu, hu yigm'leinu laad, l'hein ul'hesed ul'raḥamim
ul'revah, hatsalah v'hatslaḥah, b'rakhah vishuah, neḥamah, parnasah, v'khalkalah,
v'raḥamim v'ḥayim v'shalom, v'khol tov, umikol tov l'olam al y'has'reinu.

הָרַחֲמָן, הוּא יִמְלוֹךְ עָלֵינוּ לְעוֹלָם וָעֶד.

הָרַחֲמָן, הוּא יִתְבָּרַךְ בַּשָּׁמַיִם וּבָאָרֶץ.

הָרַחֲמָן, הוּא יִשְׁתַּבַּח לְדוֹר דּוֹרִים, וְיִתְפָּאַר בָּנוּ לָעַד וּלְנֵצַח נְצָחִים, וְיִתְהַדַּר בָּנוּ לָעַד וּלְעוֹלְמֵי עוֹלָמִים.

הָרַחֲמָן, הוּא יְפַרְנְסֵנוּ בְּכָבוֹד.

הָרַחֲמָן, הוּא יִשְׁבּוֹר עֻלֵּנוּ מֵעַל צַוָּארֵנוּ וְהוּא יוֹלִיכֵנוּ קוֹמְמִיּוּת לְאַרְצֵנוּ.

הָרַחֲמָן, הוּא יִשְׁלַח בְּרָכָה מְרֻבָּה בַּבַּיִת הַזֶּה, וְעַל שֻׁלְחָן זֶה שֶׁאָכַלְנוּ עָלָיו.

(On Rosh Ḥodesh and Festivals add)

Our God, and God of our fathers, may the remembrance and the consideration of us, and the remembrance of our fathers, and the remembrance of Messiah Yeshua, the son of David Your servant, and the remembrance of Jerusalem Your holy city, and the remembrance of all Your people, the House of Israel, arise and come, and reach, and be seen, and be accepted, and be heard, and be numbered, and be remembered before Your face; for deliverance, for favor, for grace and for loving kindness, and for compassion, and for peace on this day of...

On Rosh Ḥodesh say:	the New Month
On Pesaḥ say:	the Festival of Unleavened Bread
On Shavuot say:	the Festival of Weeks
On Rosh Hashanah say:	the Rememberance
On Sukkot say:	the Festival of Tabernacles
On Shemini Atseret say:	the Festival of the Eighth Day

Lord our God, remember us for goodness. Command blessing for us, and save us that we might live. Concerning salvation and compassion, take pity and pardon us, and have compassion on us, for You are our salvation. Our eyes are lifted to God, for You, God, are a gracious and compassionate King.

(On other days continue here)

Rebuild Jerusalem as a holy city very soon, even in our day. Blessed are You, Lord, who, in compassion, builds Jerusalem. Amen!

Blessed are You, Lord our God, King of the universe, God our Father, our King, our Mighty One, our Creator, our Redeemer, our Maker, our Holy One and the Holy One of Jacob, our Shepherd and the Shepherd of Israel. The Good King is good to all. Each day and every day, He has done good. He has done good, and He continually does good for us. He has dealt bountifully with us, He deals bountifully with us, and He will always deal bountifully with us; for grace, and for loving kindness, and for compassion, and for the wind of relief and success, blessing and deliverance, comfort, sustenance and support, and mercy, and life and peace, and with all that is good. May God, who knows our need, always provide us with good.

The Compassionate One, may He rule over us forever and ever.

The Compassionate One, may He be blessed in the heavens and in the earth.

The Compassionate One, may He be praised in all generations, and glorified in us forever and to all eternity, and honored among us forever, both in this world and in all worlds to come.

The Compassionate One, may He satisfy us with honor.

The Compassionate One, may He remove the yoke from our neck, that we might walk upright to our land.

The Compassionate One, may He multiply blessings upon us and upon this house, upon this table at which we have eaten.

הָרַחֲמָן, הוּא יִשְׁלַח לָנוּ אֶת אֵלִיָּהוּ הַנָּבִיא זָכוּר לַטּוֹב, וִיבַשֶּׂר לָנוּ בְּשׂוֹרוֹת טוֹבוֹת יְשׁוּעוֹת וְנֶחָמוֹת.

הָרַחֲמָן, הוּא יְבָרֵךְ אֶת־(אָבִי מוֹרִי,) בַּעַל הַבַּיִת הַזֶּה, וְאֶת־(אִמִּי מוֹרָתִי,) בַּעֲלַת הַבַּיִת הַזֶּה, אוֹתָם וְאֶת־בֵּיתָם וְאֶת־זַרְעָם וְאֶת־כָּל אֲשֶׁר לָהֶם.   אוֹתָנוּ וְאֶת כָּל אֲשֶׁר לָנוּ, כְּמוֹ שֶׁנִּתְבָּרְכוּ אֲבוֹתֵינוּ, אַבְרָהָם יִצְחָק וְיַעֲקֹב.   בַּכֹּל, מִכֹּל, כֹּל.   כֵּן יְבָרֵךְ אוֹתָנוּ כֻּלָּנוּ יַחַד.   בִּבְרָכָה שְׁלֵמָה, וְנֹאמַר אָמֵן.

בַּמָּרוֹם יְלַמְּדוּ עֲלֵיהֶם וְעָלֵינוּ זְכוּת, שֶׁתְּהֵא לְמִשְׁמֶרֶת שָׁלוֹם.   וְנִשָּׂא בְרָכָה מֵאֵת יְיָ וּצְדָקָה מֵאֱלֹהֵי יִשְׁעֵנוּ. וְנִמְצָא חֵן וְשֵׂכֶל טוֹב בְּעֵינֵי אֱלֹהִים וְאָדָם.

(On Shabbat say)

הָרַחֲמָן, הוּא יַנְחִילֵנוּ יוֹם שֶׁכֻּלּוֹ שַׁבָּת וּמְנוּחָה לְחַיֵּי הָעוֹלָמִים.

Haraḥaman, hu yan'ḥileinu yom she-kulo Shabbat um'uḥah l'chayei ha-olamim.

(On Rosh Ḥodesh say)

הָרַחֲמָן, הוּא יְחַדֵּשׁ עָלֵינוּ אֶת הַחֹדֶשׁ הַזֶּה לְטוֹבָה וְלִבְרָכָה.

(On a Yom Tov say)

הָרַחֲמָן, הוּא יַנְחִילֵנוּ יוֹם שֶׁכֻּלּוֹ טוֹב.

(On Rosh Hashanah say)

הָרַחֲמָן, הוּא יְחַדֵּשׁ עָלֵינוּ אֶת הַשָּׁנָה הַזֹּאת לְטוֹבָה וְלִבְרָכָה.

(On Sukkot say)

הָרַחֲמָן, הוּא יָקִים לָנוּ אֶת סֻכַּת דָּוִד.

(On other days continue here)

הָרַחֲמָן, הוּא יְבָרֵךְ אֶת־מְדִינַת יִשְׂרָאֵל, רֵאשִׁית צְמִיחַת גְּאֻלָּתֵנוּ.

Haraḥaman, hu y'vareich et M'dinat Yisraeil, reisheet ts'miḥat g'oo-lateinu.

הָרַחֲמָן, הוּא יְבָרֵךְ אֶת־אַחֵינוּ בְּנֵי יִשְׂרָאֵל הַנְּתוּנִים בְּצָרָה, וְיוֹצִיאֵם מֵאֲפֵלָה לְאוֹרָה.

Haraḥaman, hu y'vareikh et aḥeinu b'nei Yisraeil han'tunim b'tsarah, v'yotsi-eim mei-afeilah l'orah.

הָרַחֲמָן, הוּא יְזַכֵּנוּ לִימוֹת הַמָּשִׁיחַ יֵשׁוּעַ וּלְחַיֵּי הָעוֹלָם הַבָּא.

Haraḥaman, hu y'zakenu limot haMashiach Yeshua ul'ḥayei haolam haba.

מַגְדִּיל *Magdil* *(On weekdays say)*

מִגְדּוֹל *Migdol* *(On Shabbat, Festivals and Rosh Ḥodesh say)*

יְשׁוּעוֹת מַלְכּוֹ, וְעֹשֶׂה חֶסֶד לִמְשִׁיחוֹ לְדָוִד וּלְזַרְעוֹ עַד עוֹלָם. עֹשֶׂה שָׁלוֹם בִּמְרוֹמָיו, הוּא יַעֲשֶׂה שָׁלוֹם, עָלֵינוּ וְעַל כָּל יִשְׂרָאֵל, וְאִמְרוּ אָמֵן.

y'shuot malko, v'oseh ḥesed lim'shiho l'David ul'zaro ad olam. Oseh shalom bim'romav, hu ya'aseh shalom aleinu v'al kol Yisraeil, v'im'ru amein.

יְראוּ אֶת יְיָ קְדֹשָׁיו, כִּי אֵין מַחְסוֹר לִירֵאָיו. כְּפִירִים רָשׁוּ וְרָעֵבוּ, וְדֹרְשֵׁי יְיָ לֹא יַחְסְרוּ כָל טוֹב. הוֹדוּ לַיְיָ כִּי טוֹב, כִּי לְעוֹלָם חַסְדּוֹ. פּוֹתֵחַ אֶת יָדֶךָ, וּמַשְׂבִּיעַ לְכָל חַי רָצוֹן. בָּרוּךְ הַגֶּבֶר אֲשֶׁר יִבְטַח בַּיְיָ, וְהָיָה יְיָ מִבְטַחוֹ. נַעַר הָיִיתִי גַּם זָקַנְתִּי וְלֹא רָאִיתִי צַדִּיק נֶעֱזָב, וְזַרְעוֹ מְבַקֶּשׁ לָחֶם. יְיָ עֹז לְעַמּוֹ יִתֵּן, יְיָ יְבָרֵךְ אֶת עַמּוֹ בַשָּׁלוֹם.

The Compassionate One, may He send us Elijah the Prophet, of good memory, bearing good tidings of salvation and consolation.

The Compassionate One, may He bless (my father,) the master of this house, and (my mother,) the mistress of this house; and with them, this house, and their children, and all that belongs to them. Bless us as well, and all that is ours, even as our fathers Abraham, Isaac and Jacob were blessed in everything, by everything, and with everything, so may He bless all of us with perfect blessing, and let us say, Amen.

May He who is on high be called upon so that enduring peace would be upon them and upon all of us. Then we will receive blessing from the Lord, and justice from the God of our salvation, and we shall find grace and good understanding in the eyes of God and of man.

(On Shabbat say)
The Compassionate One, may He cause us to come to that day which shall always be Shabbat, with rest in life everlasting.

(On Rosh Ḥodesh say)
The Compassionate One, may He renew this month to us, for goodness and for blessing.

(On a Yom Tov say)
The Compassionate One, may He cause us to come to that day that is always good.

(On Rosh Hashanah say)
The Compassionate One, may He renew this year for us, for good and for blessing.

(On Sukkot say)
The Compassionate One, may He raise up for us the tabernacle of David.

(On other days continue here)
The Compassionate One, may He bless the State of Israel, the dawn of our redemption.

The Compassionate One, may He bless all of our people who suffer, and bring them out of darkness into light.

The Compassionate One, may He declare us worthy of Messiah Yeshua and life in the world to come.

(On weekdays say) **He makes great the**

(On Shabbat, Festivals and Rosh Hodesh say) **He fortifies the**
salvation of His Kingship, and shows loving kindness to His Anointed, to David and to his seed forever. May He who creates peace in the high heavens, may He create peace for us, and for all Israel, and let us say, Amen.

Fear the Lord, you, His holy ones, for there is no want to those who honor Him. Young lions may suffer want, but those who seek the Lord shall lack for no good thing. Give thanks to the Lord, for He is good; His loving kindness endures forever. You open Your hand and satisfy the desire of all who live. Blessed is the man whose trust is in the Lord, for the Lord will be his trust. I have been young, and now I am old, and I have never seen the righteous forsaken, and his seed having to beg for bread. The Lord will give strength to His people; the Lord will bless His people with peace.

בִּרְכַּת הַמָּזוֹן

(abridged version)

נוֹדֶה לְּךָ יְיָ אֱלֹהֵינוּ עַל שֶׁהִנְחַלְתָּ לַאֲבוֹתֵינוּ, אֶרֶץ חֶמְדָּה טוֹבָה וּרְחָבָה. בְּרִית וְתוֹרָה, חַיִּים וּמָזוֹן. יִתְבָּרַךְ שִׁמְךָ בְּפִי כָל חַי תָּמִיד לְעוֹלָם וָעֶד. כַּכָּתוּב, וְאָכַלְתָּ וְשָׂבַעְתָּ, וּבֵרַכְתָּ אֶת יְיָ אֱלֹהֶיךָ עַל הָאָרֶץ הַטֹּבָה אֲשֶׁר נָתַן לָךְ. בָּרוּךְ אַתָּה יְיָ, עַל הָאָרֶץ וְעַל הַמָּזוֹן.

Nodeh l'ka, Adonai Eloheinu, al shehin'ha'leta laavoteinu, erets ḥemdah tovah ur'ḥavah; b'rit v'Torah, ḥayim u'mazon. Yit'barakh shim'ka b'fi kol ḥai tamid l'olam va-ed. Kakatuv, v'akhal'ta v'sava'ta, uveirakhta et Adonai Eloheka al haarets hatovah asher natan lakh. Barukh atah Adonai, al haarets v'al hamazon.

(On Ḥanukah and Purim insert the appropriate blessing on page 158)

וּבְנֵה יְרוּשָׁלַיִם עִיר הַקֹּדֶשׁ בִּמְהֵרָה בְיָמֵינוּ. בָּרוּךְ אַתָּה יְיָ, בּוֹנֵה בְרַחֲמָיו יְרוּשָׁלָיִם. אָמֵן.

Uv'neih Y'rushalayim ir hakodesh bimheirah v'yameinu. Barukh atah Adonai, boneh v'raḥamav Y'rushalayim. Amen

בָּרוּךְ אַתָּה יְיָ אֱלֹהֵינוּ מֶלֶךְ הָעוֹלָם, הַמֶּלֶךְ הַטּוֹב, וְהַמֵּטִיב לַכֹּל, הוּא הֵטִיב, הוּא מֵטִיב, הוּא יֵיטִיב לָנוּ. הוּא גְמָלָנוּ, הוּא גוֹמְלֵנוּ, הוּא יִגְמְלֵנוּ לָעַד לְחֵן וּלְחֶסֶד וּלְרַחֲמִים, וּמִכָּל טוֹב לְעוֹלָם אַל יְחַסְּרֵנוּ.

Barukh atah Adonai, Eloheinu Melekh haolam, HaMelekh hatov v'hameitiv lakol, hu heitiv, hu meitiv, hu yeitiv lanu. Hu g'malanu, hu gom'leinu, hu yigm'leinu laad, l'hein ul'ḥesed ul'raḥamim, umikol tov l'olam al y'ḥas'reinu.

(On Shabbat say)

הָרַחֲמָן, הוּא יַנְחִילֵנוּ יוֹם שֶׁכֻּלּוֹ שַׁבָּת וּמְנוּחָה לְחַיֵּי הָעוֹלָמִים.

Haraḥaman, hu yan'hileinu yom she-kulo Shabbat um'uḥah l'chayei ha-olamim.

(On other days continue here)

הָרַחֲמָן, הוּא יְבָרֵךְ אֶת־מְדִינַת יִשְׂרָאֵל, רֵאשִׁית צְמִיחַת גְּאֻלָּתֵנוּ.

Haraḥaman, hu y'vareich et M'dinat Yisraeil, reisheet ts'miḥat g'oo-lateinu.

הָרַחֲמָן, הוּא יְבָרֵךְ אֶת־אַחֵינוּ בְּנֵי יִשְׂרָאֵל הַנְּתוּנִים בְּצָרָה, וְיוֹצִיאֵם מֵאֲפֵלָה לְאוֹרָה.

Haraḥaman, hu y'vareikh et aḥeinu b'nei Yisraeil han'tunim b'tsarah, v'yotsi-eim mei-afeilah l'orah.

הָרַחֲמָן, הוּא יְזַכֵּנוּ לִימוֹת הַמָּשִׁיחַ יֵשׁוּעַ וּלְחַיֵּי הָעוֹלָם הַבָּא.

Haraḥaman, hu y'zakenu limot haMashiach Yeshua ul'ḥayei haolam haba.

מַגְדִּיל *Magdil* *(On weekdays say)*

מִגְדּוֹל *Migdol* *(On Shabbat, Festivals and Rosh Ḥodesh say)*

יְשׁוּעוֹת מַלְכּוֹ, וְעֹשֶׂה חֶסֶד לִמְשִׁיחוֹ לְדָוִד וּלְזַרְעוֹ עַד עוֹלָם. עֹשֶׂה שָׁלוֹם בִּמְרוֹמָיו, הוּא יַעֲשֶׂה שָׁלוֹם, עָלֵינוּ וְעַל כָּל יִשְׂרָאֵל, וְאִמְרוּ אָמֵן.

y'shuot malko, v'oseh ḥesed lim'shiho l'David ul'zaro ad olam. Oseh shalom bim'romav, hu ya'aseh shalom aleinu v'al kol Yisraeil, v'im'ru amein.

Birkat HaMazon *(abridged version)*

Lord our God, we thank You that besides this, You have given as an inheritance to our fathers a desirable, good, and abundant land. For the covenant and Torah, for life and food. Your Name will be magnified by the mouth of all who live, forever and to all eternity. As it is written, "You shall eat and be satisfied, and give blessing to the Lord your God for the good land He has given to you." Blessed are You, Lord, for the land and for its produce.

(On Hanukah and Purim insert the appropriate blessing on page 159)

Rebuild Jerusalem as a holy city very soon, even in our day. Blessed are You, Lord, who, in compassion, builds Jerusalem. Amen!

Blessed are You, Lord our God, King of the Universe, the Good King who is good to all. He has done good, and He continually does good for us. He has dealt bountifully with us, He deals bountifully with us, and He will always deal bountifully with us; for grace, and for loving kindness, and for compassion. May God, who knows our need, always provide us with good.

(On Shabbat say)
The Compassionate One, may He cause us to come to that day which shall always be Shabbat, with rest in life everlasting.

(On other days continue here)
The Compassionate One, may He bless the State of Israel, the dawn of our redemption.

The Compassionate One, may He bless all of our people who suffer, and bring them out of darkness into light.

The Compassionate One, may He declare us worthy of Messiah Yeshua, and life in the world to come.

(On weekdays say) **He makes great the**

(On Shabbat, Festivals and Rosh Ḥodesh say) **He fortifies the**

salvation of His Kingship, and shows loving kindness to His Anointed, to David and to his seed forever. May He who creates peace in the high heavens, may He create peace for us, and for all Israel, and let us say, Amen.

Additional Readings & Blessings
Preparation for Prayer

מודה אני

מוֹדֶה (מוֹדָה) אֲנִי לְפָנֶיךָ, מֶלֶךְ חַי וְקַיָּם, שֶׁהֶחֱזַרְתָּ בִּי נִשְׁמָתִי בְּחֶמְלָה, רַבָּה אֱמוּנָתֶךָ.

(Man) *Modeh* \ (Woman) *Modah* ... *ani lefanekha, Melekh ḥai vekayam, sheheḥeza'retah bi nishmati beḥemlah, rabah emunatekhah.*

רֵאשִׁית חָכְמָה יִרְאַת יְיָ, שֵׂכֶל טוֹב לְכָל עֹשֵׂיהֶם, תְּהִלָּתוֹ עוֹמֶדֶת לָעַד. בָּרוּךְ שֵׁם כְּבוֹד מַלְכוּתוֹ לְעוֹלָם וָעֶד.

Reshit ḥakhmah yirat Adonai, seikhel tov lekhal oseihem, tehilato omedet la'ad. Barukh shem k'vod malukhuto l'olam va'ed.

(Using a cup or traditional handwashing vessel, wash first the right hand, fully washing from the wrist down to the fingertips, then the left hand, alternating hands until both have been washed three times, then say the blessing)

נטילת ידים

בָּרוּךְ אַתָּה יְיָ אֱלֹהֵינוּ מֶלֶךְ הָעוֹלָם, אֲשֶׁר קִדְּשָׁנוּ בְּמִצְוֹתָיו, וְצִוָּנוּ עַל נְטִילַת יָדָיִם.

Barukh atah Adonai, Eloheinu Melekh Ha'Olam, asher kid'shanu b'mitsvotav, v'tsivanu al netilat yadayim.

אשר יצר

בָּרוּךְ אַתָּה יְיָ אֱלֹהֵינוּ מֶלֶךְ הָעוֹלָם אֲשֶׁר יָצַר אֶת־הָאָדָם בְּחָכְמָה וּבָרָא בוֹ נְקָבִים נְקָבִים חֲלוּלִים חֲלוּלִים גָּלוּי וְיָדוּעַ לִפְנֵי כִסֵּא כְבוֹדֶךָ שֶׁאִם יִפָּתֵחַ אֶחָד מֵהֶם אוֹ יִסָּתֵם אֶחָד מֵהֶם אִי אֶפְשַׁר לְהִתְקַיֵּם וְלַעֲמֹד לְפָנֶיךָ אֲפִילוּ שָׁעָה אֶחָת. בָּרוּךְ אַתָּה יְיָ רוֹפֵא כָל־בָּשָׂר וּמַפְלִיא לַעֲשׂוֹת.

אלהי נשמה

אֱלֹהַי נְשָׁמָה שֶׁנָּתַתָּ בִּי טְהוֹרָה הִיא אַתָּה בְרָאתָהּ אַתָּה יְצַרְתָּהּ אַתָּה נְפַחְתָּהּ בִּי וְאַתָּה מְשַׁמְּרָהּ בְּקִרְבִּי וְאַתָּה עָתִיד לִטְּלָהּ מִמֶּנִּי וּלְהַחֲזִירָהּ בִּי לֶעָתִיד לָבֹא, כָּל זְמַן שֶׁהַנְּשָׁמָה בְּקִרְבִּי מוֹדֶה אֲנִי לְפָנֶיךָ יְיָ אֱלֹהַי וֵאלֹהֵי אֲבוֹתַי רִבּוֹן כָּל הַמַּעֲשִׂים אֲדוֹן כָּל הַנְּשָׁמוֹת. בָּרוּךְ אַתָּה יְיָ הַמַּחֲזִיר נְשָׁמוֹת לִפְגָרִים מֵתִים.

לבישת ציצת

בָּרוּךְ אַתָּה יְיָ אֱלֹהֵינוּ מֶלֶךְ הָעוֹלָם, אֲשֶׁר קִדְּשָׁנוּ בְּמִצְוֹתָיו, וְצִוָּנוּ עַל מִצְוַת צִיצִת.

Barukh atah Adonai, Eloheinu Melekh Ha'Olam, asher kid'shanu b'mitsvotav, v'tsivanu al mitsvat tsitsit.

עטיפת טלית

בָּרוּךְ אַתָּה יְיָ אֱלֹהֵינוּ מֶלֶךְ הָעוֹלָם, אֲשֶׁר קִדְּשָׁנוּ בְּמִצְוֹתָיו, וְצִוָּנוּ לְהִתְעַטֵּף בַּצִּיצִת.

Barukh atah Adonai, Eloheinu Melekh Ha'Olam, asher kid'shanu b'mitsvotav, v'tsivanu lehit'atef batsitsit.

Additional Readings & Blessings

Preparation for Prayer

Modeh Ani

I am thankful before You, living and eternal King, for returning my soul within me with compassion. Great is Your faithfulness.

The beginning of wisdom is the fear of the Lord, good understanding is to all who do so. His praise endures forever. Blessed is the name of His glorious kingdom forever and ever.

(Using a cup or traditional handwashing vessel, wash first the right hand, fully washing from the wrist down to the fingertips, then the left hand, alternating hands until both have been washed three times, then say the blessing)

Netilat Yadayim

Blessed are You, Lord our God, King of the Universe, who has sanctified us with His commandments and has commanded us regarding washing our hands.

Asher Yatzar

Blessed are You, Lord our God, King of the Universe, who formed man with wisdom and created within him openings and hollows. It is obvious and known in the presence of Your glorious throne that if one of them were ruptured, or if one of them were blocked, it would be impossible to exist and stand in Your Presence even for a short while. Blessed are You, Lord, who heals all flesh and performs wonders.

Elohai Neshama

My God! The soul which You bestowed in me is pure; You created it, You formed it, You breathed it into me and You preserve it within me. You will eventually take it from me and restore it in me in the time to come. So long as the soul is within me I give thanks to You, Lord my God, and God of my fathers, Lord of all creatures, Master of all souls. Blessed are You, Lord, who restores souls to dead bodies.

L'bishat Tsitsit

Blessed are You, Lord our God, King of the Universe, who has sanctified us with His commandments and has commanded us to wear garments with fringes.

Atifat Tallit

Blessed are You, Lord our God, King of the Universe, who has sanctified us with His commandments and has commanded us to wrap ourselves in tsitsit.

סדר הנחת תפילין

(While standing, recite this blessing with the arm piece in place but before tightening)

בָּרוּךְ אַתָּה יְיָ אֱלֹהֵינוּ מֶלֶךְ הָעוֹלָם, אֲשֶׁר קִדְּשָׁנוּ בְּמִצְוֹתָיו, וְצִוָּנוּ לְהָנִיחַ תְּפִלִּין.

Barukh atah Adonai, Eloheinu Melekh Ha'Olam, asher kid'shanu b'mitsvotav, v'tsivanu lehaniaḥ tefillin.

(Recite this blessing with the head piece in place but before fully positioned)

בָּרוּךְ אַתָּה יְיָ אֱלֹהֵינוּ מֶלֶךְ הָעוֹלָם, אֲשֶׁר קִדְּשָׁנוּ בְּמִצְוֹתָיו, וְצִוָּנוּ עַל מִצְוַת תְּפִלִּין.

Barukh atah Adonai, Eloheinu Melekh Ha'Olam, asher kid'shanu b'mitsvotav, v'tsivanu al mits'vat tefillin.

(Recite this blessing as you finish positioning the head piece)

בָּרוּךְ שֵׁם כְּבוֹד מַלְכוּתוֹ לְעוֹלָם וָעֶד.

Barukh shem k'vod malkhuto l'olam va'ed.

מה טבו

מַה טֹּבוּ אֹהָלֶיךָ יַעֲקֹב, מִשְׁכְּנֹתֶיךָ יִשְׂרָאֵל. וַאֲנִי בְּרֹב חַסְדְּךָ אָבוֹא בֵיתֶךָ, אֶשְׁתַּחֲוֶה אֶל הֵיכַל קָדְשְׁךָ בְּיִרְאָתֶךָ. יְיָ אָהַבְתִּי מְעוֹן בֵּיתֶךָ, וּמְקוֹם מִשְׁכַּן כְּבוֹדֶךָ. וַאֲנִי אֶשְׁתַּחֲוֶה וְאֶכְרָעָה, אֶבְרְכָה לִפְנֵי יְיָ עֹשִׂי. וַאֲנִי תְפִלָּתִי לְךָ יְיָ, עֵת רָצוֹן, אֱלֹהִים בְּרָב חַסְדֶּךָ, עֲנֵנִי בֶּאֱמֶת יִשְׁעֶךָ.

Ma tovu ohalekhah Yaakov. Mishk'notekha Yisraeil. Va'ani b'rov ḥasd'kha, avo veitekha. Eshtaḥaveh el heikhal kodsh'kha b'yiratekha. Adonai ahavti me'on beitekha. Um'kom mish'kan k'vodekha. Va'ani eshtaḥaveh v'ekhra'ah. Ev'rekha lif'nei Adonai osi. Va'ani t'filati l'kha Adonai eit ratson. Elohim berav ḥasdekha aneini be'emet yish'ekha.

ברכות השחר

בָּרוּךְ אַתָּה יְיָ אֱלֹהֵינוּ מֶלֶךְ הָעוֹלָם, אֲשֶׁר נָתַן לָנוּ דְּבַר הַחַיִּים, מָשִׁיחַ יֵשׁוּעַ.

בָּרוּךְ אַתָּה יְיָ אֱלֹהֵינוּ מֶלֶךְ הָעוֹלָם, אֲשֶׁר קִדְּשָׁנוּ בְּמִצְוֹתָיו וְצִוָּנוּ לַעֲסֹק בְּדִבְרֵי תוֹרָה.

בָּרוּךְ אַתָּה יְיָ אֱלֹהֵינוּ מֶלֶךְ הָעוֹלָם, אֲשֶׁר נָתַן לַשֶּׂכְוִי בִינָה לְהַבְחִין בֵּין יוֹם וּבֵין לָיְלָה.

בָּרוּךְ אַתָּה יְיָ אֱלֹהֵינוּ מֶלֶךְ הָעוֹלָם, שֶׁעָשַׂנִי כִּרְצוֹנוֹ.

בָּרוּךְ אַתָּה יְיָ אֱלֹהֵינוּ מֶלֶךְ הָעוֹלָם, פּוֹקֵחַ עִוְרִים.

בָּרוּךְ אַתָּה יְיָ אֱלֹהֵינוּ מֶלֶךְ הָעוֹלָם, מַלְבִּישׁ עֲרֻמִּים.

בָּרוּךְ אַתָּה יְיָ אֱלֹהֵינוּ מֶלֶךְ הָעוֹלָם, זוֹקֵף כְּפוּפִים.

בָּרוּךְ אַתָּה יְיָ אֱלֹהֵינוּ מֶלֶךְ הָעוֹלָם, רוֹקַע הָאָרֶץ עַל הַמָּיִם.

בָּרוּךְ אַתָּה יְיָ אֱלֹהֵינוּ מֶלֶךְ הָעוֹלָם, שֶׁעָשָׂה לִי כָּל־צָרְכִּי.

Seder Hanaḥat Tefillin

(While standing, recite this blessing with the arm piece in place but before tightening)

Blessed are You, Lord our God, King of the Universe, who has sanctified us with His commandments and has commanded us to put on tefillin.

(Recite this blessing with the head piece in place but before fully positioned)

Blessed are You, Lord our God, King of the Universe, who has sanctified us with His commandments and has commanded us to place upon ourselves tefillin.

(Recite this blessing as you finish positioning the head piece)

Blessed is the name of His glorious kingdom forever and ever.

Ma Tovu

How goodly are your dwellings, O Jacob; your habitations, O Israel. Thanks to Your abundant kindness, O Lord, I am able to enter Your house. I worship before Your holy temple in reverence; in this sacred place of worship. Lord, I love to be in Your house, the sanctuary dedicated to Your glory. Here I worship in Your presence, O Lord my maker. In kindness, Lord, answer my prayer; mercifully grant me Your abiding truth.

Birkhot HaShachar

Blessed are You, Lord our God, King of the Universe, who has given us the Word of Life, Messiah Yeshua.

Blessed are You, Lord our God, King of the Universe, who sanctified us with His commandments and has commanded us to absorb Your Instruction.

Blessed are You, Lord our God, King of the Universe, who gives the understanding to distinguish between day and night.

Blessed are You, Lord our God, King of the Universe, who made me according to His will.

Blessed are You, Lord our God, King of the Universe, who gives sight to the blind.

Blessed are You, Lord our God, King of the Universe, who clothes the naked.

Blessed are You, Lord our God, King of the Universe, who straightens the bent.

Blessed are You, Lord our God, King of the Universe, who spreads the earth above the waters.

Blessed are You, Lord our God, King of the Universe, who provided me with all my needs.

אַשְׁרֵי

אַשְׁרֵי יוֹשְׁבֵי בֵיתֶךָ, עוֹד יְהַלְלוּךָ, סֶלָה.
Ashrei yosh'vei veitekha, od y'hal'lukha selah.

אַשְׁרֵי הָעָם שֶׁכָּכָה לּוֹ, אַשְׁרֵי הָעָם שֶׁיְיָ אֱלֹהָיו.
Ashrei ha'am shekakha lo, ashrei ha'am she'Adonai Elohav.

Psalm 145

T'hillah l'David   תְּהִלָּה לְדָוִד,

אֲרוֹמִמְךָ אֱלוֹהַי הַמֶּלֶךְ, וַאֲבָרְכָה שִׁמְךָ לְעוֹלָם וָעֶד.
Aromim'kha Elohai hamelekh, va'avar'kha shimkha l'olam va'ed.

בְּכָל יוֹם אֲבָרְכֶךָ, וַאֲהַלְלָה שִׁמְךָ לְעוֹלָם וָעֶד.
B'khal yom avar'kheka, va'ahal'la shim'kha l'olam va'ed.

גָּדוֹל יְיָ וּמְהֻלָּל מְאֹד, וְלִגְדֻלָּתוֹ אֵין חֵקֶר.
Gadol Adonai um'hulal m'od, v'lig'dulato ein ḥeker.

דּוֹר לְדוֹר יְשַׁבַּח מַעֲשֶׂיךָ, וּגְבוּרֹתֶיךָ יַגִּידוּ.
Dor l'dor y'shabaḥ ma'asekha, ug'vurotekha yagidu.

הֲדַר כְּבוֹד הוֹדֶךָ, וְדִבְרֵי נִפְלְאֹתֶיךָ אָשִׂיחָה.
Hadar k'vod hodekha, v'divrei nifl'otekha asiḥah.

וֶעֱזוּז נוֹרְאֹתֶיךָ יֹאמֵרוּ, וּגְדוּלָּתְךָ אֲסַפְּרֶנָּה.
Ve'ezuz norotekha yomeiru, ug'dulatkha asaprenah.

זֵכֶר רַב טוּבְךָ יַבִּיעוּ, וְצִדְקָתְךָ יְרַנֵּנוּ.
Zekher rav tuv'kha yabi'u, v'tsidkatkha y'raneinu.

חַנּוּן וְרַחוּם יְיָ, אֶרֶךְ אַפַּיִם וּגְדָל חָסֶד.
Ḥanun v'raḥum Adonai, erekh apayim ug'dal ḥased.

טוֹב יְיָ לַכֹּל, וְרַחֲמָיו עַל כָּל מַעֲשָׂיו.
Tov Adonai lakol, v'raḥamayv al kal ma'asayv.

יוֹדוּךָ יְיָ כָּל מַעֲשֶׂיךָ, וַחֲסִידֶיךָ יְבָרְכוּכָה.
Yodukha Adonai kal ma'asekha, vaḥasidekha y'varkhukha.

כְּבוֹד מַלְכוּתְךָ יֹאמֵרוּ, וּגְבוּרָתְךָ יְדַבֵּרוּ.
K'vod mal'khut'kha yomeiru, ugvuratkha y'dabeiru.

לְהוֹדִיעַ לִבְנֵי הָאָדָם גְּבוּרֹתָיו, וּכְבוֹד הֲדַר מַלְכוּתוֹ.
L'hodiya liv'nei ha'adam g'vurotayv, ukh'vod hadar malkhuto.

Ashrei

Happy are they who abide in Your house; they are always praising You.

Happy are the people who are so situated. Happy are the people whose God is the Lord.

Psalm 145
A psalm of David:

My God, the King, I will exalt You, and I will bless Your Name forever and ever.

> *Each day I will bless You, and I will praise Your Name forever and ever.*

The Lord is great and most worthy to be praised; His greatness is beyond understanding.

> *One generation shall praise Your works to the next and they will tell of Your mighty deeds.*

I will meditate on the splendor of Your majesty and on Your wonders.

> *They will speak of Your awesome might; I will tell of Your greatness.*

The remembrances of Your great goodness will bubble forth, they will sing of Your righteousness.

> *The Lord is gracious and full of compassion, slow to anger, and great in mercy.*

The Lord is good to all, and His compassion is over all His works.

> *Lord, all Your works will give You praise, and Your righteous ones will bless You.*

They will speak of Your might, and of the splendor of Your kingdom;

> *To let men know of Your glorious deeds, and the majesty of Your kingdom.*

מַלְכוּתְךָ מַלְכוּת כָּל עֹלָמִים, וּמֶמְשַׁלְתְּךָ בְּכָל דּוֹר וָדֹר.

Mal'khut'kha mal'khut kal olamim, u'memshalt'kha b'khol dor vador.

סוֹמֵךְ יְיָ לְכָל הַנֹּפְלִים, וְזוֹקֵף לְכָל הַכְּפוּפִים.

Somekh Adonai l'khal hanof'lim, v'zokeif l'khal hak'fufim.

עֵינֵי כֹל אֵלֶיךָ יְשַׂבֵּרוּ, וְאַתָּה נוֹתֵן לָהֶם אֶת אָכְלָם בְּעִתּוֹ.

Einei khol eilekha y'sabeiru, v'atah notein lahem et akhlam b'ito

פּוֹתֵחַ אֶת יָדֶךָ, וּמַשְׂבִּיעַ לְכָל חַי רָצוֹן.

Potei'aḥ et yadekha, umas'bia l'khal ḥai ratson.

צַדִּיק יְיָ בְּכָל דְּרָכָיו, וְחָסִיד בְּכָל מַעֲשָׂיו.

Tsadik Adonai b'khal d'rakhayv, v'ḥasid b'khal ma'asayv.

קָרוֹב יְיָ לְכָל קֹרְאָיו, לְכֹל אֲשֶׁר יִקְרָאֻהוּ בֶאֱמֶת.

Karov Adonai l'khal korayv, l'khal asher yik'ra'uhu ve'emet.

רְצוֹן יְרֵאָיו יַעֲשֶׂה, וְאֶת שַׁוְעָתָם יִשְׁמַע וְיוֹשִׁיעֵם.

Retson y'rei'av ya'aseh, v'et shav'atam yish'ma v'yoshi'eim.

שׁוֹמֵר יְיָ אֶת כָּל אֹהֲבָיו, וְאֵת כָּל הָרְשָׁעִים יַשְׁמִיד.

Shomer Adonai et kal ohavayv, v'et kal har'shaim yash'mid.

תְּהִלַּת יְיָ יְדַבֶּר פִּי, וִיבָרֵךְ כָּל בָּשָׂר שֵׁם קָדְשׁוֹ, לְעוֹלָם וָעֶד.

T'hillat Adonai y'daber pi, vivareikh kal basar sheim kad'sho, l'olam va'ed.

וַאֲנַחְנוּ נְבָרֵךְ יָהּ, מֵעַתָּה וְעַד עוֹלָם, הַלְלוּיָהּ.

Va'anaḥnu n'vareikh Ya, mei'atah v'ad olam, halleluyah.

תפילה למען ישראל

אֱלֹהֵינוּ וֵאלֹהֵי אֲבוֹתֵינוּ, יַעֲלֶה וְיָבֹא וְיַגִּיעַ וְיֵרָאֶה וְיֵרָצֶה וְיִשָּׁמַע וְיִפָּקֵד וְיִזָּכֵר זִכְרוֹנֵנוּ, וְזִכְרוֹן אֲבוֹתֵינוּ,
וְזִכְרוֹן מָשִׁיחַ יֵשׁוּעַ בֶּן דָּוִד עַבְדֶּךָ, וְזִכְרוֹן יְרוּשָׁלַיִם עִיר קָדְשֶׁךָ, וְזִכְרוֹן כָּל
עַמְּךָ בֵּית יִשְׂרָאֵל לְפָנֶךָ, לְטוֹבָה, וּלְחֵן, וּלְחֶסֶד, וּלְרַחֲמִים, וּלְחַיִּים, וּלְשָׁלוֹם.
זָכְרֵנוּ יְיָ אֱלֹהֵינוּ בּוֹ לְטוֹבָה, וּפָקְדֵנוּ בּוֹ לִבְרָכָה, וְהוֹשִׁיעֵנוּ בּוֹ לְחַיִּים
וּבִדְבַר יְשׁוּעָה וְרַחֲמִים חוּס וְחָנֵּנוּ וְרַחֵם עָלֵינוּ וְהוֹשִׁיעֵנוּ.   אֵלֶיךָ עֵינֵינוּ, כִּי
אֵל מֶלֶךְ חַנּוּן וְרַחוּם אָתָּה.

Your kingdom is an everlasting kingdom; Your dominion is over all generations.

The Lord upholds all who fall, and lifts up all who are bowed down.

All eyes will look to You with hope, and You give them food in due season.

You open Your hand, and satisfy the needs of every living thing.

The Lord is righteous in all His ways, and gracious in all His deeds.

The Lord is near to all who call on Him; to all who truly will call on Him.

He will fulfill the desire of those who fear Him; He will hear their cry and save them.

The Lord will keep all who love Him, but the wicked will be destroyed.

My mouth will declare the praise of the Lord, and His Holy Name will forever be blessed by all flesh.

We will bless the Lord both now and forever. Praise the Lord.

A Prayer for Israel

Our God and God of our fathers, may our remembrance and the remembrance of our fathers, and the remembrance of Your Servant, Messiah Yeshua the son of David, and the remembrance of Jerusalem, Your holy city, and the remembrance of all Your people, the house of Israel rise up and reach You, and be seen and be heard before Your Presence, for goodness and for favor, for loving kindness and for compassion, for life and for peace. Remember us, Lord our God, for goodness, and command blessing for us, and save us unto life. Have pity, and spare us, and be merciful upon us and rescue us, and speak salvation and compassion to us. Our eyes are upon You, Lord, for You, God, are a merciful and compassionate King.

מוסף עמידה לשבת ויום טוב

(All rise and face east or toward an open ark - take three steps back, then three steps forward)

Ki shem Adonai ekra, havu godel lelohenu   כִּי שֵׁם יְיָ אֶקְרָא, הָבוּ גֹדֶל לֵאלֹהֵינוּ.

Adonai s'fatai tiftah u'fi yagid tehila'tekhah.   אֲדֹנָי שְׂפָתַי תִּפְתָּח וּפִי יַגִּיד תְּהִלָּתֶךָ.

אבות

(Bend the knees at בָּרוּךְ *Bow at* אַתָּה *Straighten at* יְיָ*)*

בָּרוּךְ אַתָּה יְיָ אֱלֹהֵינוּ וֵאלֹהֵי אֲבוֹתֵינוּ, אֱלֹהֵי אַבְרָהָם, אֱלֹהֵי יִצְחָק, וֵאלֹהֵי יַעֲקֹב, הָאֵל הַגָּדוֹל הַגִּבּוֹר וְהַנּוֹרָא, אֵל עֶלְיוֹן, גּוֹמֵל חֲסָדִים טוֹבִים, וְקוֹנֵה הַכֹּל, וְזוֹכֵר חַסְדֵי אָבוֹת אֲשֶׁר הֵבִי, וּמֵבִיא, גּוֹאֵל לִבְנֵי בְנֵיהֶם לְמַעַן שְׁמוֹ בְּאַהֲבָה.

Barukh atah Adonai, Eloheinu velohei avoteinu: Elohei Avraham, Elohei Yitshak, v'Eilohei Ya'akòv. Ha'Eil hagadol hagibor v'hanorah, Eil Elyon, Gomeil ḥasadim tovim, v'koneih hakol, v'zokheir ḥas'deh avot, asher heivi, u'meivi, Go'eil liv'nei v'neihem, l'ma-an sh'mo, b'ahavah.

(From Rosh Hashanah to Yom Kippur add)

זָכְרֵנוּ לְחַיִּים בְּיֵשׁוּעַ, מֶלֶךְ חָפֵץ בַּחַיִּים, וְכָתְבֵנוּ בְּסֵפֶר הַחַיִּים, לְמַעַנְךָ אֱלֹהִים חַיִּים.

Zokh'reinu l'ḥaim be-Yeshua, Melekh ḥafetz baḥayim, v'khot'veinu b'sefer haḥayim, l'ma'ankha Elohim ḥayim.

(Bend the knees at בָּרוּךְ *Bow at* אַתָּה *Straighten at* יְיָ*)*

מֶלֶךְ עוֹזֵר וּמוֹשִׁיעַ וּמָגֵן.   בָּרוּךְ אַתָּה יְיָ, מָגֵן אַבְרָהָם.

Melekh ozer umoshia umagein. Barukh atah Adonai, magein Avraham.

גבורות

אַתָּה גִּבּוֹר לְעוֹלָם אֲדֹנָי, מְחַיֵּה מֵתִים אַתָּה, רַב לְהוֹשִׁיעַ.

Atah gibor l'olam, Adonai, m'chayei meitim atah, rav l'hoshia.

(Between Shemini Atseret and Pesah add)

Mashiv ha'ruaḥ u'morid ha-geshem.   מַשִּׁיב הָרוּחַ וּמוֹרִיד הַגָּשֶׁם.

מְכַלְכֵּל חַיִּים בְּחֶסֶד, מְחַיֵּה מֵתִים בְּרַחֲמִים רַבִּים, סוֹמֵךְ נוֹפְלִים, וְרוֹפֵא חוֹלִים, וּמַתִּיר אֲסוּרִים, וּמְקַיֵּם אֱמוּנָתוֹ לִישֵׁנֵי עָפָר, מִי כָמוֹךָ בַּעַל גְּבוּרוֹת וּמִי דוֹמֶה לָךְ, מֶלֶךְ מֵמִית וּמְחַיֵּה וּמַצְמִיחַ יְשׁוּעָה.

M'khalkeil ḥayim b'hesed, m'hayei meitim b'raḥamim rabim. Someiḥ nof'lim, v'rofeh holim, umatir asurim, um'kayeim emunatoh lisheinei afar. Mi khamokha ba'al g'vurot, umi domeh lakh, Melekh meimit um'hayeh u'matsmiaḥ yeshua.

(From Rosh Hashanah to Yom Kippur add)

מִי כָמוֹךָ אַב הָרַחֲמִים, זוֹכֵר יְצוּרָיו לְחַיִּים בְּרַחֲמִים.

Mi khamokha av haraḥamim, zokheir yetzurav l'ḥaim b'rachamim.

וְנֶאֱמָן אַתָּה לְהַחֲיוֹת מֵתִים. בָּרוּךְ אַתָּה יְיָ, מְחַיֵּה הַמֵּתִים.

V'ne'eman atah l'haḥayot meitim. Barukh atah Adonai, m'hayei hameitim.

Musaf Amidah L'Shabbat v'Yom Tov

(All rise and face east or toward an open ark - take three steps back, then three steps forward)

When I proclaim the Name of Adonai, give glory to our God!
Lord, you will open my lips that my mouth may declare Your praise.

Avot

*(Bend the knees at **Blessed**, Bow at **Are You**, Straighten at **Lord**)*

Blessed are You, Lord our God and God of our fathers, God of Abraham, God of Isaac and God of Jacob, the great, mighty and awesome God, Most High God, who grants loving kindness and is Master of all. You remember the deeds of our fathers, and in Your love You have brought, and You bring, a Redeemer to their children's children for the sake of Your Name.

(From Rosh Hashanah to Yom Kippur add)
Remember us to life in Yeshua, O King who takes delight in life. Inscribe us in the book of life, for Your sake, O God of life.

*(Bend the knees at **Blessed**, Bow at **Are You**, Straighten at **Lord**)*
King, Supporter, Savior and Shield, blessed are You, Lord, Shield of Abraham.

G'vurot

Lord, You are mighty forever. You call the dead to life. You are mighty to save.

(Between Shemini Atseret and Pesah add)
You cause the wind to return and the rain to come down.

You sustain the living with loving kindness, and with great mercy You revive the dead. You uphold those who fall, heal the sick, set the captive free and keep faith with those who sleep in the dust. Lord of might, who is like You? King, who can be compared to You? You decree death and restore life, causing salvation to come forth.

(From Rosh Hashanah to Yom Kippur add)
Compassionate Father, who is like You, remembering with mercy your creatures for life?

You are faithful to revive the dead. Blessed are You, Lord, who calls the dead to life.

(During the silent Amidah continue with אַתָּה קָדוֹשׁ *at the bottom of the page.*
During the Reader's repetition begin here.
Rise on your toes at בָּרוּךְ *and* (יִמְלֹךְ) *,* קָדוֹשׁ, קָדוֹשׁ, קָדוֹשׁ

קדושה

(Reader then All) נַעֲרִיצְךָ וְנַקְדִּישְׁךָ כְּסוֹד שִׂיחַ שַׂרְפֵי קֹדֶשׁ הַמַּקְדִּישִׁים שִׁמְךָ בַּקֹּדֶשׁ,
כַּכָּתוּב עַל יַד נְבִיאֶךָ, וְקָרָא זֶה אֶל זֶה וְאָמַר:

Na'arits'ka v'nak'dish'ka k'sod siaḥ sar'fei kodesh hamk'dishim shim'ka ba'kodesh, kakatuv al yad n'vi'ekha, v'kara ze el ze v'amar:

(All) קָדוֹשׁ, קָדוֹשׁ, קָדוֹשׁ, יְיָ צְבָאוֹת, מְלֹא כָל הָאָרֶץ כְּבוֹדוֹ.

Kadosh, kadosh, kadosh, Adonai Ts'vaot, m'lo khol ha'arets k'vodo.

(Reader) כְּבוֹדוֹ מָלֵא עוֹלָם. מְשָׁרְתָיו שׁוֹאֲלִים זֶה לָזֶה אַיֵּה מְקוֹם כְּבוֹדוֹ לְעֻמָּתָם בָּרוּךְ יֹאמֵרוּ.

Barukh k'vod Adonai mim'komo **(All)** בָּרוּךְ כְּבוֹד יְיָ, מִמְּקוֹמוֹ.

(Reader) מִמְּקוֹמוֹ הוּא יִפֶן בְּרַחֲמִים וְיָחֹן עַם הַמְיַחֲדִים שְׁמוֹ, עֶרֶב וָבֹקֶר, בְּכָל יוֹם תָּמִיד, פַּעֲמַיִם בְּאַהֲבָה שְׁמַע אוֹמְרִים.

Sh'ma Yisraeil, Adonai Eloheinu, Adonai Eḥad. **(All)** שְׁמַע יִשְׂרָאֵל יְיָ אֱלֹהֵינוּ יְיָ אֶחָד.

(Reader) הוּא אֱלֹהֵינוּ, הוּא אָבִינוּ, הוּא מַלְכֵּנוּ, הוּא מוֹשִׁיעֵנוּ, וְהוּא יַשְׁמִיעֵנוּ בְּרַחֲמָיו שֵׁנִית לְעֵינֵי כָּל חָי, לִהְיוֹת לָכֶם לֵאלֹהִים.

Ani Adonai Eloheikhem. **(All)** אֲנִי יְיָ אֱלֹהֵיכֶם.

(Reader) וּבְדִבְרֵי קָדְשְׁךָ כָּתוּב לֵאמֹר,

(All) יִמְלֹךְ יְיָ לְעוֹלָם, אֱלֹהַיִךְ צִיּוֹן לְדֹר וָדֹר, הַלְלוּיָהּ.

Yim'lokh Adonai l'olam ElohayikhTsiyon, l'dor vador, halleluyah

(Reader) לְדוֹר וָדוֹר נַגִּיד גָּדְלֶךָ וּלְנֵצַח נְצָחִים קְדֻשָּׁתְךָ נַקְדִּישׁ, וְשִׁבְחֲךָ אֱלֹהֵינוּ מִפִּינוּ לֹא יָמוּשׁ לְעוֹלָם וָעֶד, כִּי אֵל מֶלֶךְ גָּדוֹל וְקָדוֹשׁ אָתָּה.
*בָּרוּךְ אַתָּה יְיָ, הָאֵל, הַקָּדוֹשׁ.

(From Rosh Hashanah to Yom Kippur substitute)
*בָּרוּךְ אַתָּה יְיָ, הַמֶּלֶךְ הַקָּדוֹשׁ.

(During the silent Amidah continue here)
אַתָּה קָדוֹשׁ וְשִׁמְךָ קָדוֹשׁ, וּקְדוֹשִׁים בְּכָל יוֹם יְהַלְלוּךָ, סֶּלָה.
*בָּרוּךְ אַתָּה יְיָ, הָאֵל הַקָּדוֹשׁ.

(From Rosh Hashanah to Yom Kippur substitute)
*בָּרוּךְ אַתָּה יְיָ, הַמֶּלֶךְ הַקָּדוֹשׁ.

*(During the silent Amidah continue with **You are Holy** at the bottom of the page.*
During the Reader's repetition begin here.
*Rise on your toes at **Holy, Holy, Holy, Blessed** and **The Lord will Reign**)*

Kedushah

(Reader then All) We revere and sanctify You using the words of the holy serafim who assemble to hallow Your name, as it is written by Your prophet, They continuously call to one another:

Holy, holy, holy is the Lord of Hosts; the whole earth is filled with His glory.

(Reader) His glory fills the universe; His attending angels ask one another, Where is His glorious place? They say to one another:

(All) Blessed. . . Blessed is the glory of the Lord from His abode.

(Reader) From His abode may he turn with compassion and be gracious to the people who proclaim His oneness evening and morning, twice each day, and with passion recite the Shema,

(All) Hear, O Israel, the Lord our God, the Lord is One!

(Reader) He is our God, He is our Father, He is our King, He is our Savior. He will again in his mercy proclaim to us in the presence of all living to be their God.

(All) I am the Lord your God.

(Reader) And in the Scriptures it is written:

> *(All)* The Lord will reign forever; your God, O Tsiyon,
> from generation to generation. Halleluyah!

(Reader) We will declare Your greatness from generation to generation. We will proclaim Your holiness to all eternity. Your praise, our God, will never depart from our mouth, for You, God, are a great and mighty King.

* Blessed are You, Lord, holy God.

(From Rosh Hashana to Yom Kippur substitute)
***Blessed are You, Lord, the Holy King.**

(During the silent Amidah continue here)

You are holy, and Your Name is holy, and holy ones proclaim Your praise daily.
* Blessed are You, Lord, holy God.

(From Rosh Hashana to Yom Kippur substitute)
***Blessed are You, Lord, the Holy King.**

קדושת היום

תִּכַּנְתָּ שַׁבָּת, רָצִיתָ קָרְבְּנוֹתֶיהָ. צִוִּיתָ פֵּרוּשֶׁיהָ עִם סִדּוּרֵי נְסָכֶיהָ. מְעַנְּגֶיהָ לְעוֹלָם כָּבוֹד יִנְחָלוּ; טוֹעֲמֶיהָ חַיִּים זָכוּ; וְגַם הָאוֹהֲבִים דְּבָרֶיהָ גְּדֻלָּה בָּחֲרוּ. אָז מִסִּינַי נִצְטַוּוּ עָלֶיהָ. וַתְּצַוֵּנוּ, יְיָ אֱלֹהֵינוּ, לְהַקְרִיב בָּהּ קָרְבַּן מוּסַף שַׁבָּת כָּרָאוּי. יְהִי רָצוֹן מִלְּפָנֶיךָ, יְיָ אֱלֹהֵינוּ וֵאלֹהֵי אֲבוֹתֵינוּ, שֶׁתַּעֲלֵנוּ בְשִׂמְחָה לְאַרְצֵנוּ, וְתִטָּעֵנוּ בִּגְבוּלֵנוּ; וְשָׁם נַעֲשֶׂה לְפָנֶיךָ אֶת קָרְבְּנוֹת חוֹבוֹתֵינוּ, תְּמִידִים כְּסִדְרָם וּמוּסָפִים כְּהִלְכָתָם. וְאֶת מוּסַף יוֹם הַשַּׁבָּת הַזֶּה נַעֲשֶׂה וְנַקְרִיב לְפָנֶיךָ בְּאַהֲבָה, כְּמִצְוַת רְצוֹנֶךָ, כְּמוֹ שֶׁכָּתַבְתָּ עָלֵינוּ בְּתוֹרָתֶךָ, עַל יְדֵי מֹשֶׁה עַבְדֶּךָ, מִפִּי כְבוֹדֶךָ, כָּאָמוּר.

וּבְיוֹם הַשַּׁבָּת, שְׁנֵי כְבָשִׂים בְּנֵי שָׁנָה תְּמִימִם; וּשְׁנֵי עֶשְׂרֹנִים סֹלֶת, מִנְחָה בְּלוּלָה בַשֶּׁמֶן, וְנִסְכּוֹ. עֹלַת שַׁבַּת בְּשַׁבַּתּוֹ, עַל עֹלַת הַתָּמִיד וְנִסְכָּהּ.

יִשְׂמְחוּ בְמַלְכוּתְךָ שׁוֹמְרֵי שַׁבָּת וְקוֹרְאֵי עֹנֶג, עַם מְקַדְּשֵׁי שְׁבִיעִי, כֻּלָּם יִשְׂבְּעוּ וְיִתְעַנְּגוּ מִטּוּבֶךָ, וּבַשְּׁבִיעִי רָצִיתָ בּוֹ וְקִדַּשְׁתּוֹ, חֶמְדַּת יָמִים אוֹתוֹ קָרָאתָ, זֵכֶר לְמַעֲשֵׂה בְרֵאשִׁית.

אלהינו ואלהי

אֱלֹהֵינוּ וֵאלֹהֵי אֲבוֹתֵינוּ, רְצֵה בִמְנוּחָתֵנוּ. קַדְּשֵׁנוּ בְּמִצְוֹתֶיךָ וְתֵן חֶלְקֵנוּ בְּתוֹרָתֶךָ, שַׂבְּעֵנוּ מִטּוּבֶךָ, וְשַׂמְּחֵנוּ בִּישׁוּעָתֶךָ, וְטַהֵר לִבֵּנוּ לְעָבְדְּךָ בֶּאֱמֶת, וְהַנְחִילֵנוּ יְיָ אֱלֹהֵינוּ בְּאַהֲבָה וּבְרָצוֹן שַׁבַּת קָדְשֶׁךָ, וְיָנוּחוּ בָהּ יִשְׂרָאֵל, מְקַדְּשֵׁי שְׁמֶךָ. בָּרוּךְ אַתָּה יְיָ, מְקַדֵּשׁ הַשַּׁבָּת.

רְצֵה, יְיָ אֱלֹהֵינוּ, בְּעַמְּךָ יִשְׂרָאֵל וּבִתְפִלָּתָם, וְהָשֵׁב אֶת הָעֲבוֹדָה לִדְבִיר בֵּיתֶךָ, וְאִשֵּׁי יִשְׂרָאֵל, וּתְפִלָּתָם בְּאַהֲבָה תְקַבֵּל בְּרָצוֹן, וּתְהִי לְרָצוֹן תָּמִיד עֲבוֹדַת יִשְׂרָאֵל עַמֶּךָ.

וְתֶחֱזֶינָה עֵינֵינוּ בְּשׁוּבְךָ לְצִיּוֹן בְּרַחֲמִים. בָּרוּךְ אַתָּה יְיָ, הַמַּחֲזִיר שְׁכִינָתוֹ לְצִיּוֹן.

מודים אנחנו

(While the Reader recites out loud מוֹדִים אֲנַחְנוּ, *the Congregation recites* מוֹדִים דְּרַבָּנָן *softly.*
Bend the knees at מוֹדִים אֲנַחְנוּ *and straighten at* יְיָ)

מוֹדִים אֲנַחְנוּ לָךְ שָׁאַתָּה הוּא יְיָ אֱלֹהֵינוּ וֵאלֹהֵי אֲבוֹתֵינוּ לְעוֹלָם וָעֶד. צוּר חַיֵּינוּ, מָגֵן יִשְׁעֵנוּ, אַתָּה הוּא לְדוֹר וָדוֹר, נוֹדֶה לְּךָ וּנְסַפֵּר תְּהִלָּתֶךָ, עַל חַיֵּינוּ הַמְּסוּרִים בְּיָדֶךָ, וְעַל נִשְׁמוֹתֵינוּ הַפְּקוּדוֹת לָךְ, וְעַל נִסֶּיךָ שֶׁבְּכָל יוֹם עִמָּנוּ, וְעַל נִפְלְאוֹתֶיךָ וְטוֹבוֹתֶיךָ שֶׁבְּכָל עֵת, עֶרֶב וָבֹקֶר וְצָהֳרָיִם, הַטּוֹב, כִּי לֹא כָלוּ רַחֲמֶיךָ, וְהַמְרַחֵם, כִּי לֹא תַמּוּ חֲסָדֶיךָ, מֵעוֹלָם קִוִּינוּ לָךְ.

מודים דרבנן

מוֹדִים אֲנַחְנוּ לָךְ, שָׁאַתָּה הוּא יְיָ אֱלֹהֵינוּ וֵאלֹהֵי אֲבוֹתֵינוּ, אֱלֹהֵי כָל בָּשָׂר, יוֹצְרֵנוּ, יוֹצֵר בְּרֵאשִׁית. בְּרָכוֹת וְהוֹדָאוֹת לְשִׁמְךָ הַגָּדוֹל וְהַקָּדוֹשׁ, עַל שֶׁהֶחֱיִיתָנוּ וְקִיַּמְתָּנוּ. כֵּן תְּחַיֵּנוּ וּתְקַיְּמֵנוּ, וְתֶאֱסוֹף גָּלֻיּוֹתֵינוּ לְחַצְרוֹת קָדְשֶׁךָ, לִשְׁמוֹר חֻקֶּיךָ וְלַעֲשׂוֹת רְצוֹנֶךָ, וּלְעָבְדְּךָ בְּלֵבָב שָׁלֵם עַל שֶׁאֲנַחְנוּ מוֹדִים לָךְ. בָּרוּךְ אֵל הַהוֹדָאוֹת.

Kedushot HaYom

You instituted the Sabbath; You favored its offerings. You commanded its specific laws along with the order of its libations. Those who delight in it inherit eternal glory, those who relish it merit life, and those who love its teachings have chosen greatness. Even before Sinai they were commanded about it. Then You, Lord our God, commanded us to offer on it the additional offering of the Sabbath in the proper way. May it be Your will, Lord our God and God of our ancestors, to lead us back in joy to our land and to plant us within our borders. There we will prepare for You our obligatory offerings: the regular daily offerings in their order, and the additional offerings according to their laws.

And the additional offerings of this Sabbath day we will prepare and offer before You in love, in accord with Your will's commandment, as You wrote for us in Your Torah through Your servant Moses, by Your own word, as it is said: On the Sabbath day, make an offering of two lambs a year old, without blemish, together with two-tenths of an ephor of fine flour mixed with oil as a meal-offering, and its appropriate libation. This is the burnt-offering for every Sabbath, in addition to the regular daily burnt-offering and its libation.

Those who keep the Sabbath and call it a delight shall rejoice in Your kingship. The people who sanctify the seventh day shall all be satisfied and take delight in Your goodness, for You favored the seventh day and declared it holy. You called it "most desirable of days" in remembrance of Creation.

Eloheinu Ve'lohei

Our God, and God of our fathers, be pleased with our rest. Set us apart through Your commandments, and grant us a portion in Your Torah. Satisfy us with Your goodness, and make us glad in Your salvation. Purify our hearts to serve you in truth, and grant us, Lord our God, in love and in grace, that Your holy Shabbat remain an inheritance, and that Israel, who sanctifies Your Name, will rest on it. Blessed are You, Lord, who makes the Shabbat holy!

Take pleasure, Lord our God, in Your people Israel, and in their prayer. Restore the service to Your most holy house, and receive Israel's offerings by fire, and their prayer with gracious love. May the worship of Your people Israel always be pleasing to You.

May we see, with our own eyes, Your return to Tsiyon in compassion. Blessed are You, Lord, whose Presence is the restoration of Tsiyon.

Modim Anaḥnu

(While the Reader recites out loud **Modim Anaḥnu,** *the Congregation recites* **Modim of the Rabbis** *softly. Bend the knees at* **Lord, we are eternally grateful** *and straighten at* **Lord)**

Modim of the Rabbis

Lord, we are eternally grateful that You are the Lord our God and the God of our fathers. God of all flesh, our Creator and Creator in the beginning; blessings and thanks are due Your great and holy Name, for You have kept us alive and You sustained us. May You continue to grant us life and to sustain us. Bring our dispersed to Your courts, that in holiness they would observe Your laws, do Your will and serve You with all their heart; for these things we give You thanks. Blessed is the God of thanksgiving.

Lord, we are eternally grateful that You are the Lord our God and the God of our fathers. You are the strength of our life and the Shield of our Salvation. We thank You from generation to generation, and recount Your praise; for our lives which are in Your hand; and for our souls which are in Your care; and for Your miracles which are seen every day; and for Your wondrous deeds and favors which are always with us - evening, morning and noon. Beneficent One, Your compassion never fails; Merciful One, Your loving kindness never ends; You have always been our hope.

(On Ḥanukah and Purim insert the appropriate blessing on page 158)

וְעַל כֻּלָּם יִתְבָּרַךְ וְיִתְרוֹמַם שִׁמְךָ מַלְכֵּנוּ תָּמִיד לְעוֹלָם וָעֶד.

(From Rosh Hashanah to Yom Kippur add)

וּכְתוֹב לְחַיִּים טוֹבִים כָּל בְּנֵי בְרִיתֶךָ.

וְכֹל הַחַיִּים יוֹדוּךָ סֶּלָה, וִיהַלְלוּ אֶת שִׁמְךָ בֶּאֱמֶת, הָאֵל יְשׁוּעָתֵנוּ וְעֶזְרָתֵנוּ, סֶלָה.

(Bend the knees at בָּרוּךְ *Bow at* אַתָּה *Straighten at* יְיָ *)*

בָּרוּךְ אַתָּה יְיָ, הַטּוֹב שִׁמְךָ וּלְךָ נָאֶה לְהוֹדוֹת.

(The Service Leader recites the Aaronic Blessing during his repetition)

אֱלֹהֵינוּ וֵאלֹהֵי אֲבוֹתֵינוּ, בָּרְכֵנוּ בַבְּרָכָה הַמְשֻׁלֶּשֶׁת בַּתּוֹרָה הַכְּתוּבָה עַל יְדֵי מֹשֶׁה עַבְדֶּךָ, הָאֲמוּרָה מִפִּי אַהֲרֹן וּבָנָיו כֹּהֲנִים, עַם קְדוֹשֶׁךָ, כָּאָמוּר.

Cong – *Kein yehi ratson* (קהל–כֵּן יְהִי רָצוֹן)   יְבָרֶכְךָ יְיָ וְיִשְׁמְרֶךָ.

Cong – *Kein yehi ratson* (קהל–כֵּן יְהִי רָצוֹן)   יָאֵר יְיָ פָּנָיו אֵלֶיךָ וִיחֻנֶּךָּ.

Cong – *Kein yehi ratson* (קהל–כֵּן יְהִי רָצוֹן)   יִשָּׂא יְיָ פָּנָיו אֵלֶיךָ וְיָשֵׂם לְךָ שָׁלוֹם.

שִׂים שָׁלוֹם

שִׂים שָׁלוֹם טוֹבָה וּבְרָכָה, חֵן וָחֶסֶד וְרַחֲמִים, עָלֵינוּ וְעַל כָּל יִשְׂרָאֵל עַמֶּךָ. בָּרְכֵנוּ, אָבִינוּ, כֻּלָּנוּ כְּאֶחָד בְּאוֹר פָּנֶיךָ, כִּי בְאוֹר פָּנֶיךָ נָתַתָּ לָּנוּ, יְיָ אֱלֹהֵינוּ, תּוֹרַת חַיִּים וְאַהֲבַת חֶסֶד, וּצְדָקָה וּבְרָכָה וְרַחֲמִים וְחַיִּים וְשָׁלוֹם, וְטוֹב בְּעֵינֶיךָ לְבָרֵךְ אֶת עַמְּךָ יִשְׂרָאֵל בְּכָל עֵת וּבְכָל שָׁעָה בִּשְׁלוֹמֶךָ.

Sim Shalom tovah uvrakha hein vaḥesed v'raḥamim aleinu v'al kol Yisraeil amekha. Barkheinu avinu kulanu ke'eḥad b'or panekha, ki v'or panekha natahta lanu, Adonai Eloheinu, Torat ḥayim v'ahavat ḥesed, uts'daka uv'rakha v'raḥamim v'ḥayim v'shalom, v'tov b'einekha l'varekh et am'kha Yisraeil b'khol et uv'khol sha'ah bish'lomekha.

*בָּרוּךְ אַתָּה יְיָ, הַמְבָרֵךְ אֶת עַמּוֹ יִשְׂרָאֵל בַּשָּׁלוֹם.

**Barukh atah Adonai, ham'varekh et amo Yisraeil ba'shalom.*

(From Rosh Hashanah to Yom Kippur substitute)

*בְּסֵפֶר חַיִּים, בְּרָכָה וְשָׁלוֹם, וּפַרְנָסָה טוֹבָה, נִזָּכֵר וְנִכָּתֵב לְפָנֶיךָ, אֲנַחְנוּ וְכָל עַמְּךָ בֵּית יִשְׂרָאֵל, לְחַיִּים טוֹבִים וּלְשָׁלוֹם. בָּרוּךְ אַתָּה יְיָ, עֹשֶׂה הַשָּׁלוֹם.

**B'sefer ḥayim, b'rachah, b'shalom, u-far'nasah tovah, ni'zakher v'nikataiv l'fahnekhah, anakhnu v'chol am'khah bait Yisrael, l'ḥayim tovim ul'shalom. Baruch atah Adonai, oseh ha'shalom.*

(After the Amidah the following meditation is added)

אֱלֹהַי, נְצוֹר לְשׁוֹנִי מֵרָע, וּשְׂפָתַי מִדַּבֵּר מִרְמָה. וְלִמְקַלְלַי נַפְשִׁי תִדּוֹם, וְנַפְשִׁי כֶּעָפָר לַכֹּל תִּהְיֶה. פְּתַח לִבִּי בְּתוֹרָתֶךָ, וּבְמִצְוֺתֶיךָ תִּרְדּוֹף נַפְשִׁי. וְכָל הַחוֹשְׁבִים עָלַי רָעָה, מְהֵרָה הָפֵר עֲצָתָם וְקַלְקֵל מַחֲשַׁבְתָּם. עֲשֵׂה לְמַעַן שְׁמֶךָ, עֲשֵׂה לְמַעַן יְמִינֶךָ, עֲשֵׂה לְמַעַן קְדֻשָּׁתֶךָ, עֲשֵׂה לְמַעַן תּוֹרָתֶךָ. לְמַעַן יֵחָלְצוּן יְדִידֶיךָ, הוֹשִׁיעָה יְמִינְךָ וַעֲנֵנִי. יִהְיוּ לְרָצוֹן אִמְרֵי פִי וְהֶגְיוֹן לִבִּי לְפָנֶיךָ, יְיָ צוּרִי וְגוֹאֲלִי. עֹשֶׂה שָׁלוֹם בִּמְרוֹמָיו, הוּא יַעֲשֶׂה שָׁלוֹם עָלֵינוּ, וְעַל כָּל יִשְׂרָאֵל, וְאִמְרוּ, אָמֵן.

(The Full Kaddish is traditionally recited here, see page 202.
Turn back to continue Shabbat service on page 104)

(On Hanukah and Purim insert the appropriate blessing on page 159)

For all these things we will bless and we will lift up Your name, our King, always, to the end of the age, and until.

(From Rosh Hashanah to Yom Kippur add)

Remember for life and good all the Children of your Covenant

And all the living will thank You, and in truth they will praise Your Name; the God of our Salvation and our Help at all times.

*(Bend the knees at **Blessed**, Bow at **Are You**, Straighten at **Lord**)*

Blessed are You, Lord; it is right to give thanks to You for Your Name is good.

(The Service Leader recites the Aaronic Blessing during his repetition)

Our God and God of our fathers, bless us with the threefold blessing written in Torah by Moses, Your servant, and spoken through the mouth of Aaron; and his sons, the priests, Your holy people, as it is said:

May the Lord bless you and keep you!
(Congregation: ***May it Be Your Will!***)
May the Lord lift up His countenance to you, and be gracious to you!
(Congregation: ***May it Be Your Will!***)
May the Lord turn His countenance toward you, and establish peace for you!
(Congregation: ***May it Be Your Will!***)

Sim Shalom

Grant peace, happiness, blessing, grace, kindness and mercy to us and all Israel, Your people. Our Father, bless us all alike with the light of Your countenance. Lord our God, by the light of Your countenance You have given us a Torah of life, loving kindness, charity, blessing, mercy, life and peace. May it be good in Your sight to bless Your people Israel with peace at all times and at every hour.

* Blessed are You, Lord, the one who blessed His nation Israel with peace.

(From Rosh Hashanah to Yom Kippur substitute)

*Our Father, and the Father of all Israel, remember us, and inscribe us in the Book of Life, for blessing and for peace, and good provision, for good life and for peace. Blessed are You, Lord, who makes peace.

(After the Amidah the following meditation is added)

My God, guard my tongue from evil, and my lips from speaking falsehood. May my soul be silent to those who insult me, and may my soul be humble before all. Open my heart to Your Torah, that my soul might follow Your commands. As for all who plot evil against me, thwart their counsel and upset their plans. Do it for the sake of Your Name. Do it for the sake of Your power. Do it for the sake of Your holiness. Do it for the sake of Your Torah, that the one on whom You have set Your love might be rescued; save with Your right hand and answer us. May the words that proceed from my mouth and the secret thoughts that are in my heart be pleasing to You, O Lord, for You are my Stronghold as well as my Redeemer. May He who creates peace in His high heavens create peace for us and for all Israel, and say, "Amen."

(The Full Kaddish is traditionally recited here, see page 203.
Turn back to continue Shabbat service on page 105)

עֲמִידָה לְחֹל

(All rise and face east or toward an open ark - take three steps back, then three steps forward)

Minḥah only – כִּי שֵׁם יְיָ אֶקְרָא, הָבוּ גֹדֶל לֵאלֹהֵינוּ.
אֲדֹנָי שְׂפָתַי תִּפְתָּח וּפִי יַגִּיד תְּהִלָּתֶךָ:

*Minḥah only - **Ki sheim Adonai ekra, havu godel leiEloheinu.
Adonai s'fatay tif'taḥ u-fi yagid t'hilate-kha.***

אָבוֹת

(Bend the knees at בָּרוּךְ Bow at אַתָּה Straighten at יְיָ)

בָּרוּךְ אַתָּה יְיָ אֱלֹהֵינוּ וֵאלֹהֵי אֲבוֹתֵינוּ, אֱלֹהֵי אַבְרָהָם, אֱלֹהֵי יִצְחָק, וֵאלֹהֵי יַעֲקֹב, הָאֵל הַגָּדוֹל הַגִּבּוֹר וְהַנּוֹרָא, אֵל עֶלְיוֹן, גּוֹמֵל חֲסָדִים טוֹבִים, וְקוֹנֵה הַכֹּל, וְזוֹכֵר חַסְדֵי אָבוֹת אֲשֶׁר הֵבִיא, וּמֵבִיא, גּוֹאֵל לִבְנֵי בְנֵיהֶם לְמַעַן שְׁמוֹ בְּאַהֲבָה.

*Barukh atah Adonai, Eloheinu velohei avoteinu: Elohei Avraham, Elohei Yitsḥak,
v'Eilohei Ya'akov. Ha'Eil hagadol hagibor v'hanorah, Eil Elyon, Gomeil ḥasadim
tovim, v'koneih hakal, v'zokheir has'deh avot, asher heivi, u'meivi, Go'eil liv'nei
v'neihem, l'ma-an sh'mo, b'ahavah.*

(From Rosh Hashanah to Yom Kippur add)

זָכְרֵנוּ לְחַיִּים בְּיֵשׁוּעַ, מֶלֶךְ חָפֵץ בַּחַיִּים, וְכָתְבֵנוּ בְּסֵפֶר הַחַיִּים, לְמַעַנְךָ אֱלֹהִים חַיִּים.
*Zokh'reinu l'ḥaim be-Yeshua, Melekh ḥafetz baḥayim, v'khot'veinu b'sefer haḥayim,
l'ma'ankha Elohim ḥayim.*

(Bend the knees at בָּרוּךְ Bow at אַתָּה Straighten at יְיָ)

מֶלֶךְ עוֹזֵר וּמוֹשִׁיעַ וּמָגֵן.   בָּרוּךְ אַתָּה יְיָ, מָגֵן אַבְרָהָם.
Melekh ozer umoshia umagein. Barukh atah Adonai, magein Avraham.

גְּבוּרוֹת

אַתָּה גִּבּוֹר לְעוֹלָם אֲדֹנָי, מְחַיֵּה מֵתִים אַתָּה, רַב לְהוֹשִׁיעַ.
Atah gibor l'olam, Adonai, m'chayei meitim atah, rav l'hoshia.

(Between Shemini Atseret and Pesaḥ add)

Mashiv haruaḥ u'morid ha-geshem.   מַשִּׁיב הָרוּחַ וּמוֹרִיד הַגָּשֶׁם.

מְכַלְכֵּל חַיִּים בְּחֶסֶד, מְחַיֵּה מֵתִים בְּרַחֲמִים רַבִּים, סוֹמֵךְ נוֹפְלִים, וְרוֹפֵא חוֹלִים, וּמַתִּיר אֲסוּרִים, וּמְקַיֵּם אֱמוּנָתוֹ לִישֵׁנֵי עָפָר, מִי כָמוֹךָ בַּעַל גְּבוּרוֹת וּמִי דוֹמֶה לָּךְ, מֶלֶךְ מֵמִית וּמְחַיֶּה וּמַצְמִיחַ יְשׁוּעָה.

*M'khalkeil ḥayim b'ḥesed, m'ḥayei meitim b'raḥamim rabim. Someiḥ nof'lim, v'rofeh
holim, umatir asurim, um'kayeim emunatoh lisheinei afar. Mi khamokha ba'al g'vurot,
umi domeh lakh, Melekh meimit um'ḥayeh u'matsmiaḥ yeshua.*

(From Rosh Hashanah to Yom Kippur add)

מִי כָמוֹךָ אַב הָרַחֲמִים, זוֹכֵר יְצוּרָיו לְחַיִּים בְּרַחֲמִים.
Mi khamokha av haraḥamim, zokheir yetzurav l'ḥaim b'rachamim.

וְנֶאֱמָן אַתָּה לְהַחֲיוֹת מֵתִים. בָּרוּךְ אַתָּה יְיָ, מְחַיֵּה הַמֵּתִים.
V'ne'eman atah l'haḥayot meitim. Barukh atah Adonai, m'ḥayei hameitim.

Amidah L'Ḥol

(All rise and face east or toward an open ark - take three steps back, then three steps forward)

Minhah only - When I proclaim the Name of Adonai, give glory to our God!
Lord, you will open my lips that my mouth may declare Your praise.

Avot

*(Bend the knees at **Blessed**, Bow at **Are You,** Straighten at **Lord**)*

Blessed are You, Lord our God and God of our fathers, God of Abraham, God of Isaac and God of Jacob, the great, mighty and awesome God, Most High God, who grants loving kindness and is Master of all. You remember the deeds of our fathers, and in Your love You have brought, and you bring, a Redeemer to their children's children for the sake of Your Name.

(From Rosh Hashanah to Yom Kippur add)
Remember us to life in Yeshua, O King who takes delight in life. Inscribe us in the book of life, for Your sake, O God of life.

*(Bend the knees at **Blessed**, Bow at **Are You,** Straighten at **Lord**)*

King, Supporter, Savior and Shield, blessed are You, Lord, Shield of Abraham.

G'vurot

Lord, You are mighty forever. You call the dead to life. You are mighty to save.

(Between Shemini Atseret and Pesah add)
You cause the wind to return and the rain to come down.

You sustain the living with loving kindness, and with great mercy You revive the dead. You uphold those who fall, heal the sick, set the captive free and keep faith with those who sleep in the dust. Lord of might, who is like You? King, who can be compared to You? You decree death and restore life, causing salvation to come forth.

(From Rosh Hashanah to Yom Kippur add)
Compassionate Father, who is like You, remembering with mercy your creatures for life?

You are faithful to revive the dead. Blessed are You, Lord, who calls the dead to life.

(During the silent Amidah continue with אַתָּה קָדוֹשׁ *at the bottom of the page.*
During the Reader's repetition continue here. For Minhah Kedushah turn to page 148.

Rise on your toes at קָדוֹשׁ, קָדוֹשׁ, קָדוֹשׁ *,* בָּרוּךְ *and* (יִמְלֹךְ

קְדוּשָׁה

(All) נְקַדֵּשׁ אֶת שִׁמְךָ בָּעוֹלָם, כְּשֵׁם שֶׁמַּקְדִּישִׁים אוֹתוֹ בִּשְׁמֵי מָרוֹם, כַּכָּתוּב עַל יַד נְבִיאֶךָ, וְקָרָא זֶה אֶל זֶה וְאָמַר:

N'kadeish et shim'kha ba'olam, k'shem shemak'dishim otoh bish'mei marom,
kakatuv al yad nevi'ekha, v'karah ze el ze v'amar:

קָדוֹשׁ, קָדוֹשׁ, קָדוֹשׁ, יְיָ צְבָאוֹת, מְלֹא כָל הָאָרֶץ כְּבוֹדוֹ.

Kadosh, kadosh, kadosh, Adonai ts'vaot, m'lo khol ha'arets k'vohdoh.

(Reader) לְעֻמָּתָם בָּרוּךְ יֹאמֵרוּ:

Barukh k'vod Adonai mim'komoh   *(All)* בָּרוּךְ כְּבוֹד יְיָ, מִמְּקוֹמוֹ.

(Reader) וּבְדִבְרֵי קָדְשְׁךָ כָּתוּב לֵאמֹר:

(All) יִמְלֹךְ יְיָ לְעוֹלָם, אֱלֹהַיִךְ צִיּוֹן לְדֹר וָדֹר, הַלְלוּיָהּ.

Yimlokh Adonai l'olam elohayikh Tsiyon, l'dor vador, halelluyah

(Reader) לְדוֹר וָדוֹר נַגִּיד גָּדְלֶךָ וּלְנֵצַח נְצָחִים קְדֻשָּׁתְךָ נַקְדִּישׁ, וְשִׁבְחֲךָ אֱלֹהֵינוּ מִפִּינוּ לֹא יָמוּשׁ לְעוֹלָם וָעֶד, כִּי אֵל מֶלֶךְ גָּדוֹל וְקָדוֹשׁ אָתָּה.
*בָּרוּךְ אַתָּה יְיָ, הָאֵל הַקָּדוֹשׁ.

(From Rosh Hashanah to Yom Kippur substitute)
*בָּרוּךְ אַתָּה יְיָ, הַמֶּלֶךְ הַקָּדוֹשׁ

(Recitation of the silent Amidah continues here)

קְדוּשַׁת הַשֵּׁם

אַתָּה קָדוֹשׁ וְשִׁמְךָ קָדוֹשׁ, וּקְדוֹשִׁים בְּכָל יוֹם יְהַלְלוּךָ, סֶּלָה.
*בָּרוּךְ אַתָּה יְיָ, הָאֵל הַקָּדוֹשׁ.

(From Rosh Hashanah to Yom Kippur substitute)
*בָּרוּךְ אַתָּה יְיָ, הַמֶּלֶךְ הַקָּדוֹשׁ

*(During the silent Amidah continue with **You are Holy** at the bottom of the page.
During the Reader's repetition continue here. For Minhah Kedusah turn to page 149.
Rise on your toes at **Holy, Holy, Holy, Blessed** and **The Lord will Reign**)*

Kedushah

(All) We will sanctify Your Name in this world, even as they sanctify it in
the heavens above, as it is written by Your prophet, They continuously call to one
another:

> Holy, holy, holy is the Lord of Hosts;
> the whole earth is filled with His glory.

(Reader) They respond by saying, Blessed:

(All) Blessed is the glory of the Lord from His abode.

(Reader) In your Holy Writings you say:

(All) The Lord will reign forever; your God, O Tsiyon, from generation to
generation. Halleluyah!

(Reader) We will declare Your greatness from generation to generation.
We will proclaim Your holiness to all eternity. Your praise, our God, will never
depart from our mouth, for You, God, are a great and mighty King.

*Blessed are You, Lord, holy God.

(From Rosh Hashana to Yom Kippur substitute)
*Blessed are You, Lord, the Holy King.

(Recitation of the silent Amidah continues here)

Kedushot HaSheim

You are holy, and Your Name is holy, and holy ones proclaim Your praise daily.

*Blessed are You, Lord, holy God.

(From Rosh Hashanah to Yom Kippur substitute)
*Blessed are You, Lord, the Holy King.

(During the silent Amidah continue with אַתָּה קָדוֹשׁ *at the bottom of the page.*
During the Reader's repetition continue here)

(Rise on your toes at בָּרוּךְ , קָדוֹשׁ, קָדוֹשׁ, קָדוֹשׁ *and* יִמְלֹךְ)

קְדוּשָׁה לְמִנְחָה

(All) נְקַדֵּשׁ אֶת שִׁמְךָ בָּעוֹלָם, כְּשֵׁם שֶׁמַּקְדִּישִׁים אוֹתוֹ בִּשְׁמֵי מָרוֹם, כַּכָּתוּב
עַל יַד נְבִיאֶךָ, וְקָרָא זֶה אֶל זֶה וְאָמַר:

N'kadeish et shim'kha ba'olam, k'shem shemak'dishim otoh bish'mei marom,
kakatuv al yad nevi'echa, v'karah ze el ze v'amar:

קָדוֹשׁ, קָדוֹשׁ, קָדוֹשׁ, יְיָ צְבָאוֹת, מְלֹא כָל הָאָרֶץ כְּבוֹדוֹ.

Kadosh, kadosh, kadosh, Adonai ts'vaot, m'lo khol haarets k'vohdoh.

(Reader) לְעֻמָּתָם בָּרוּךְ יֹאמֵרוּ.

Barukh k'vod Adonai mim'komo (All) בָּרוּךְ כְּבוֹד יְיָ, מִמְּקוֹמוֹ.

(Reader) וּבְדִבְרֵי קָדְשְׁךָ כָּתוּב לֵאמֹר:

(All) יִמְלֹךְ יְיָ לְעוֹלָם, אֱלֹהַיִךְ צִיּוֹן לְדֹר וָדֹר, הַלְלוּיָהּ.

Yim'lokh Adonai l'olam elohayikhTsiyon, l'dor vador, halleluyah

(Reader) לְדוֹר וָדוֹר נַגִּיד גָּדְלֶךָ וּלְנֵצַח נְצָחִים קְדֻשָּׁתְךָ נַקְדִּישׁ, וְשִׁבְחֲךָ
אֱלֹהֵינוּ מִפִּינוּ לֹא יָמוּשׁ לְעוֹלָם וָעֶד, כִּי אֵל מֶלֶךְ גָּדוֹל וְקָדוֹשׁ אָתָּה.
*בָּרוּךְ אַתָּה יְיָ, הָאֵל הַקָּדוֹשׁ.

(From Rosh Hashanah to Yom Kippur substitute)
*בָּרוּךְ אַתָּה יְיָ, הַמֶּלֶךְ הַקָּדוֹשׁ

(Recitation of the silent Amidah continues here)

אַתָּה קָדוֹשׁ וְשִׁמְךָ קָדוֹשׁ, וּקְדוֹשִׁים בְּכָל יוֹם יְהַלְלוּךָ, סֶּלָה.
*בָּרוּךְ אַתָּה יְיָ, הָאֵל הַקָּדוֹשׁ.

(From Rosh Hashanah to Yom Kippur substitute)
*בָּרוּךְ אַתָּה יְיָ, הַמֶּלֶךְ הַקָּדוֹשׁ

*(During the silent Amidah continue with **You are Holy** at the bottom of the page.
During the Reader's repetition begin here.
(Rise on your toes at "**Holy, holy, holy**" , "**Blessed**" and "**The Lord will reign**")*

Kedushah L'Minḥah

(All) We will sanctify Your Name in this world, even as they sanctify it in the heavens above, as it is written by Your prophet: They continuously call to one another

Holy, holy, holy is the Lord of Hosts; the whole earth is filled with His glory.

(Reader) They respond by saying:

(All) Blessed. . . Blessed is the glory of the Lord from His abode.

(Reader) And in your holy Scriptures is written...

(All) The Lord will reign forever; your God, O Tsiyon, from generation to generation. Halleluyah!

(Reader) We will declare Your greatness from generation to generation. We will proclaim Your holiness to all eternity. Your praise, our God, will never depart from our mouth, for You, God, are a great and mighty King.

*Blessed are You, Lord, the holy God.

(From Rosh Hashana to Yom Kippur substitute)
Blessed are You, Lord, the Holy King.

(Recitation of the silent Amidah continues here)

You are holy, and Your Name is holy, and holy ones proclaim Your praise daily.
*Blessed are You, Lord, the holy God.

(From Rosh Hashanah to Yom Kippur substitute)
Blessed are You, Lord, the Holy King.

בינה

אַתָּה חוֹנֵן לְאָדָם דַּעַת, וּמְלַמֵּד לֶאֱנוֹשׁ בִּינָה. חָנֵּנוּ מֵאִתְּךָ דֵּעָה, בִּינָה וְהַשְׂכֵּל. בָּרוּךְ אַתָּה יְיָ, חוֹנֵן הַדָּעַת.

תשובה

הֲשִׁיבֵנוּ אָבִינוּ לְתוֹרָתֶךָ, וְקָרְבֵנוּ מַלְכֵּנוּ לַעֲבוֹדָתֶךָ, וְהַחֲזִירֵנוּ בִּתְשׁוּבָה שְׁלֵמָה לְפָנֶיךָ. בָּרוּךְ אַתָּה יְיָ, הָרוֹצֶה בִּתְשׁוּבָה.

סליחה

(Using your right fist, beat your chest when you recite פָּשָׁעְנוּ *and* חָטָאנוּ*)*

סְלַח לָנוּ, אָבִינוּ, כִּי חָטָאנוּ, מְחַל לָנוּ, מַלְכֵּנוּ, כִּי פָשָׁעְנוּ, כִּי מוֹחֵל וְסוֹלֵחַ אָתָּה. בָּרוּךְ אַתָּה יְיָ, חַנּוּן הַמַּרְבֶּה לִסְלוֹחַ.

גאולה

רְאֵה בְעָנְיֵנוּ, וְרִיבָה רִיבֵנוּ, וּגְאָלֵנוּ מְהֵרָה לְמַעַן שְׁמֶךָ, כִּי גּוֹאֵל חָזָק אָתָּה. בָּרוּךְ אַתָּה יְיָ, גּוֹאֵל יִשְׂרָאֵל.

(On fast days other than Tisha b'Av during Shaharit and Minhah, the Reader adds)

עֲנֵנוּ, יְיָ, עֲנֵנוּ, בְּיוֹם צוֹם תַּעֲנִיתֵנוּ, כִּי בְצָרָה גְדוֹלָה אֲנַחְנוּ. אַל תֵּפֶן אֶל רִשְׁעֵנוּ, וְאַל תַּסְתֵּר פָּנֶיךָ מִמֶּנּוּ, וְאַל תִּתְעַלַּם מִתְּחִנָּתֵנוּ. הֱיֵה נָא קָרוֹב לְשַׁוְעָתֵנוּ, יְהִי נָא חַסְדְּךָ לְנַחֲמֵנוּ, טֶרֶם נִקְרָא אֵלֶיךָ עֲנֵנוּ, כַּדָּבָר שֶׁנֶּאֱמַר: וְהָיָה טֶרֶם יִקְרָאוּ וַאֲנִי אֶעֱנֶה, עוֹד הֵם מְדַבְּרִים וַאֲנִי אֶשְׁמָע. כִּי אַתָּה, יְיָ, הָעוֹנֶה בְּעֵת צָרָה, פּוֹדֶה וּמַצִּיל בְּכָל עֵת צָרָה וְצוּקָה. בָּרוּךְ אַתָּה יְיָ, הָעוֹנֶה בְּעֵת צָרָה.

Binah

You have favored man with knowledge, and have taught mankind with understanding. From Your knowledge, understanding, and wisdom be gracious to us. Blessed are You Lord, who has favored us with knowledge.

Teshuvah

Turn us, our Father, to Your Torah, and draw near to us, our King, that we would serve You, and return us, in perfect repentance, to Your presence. Blessed are You Lord, who desires our return.

Seliḥah

(Using your right fist, beat your chest when you recite **sinned** *and* **misdeeds)**

Forgive us, our Father, for we have sinned; pardon us, our King, for our misdeeds, for from You are pardon and forgiveness. Blessed are You Lord, who pardons us out of the abundance of Your compassion.

Geulah

Consider now our poverty, and fight our fight, and redeem us quickly for the sake of Your name, for You are the Mighty Redeemer. Blessed are You Lord, Redeemer of Israel.

(On fast days other than Tisha b'Av during Shaharit and Minhah, the Reader adds)

Answer us Lord, answer us in the day we are called upon to fast, for we are in great distress. Do not consider our iniquity; do not turn Your face from us; do not ignore our supplication. Be near when we call out now, and in time to come let us be comforted by Your loving kindness. Before we call out to You, answer us, speaking even as we speak. "And it will be before they call I will answer; while they yet speak I will hear." For You Lord, answer us in the season of trouble; ransoming and rescuing from all trouble and distress. Blessed are You Lord, who answers in time of trouble.

רפואה

רְפָאֵנוּ, יְיָ, וְנֵרָפֵא, הוֹשִׁיעֵנוּ וְנִוָּשֵׁעָה, כִּי תְהִלָּתֵנוּ אָתָּה, וְהַעֲלֵה רְפוּאָה שְׁלֵמָה לְכָל מַכּוֹתֵינוּ. * כִּי אֵל מֶלֶךְ רוֹפֵא נֶאֱמָן וְרַחֲמָן אָתָּה. בָּרוּךְ אַתָּה יְיָ, רוֹפֵא חוֹלֵי עַמּוֹ יִשְׂרָאֵל.

*At this point, Jewish tradition encourages the one praying to pause and pray for the healing of individuals.

ברכת השנים

בָּרֵךְ עָלֵינוּ, יְיָ אֱלֹהֵינוּ, אֶת הַשָּׁנָה הַזֹּאת וְאֶת כָּל מִינֵי תְבוּאָתָהּ לְטוֹבָה,

(From December 4th until Pesah add)	*(From Pesah until December 4th add)*
וְתֵן בְּרָכָה	וְתֵן טַל וּמָטָר לִבְרָכָה

עַל פְּנֵי הָאֲדָמָה, וְשַׂבְּעֵנוּ מִטּוּבֶךָ, וּבָרֵךְ שְׁנָתֵנוּ כַּשָּׁנִים הַטּוֹבוֹת. בָּרוּךְ אַתָּה יְיָ, מְבָרֵךְ הַשָּׁנִים.

קבוץ גלויות

תְּקַע בְּשׁוֹפָר גָּדוֹל לְחֵרוּתֵנוּ, וְשָׂא נֵס לְקַבֵּץ גָּלֻיּוֹתֵינוּ, וְקַבְּצֵנוּ יַחַד מֵאַרְבַּע כַּנְפוֹת הָאָרֶץ. בָּרוּךְ אַתָּה יְיָ, מְקַבֵּץ נִדְחֵי עַמּוֹ יִשְׂרָאֵל.

משפט

הָשִׁיבָה שׁוֹפְטֵינוּ כְּבָרִאשׁוֹנָה וְיוֹעֲצֵינוּ כְּבַתְּחִלָּה, וְהָסֵר מִמֶּנּוּ יָגוֹן וַאֲנָחָה, וּמְלוֹךְ עָלֵינוּ אַתָּה, יְיָ, לְבַדְּךָ בְּחֶסֶד וּבְרַחֲמִים, וְצַדְּקֵנוּ בַּמִּשְׁפָּט. *בָּרוּךְ אַתָּה יְיָ, מֶלֶךְ אוֹהֵב צְדָקָה וּמִשְׁפָּט.

(From Rosh Hashanah to Yom Kippur substitute)

*בָּרוּךְ אַתָּה יְיָ, הַמֶּלֶךְ הַמִּשְׁפָּט

Refuah

Heal us, O Lord, and we will be healed, save us and we will be saved, for You are our praise, and perfect healing has risen upon all our wounds. *

For unto You, King, is healing, faithfulness, and compassion. Blessed are You Lord, who heals the sick among His people Israel.

**(At this point, Jewish tradition encourages the one praying to pause and pray for the healing of individuals)*

Bir'kat HaShanim

Your blessing be upon us, Lord our God, this year with various kinds of produce, for goodness.

(From December 4th until Pesaḥ add)	*(From Pesah until December 4th add)*
And send dew and rain as blessing	And give blessing

...upon the surface of the land, and satisfy us with Your goodness, and bless our year and the years *to come* with goodness.
Blessed are You Lord, who blesses the years *to come*.

Kibbuts Galuyot

Sound the great shofar of our freedom; and raise the banner for the gathering of our exiles. Gather us together from the four corners of the earth. Blessed are You, Lord, who gathers the outcasts of your people Israel.

Mish'pat

Restore our judges and our counselors as in the beginning; and turn away from us sorrow and sighing. And, rule over us Lord, You and only You, in loving kindness, and compassion, and justice. *Blessed are You, Lord, King, who loves righteous judgment.

(From Rosh Hashanah to Yom Kippur substitute)
**Blessed are You Lord, King and Judge*

עֲנָוָה

וְכָל הָרִשְׁעָה כְּרֶגַע תֹּאבֵד, וְכָל אוֹיְבֶיךָ מְהֵרָה יִכָּרֵתוּ.
בִּמְהֵרָה בְיָמֵינוּ לְבוֹא יֵשׁוּעַ מְשִׁיחֵנוּ. וְהַזֵּדִים יֵדְעוּ אֲהַבָתֶךָ וְכָל אוֹיְבֶיךָ
יָשׁוּבוּ בִּתְשׁוּבָה שְׁלֵמָה לְפָנֶיךָ. בָּרוּךְ אַתָּה יְיָ, שֹׁבֵר אוֹיְבִים וּמַכְנִיעַ זֵדִים.

הַצַדִיקִים

עַל הַצַדִיקִים וְעַל הַחֲסִידִים וְעַל זִקְנֵי עַמְּךָ בֵּית יִשְׂרָאֵל, וְעַל פְּלֵיטַת
סוֹפְרֵיהֶם, וְעַל גֵּרֵי הַצֶּדֶק וְעָלֵינוּ, יֶהֱמוּ נָא רַחֲמֶיךָ, יְיָ אֱלֹהֵינוּ, וְתֵן שָׂכָר
טוֹב לְכָל הַבּוֹטְחִים בְּשִׁמְךָ בֶּאֱמֶת, וְשִׂים חֶלְקֵנוּ עִמָּהֶם לְעוֹלָם, וְלֹא נֵבוֹשׁ
כִּי בְךָ בָּטָחְנוּ. בָּרוּךְ אַתָּה יְיָ, מִשְׁעָן וּמִבְטָח לַצַּדִיקִים.

בנין ירושלים

וְלִירוּשָׁלַיִם עִירְךָ בְּרַחֲמִים תָּשׁוּב, וְתִשְׁכּוֹן בְּתוֹכָהּ כַּאֲשֶׁר דִּבַּרְתָּ, וּבְנֵה
אוֹתָהּ בְּקָרוֹב בְּיָמֵינוּ בִּנְיַן עוֹלָם, וְכִסֵּא דָוִד מְהֵרָה לְתוֹכָהּ תָּכִין. בָּרוּךְ
אַתָּה יְיָ, בּוֹנֵה יְרוּשָׁלָיִם.

מלכות בית דוד

אֶת צֶמַח דָּוִד עַבְדְּךָ מְהֵרָה תַצְמִיחַ, וְקַרְנוֹ תָּרוּם בִּישׁוּעָתֶךָ, יֵשׁוּעַ
מְשִׁיחֵנוּ, כִּי לִישׁוּעָתְךָ קִוִּינוּ כָּל הַיּוֹם. בָּרוּךְ אַתָּה יְיָ, מַצְמִיחַ קֶרֶן יְשׁוּעָה.

שומע תפלה

שְׁמַע קוֹלֵנוּ, יְיָ אֱלֹהֵינוּ, חוּס וְרַחֵם עָלֵינוּ, וְקַבֵּל בְּרַחֲמִים וּבְרָצוֹן אֶת
תְּפִלָּתֵנוּ, כִּי אֵל שׁוֹמֵעַ תְּפִלוֹת וְתַחֲנוּנִים אָתָּה, וּמִלְּפָנֶיךָ, מַלְכֵּנוּ, רֵיקָם אַל
תְּשִׁיבֵנוּ. כִּי אַתָּה שׁוֹמֵעַ תְּפִלַּת עַמְּךָ יִשְׂרָאֵל בְּרַחֲמִים. בָּרוּךְ אַתָּה יְיָ,
שׁוֹמֵעַ תְּפִלָּה.

Anavah

May all wickedness perish; may all your enemies be soon cut down. Do this quickly and even in our days with the coming of our Messiah Yeshua. May the arrogant come to know your love, and may all Your enemies turn in sincere repentance before You. Blessed are you, Lord, who breaks the enemies and humbles the arrogant.

Tsadikim

Upon the upright, and upon the devoted, and upon the elders of Your people, the house of Israel, and upon the remnant of their scribes; and upon the righteous who are among us, please call out from Your compassion, Lord our God, a good reward to all who trusted in the truth of Your name. And place our portion with them, forever. And do not shame us, for we put our trust in You. Blessed are You, Lord, the support and the confidence of the righteous.

Binyan Yerushalayim

Return in compassion to Your city, Jerusalem, and dwell in her midst as You have spoken; build her soon, even in our days, and for our offspring forever. And speedily establish the throne of David in the midst of her. Blessed are You, Lord, the builder of Jerusalem.

Mal'khut Beit David

May You cause David, Your servant, to blossom, as a pregnant woman blossoms, and quickly establish the Horn of Your Salvation, our Messiah Yeshua, for we have hoped for Your salvation every day. Blessed are You, Lord, who causes the Horn of Your Salvation to blossom.

Shomei'a Tefillah

Hear our cry, Lord our God, spare us and have compassion upon us, and in compassion receive our prayer with pleasure, for You, God, hear prayer and supplications. Do not cause us to turn us away from Your presence empty handed our King, for You hear the prayer of Your people, Israel, in compassion. Blessed are You, Lord, who hears our prayer.

עבודה

רְצֵה, יְיָ אֱלֹהֵינוּ, בְּעַמְּךָ יִשְׂרָאֵל וּבִתְפִלָּתָם, וְהָשֵׁב אֶת הָעֲבוֹדָה לִדְבִיר בֵּיתֶךָ, וְאִשֵּׁי יִשְׂרָאֵל, וּתְפִלָּתָם בְּאַהֲבָה תְקַבֵּל בְּרָצוֹן, וּתְהִי לְרָצוֹן תָּמִיד עֲבוֹדַת יִשְׂרָאֵל עַמֶּךָ.

(On Rosh Hodesh and Hol HaMoed Pesah and Sukkot add)

אֱלֹהֵינוּ וֵאלֹהֵי אֲבוֹתֵינוּ, יַעֲלֶה וְיָבֹא, וְיַגִּיעַ, וְיֵרָאֶה, וְיֵרָצֶה, וְיִשָּׁמַע, וְיִפָּקֵד, וְיִזָּכֵר זִכְרוֹנֵנוּ וּפִקְדוֹנֵנוּ, וְזִכְרוֹן אֲבוֹתֵינוּ, וְזִכְרוֹן מָשִׁיחַ יֵשׁוּעַ בֶּן דָּוִד עַבְדֶּךָ, וְזִכְרוֹן יְרוּשָׁלַיִם עִיר קָדְשֶׁךָ, וְזִכְרוֹן כָּל עַמְּךָ בֵּית יִשְׂרָאֵל לְפָנֶיךָ, לִפְלֵיטָה, לְטוֹבָה, לְחֵן וּלְחֶסֶד וּלְרַחֲמִים, לְחַיִּים וּלְשָׁלוֹם, בְּיוֹם

רֹאשׁ הַחֹדֶשׁ הַזֶּה.	לְרֹאשׁ חֹדֶשׁ:
חַג הַמַּצּוֹת הַזֶּה.	לְפֶסַח:
חַג הַסֻּכּוֹת הַזֶּה.	לְסֻכּוֹת:

זָכְרֵנוּ, יְיָ אֱלֹהֵינוּ, בּוֹ לְטוֹבָה, וּפָקְדֵנוּ בוֹ לִבְרָכָה, וְהוֹשִׁיעֵנוּ בוֹ לְחַיִּים, וּבִדְבַר יְשׁוּעָה וְרַחֲמִים, חוּס וְחָנֵּנוּ, וְרַחֵם עָלֵינוּ וְהוֹשִׁיעֵנוּ, כִּי אֵלֶיךָ עֵינֵינוּ, כִּי אֵל מֶלֶךְ חַנּוּן וְרַחוּם אָתָּה.

וְתֶחֱזֶינָה עֵינֵינוּ בְּשׁוּבְךָ לְצִיּוֹן בְּרַחֲמִים. בָּרוּךְ אַתָּה יְיָ, הַמַּחֲזִיר שְׁכִינָתוֹ לְצִיּוֹן.

Avodah

Lord our God, favor Your people Israel, and their prayer, and bring about the restoration of their service to the Most Holy Place in Your house; as well as the offerings of Israel. And, receive their prayer in love and favor, and may it be so always concerning the service of Israel, Your people.

(On Rosh Hodesh and Hol HaMoed Pesah and Sukkot add)

Our God, and God of our fathers, arise, and bring, and labor, and see, and want, and hear, and count, and remember our remembrance and our charge, and the remembrance of our fathers, and the remembrance of Messiah Yeshua, the son of David, Your Servant, and the remembrance of Jerusalem, Your holy city, and the remembrance of all Your people, the House of Israel, who are before You, for refuge, for goodness, for grace, and for loving kindness, and for compassion, for life, and for peace in the day of:

On Rosh Ḥodesh add: this Rosh Ḥodesh.
On Pesaḥ add: this Festival of Matzah.
On Sukkot add: this Festival of Sukkot.

Remember us, Lord our God, in Him, for goodness; and command us, in Him, for blessing; and save us, in Him, unto life; and speak salvation and compassion, sparing and being gracious to us, and have compassion upon us and save us, for to You do we look. For You, God, reign with grace and with compassion.

And may we see, with our own eyes, Your return to Tsiyon in compassion. Blessed are You Lord, whose Presence is the restoration of Tsiyon.

מודים אנחנו

(While the Reader recites out loud מוֹדִים אֲנַחְנוּ*, the Congregation recites* מוֹדִים דְּרַבָּנָן *softly.*
Bend the knees at מוֹדִים אֲנַחְנוּ *and straighten at* יְיָ *)*

מוֹדִים אֲנַחְנוּ לָךְ, שָׁאַתָּה הוּא, יְיָ
אֱלֹהֵינוּ וֵאלֹהֵי אֲבוֹתֵינוּ, לְעוֹלָם וָעֶד,
צוּר חַיֵּינוּ, מָגֵן יִשְׁעֵנוּ, אַתָּה הוּא
לְדוֹר וָדוֹר, נוֹדֶה לְךָ וּנְסַפֵּר
תְּהִלָּתֶךָ, עַל חַיֵּינוּ הַמְּסוּרִים בְּיָדֶךָ,
וְעַל נִשְׁמוֹתֵינוּ הַפְּקוּדוֹת לָךְ, וְעַל
נִסֶּיךָ שֶׁבְּכָל יוֹם עִמָּנוּ, וְעַל
נִפְלְאוֹתֶיךָ וְטוֹבוֹתֶיךָ שֶׁבְּכָל עֵת,
עֶרֶב וָבֹקֶר וְצָהֳרָיִם, הַטּוֹב, כִּי לֹא
כָלוּ רַחֲמֶיךָ, וְהַמְרַחֵם, כִּי לֹא תַמּוּ
חֲסָדֶיךָ, מֵעוֹלָם קִוִּינוּ לָךְ.

מודים דרבנן

מוֹדִים אֲנַחְנוּ לָךְ, שָׁאַתָּה הוּא יְיָ
אֱלֹהֵינוּ וֵאלֹהֵי אֲבוֹתֵינוּ, אֱלֹהֵי כָל
בָּשָׂר, יוֹצְרֵנוּ, יוֹצֵר בְּרֵאשִׁית.
בְּרָכוֹת וְהוֹדָאוֹת לְשִׁמְךָ הַגָּדוֹל
וְהַקָּדוֹשׁ, עַל שֶׁהֶחֱיִיתָנוּ וְקִיַּמְתָּנוּ.
כֵּן תְּחַיֵּנוּ וּתְקַיְּמֵנוּ, וְתֶאֱסוֹף
גָּלֻיּוֹתֵינוּ לְחַצְרוֹת קָדְשֶׁךָ, לִשְׁמוֹר
חֻקֶּיךָ וְלַעֲשׂוֹת רְצוֹנֶךָ, וּלְעָבְדְּךָ
בְּלֵבָב שָׁלֵם, עַל שֶׁאֲנַחְנוּ מוֹדִים
לָךְ. בָּרוּךְ אֵל הַהוֹדָאוֹת.

לַחֲנֻכָּה וּפוּרִים:

עַל הַנִּסִּים, וְעַל הַפֻּרְקָן, וְעַל הַגְּבוּרוֹת, וְעַל הַתְּשׁוּעוֹת, וְעַל הַמִּלְחָמוֹת, שֶׁעָשִׂיתָ לַאֲבוֹתֵינוּ בַּיָּמִים הָהֵם בַּזְּמַן הַזֶּה.

Al hanisim v'al hafurkan, v'al hag'vurot, v'al hat'shu-ot, v'al hamil'hamot
sheh-asitah la-avoteinu bayameem hahem baz'man hazeh

לַחֲנֻכָּה:

בִּימֵי מַתִּתְיָהוּ בֶּן יוֹחָנָן כֹּהֵן גָּדוֹל, חַשְׁמוֹנַאי וּבָנָיו, כְּשֶׁעָמְדָה מַלְכוּת יָוָן הָרְשָׁעָה עַל עַמְּךָ יִשְׂרָאֵל
לְהַשְׁכִּיחָם תּוֹרָתֶךָ, וּלְהַעֲבִירָם מֵחֻקֵּי רְצוֹנֶךָ, וְאַתָּה בְּרַחֲמֶיךָ הָרַבִּים עָמַדְתָּ לָהֶם בְּעֵת צָרָתָם, רַבְתָּ
אֶת רִיבָם, דַּנְתָּ אֶת דִּינָם, נָקַמְתָּ אֶת נִקְמָתָם, מָסַרְתָּ גִבּוֹרִים בְּיַד חַלָּשִׁים, וְרַבִּים בְּיַד מְעַטִּים,
וּטְמֵאִים בְּיַד טְהוֹרִים, וּרְשָׁעִים בְּיַד צַדִּיקִים, וְזֵדִים בְּיַד עוֹסְקֵי תוֹרָתֶךָ. וּלְךָ עָשִׂיתָ שֵׁם גָּדוֹל וְקָדוֹשׁ
בְּעוֹלָמֶךָ, וּלְעַמְּךָ יִשְׂרָאֵל עָשִׂיתָ תְּשׁוּעָה גְדוֹלָה וּפֻרְקָן כְּהַיּוֹם הַזֶּה. וְאַחַר כֵּן בָּאוּ בָנֶיךָ לִדְבִיר
בֵּיתֶךָ, וּפִנּוּ אֶת הֵיכָלֶךָ, וְטִהֲרוּ אֶת מִקְדָּשֶׁךָ, וְהִדְלִיקוּ נֵרוֹת בְּחַצְרוֹת קָדְשֶׁךָ, וְקָבְעוּ שְׁמוֹנַת יְמֵי
חֲנֻכָּה אֵלּוּ, לְהוֹדוֹת וּלְהַלֵּל לְשִׁמְךָ הַגָּדוֹל.

לְפוּרִים:

בִּימֵי מָרְדְּכַי וְאֶסְתֵּר בְּשׁוּשַׁן הַבִּירָה, כְּשֶׁעָמַד עֲלֵיהֶם הָמָן הָרָשָׁע, בִּקֵּשׁ לְהַשְׁמִיד לַהֲרֹג וּלְאַבֵּד אֶת
כָּל הַיְּהוּדִים, מִנַּעַר וְעַד זָקֵן, טַף וְנָשִׁים, בְּיוֹם אֶחָד, בִּשְׁלוֹשָׁה עָשָׂר לְחֹדֶשׁ שְׁנֵים עָשָׂר, הוּא חֹדֶשׁ
אֲדָר, וּשְׁלָלָם לָבוֹז. וְאַתָּה בְּרַחֲמֶיךָ הָרַבִּים הֵפַרְתָּ אֶת עֲצָתוֹ, וְקִלְקַלְתָּ אֶת מַחֲשַׁבְתּוֹ, וַהֲשֵׁבוֹתָ לּוֹ
גְּמוּלוֹ בְּרֹאשׁוֹ, וְתָלוּ אוֹתוֹ וְאֶת בָּנָיו עַל הָעֵץ.

וְעַל כֻּלָּם יִתְבָּרַךְ וְיִתְרוֹמַם שִׁמְךָ מַלְכֵּנוּ תָּמִיד לְעוֹלָם וָעֶד.

(From Rosh Hashanah to Yom Kippur add)

וּכְתוֹב לְחַיִּים טוֹבִים כָּל בְּנֵי בְרִיתֶךָ.

Modim Anaḥnu

(While the Reader recites out loud **Modim Anaḥnu***, the Congregation recites* **Modim of the Rabbis** *softly.*
Bend the knees at **Lord, we are eternally grateful** *and straighten at* **Lord)**

Modim of the Rabbis

Lord, we are eternally grateful that You are the Lord our God and the God of our fathers. God of all flesh, our Creator and Creator in the beginning; blessings and thanks are due Your great and holy Name, for You have kept us alive and You sustained us. May You continue to grant us life and to sustain us. Bring our dispersed to Your courts, that in holiness they would observe Your laws, do Your will and serve You with all their heart; for these things we give You thanks. Blessed is the God of thanksgiving.

Lord, we are eternally grateful that You are the Lord our God and the God of our fathers. You are the strength of our life and the Shield of our Salvation. We thank You from generation to generation, and recount Your praise; for our lives which are in Your hand; and for our souls which are in Your care; and for Your miracles which are seen every day; and for Your wondrous deeds and favors which are always with us evening, morning and noon. Beneficent One, Your compassion never fails; Merciful One, Your loving kindness never ends; You have always been our hope.

(On Hanukah and Purim add)

For the miracles, and for the deliverance, and for the mightinesses, and for the salvations, and for the battles that You have brought to our fathers in this season, in those days...

(On Hanukah add)

In the days of the Hasmonean Matityahu son of Yochanan the High Priest, and his sons, when stood the wicked kingdom of the Hellenists against Your people Israel to cause them to abandon Your Torah and to turn from the statutes of will, You in Your great compassion stood for them in their time of tribulation. You contended for them in their fight, judged for them in their judgment, avenged them in their vengeance, and delivered them by means of heros when they were weak; the many into the hands of the few, the unclean into the hands of the clean, the wicked into the hands of the righteous, and the deceiver into the hands of they who practiced Your Torah. Your great and holy name is established in Your world, and You have established a great salvation for Your people Israel, and have relieved them from that day to this. Indeed, after this Your children came into the Holy Place of Your House, we cleared Your Temple of defilement, and purified Your holy sanctuary, and lit the lights in Your holy court, and established the lighting of the lights in the eight days of Chanukah, to thank and to praise the greatness of Your name.

(On Purim add)

And in the days of Mordecai and Esther, in the capital city of Shushan, when the wicked Hamen stood against them, asking that all the Jews be annihilated, murdered, and destroyed, both young boys and the old, infants and women, and to take their plunder, in one day, on the thirteenth day of the twelfth month, which is Adar. And You, in Your great compassion, annulled this decree, spoiling his purposes, and returning to him recompense upon his head, that both he and his sons would hang upon the tree.

For all these things we will bless and we will lift up Your name, our King, always, to the end of the age, and until.

(From Rosh Hashanah to Yom Kippur add)

Remember for life and good all the Children of your Covenant

וְכֹל הַחַיִּים יוֹדְוּךָ סֶּלָה, וִיהַלְלוּ אֶת שִׁמְךָ בֶּאֱמֶת, הָאֵל יְשׁוּעָתֵנוּ וְעֶזְרָתֵנוּ סֶלָה.

(Bend the knees at בָּרוּךְ Bow at אַתָּה Straighten at יְיָ)

בָּרוּךְ אַתָּה יְיָ, הַטּוֹב שִׁמְךָ וּלְךָ נָאֶה לְהוֹדוֹת.

(The Reader recites the Aaronic Blessing during his repetition
except in a House of Mourning)

אֱלֹהֵינוּ וֵאלֹהֵי אֲבוֹתֵינוּ, בָּרְכֵנוּ בַבְּרָכָה הַמְשֻׁלֶּשֶׁת בַּתּוֹרָה הַכְּתוּבָה עַל יְדֵי מֹשֶׁה עַבְדֶּךָ, הָאֲמוּרָה מִפִּי אַהֲרֹן וּבָנָיו כֹּהֲנִים, עַם קְדוֹשֶׁךָ, כָּאָמוּר.

Cong - *Kein yehi ratson* (קהל–כֵּן יְהִי רָצוֹן)   יְבָרֶכְךָ יְיָ וְיִשְׁמְרֶךָ.

Cong - *Kein yehi ratson* (קהל–כֵּן יְהִי רָצוֹן)   יָאֵר יְיָ פָּנָיו אֵלֶיךָ וִיחֻנֶּךָּ.

Cong - *Kein yehi ratson* (קהל–כֵּן יְהִי רָצוֹן)   יִשָּׂא יְיָ פָּנָיו אֵלֶיךָ וְיָשֵׂם לְךָ שָׁלוֹם.

(During Shaharit recite)

שִׂים שָׁלוֹם

שִׂים שָׁלוֹם טוֹבָה וּבְרָכָה, חֵן וָחֶסֶד וְרַחֲמִים, עָלֵינוּ וְעַל כָּל יִשְׂרָאֵל עַמֶּךָ. בָּרְכֵנוּ, אָבִינוּ, כֻּלָּנוּ כְּאֶחָד בְּאוֹר פָּנֶיךָ, כִּי בְאוֹר פָּנֶיךָ נָתַתָּ לָנוּ, יְיָ אֱלֹהֵינוּ, תּוֹרַת חַיִּים וְאַהֲבַת חֶסֶד, וּצְדָקָה וּבְרָכָה וְרַחֲמִים וְחַיִּים וְשָׁלוֹם, וְטוֹב בְּעֵינֶיךָ לְבָרֵךְ אֶת עַמְּךָ יִשְׂרָאֵל בְּכָל עֵת וּבְכָל שָׁעָה בִּשְׁלוֹמֶךָ.
*בָּרוּךְ אַתָּה יְיָ, הַמְבָרֵךְ אֶת עַמּוֹ יִשְׂרָאֵל בַּשָּׁלוֹם.

Sim Shalom tova uv'rakha hein vahesed verahamim aleinu v'al kol Yisraeil amekha. Barkheinu avinu kulanu ki'ehad b'or panekha, ki v'or panekha natata lanu, Adonai Eloheinu, Torat hayim v'ahavat hesed, uts'dakah uv'rakhah v'rahamim v'hayim v'shalom, v'tov b'einekhah l'varekh et am'kha Yisraeil b'khol et uv'khol sha'ah bish'lomekhah.

**Barukh atah Adonai, ham'vareikh et amo Yisraeil bashalom.*

(From Rosh Hashanah to Yom Kippur substitute)

*בְּסֵפֶר חַיִּים, בְּרָכָה וְשָׁלוֹם, וּפַרְנָסָה טוֹבָה, נִזָּכֵר וְנִכָּתֵב לְפָנֶיךָ, אֲנַחְנוּ וְכָל עַמְּךָ בֵּית יִשְׂרָאֵל, לְחַיִּים טוֹבִים וּלְשָׁלוֹם.
בָּרוּךְ אַתָּה יְיָ, עֹשֶׂה הַשָּׁלוֹם.

**B'sefer hayim, b'rachah, b'shalom, u-far'nasah tovah, ni'zakher v'nikataiv l'fahnekhah, anakhnu v'chol am'khah bait Yisrael, l'hayim tovim ul'shalom. Baruch atah Adonai, oseh ha'shalom.*

And all the living will thank You, and in truth they will praise Your Name; the God of our Salvation and our Help at all times.

*(Bend the knees at **Blessed**, Bow at **Are You**, Straighten at **Lord**)*

Blessed are You, Lord; it is right to give thanks to You for Your Name is good.

*(The Reader recites the Aaronic Blessing during his repetition
except in a House of Mourning)*

Our God and God of our fathers, bless us with the threefold blessing written in Torah by Moses, Your servant, and spoken through the mouth of Aaron; and his sons, the priests, Your holy people, as it is said:

May the Lord bless you and keep you!
(Congregation: *May it Be Your Will!*)
May the Lord lift up His countenance to you, and be gracious to you!
(Congregation: *May it Be Your Will!*)
**May the Lord turn His countenance toward you,
and establish peace for you!**
(Congregation: *May it Be Your Will!*)

(During Shaharit recite)
Sim Shalom

Grant peace, happiness, blessing, grace, kindness and mercy to us and all Israel, Your people. Our Father, bless us all alike with the light of Your countenance. Lord our God, by the light of Your countenance You have given us a Torah of life, loving kindness, charity, blessing, mercy, life and peace. May it be good in Your sight to bless Your people Israel with peace at all times and at every hour.

*Blessed are You, Lord, who is blessing His people Israel with peace.

(From Rosh Hashanah to Yom Kippur substitute)
*Our Father, and the Father of all Israel, remember us, and inscribe us in the Book of Life, for blessing and for peace, and good provision, for good life and for peace. Blessed are You, Lord, who makes peace.

(During Minhah and Maariv Recite)

שָׁלוֹם רָב

שָׁלוֹם רָב עַל יִשְׂרָאֵל עַמְּךָ תָּשִׂים לְעוֹלָם, כִּי אַתָּה הוּא מֶלֶךְ אָדוֹן לְכָל הַשָּׁלוֹם. וְטוֹב בְּעֵינֶיךָ לְבָרֵךְ אֶת עַמְּךָ יִשְׂרָאֵל, בְּכָל עֵת וּבְכָל שָׁעָה בִּשְׁלוֹמֶךָ. *בָּרוּךְ אַתָּה יְיָ, הַמְבָרֵךְ אֶת עַמּוֹ יִשְׂרָאֵל בַּשָּׁלוֹם.

Shalom Rav al Yisraeil am'kha tasim l'olam. Ki Atah hu melech adon l'khol hashalom. V'tov b'einekha l'vareikh et am'kha Yisraeil, b'chol eit uv'khol sha'ah bish'lomekha.
**Barukh atah Adonai, hamivareikh et amo Yisraeil ba'shalom.*

(From Rosh Hashanah to Yom Kippur substitute)

*בְּסֵפֶר חַיִּים, בְּרָכָה וְשָׁלוֹם, וּפַרְנָסָה טוֹבָה, נִזָּכֵר וְנִכָּתֵב לְפָנֶיךָ, אֲנַחְנוּ וְכָל עַמְּךָ בֵּית יִשְׂרָאֵל, לְחַיִּים טוֹבִים וּלְשָׁלוֹם. בָּרוּךְ אַתָּה יְיָ, עֹשֵׂה הַשָּׁלוֹם.

**B'sefer hayim, b'rakhah, b'shalom, u-far'nasah tovah, ni'zakheir v'nikateiv l'fahnekhah, anakhnu v'chol am'khah beit Yisrael, l'hayim tovim ul'shalom.*
Barukh atah Adonai, oseh ha'shalom.

(Continue all services here)

יִהְיוּ לְרָצוֹן אִמְרֵי פִי וְהֶגְיוֹן לִבִּי לְפָנֶיךָ, יְיָ צוּרִי וְגֹאֲלִי.

Yih'yu l'ratson im'rei fi veheg'yon libi le'fanekha, Adonai tsuri v'goali.

(The Reader's repetition of the Amidah ends here. Individuals continue to the bottom of the page)

אֱלֹהַי, נְצוֹר לְשׁוֹנִי מֵרָע. וּשְׂפָתַי מִדַּבֵּר מִרְמָה. וְלִמְקַלְלַי נַפְשִׁי תִדּוֹם, וְנַפְשִׁי כֶּעָפָר לַכֹּל תִּהְיֶה. פְּתַח לִבִּי בְּתוֹרָתֶךָ, וּבְמִצְוֹתֶיךָ תִּרְדוֹף נַפְשִׁי. וְכָל הַחוֹשְׁבִים עָלַי רָעָה, מְהֵרָה הָפֵר עֲצָתָם וְקַלְקֵל מַחֲשַׁבְתָּם. עֲשֵׂה לְמַעַן שְׁמֶךָ, עֲשֵׂה לְמַעַן יְמִינֶךָ, עֲשֵׂה לְמַעַן קְדֻשָּׁתֶךָ. עֲשֵׂה לְמַעַן תּוֹרָתֶךָ. לְמַעַן יֵחָלְצוּן יְדִידֶיךָ, הוֹשִׁיעָה יְמִינְךָ וַעֲנֵנִי. יִהְיוּ לְרָצוֹן אִמְרֵי פִי וְהֶגְיוֹן לִבִּי לְפָנֶיךָ, יְיָ צוּרִי וְגֹאֲלִי.

(Take three steps back. Bow first left, then right and finally forward as you recite)

עֹשֵׂה שָׁלוֹם בִּמְרוֹמָיו, הוּא יַעֲשֶׂה שָׁלוֹם עָלֵינוּ, וְעַל כָּל יִשְׂרָאֵל, וְאִמְרוּ אָמֵן.

Oseh shalom bim'romav Hu ya'aseh shalom aleinu, v'al kol Yisraeil v'imru, Amen.

יְהִי רָצוֹן מִלְּפָנֶיךָ, יְיָ אֱלֹהֵינוּ וֵאלֹהֵי אֲבוֹתֵינוּ, שֶׁיִּבָּנֶה בֵּית הַמִּקְדָּשׁ בִּמְהֵרָה בְיָמֵינוּ, וְתֵן חֶלְקֵנוּ בְּתוֹרָתֶךָ, וְשָׁם נַעֲבָדְךָ בְּיִרְאָה כִּימֵי עוֹלָם וּכְשָׁנִים קַדְמוֹנִיּוֹת. וְעָרְבָה לַיְיָ מִנְחַת יְהוּדָה וִירוּשָׁלָיִם, כִּימֵי עוֹלָם וּכְשָׁנִים קַדְמוֹנִיּוֹת.

(For Shaharit and Minhah continue with Tahanun. For Maariv turn to page 40 for Aleinu)

(During Minhah and Maariv Recite)

Shalom Rav

Grant abundant peace to Israel, who will always be Your people, for You are He, King, who is Lord of all peace. May it be good in Your sight to bless Your people Israel at all times and in all hours with Your peace.

*Blessed are You, Lord, who is blessing His people Israel with peace.

(From Rosh Hashanah to Yom Kippur substitute)

*Our Father, and the Father of all Israel, remember us, and inscribe us in the Book of Life, for blessing and for peace, and good provision, for good life and for peace. Blessed are You, Lord, who makes peace.

(Continue all services here)

May the words that proceed from my mouth and the secret thoughts that are in my heart be pleasing to You, O Lord, for You are my Stronghold as well as my Redeemer.

(The Reader's repetition of the Amidah ends here. Individuals continue to the bottom of the page)

My God, guard my tongue from evil, and my lips from speaking falsehood. May my soul be silent to those who insult me, and may my soul be humble before all. Open my heart to Your Torah, that my soul might follow Your commands. As for all who plot evil against me, thwart their counsel and upset their plans. Do it for the sake of Your Name. Do it for the sake of Your power. Do it for the sake of Your holiness. Do it for the sake of Your Torah, that the one on whom You have set Your love might be rescued; save with Your right hand and answer us. May the words that proceed from my mouth and the secret thoughts that are in my heart be pleasing to You, O Lord, for You are my Stronghold as well as my Redeemer.

(Take three steps back. Bow first left, then right and finally forward as you recite)

May He who creates peace in His high heavens create peace for us and for all Israel, and say, "Amen."

May it be Your will, Lord our God, and God or our fathers, to rebuild Your holy Temple, speedily, and in our days, and give to us our portion in Your Torah. Then we will serve You in reverence, as we did in days of old and in former years. And the evening offerings of Judah and Jerusalem shall be a surety to the Lord, as in days of old, and in former years.

(For Shaharit and Minhah continue with Tahanun. For Maariv turn to page 41 for Aleinu)

תחנון

(Taḥanun is recited after the weekday Amidah for Shaharit and Minhah. Consult a Rabbi or a Madrikh for occasions and days when Tahunun is omitted)
(Begin Tahanun here while standing on Monday and Thursday for Shaharit only, then continue below)

וְהוּא רַחוּם יְכַפֵּר עָוֹן וְלֹא יַשְׁחִית, וְהִרְבָּה לְהָשִׁיב אַפּוֹ, וְלֹא יָעִיר כָּל חֲמָתוֹ.

אַתָּה, יְיָ, לֹא תִכְלָא רַחֲמֶיךָ מִמֶּנּוּ, חַסְדְּךָ וַאֲמִתְּךָ תָּמִיד יִצְּרוּנוּ.

(Begin Tahanun here while seated on Sunday, Tuesday, Wednesday & Friday for Shaharit and daily for Minhah. Rest one's head on an arm not wearing tefillan if in the presence of a Torah scroll until the end of Psalm 6)

וַיֹּאמֶר דָּוִד אֶל גָּד, צַר לִי מְאֹד, נִפְּלָה נָּא בְיַד יְיָ, כִּי רַבִּים רַחֲמָיו, וּבְיַד אָדָם אַל אֶפֹּלָה.

Psalm 6:2-11

יְיָ אַל־בְּאַפְּךָ תוֹכִיחֵנִי וְאַל־בַּחֲמָתְךָ תְיַסְּרֵנִי. חָנֵּנִי יְיָ כִּי אֻמְלַל אָנִי רְפָאֵנִי יְיָ כִּי נִבְהֲלוּ עֲצָמָי. וְנַפְשִׁי נִבְהֲלָה מְאֹד וְאַתָּה יְיָ עַד־מָתָי. שׁוּבָה יְיָ חַלְּצָה נַפְשִׁי הוֹשִׁיעֵנִי לְמַעַן חַסְדֶּךָ. כִּי אֵין בַּמָּוֶת זִכְרֶךָ בִּשְׁאוֹל מִי יוֹדֶה־לָּךְ. יָגַעְתִּי בְּאַנְחָתִי אַשְׂחֶה בְכָל־לַיְלָה מִטָּתִי בְּדִמְעָתִי עַרְשִׂי אַמְסֶה. עָשְׁשָׁה מִכַּעַס עֵינִי עָתְקָה בְּכָל־צוֹרְרָי. סוּרוּ מִמֶּנִּי כָּל־פֹּעֲלֵי אָוֶן כִּי־שָׁמַע יְיָ קוֹל בִּכְיִי. שָׁמַע יְיָ תְּחִנָּתִי יְיָ תְּפִלָּתִי יִקָּח. יֵבֹשׁוּ וְיִבָּהֲלוּ מְאֹד כָּל־אֹיְבָי יָשֻׁבוּ יֵבֹשׁוּ רָגַע.

1 John 1:8-9

אִם־נֹאמַר כִּי אֵין־בָּנוּ עָוֹן מַתְעִים אֲנַחְנוּ אֶת־נַפְשֹׁתֵינוּ וְהָאֱמֶת אֵין בָּנוּ.

וְאִם־נִתְוַדֶּה אֶת־חַטֹּאתֵינוּ נֶאֱמָן הוּא וְצַדִּיק לִסְלֹחַ לָנוּ אֶת־חַטֹּאתֵינוּ וּלְטַהֲרֵנוּ מִכָּל־עָוֹן.

שומר ישראל

שׁוֹמֵר יִשְׂרָאֵל, שְׁמוֹר שְׁאֵרִית יִשְׂרָאֵל,

וְאַל יֹאבַד יִשְׂרָאֵל, הָאוֹמְרִים שְׁמַע יִשְׂרָאֵל.

שׁוֹמֵר גּוֹי אֶחָד, שְׁמוֹר שְׁאֵרִית עַם אֶחָד,

וְאַל יֹאבַד גּוֹי אֶחָד, הַמְיַחֲדִים שִׁמְךָ יְיָ אֱלֹהֵינוּ יְיָ אֶחָד.

שׁוֹמֵר גּוֹי קָדוֹשׁ, שְׁמוֹר שְׁאֵרִית עַם קָדוֹשׁ,

וְאַל יֹאבַד גּוֹי קָדוֹשׁ, הַמְשַׁלְּשִׁים בְּשָׁלֹשׁ קְדֻשּׁוֹת לְקָדוֹשׁ.

מִתְרַצֶּה בְרַחֲמִים וּמִתְפַּיֵּס בְּתַחֲנוּנִים, הִתְרַצֵּה וְהִתְפַּיֵּס לְדוֹר עָנִי, כִּי אֵין עוֹזֵר.

אָבִינוּ מַלְכֵּנוּ, חָנֵּנוּ וַעֲנֵנוּ, כִּי אֵין בָּנוּ מַעֲשִׂים,

עֲשֵׂה עִמָּנוּ צְדָקָה וָחֶסֶד וְהוֹשִׁיעֵנוּ.

Romans 8:1-2

לָכֵן אֵין עַכְשָׁו שׁוּם הַרְשָׁעָה עַל אֵלֶּה שֶׁנִּמְצָאִים בַּמָּשִׁיחַ יֵשׁוּעַ, כִּי חֹק רוּחַ הַחַיִּים שֶׁבַּמָּשִׁיחַ יֵשׁוּעַ שִׁחְרֵר אוֹתִי מֵחֹק הַחֵטְא וְהַמָּוֶת.

(For Shaharit and Minhah turn to page 106 for Aleinu. On Mondays and Thurdays during Shaharit turn to page 92 for the reading of the Torah)

Taḥanun

(Taḥanun is recited after the weekday Amidah for Shaḥarit and Minḥah. Consult a Rabbi or a Madrikh for occasions and days when Taḥunun is omitted)
(Begin Taḥanun here while standing on Monday and Thursday for Shaḥarit only, then continue below)

He is merciful, forgives iniquity, and does not destroy. Frequently He turns back His anger, and does not stir up all His wrath. You, Lord, will not hold back Your mercy from us, and Your truth will always protect us.

(Begin Taḥanun here while seated on Sunday, Tuesday, Wednesday & Friday for Shaḥarit and daily for Minḥah. Rest one's head on an arm not wearing tefillan if in the presence of a Torah scroll until the end of Psalm 6)

And David said to Gad, I am extremely distressed. Let us fall into the hand of the Lord for He is abundantly merciful, but let me not fall into the hand of man.

Psalm 6:2-11

Have mercy upon me, O Lord; for I am wasted away. O Lord, heal me; for my bones are troubled. My soul also is sorely troubled. And You, O Lord, how long? Return, O Lord, deliver my soul. Save me for Your lovingkindness' sake. For in death there is no remembrance of You. In Sheol who will give You thanks? I am weary with my groaning. Every night I make my bed to swim and I water my couch with my tears. My eye wastes away because of grief and my life waxes old because of all my enemies. Depart from me, all you workers of iniquity, for the Lord has heard the voice of my crying. The Lord has heard my supplication, the Lord has received my prayer. All my enemies shall be put to shame and severely trouble. They shall be turned back; they shall be put to shame suddenly.

1 John 1:8-9

If we say we have no sin in us, we are deceiving ourselves and the truth is not in us. But, if we confess our sins He is faithful and just to forgive us our sins and to make us pure from all our iniquities.

Shomeir Yisraeil

O Guardian of Israel, protect the remnant of Israel, let not Israel be destroyed. Let them proclaim: Hear O Israel!

O Guardian of the Unique Nation, protect the remnant of the unique people. Let not the unique nation be destroyed. Let them proclaim the oneness of Your name: The Lord is our God, the Lord is One!

O Guardian of the Holy Nation, protect the remnant of the holy people. Let not the holy nation be destroyed. Let them proclaim: A Threefold Nature of Holiness is the Holy One!

You are merciful and compassionate and You hear our prayers. Our Father, our King, be gracious and answer us, though there is nothing of merit in us, deal with us in justice and in loving kindness, and save us.

Romans 8:1-2

There is therefore now no condemnation to those who are in Messiah Yeshua who do not walk by their flesh but by the Spirit. For the law of the Spirit of life in Messiah Yeshua has made me free from the law of sin and of death.

(For Shaharit and Minhah turn to page 107 for Aleinu. On Mondays and Thurdays during Shaharit turn to page 93 for the reading of the Torah)

עֲמִידָה לְיוֹם טוֹב

(All rise and face east or toward an open ark - take three steps back, then three steps forward)

Minhah only – כִּי שֵׁם יְיָ אֶקְרָא, הָבוּ גֹדֶל לֵאלֹהֵינוּ.

אֲדֹנָי שְׂפָתַי תִּפְתָּח וּפִי יַגִּיד תְּהִלָּתֶךָ:

Minhah only - *Ki sheim Adonai ekra, havu godel lelohenu.*
Adonai s'fatai tiftah u'fi yagid tehila'tekhah.

אָבוֹת

(Bend the knees at בָּרוּךְ *Bow at* אַתָּה *Straighten at* יְיָ*)*

בָּרוּךְ אַתָּה יְיָ אֱלֹהֵינוּ וֵאלֹהֵי אֲבוֹתֵינוּ, אֱלֹהֵי אַבְרָהָם, אֱלֹהֵי יִצְחָק, וֵאלֹהֵי יַעֲקֹב, הָאֵל הַגָּדוֹל הַגִּבּוֹר וְהַנּוֹרָא, אֵל עֶלְיוֹן, גּוֹמֵל חֲסָדִים טוֹבִים, וְקוֹנֵה הַכֹּל, וְזוֹכֵר חַסְדֵי אָבוֹת אֲשֶׁר הֵבִי, וּמֵבִיא, גּוֹאֵל לִבְנֵי בְנֵיהֶם לְמַעַן שְׁמוֹ בְּאַהֲבָה.

Barukh atah Adonai, Eloheinu velohei avoteinu: Elohei Avraham, Elohei Yitzhak,
v'Elohei Ya'akov. Ha'Eil hagadol hagibor v'hanorah, Eil Elyon, Gomeil hasadim tovim,
v'koneih hakol, v'zokheir has'deih avot, asher hevi, u'meivi, Go'eil liv'nei v'neihem,
l'ma-an sh'mo, b'ahavah.

(From Rosh Hashanah to Yom Kippur add)

זָכְרֵנוּ לְחַיִּים בְּיֵשׁוּעַ, מֶלֶךְ חָפֵץ בַּחַיִּים, וְכָתְבֵנוּ בְּסֵפֶר הַחַיִּים, לְמַעַנְךָ אֱלֹהִים חַיִּים.
Zokh'reinu l'haim be-Yeshua, Melekh hafetz bahayim, v'khot'veinu b'sefer hahayim,
l'ma'ankha Elohim hayim.

(Bend the knees at בָּרוּךְ *Bow at* אַתָּה *Straighten at* יְיָ*)*

מֶלֶךְ עוֹזֵר וּמוֹשִׁיעַ וּמָגֵן. בָּרוּךְ אַתָּה יְיָ, מָגֵן אַבְרָהָם.
Melekh ozer umoshia umagein. Barukh atah Adonai, magein Avraham.

גְּבוּרוֹת

אַתָּה גִּבּוֹר לְעוֹלָם אֲדֹנָי, מְחַיֵּה מֵתִים אַתָּה, רַב לְהוֹשִׁיעַ.
Atah gibor l'olam, Adonai, m'hayei meitim atah, rav l'hoshia.

(On the morning of Shemini Atseret add תְּפִלַּת גֶּשֶׁם *on page 186.*
Between Shemini Atseret and Pesah add)

Mashiv haruah u'morid ha-geshem. מַשִּׁיב הָרוּחַ וּמוֹרִיד הַגֶּשֶׁם.

מְכַלְכֵּל חַיִּים בְּחֶסֶד, מְחַיֵּה מֵתִים בְּרַחֲמִים רַבִּים, סוֹמֵךְ נוֹפְלִים, וְרוֹפֵא חוֹלִים, וּמַתִּיר אֲסוּרִים, וּמְקַיֵּם אֱמוּנָתוֹ לִישֵׁנֵי עָפָר, מִי כָמוֹךָ בַּעַל גְּבוּרוֹת וּמִי דוֹמֶה לָךְ, מֶלֶךְ מֵמִית וּמְחַיֶּה וּמַצְמִיחַ יְשׁוּעָה.

M'khalkeil hayim b'hesed, M'hayai meitim b'rahamim rabim. Someih nof'lim, v'rofeh
holim, umatir asurim, um'kayeim emunatoh l'sheinei afar. Mi khamokha ba'al g'vurot,
umi domeh lakh, Melekh meimit um'hayeh u'matsmiah yeshua.

(From Rosh Hashanah to Yom Kippur add)

מִי כָמוֹךָ אַב הָרַחֲמִים, זוֹכֵר יְצוּרָיו לְחַיִּים בְּרַחֲמִים.
Mi khamokha av harahamim zokher yetzurav l'haim b'rachamim.

וְנֶאֱמָן אַתָּה לְהַחֲיוֹת מֵתִים. בָּרוּךְ אַתָּה יְיָ, מְחַיֵּה הַמֵּתִים.
V'ne'eman atah l'hahayot meitim. Barukh atah Adonai, m'hayei hameitim.

Amidah L'Yom Tov

(All rise and face east or toward an open ark - take three steps back, then three steps forward)

Minhah only - When I proclaim the Name of Adonai, give glory to our God!
Lord, you will open my lips that my mouth may declare Your praise.

Avot

*Bend the knees at **Blessed**, Bow at **Are You**, Straighten at **Lord**)*

Blessed are You, Lord our God and God of our fathers, God of Abraham, God of Isaac and God of Jacob, the great, mighty and awesome God, Most High God, who grants loving kindness and is Master of all. You remember the deeds of our fathers, and in Your love You have brought, and you bring, a Redeemer to their children's children for the sake of Your Name.

(From Rosh Hashanah to Yom Kippur add)
Remember us to life in Yeshua, O King who takes delight in life. Inscribe us in the book of life, for Your sake, O God of life.

*(Bend the knees at **Blessed**, Bow at **Are You**, Straighten at **Lord**)*

King, Supporter, Savior and Shield, blessed are You, Lord, Shield of Abraham.

Gevurot

Lord, You are mighty forever. You call the dead to life. You are mighty to save.

*(On the morning of Shemini Atseret add **Prayer for Rain** page 187.
Between Shemini Atseret and Pesah add)*
You cause the wind to return and the rain to come down.

You sustain the living with loving kindness, and with great mercy You revive the dead. You uphold those who fall, heal the sick, set the captive free and keep faith with those who sleep in the dust. Lord of might, who is like You? King, who can be compared to You? You decree death and restore life, causing salvation to come forth.

(From Rosh Hashanah to Yom Kippur add)
Compassionate Father, who is like You, remembering with mercy
your creatures for life?

You are faithful to revive the dead. Blessed are You, Lord, who calls the dead to life.

(During the silent Amidah continue with אַתָּה קָדוֹש *at the bottom of the page.*
During the Reader's repetition continue here.
For Minhah Kedushah turn to page 170)

קְדוּשָׁה

(Rise on your toes at קָדוֹש, קָדוֹש, קָדוֹש *,* בָּרוּךְ *and* יִמְלֹךְ*)*

(All) נְקַדֵּש אֶת שִׁמְךָ בָּעוֹלָם, כְּשֵׁם שֶׁמַּקְדִּישִׁים אוֹתוֹ בִּשְׁמֵי מָרוֹם, כַּכָּתוּב עַל יַד נְבִיאֶךָ, וְקָרָא זֶה אֶל זֶה וְאָמַר:

N'kadeish et shim'kha ba'olam, k'shem shemak'dishim otoh bish'mei marom,
kakatuv al yad nevi'echa, v'karah ze el ze v'amar:

קָדוֹש, קָדוֹש, קָדוֹש, יְיָ צְבָאוֹת, מְלֹא כָל הָאָרֶץ כְּבוֹדוֹ.

Kadosh, kadosh, kadosh, Adonai ts'vaot, m'lo khol ha'arets k'vohdoh.

(Reader) אָז בְּקוֹל רַעַשׁ גָּדוֹל אַדִּיר וְחָזָק מַשְׁמִיעִים קוֹל, מִתְנַשְּׂאִים לְעֻמַּת שְׂרָפִים, לְעֻמָּתָם בָּרוּךְ יֹאמֵרוּ.

(All) *Barukh k'vod Adonai mim'komo* בָּרוּךְ כְּבוֹד יְיָ, מִמְּקוֹמוֹ.

(Reader) מִמְּקוֹמְךָ מַלְכֵּנוּ תוֹפִיעַ, וְתִמְלֹךְ עָלֵינוּ, כִּי מְחַכִּים אֲנַחְנוּ לָךְ. מָתַי תִּמְלֹךְ בְּצִיּוֹן, בְּקָרוֹב בְּיָמֵינוּ, לְעוֹלָם וָעֶד תִּשְׁכּוֹן. תִּתְגַּדַּל וְתִתְקַדַּשׁ בְּתוֹךְ יְרוּשָׁלַיִם עִירְךָ, לְדוֹר וָדוֹר וּלְנֵצַח נְצָחִים. וְעֵינֵינוּ תִרְאֶינָה מַלְכוּתֶךָ, כַּדָּבָר הָאָמוּר בְּשִׁירֵי עֻזֶּךָ, עַל יְדֵי דָוִד מְשִׁיחַ צִדְקֶךָ,

(All) יִמְלֹךְ יְיָ לְעוֹלָם, אֱלֹהַיִךְ צִיּוֹן לְדֹר וָדֹר, הַלְלוּיָהּ.

Yim'lokh Adonai l'olam elohayikhTsiyon, l'dor vador, halleluyah

(Reader) לְדוֹר וָדוֹר נַגִּיד גָּדְלֶךָ וּלְנֵצַח נְצָחִים קְדֻשָּׁתְךָ נַקְדִּישׁ, וְשִׁבְחֲךָ אֱלֹהֵינוּ מִפִּינוּ לֹא יָמוּשׁ לְעוֹלָם וָעֶד, כִּי אֵל מֶלֶךְ גָּדוֹל וְקָדוֹשׁ אָתָּה.

*בָּרוּךְ אַתָּה יְיָ, הָאֵל הַקָּדוֹשׁ.

(From Rosh Hashanah to Yom Kippur substitute)

*בָּרוּךְ אַתָּה יְיָ. הַמֶּלֶךְ הַקָּדוֹשׁ

(Recitation of the silent Amidah continues here)

אַתָּה קָדוֹשׁ וְשִׁמְךָ קָדוֹשׁ, וּקְדוֹשִׁים בְּכָל יוֹם יְהַלְלוּךָ, סֶּלָה.

*בָּרוּךְ אַתָּה יְיָ, הָאֵל הַקָּדוֹשׁ.

*(During the silent Amidah continue with **You are Holy** at the bottom of the page.*
During the Reader's repetition begin here.
For Minhah Kedusahah turn to page 171)

Kedushah

*(Rise on your toes at "**Holy, holy, holy**" , "**Blessed**" and "**The Lord will reign**)*

(All) We will sanctify Your Name in this world, even as they sanctify it in the heavens above, as it is written by Your prophet: They continuously call to one another

Holy, holy, holy is the Lord of Hosts; the whole earth is filled with His glory.

(Reader) Then with a loud sound, mighty and strong, they make their voices heard, raising themselves toward the Seraphim, they respond by saying:

(All) Blessed. . . Blessed is the glory of the Lord from His abode.

(Reader) Our King, You will come forth from Your abode and you will reign over us, for we wait for You. When will You reign in Tsiyon? Quickly, indeed, in our days, dwell there forever. May Your greatness and Your holiness be seen in Your city, Jerusalem, through all generations and to all eternity. May our eyes behold your Kingdom, as it is said by your righteous anointed one David, in Your songs of glory,

(All) The Lord will reign forever; your God, O Tsiyon, from generation to generation. Halleluyah!

(Reader) We will declare Your greatness from generation to generation. We will proclaim Your holiness to all eternity. Your praise, our God, will never depart from our mouth, for You, God, are a great and mighty King.

*Blessed are You, Lord, the holy God.

(From Rosh Hashana to Yom Kippur substitute)
*Blessed are You, Lord, the Holy King.

(Recitation of the silent Amidah continues here)

You are holy, and Your Name is holy, and holy ones proclaim Your praise daily.

*Blessed are You, Lord, the holy God.

(During the silent Amidah continue with אַתָּה קָדוֹשׁ *at the bottom of the page.*
During the Reader's repetition continue here)

קדושה למנחה

(Rise on your toes at בָּרוּךְ , קָדוֹשׁ. קָדוֹשׁ. קָדוֹשׁ *and* יִמְלֹךְ*)*

(All) נְקַדֵּשׁ אֶת שִׁמְךָ בָּעוֹלָם, כְּשֵׁם שֶׁמַּקְדִּישִׁים אוֹתוֹ בִּשְׁמֵי מָרוֹם, כַּכָּתוּב
עַל יַד נְבִיאֶךָ, וְקָרָא זֶה אֶל זֶה וְאָמַר:

N'kadeish et shim'kha ba'olam, k'shem shemak'dishim otoh bish'mei marom,
kakatuv al yad nevi'echa, v'karah ze el ze v'amar:

קָדוֹשׁ, קָדוֹשׁ, קָדוֹשׁ, יְיָ צְבָאוֹת, מְלֹא כָל הָאָרֶץ כְּבוֹדוֹ.

Kadosh, kadosh, kadosh, Adonai ts'vaot, m'lo khol haarets k'vohdoh.

(Reader) לְעֻמָּתָם בָּרוּךְ יֹאמֵרוּ.

(All) בָּרוּךְ כְּבוֹד יְיָ, מִמְּקוֹמוֹ.   *Barukh k'vod Adonai mim'komo*

(Reader) וּבְדִבְרֵי קָדְשְׁךָ כָּתוּב לֵאמֹר:

(All) יִמְלֹךְ יְיָ לְעוֹלָם, אֱלֹהַיִךְ צִיּוֹן לְדֹר וָדֹר, הַלְלוּיָהּ.
Yim'lokh Adonai l'olam elohayikhTsiyon, l'dor vador, halleluyah

(Reader) לְדוֹר וָדוֹר נַגִּיד גָּדְלֶךָ וּלְנֵצַח נְצָחִים קְדֻשָּׁתְךָ נַקְדִּישׁ, וְשִׁבְחֲךָ
אֱלֹהֵינוּ מִפִּינוּ לֹא יָמוּשׁ לְעוֹלָם וָעֶד, כִּי אֵל מֶלֶךְ גָּדוֹל וְקָדוֹשׁ אָתָּה.
*בָּרוּךְ אַתָּה יְיָ, הָאֵל הַקָּדוֹשׁ.

(From Rosh Hashanah to Yom Kippur substitute)
*בָּרוּךְ אַתָּה יְיָ. הַמֶּלֶךְ הַקָּדוֹשׁ

(Recitation of the silent Amidah continues here)

אַתָּה קָדוֹשׁ וְשִׁמְךָ קָדוֹשׁ, וּקְדוֹשִׁים בְּכָל יוֹם יְהַלְלוּךָ, סֶּלָה.

*בָּרוּךְ אַתָּה יְיָ, הָאֵל הַקָּדוֹשׁ.

*(During the silent Amidah continue with **You are Holy** at the bottom of the page.
During the Reader's repetition begin here)*

Kedushah L'Minḥah

*(Rise on your toes at "**Holy, holy, holy**", "**Blessed**" and "**The Lord will reign**)*

(All) We will sanctify Your Name in this world, even as they sanctify it in the heavens above, as it is written by Your prophet: They continuously call to one another

Holy, holy, holy is the Lord of Hosts; the whole earth is filled with His glory.

(Reader) They respond by saying:

(All) Blessed. . . Blessed is the glory of the Lord from His abode.

(Reader) And in your holy Scriptures is written...

(All) The Lord will reign forever; your God, O Tsiyon, from generation to generation. Halleluyah!

(Reader) We will declare Your greatness from generation to generation. We will proclaim Your holiness to all eternity. Your praise, our God, will never depart from our mouth, for You, God, are a great and mighty King.

*Blessed are You, Lord, the holy God.

(From Rosh Hashana to Yom Kippur substitute)
***Blessed are You, Lord, the Holy King.**

(Recitation of the silent Amidah continues here)

You are holy, and Your Name is holy, and holy ones proclaim Your praise daily.

*Blessed are You, Lord, the holy God.

לשלש רגלים

(On Shabbat start with וישמרו *and add the words in parentheses)*

וישמרו

(וְשָׁמְרוּ בְנֵי יִשְׂרָאֵל אֶת הַשַּׁבָּת, לַעֲשׂוֹת אֶת הַשַּׁבָּת לְדֹרֹתָם בְּרִית עוֹלָם. בֵּינִי וּבֵין בְּנֵי יִשְׂרָאֵל אוֹת הִיא לְעֹלָם, כִּי שֵׁשֶׁת יָמִים עָשָׂה יְיָ אֶת הַשָּׁמַיִם וְאֶת הָאָרֶץ, וּבַיוֹם הַשְּׁבִיעִי שָׁבַת וַיִּנָּפַשׁ.

V'shamru v'nei Yisraeil et ha'shabbat, la'asot et ha'shabbat l'dorotam b'rit olam. Beini u'vein b'nei Yisraeil ot hi l'olam, ki sheshet yamim asah Adonai et hashamayim v'et ha'arets, uvayom hash'vi'i shavat vayinafash.

עַם מְקַדְשֵׁי שְׁבִיעִי, כֻּלָּם יִשְׂבְּעוּ וְיִתְעַנְגוּ מִטּוּבֶךָ, וּבַשְּׁבִיעִי רָצִיתָ בּוֹ וְקִדַּשְׁתּוֹ, חֶמְדַּת יָמִים אוֹתוֹ קָרָאתָ, זֵכֶר לְמַעֲשֵׂה בְרֵאשִׁית.)

(On weekdays begin here and omit words in parentheses)

וַתִּתֶּן לָנוּ יְיָ אֱלֹהֵינוּ בְּאַהֲבָה (שַׁבָּתוֹת לִמְנוּחָה וּ) מוֹעֲדִים לְשִׂמְחָה, חַגִּים וּזְמַנִּים לְשָׂשׂוֹן, אֶת יוֹם (הַשַּׁבָּת הַזֶּה וְאֶת יוֹם)

חַג הַמַּצּוֹת הַזֶּה, זְמַן חֵרוּתֵנוּ	לְפֶסַח:
חַג הַשָּׁבֻעוֹת הַזֶּה, זְמַן מַתַּן תּוֹרָתֵנוּ	לְשָׁבֻעוֹת:
חַג הַסֻּכּוֹת הַזֶּה, זְמַן שִׂמְחָתֵנוּ	לְסֻכּוֹת:
הַשְּׁמִינִי חַג הָעֲצֶרֶת הַזֶּה, זְמַן שִׂמְחָתֵנוּ	לִשְׁמִינִי עֲצֶרֶת:

(בְּאַהֲבָה) מִקְרָא קֹדֶשׁ, זֵכֶר לִיצִיאַת מִצְרָיִם.

אֱלֹהֵינוּ וֵאלֹהֵי אֲבוֹתֵינוּ, יַעֲלֶה וְיָבֹא, וְיַגִּיעַ, וְיֵרָאֶה, וְיֵרָצֶה, וְיִשָּׁמַע, וְיִפָּקֵד, וְיִזָּכֵר זִכְרוֹנֵנוּ וּפִקְדוֹנֵנוּ, וְזִכְרוֹן אֲבוֹתֵינוּ, וְזִכְרוֹן מָשִׁיחַ יֵשׁוּעַ בֶּן דָּוִד עַבְדֶּךָ, וְזִכְרוֹן יְרוּשָׁלַיִם עִיר קָדְשֶׁךָ, וְזִכְרוֹן כָּל עַמְּךָ בֵּית יִשְׂרָאֵל לְפָנֶיךָ, לִפְלֵיטָה, לְטוֹבָה, לְחֵן וּלְחֶסֶד וּלְרַחֲמִים, לְחַיִּים וּלְשָׁלוֹם, בְּיוֹם

חַג הַמַּצּוֹת הַזֶּה.	לְפֶסַח:
חַג הַשָּׁבוּעוֹת הַזֶּה.	לְשָׁבֻעוֹת:
חַג הַסֻּכּוֹת הַזֶּה.	לְסֻכּוֹת:
הַשְּׁמִינִי חַג הָעֲצֶרֶת הַזֶּה.	לִשְׁמִינִי עֲצֶרֶת:

זָכְרֵנוּ, יְיָ אֱלֹהֵינוּ, בּוֹ לְטוֹבָה, וּפָקְדֵנוּ בוֹ לִבְרָכָה, וְהוֹשִׁיעֵנוּ בוֹ לְחַיִּים. וּבִדְבַר יְשׁוּעָה וְרַחֲמִים, חוּס וְחָנֵּנוּ, וְרַחֵם עָלֵינוּ וְהוֹשִׁיעֵנוּ, כִּי אֵלֶיךָ עֵינֵינוּ, כִּי אֵל מֶלֶךְ חַנּוּן וְרַחוּם אָתָּה.

רצה

רְצֵה, יְיָ אֱלֹהֵינוּ, בְּעַמְּךָ יִשְׂרָאֵל וּבִתְפִלָּתָם, וְהָשֵׁב אֶת הָעֲבוֹדָה לִדְבִיר בֵּיתֶךָ, וְאִשֵּׁי יִשְׂרָאֵל וּתְפִלָּתָם בְּאַהֲבָה תְקַבֵּל בְּרָצוֹן, וּתְהִי לְרָצוֹן תָּמִיד עֲבוֹדַת יִשְׂרָאֵל עַמֶּךָ.

וְתֶחֱזֶינָה עֵינֵינוּ בְּשׁוּבְךָ לְצִיּוֹן בְּרַחֲמִים. בָּרוּךְ אַתָּה יְיָ, הַמַּחֲזִיר שְׁכִינָתוֹ לְצִיּוֹן.

L'Shalosh Regalim

*(On Shabbat start with **V'Shamru** and add the words in parentheses)*

V'shamru

(And the children of Israel will keep the Shabbat, observing the Shabbat to all generations as an everlasting covenant. It shall be a sign between Me and the children of Israel forever, for in six days the Lord made the heavens and the earth, and on the seventh day He ceased from work and He rested.

The people who set apart the seventh day shall all be satisfied and will delight in Your goodness. You took pleasure in the seventh day and made it holy, proclaiming it the most desirable of days; a remembrance of the beginning.)

(On weekdays begin here and omit words in parentheses)

And You, Lord our God, have given us (Shabbats for rest,) holidays for gladness and festival seasons for joy, (this Shabbat day and) this:

On Pesaḥ add: Festival of Matsah, our Festival of Freedom,
On Shavuot add: Festival of Shavuot, our Festival of the Gift, of the Torah,
On Sukkot add: Festival of Sukkot, our Festival of Rejoicing,
On Shemini Atseret add: Festival of Shemini Atseret, our Festival of Joy,

(in love), a holy assembly in remembrance of the exodus from Egypt.

Our God, and God of our fathers, arise, and bring, and labor, and see, and want, and hear, and count, and remember our remembrance and our charge, and the remembrance of our fathers, and the remembrance of Messiah Yeshua, the son of David, Your Servant, and the remembrance of Jerusalem, Your holy city, and the remembrance of all Your people, the House of Israel, who are before You, for refuge, for goodness, for grace, and for loving kindness, and for compassion, for life, and for peace in the day of:

On Pesaḥ add: this Festival of Matsah.
On Shavuot add: this Festival of Shavuot.
On Sukkot add: this Festival of Sukkot.
On Shemini Atseret add: this Festival of Shemini Atseret.

Remember us, Lord our God, in Him, for goodness; and command us, in Him, for blessing; and save us, in Him, unto life; and speak salvation and compassion, sparing and being gracious to us, and have compassion upon us and save us, for to You do we look. For You, God, reign with grace and with compassion.

Retsei

Lord our God, favor Your people Israel, and their prayer, and bring about the restoration of their service to the Most Holy Place in Your house; as well as the offerings of Israel. And, receive their prayer in love and favor, and may it be so always concerning the service of Israel, Your people.

And may we see, with our own eyes, Your return to Tsiyon in compassion. Blessed are You Lord, whose Presence is the restoration of Tsiyon.

מוֹדִים אֲנַחְנוּ

(While the Reader recites out loud מוֹדִים דְּרַבָּנָן, *the Congregation recites* מוֹדִים אֲנַחְנוּ *softly.*
Bend the knees at מוֹדִים אֲנַחְנוּ *and straighten at* יְיָ)

מוֹדִים אֲנַחְנוּ לָךְ, שָׁאַתָּה הוּא, יְיָ
אֱלֹהֵינוּ וֵאלֹהֵי אֲבוֹתֵינוּ, לְעוֹלָם וָעֶד,
צוּר חַיֵּינוּ, מָגֵן יִשְׁעֵנוּ, אַתָּה הוּא
לְדוֹר וָדוֹר, נוֹדֶה לְךָ וּנְסַפֵּר
תְּהִלָּתֶךָ, עַל חַיֵּינוּ הַמְּסוּרִים בְּיָדֶךָ,
וְעַל נִשְׁמוֹתֵינוּ הַפְּקוּדוֹת לָךְ, וְעַל
נִסֶּיךָ שֶׁבְּכָל יוֹם עִמָּנוּ, וְעַל
נִפְלְאוֹתֶיךָ וְטוֹבוֹתֶיךָ שֶׁבְּכָל עֵת,
עֶרֶב וָבֹקֶר וְצָהֳרָיִם, הַטּוֹב, כִּי לֹא
כָלוּ רַחֲמֶיךָ, וְהַמְרַחֵם, כִּי לֹא תַמּוּ
חֲסָדֶיךָ, מֵעוֹלָם קִוִּינוּ לָךְ.

מוֹדִים דְּרַבָּנָן

מוֹדִים אֲנַחְנוּ לָךְ, שָׁאַתָּה הוּא יְיָ
אֱלֹהֵינוּ וֵאלֹהֵי אֲבוֹתֵינוּ, אֱלֹהֵי כָל
בָּשָׂר, יוֹצְרֵנוּ, יוֹצֵר בְּרֵאשִׁית.
בְּרָכוֹת וְהוֹדָאוֹת לְשִׁמְךָ הַגָּדוֹל
וְהַקָּדוֹשׁ, עַל שֶׁהֶחֱיִיתָנוּ וְקִיַּמְתָּנוּ.
כֵּן תְּחַיֵּינוּ וּתְקַיְּמֵנוּ, וְתֶאֱסוֹף
גָּלֻיּוֹתֵינוּ לְחַצְרוֹת קָדְשֶׁךָ, לִשְׁמוֹר
חֻקֶּיךָ וְלַעֲשׂוֹת רְצוֹנֶךָ, וּלְעָבְדְּךָ
בְּלֵבָב שָׁלֵם, עַל שֶׁאֲנַחְנוּ מוֹדִים
לָךְ. בָּרוּךְ אֵל הַהוֹדָאוֹת.

לַחֲנֻכָּה וּפוּרִים:

עַל הַנִּסִּים, וְעַל הַפֻּרְקָן, וְעַל הַגְּבוּרוֹת, וְעַל הַתְּשׁוּעוֹת, וְעַל הַמִּלְחָמוֹת, שֶׁעָשִׂיתָ לַאֲבוֹתֵינוּ בַּיָּמִים
הָהֵם בַּזְּמַן הַזֶּה.
Al hanisim v'al hafurkan, v'al hag'vurot, v'al hat'shu-ot, v'al hamil'hamot
sheh-asitah la-avoteinu bayameem hahem baz'man hazeh

לַחֲנֻכָּה:

בִּימֵי מַתִּתְיָהוּ בֶּן יוֹחָנָן כֹּהֵן גָּדוֹל, חַשְׁמוֹנַאי וּבָנָיו, כְּשֶׁעָמְדָה מַלְכוּת יָוָן הָרְשָׁעָה עַל עַמְּךָ יִשְׂרָאֵל
לְהַשְׁכִּיחָם תּוֹרָתֶךָ, וּלְהַעֲבִירָם מֵחֻקֵּי רְצוֹנֶךָ, וְאַתָּה בְּרַחֲמֶיךָ הָרַבִּים עָמַדְתָּ לָהֶם בְּעֵת צָרָתָם, רַבְתָּ
אֶת רִיבָם, דַּנְתָּ אֶת דִּינָם, נָקַמְתָּ אֶת נִקְמָתָם, מָסַרְתָּ גִבּוֹרִים בְּיַד חַלָּשִׁים, וְרַבִּים בְּיַד מְעַטִּים,
וּטְמֵאִים בְּיַד טְהוֹרִים, וּרְשָׁעִים בְּיַד צַדִּיקִים, וְזֵדִים בְּיַד עוֹסְקֵי תוֹרָתֶךָ. וּלְךָ עָשִׂיתָ שֵׁם גָּדוֹל וְקָדוֹשׁ
בְּעוֹלָמֶךָ, וּלְעַמְּךָ יִשְׂרָאֵל עָשִׂיתָ תְּשׁוּעָה גְדוֹלָה וּפֻרְקָן כְּהַיּוֹם הַזֶּה. וְאַחַר כֵּן בָּאוּ בָנֶיךָ לִדְבִיר
בֵּיתֶךָ, וּפִנּוּ אֶת הֵיכָלֶךָ, וְטִהֲרוּ אֶת מִקְדָּשֶׁךָ, וְהִדְלִיקוּ נֵרוֹת בְּחַצְרוֹת קָדְשֶׁךָ, וְקָבְעוּ שְׁמוֹנַת יְמֵי
חֲנֻכָּה אֵלּוּ, לְהוֹדוֹת וּלְהַלֵּל לְשִׁמְךָ הַגָּדוֹל.

לְפוּרִים:

בִּימֵי מָרְדְּכַי וְאֶסְתֵּר בְּשׁוּשַׁן הַבִּירָה, כְּשֶׁעָמַד עֲלֵיהֶם הָמָן הָרָשָׁע, בִּקֵּשׁ לְהַשְׁמִיד לַהֲרֹג וּלְאַבֵּד אֶת
כָּל הַיְּהוּדִים, מִנַּעַר וְעַד זָקֵן, טַף וְנָשִׁים, בְּיוֹם אֶחָד, בִּשְׁלוֹשָׁה עָשָׂר לְחֹדֶשׁ שְׁנֵים עָשָׂר, הוּא חֹדֶשׁ
אֲדָר, וּשְׁלָלָם לָבוֹז. וְאַתָּה בְּרַחֲמֶיךָ הָרַבִּים הֵפַרְתָּ אֶת עֲצָתוֹ, וְקִלְקַלְתָּ אֶת מַחֲשַׁבְתּוֹ, וַהֲשֵׁבוֹתָ לּוֹ
גְּמוּלוֹ בְּרֹאשׁוֹ, וְתָלוּ אוֹתוֹ וְאֶת בָּנָיו עַל הָעֵץ.

וְעַל כֻּלָּם יִתְבָּרַךְ וְיִתְרוֹמַם שִׁמְךָ מַלְכֵּנוּ תָּמִיד לְעוֹלָם וָעֶד.

(From Rosh Hashanah to Yom Kippur add)

וּכְתוֹב לְחַיִּים טוֹבִים כָּל בְּנֵי בְרִיתֶךָ.

Modim Anaḥnu

*(While the Reader recites out loud **Modim Anaḥnu**, the Congregation recites **Modim of the Rabbis** softly. Bend the knees at **Lord, we are eternally grateful** and straighten at **Lord**)*

Modim of the Rabbis

Lord, we are eternally grateful that You are the Lord our God and the God of our fathers. God of all flesh, our Creator and Creator in the beginning; blessings and thanks are due Your great and holy Name, for You have kept us alive and You sustained us. May You continue to grant us life and to sustain us. Bring our dispersed to Your courts, that in holiness they would observe Your laws, do Your will and serve You with all their heart; for these things we give You thanks. Blessed is the God of thanksgiving.

Lord, we are eternally grateful that You are the Lord our God and the God of our fathers. You are the strength of our life and the Shield of our Salvation. We thank You from generation to generation, and recount Your praise; for our lives which are in Your hand; and for our souls which are in Your care; and for Your miracles which are seen every day; and for Your wondrous deeds and favors which are always with us evening, morning and noon. Beneficent One, Your compassion never fails; Merciful One, Your loving kindness never ends; You have always been our hope.

(On Hanukah and Purim add)

For the miracles, and for the deliverance, and for the mightinesses, and for the salvations, and for the battles that You have brought to our fathers in this season, in those days...

(On Hanukah add)

In the days of the Hasmonean Matityahu son of Yochanan the High Priest, and his sons, when stood the wicked kingdom of the Hellenists against Your people Israel to cause them to abandon Your Torah and to turn from the statutes of will, You in Your great compassion stood for them in their time of tribulation. You contended for them in their fight, judged for them in their judgment, avenged them in their vengeance, and delivered them by means of heros when they were weak; the many into the hands of the few, the unclean into the hands of the clean, the wicked into the hands of the righteous, and the deceiver into the hands of they who practiced Your Torah. Your great and holy name is established in Your world, and You have established a great salvation for Your people Israel, and have relieved them from that day to this. Indeed, after this Your children came into the Holy Place of Your House, we cleared Your Temple of defilement, and purified Your holy sanctuary, and lit the lights in Your holy court, and established the lighting of the lights in the eight days of Chanukah, to thank and to praise the greatness of Your name.

(On Purim add)

And in the days of Mordecai and Esther, in the capital city of Shushan, when the wicked Hamen stood against them, asking that all the Jews be annihilated, murdered, and destroyed, both young boys and the old, infants and women, and to take their plunder, in one day, on the thirteenth day of the twelfth month, which is Adar. And You, in Your great compassion, annulled this decree, spoiling his purposes, and returning to him recompense upon his head, that both he and his sons would hang upon the tree.

For all these things we will bless and we will lift up Your name, our King, always, to the end of the age, and until.

(From Rosh Hashanah to Yom Kippur add)

Remember for life and good all the Children of your Covenant

וְכֹל הַחַיִּים יוֹדְוּךָ סֶּלָה, וִיהַלְלוּ אֶת שִׁמְךָ בֶּאֱמֶת, הָאֵל יְשׁוּעָתֵנוּ וְעֶזְרָתֵנוּ סֶלָה.

(Bend the knees at בָּרוּךְ *Bow at* אַתָּה *Straighten at* יְיָ*)*

בָּרוּךְ אַתָּה יְיָ, הַטּוֹב שִׁמְךָ וּלְךָ נָאֶה לְהוֹדוֹת.

*(The Reader recites the Aaronic Blessing during his repetition
except in a House of Mourning)*

אֱלֹהֵינוּ וֵאלֹהֵי אֲבוֹתֵינוּ, בָּרְכֵנוּ בַּבְּרָכָה הַמְשֻׁלֶּשֶׁת בַּתּוֹרָה הַכְּתוּבָה עַל יְדֵי מֹשֶׁה עַבְדֶּךָ, הָאֲמוּרָה מִפִּי אַהֲרֹן וּבָנָיו כֹּהֲנִים, עַם קְדוֹשֶׁךָ, כָּאָמוּר.

יְבָרֶכְךָ יְיָ וְיִשְׁמְרֶךָ. ‏(קהל-כֵּן יְהִי רָצוֹן) ***Cong** - Kein yehi ratson*

יָאֵר יְיָ פָּנָיו אֵלֶיךָ וִיחֻנֶּךָּ. ‏(קהל-כֵּן יְהִי רָצוֹן) ***Cong** - Kein yehi ratson*

יִשָּׂא יְיָ פָּנָיו אֵלֶיךָ וְיָשֵׂם לְךָ שָׁלוֹם. ‏(קהל-כֵּן יְהִי רָצוֹן) ***Cong** - Kein yehi ratson*

(During Shaharit Recite)

שִׂים שָׁלוֹם

שִׂים שָׁלוֹם טוֹבָה וּבְרָכָה, חֵן וָחֶסֶד וְרַחֲמִים, עָלֵינוּ וְעַל כָּל יִשְׂרָאֵל עַמֶּךָ. בָּרְכֵנוּ, אָבִינוּ, כֻּלָּנוּ כְּאֶחָד בְּאוֹר פָּנֶיךָ, כִּי בְאוֹר פָּנֶיךָ נָתַתָּ לָּנוּ, יְיָ אֱלֹהֵינוּ, תּוֹרַת חַיִּים וְאַהֲבַת חֶסֶד, וּצְדָקָה וּבְרָכָה וְרַחֲמִים וְחַיִּים וְשָׁלוֹם, וְטוֹב בְּעֵינֶיךָ לְבָרֵךְ אֶת עַמְּךָ יִשְׂרָאֵל בְּכָל עֵת וּבְכָל שָׁעָה בִּשְׁלוֹמֶךָ. *בָּרוּךְ אַתָּה יְיָ, הַמְבָרֵךְ אֶת עַמּוֹ יִשְׂרָאֵל בַּשָּׁלוֹם.

*Sim Shalom tova uv'rakha ḥein vaḥesed veraḥamim aleinu v'al kol Yisraeil amekha.
Barkheinu avinu kulanu ki'eḥad b'or panekha, ki v'or panekha natata lanu, Adonai
Eloheinu, Torat ḥayim v'ahavat ḥesed, uts'dakah uv'rakhah v'raḥamim v'ḥayim
v'shalom, v'tov b'einekhah l'varekh et am'kha Yisraeil b'khol et uv'khol sha'ah
bish'lomekhah.
Barukh atah Adonai, ham'vareikh et amo Yisraeil bashalom.

(From Rosh Hashanah to Yom Kippur substitute)

*בְּסֵפֶר חַיִּים, בְּרָכָה וְשָׁלוֹם, וּפַרְנָסָה טוֹבָה, נִזָּכֵר וְנִכָּתֵב לְפָנֶיךָ, אֲנַחְנוּ וְכָל עַמְּךָ בֵּית יִשְׂרָאֵל, לְחַיִּים טוֹבִים וּלְשָׁלוֹם. בָּרוּךְ אַתָּה יְיָ, עֹשֶׂה הַשָּׁלוֹם.

*B'sefer ḥah-yeem, b'rah-khah, b'shalom, ufar'nasah tovah, nizakher v'nikahtaiv
l'fanekhah, anaḥnu v'khol am'khah beit Yisrael, l'ḥayim tovim ul'shalom. Barukh atah
Adonai, oseh ha'shalom.

And all the living will thank You, and in truth they will praise Your Name; the God of our Salvation and our Help at all times.

*(Bend the knees at **Blessed**, Bow at **Are You,** Straighten at **Lord**)*

Blessed are You, Lord; it is right to give thanks to You for Your Name is good.

(The Reader recites the Aaronic Blessing during his repetition
except in a House of Mourning)

Our God and God of our fathers, bless us with the threefold blessing written in Torah by Moses, Your servant, and spoken through the mouth of Aaron; and his sons, the priests, Your holy people, as it is said:

May the Lord bless you and keep you!
(Congregation: *May it Be Your Will!*)
May the Lord lift up His countenance to you, and be gracious to you!
(Congregation: *May it Be Your Will!*)
May the Lord turn His countenance toward you,
and establish peace for you!
(Congregation: *May it Be Your Will!*)

(During Shaharit Recite)

Sim Shalom

Grant peace, happiness, blessing, grace, kindness and mercy to us and all Israel, Your people. Our Father, bless us all alike with the light of Your countenance. Lord our God, by the light of Your countenance You have given us a Torah of life, loving kindness, charity, blessing, mercy, life and peace. May it be good in Your sight to bless Your people Israel with peace at all times and at every hour.

*Blessed are You, Lord, who is blessing His people Israel with peace.

(From Rosh Hashanah to Yom Kippur substitute)

*Our Father, and the Father of all Israel, remember us, and inscribe us in the Book of Life, for blessing and for peace, and good provision, for good life and for peace. Blessed are You, Lord, who makes peace.

(During Minḥah and Maariv Recite)

שלום רב

שָׁלוֹם רָב עַל יִשְׂרָאֵל עַמְּךָ תָּשִׂים לְעוֹלָם, כִּי אַתָּה הוּא מֶלֶךְ אָדוֹן לְכָל הַשָּׁלוֹם. וְטוֹב בְּעֵינֶיךָ לְבָרֵךְ אֶת עַמְּךָ יִשְׂרָאֵל, בְּכָל עֵת וּבְכָל שָׁעָה בִּשְׁלוֹמֶךָ. *בָּרוּךְ אַתָּה יְיָ, הַמְבָרֵךְ אֶת עַמּוֹ יִשְׂרָאֵל בַּשָּׁלוֹם.

Shalom Rav al Yisraeil am'kha tasim l'olam. Ki atah hu Melekh Adon l'khol hashalom.
V'tov b'einekha l'varekh et am'kha Yisraeil, b'chol eit uv'khol sha'ah bish'lomekha.

**Barukh atah Adonai, hamivarekh et amo Yisraeil ba'shalom.*

(From Rosh Hashanah to Yom Kippur substitute)

*בְּסֵפֶר חַיִּים, בְּרָכָה וְשָׁלוֹם, וּפַרְנָסָה טוֹבָה, נִזָּכֵר וְנִכָּתֵב לְפָנֶיךָ, אֲנַחְנוּ וְכָל עַמְּךָ בֵּית יִשְׂרָאֵל, לְחַיִּים טוֹבִים וּלְשָׁלוֹם. בָּרוּךְ אַתָּה יְיָ, עֹשֵׂה הַשָּׁלוֹם.

**B'sefer ḥah-yeem, b'rah-khah, b'shalom, ufar'nasah tovah, nizakher v'nikahtaiv*
l'fanekhah, anaḥnu v'khol am'khah beit Yisrael, l'ḥayim tovim ul'shalom. Barukh atah
Adonai, oseh ha'shalom.

(Continue all services here)

יִהְיוּ לְרָצוֹן אִמְרֵי פִי וְהֶגְיוֹן לִבִּי לְפָנֶיךָ, יְיָ צוּרִי וְגוֹאֲלִי.

Yih'yu l'ratson im'ri fi veheg'yon libi le'fanekha, Adonai tsuri v'goali.

(The Reader's Repetition of the Amidah ends here. Individuals continue to the bottom of the page)

אֱלֹהַי, נְצוֹר לְשׁוֹנִי מֵרָע. וּשְׂפָתַי מִדַּבֵּר מִרְמָה. וְלִמְקַלְלַי נַפְשִׁי תִדּוֹם, וְנַפְשִׁי כֶּעָפָר לַכֹּל תִּהְיֶה. פְּתַח לִבִּי בְּתוֹרָתֶךָ, וּבְמִצְוֹתֶיךָ תִּרְדּוֹף נַפְשִׁי. וְכָל הַחוֹשְׁבִים עָלַי רָעָה, מְהֵרָה הָפֵר עֲצָתָם וְקַלְקֵל מַחֲשַׁבְתָּם. עֲשֵׂה לְמַעַן שְׁמֶךָ, עֲשֵׂה לְמַעַן יְמִינֶךָ, עֲשֵׂה לְמַעַן קְדֻשָּׁתֶךָ. עֲשֵׂה לְמַעַן תּוֹרָתֶךָ. לְמַעַן יֵחָלְצוּן יְדִידֶיךָ, הוֹשִׁיעָה יְמִינְךָ וַעֲנֵנִי. יִהְיוּ לְרָצוֹן אִמְרֵי פִי וְהֶגְיוֹן לִבִּי לְפָנֶיךָ, יְיָ צוּרִי וְגוֹאֲלִי.

(Take three steps back. Bow first left, then right and finally forward as you recite)

עֹשֶׂה שָׁלוֹם בִּמְרוֹמָיו, הוּא יַעֲשֶׂה שָׁלוֹם עָלֵינוּ, וְעַל כָּל יִשְׂרָאֵל, וְאִמְרוּ, אָמֵן.

Oseh shalom bim'romav Hu ya'aseh shalom aleinu,
v'al kol Yisraeil v'imru, Amen.

יְהִי רָצוֹן מִלְּפָנֶיךָ, יְיָ אֱלֹהֵינוּ וֵאלֹהֵי אֲבוֹתֵינוּ, שֶׁיִּבָּנֶה בֵּית הַמִּקְדָּשׁ בִּמְהֵרָה בְיָמֵינוּ, וְתֵן חֶלְקֵנוּ בְּתוֹרָתֶךָ, וְשָׁם נַעֲבָדְךָ בְּיִרְאָה כִּימֵי עוֹלָם וּכְשָׁנִים קַדְמוֹנִיּוֹת. וְעָרְבָה לַייָ מִנְחַת יְהוּדָה וִירוּשָׁלָיִם, כִּימֵי עוֹלָם וּכְשָׁנִים קַדְמוֹנִיּוֹת.

(At Shaharit continue with Hallel on page 180, followed by the reading of the Torah on page 92.
At Minḥah recite Aleinu on page 106; at Maariv recite Aleinu on page 40)

(During Minhah and Maariv Recite)

Shalom Rav

Grant abundant peace to Israel, who will always be Your people, for You are He, King, who is Lord of all peace. May it be good in Your sight to bless Your people Israel in all times and in all hours with Your peace.

*Blessed are You, Lord, who is blessing His people Israel with peace.

(From Rosh Hashanah to Yom Kippur substitute)

*Our Father, and the Father of all Israel, remember us, and inscribe us in the Book of Life, for blessing and for peace, and good provision, for good life and for peace. Blessed are You, Lord, who makes peace.

(Continue all services here)

May the words that proceed from my mouth and the secret thoughts that are in my heart be pleasing to You, O Lord, for You are my Stronghold as well as my Redeemer.

(The Reader's Repetition of the Amidah ends here. Individuals continue to the bottom of the page)

My God, guard my tongue from evil, and my lips from speaking falsehood. May my soul be silent to those who insult me, and may my soul be humble before all. Open my heart to Your Torah, that my soul might follow Your commands. As for all who plot evil against me, thwart their counsel and upset their plans. Do it for the sake of Your Name. Do it for the sake of Your power. Do it for the sake of Your holiness. Do it for the sake of Your Torah, that the one on whom You have set Your love might be rescued; save with Your right hand and answer us. May the words that proceed from my mouth and the secret thoughts that are in my heart be pleasing to You, O Lord, for You are my Stronghold as well as my Redeemer.

(Take three steps back. Bow first left, then right and finally forward as you recite)

May He who creates peace in His high heavens create peace for us and for all Israel, and say, Amen.

May it be Your will, Lord our God, and God or our fathers, to rebuild Your holy Temple, speedily, and in our days, and give to us our portion in Your Torah. Then we will serve You in reverence, as we did in days of old and in former years. And the evening offerings of Judah and Jerusalem shall be a surety to the Lord, as in days of old, and in former years.

(At Shaharit continue with Hallel on page 181, followed by the reading of the Torah on page 93. At Minhah recite Aleinu on page 107; at Maariv recite Aleinu on page 41)

הלל

(Recited in the morning service after the Amidah on the Yomim Tovim of
Pesah, Shavuot, Sukkot, Shemini Atseret, Hanukkah and Rosh Hodesh)

Blessing for Reciting Hallel

בָּרוּךְ אַתָּה יְיָ אֱלֹהֵינוּ מֶלֶךְ הָעוֹלָם, אֲשֶׁר קִדְּשָׁנוּ בְּמִצְוֹתָיו, וְצִוָּנוּ לִקְרֹא אֶת
הַהַלֵּל.

Barukh atah Adonai, Eloheinu Melekh Ha'Olam, asher kid'shanu b'mitsvotav
v'tsivanu likro et hahallel.

Psalm 113

הַלְלוּיָהּ, הַלְלוּ עַבְדֵי יְיָ, הַלְלוּ אֶת שֵׁם יְיָ. יְהִי שֵׁם יְיָ מְבֹרָךְ, מֵעַתָּה וְעַד
עוֹלָם. מִמִּזְרַח שֶׁמֶשׁ עַד מְבוֹאוֹ, מְהֻלָּל שֵׁם יְיָ. רָם עַל כָּל גּוֹיִם יְיָ, עַל
הַשָּׁמַיִם כְּבוֹדוֹ. מִי כַּיְיָ אֱלֹהֵינוּ, הַמַּגְבִּיהִי לָשָׁבֶת. הַמַּשְׁפִּילִי לִרְאוֹת, בַּשָּׁמַיִם
וּבָאָרֶץ. מְקִימִי מֵעָפָר דָּל, מֵאַשְׁפֹּת יָרִים אֶבְיוֹן. לְהוֹשִׁיבִי עִם נְדִיבִים, עִם
נְדִיבֵי עַמּוֹ. מוֹשִׁיבִי עֲקֶרֶת הַבַּיִת, אֵם הַבָּנִים שְׂמֵחָה, הַלְלוּיָהּ.

Psalm 114

בְּצֵאת יִשְׂרָאֵל מִמִּצְרָיִם, בֵּית יַעֲקֹב מֵעַם לֹעֵז. הָיְתָה יְהוּדָה לְקָדְשׁוֹ, יִשְׂרָאֵל
מַמְשְׁלוֹתָיו. הַיָּם רָאָה וַיָּנֹס, הַיַּרְדֵּן יִסֹּב לְאָחוֹר. הֶהָרִים רָקְדוּ כְאֵילִים,
גְּבָעוֹת כִּבְנֵי צֹאן. מַה לְּךָ הַיָּם כִּי תָנוּס, הַיַּרְדֵּן תִּסֹּב לְאָחוֹר. הֶהָרִים
תִּרְקְדוּ כְאֵילִים, גְּבָעוֹת כִּבְנֵי צֹאן. מִלְּפְנֵי אָדוֹן חוּלִי אָרֶץ, מִלְּפְנֵי אֱלוֹהַ
יַעֲקֹב. הַהֹפְכִי הַצּוּר אֲגַם מָיִם, חַלָּמִישׁ לְמַעְיְנוֹ מָיִם.

(Psalm 115:1-11 is omitted on Rosh Ḥodesh and the last six days of Passover. Continue with Psalm 115:12-18)

Psalm 115:1-11

לֹא לָנוּ, יְיָ, לֹא לָנוּ, כִּי לְשִׁמְךָ תֵּן כָּבוֹד, עַל חַסְדְּךָ עַל אֲמִתֶּךָ. לָמָּה יֹאמְרוּ
הַגּוֹיִם, אַיֵּה נָא אֱלֹהֵיהֶם. וֵאלֹהֵינוּ בַשָּׁמָיִם, כֹּל אֲשֶׁר חָפֵץ עָשָׂה. עֲצַבֵּיהֶם
כֶּסֶף וְזָהָב, מַעֲשֵׂה יְדֵי אָדָם. פֶּה לָהֶם וְלֹא יְדַבֵּרוּ, עֵינַיִם לָהֶם וְלֹא יִרְאוּ.
אָזְנַיִם לָהֶם וְלֹא יִשְׁמָעוּ, אַף לָהֶם וְלֹא יְרִיחוּן. יְדֵיהֶם וְלֹא יְמִישׁוּן, רַגְלֵיהֶם
וְלֹא יְהַלֵּכוּ, לֹא יֶהְגּוּ בִּגְרוֹנָם. כְּמוֹהֶם יִהְיוּ עֹשֵׂיהֶם, כֹּל אֲשֶׁר בֹּטֵחַ בָּהֶם.
יִשְׂרָאֵל בְּטַח בַּיְיָ, עֶזְרָם וּמָגִנָּם הוּא. בֵּית אַהֲרֹן בִּטְחוּ בַיְיָ, עֶזְרָם וּמָגִנָּם
הוּא. יִרְאֵי יְיָ בִּטְחוּ בַיְיָ, עֶזְרָם וּמָגִנָּם הוּא.

Hallel

*(Recited in the morning service after the Amidah on the Yomim Tovim of
Pesah, Shavuot, Sukkot, Shemini Atseret, Hanukkah and Rosh Hodesh)*

Blessing for Reciting Hallel

Blessed are You, Lord our God, King of the Universe, who sanctifies us by His commandments and who has commanded us to read the Hallel.

Psalm 113

Praise the Lord. Praise Him, you the servants of the Lord. Praise the name of the Lord. Blessed be the name of the Lord, from this time forth and forevermore. From the rising of the sun unto the going down of the same, the Lord's name is to be praised. The Lord is high above all nations and His glory is above the heavens. Who is like the Lord our God, whose seat is lifted up, yet humbles Himself to behold the things that are in heaven and in the earth? He raises up the poor out of the dust, and lifts up the needy from the dirt, that He may set him with princes, even with the princes of His people. He makes the barren woman to keep house, and to be a joyful mother of children. Praise the Lord.

Psalm 114

When Israel went out from Egypt, the house of Jacob from a people of strange language, Judah became His sanctuary, Israel His dominion. The sea saw it, and fled; the Jordan was driven back. The mountains skipped like rams and the little hills like lambs. What ailes you, oh sea, that you flee? You Jordan, that you turn back? You mountains, that you skip like rams, you little hills like lambs? Tremble, all the earth, at the presence of the Lord, at the presence of the God of Jacob, who turned the rock into a pool of water, the flint into a fountain of waters.

(Psalm 115:1-11 is omitted on Rosh Hodesh and the last six days of Passover. Continue with Psalm 115:12-18)

Psalm 115:1-11

Not unto us, oh Lord, not unto us, but unto Thy name give glory. For Thy lovingkindness, and for Thy truth's sake. Wherefore should the nations say, where is now their God? But our God is in the heavens: He has done whatsoever He desired. Their idols are silver and gold, the work of men's hands. They have mouths, but they cannot speak, eyes but they cannot see, ears, but they cannot hear, noses but they cannot smell. They have hands, but they cannot handle, feet but they cannot walk, throats but they cannot speak. They that make them shall be like them. Yes, every one that trusts in them. Oh Israel, trust in the Lord. He is your help and your shield. Oh House of Aaron, trust in the Lord. He is your help and your shield. You that fear the Lord, trust in the Lord. He is your help and your shield.

Psalm 115:12-18

יְיָ זְכָרָנוּ יְבָרֵךְ, יְבָרֵךְ אֶת בֵּית יִשְׂרָאֵל, יְבָרֵךְ אֶת בֵּית אַהֲרֹן. יְבָרֵךְ יִרְאֵי יְיָ,
הַקְּטַנִּים עִם הַגְּדֹלִים. יֹסֵף יְיָ עֲלֵיכֶם, עֲלֵיכֶם וְעַל בְּנֵיכֶם. בְּרוּכִים אַתֶּם לַיְיָ, עֹשֵׂה
שָׁמַיִם וָאָרֶץ. הַשָּׁמַיִם שָׁמַיִם לַיְיָ, וְהָאָרֶץ נָתַן לִבְנֵי אָדָם. לֹא הַמֵּתִים יְהַלְלוּ יָהּ,
וְלֹא כָּל יֹרְדֵי דוּמָה. וַאֲנַחְנוּ נְבָרֵךְ יָהּ, מֵעַתָּה וְעַד עוֹלָם, הַלְלוּיָהּ.

(Psalm 116:1-11 is omitted on Rosh Hodesh and the last six days of Passover. Continue with Psalm 116:12-19)

Psalm 116:1-11

אָהַבְתִּי כִּי יִשְׁמַע יְיָ, אֶת קוֹלִי תַּחֲנוּנָי. כִּי הִטָּה אָזְנוֹ לִי, וּבְיָמַי אֶקְרָא. אֲפָפוּנִי
חֶבְלֵי מָוֶת, וּמְצָרֵי שְׁאוֹל מְצָאוּנִי, צָרָה וְיָגוֹן אֶמְצָא. וּבְשֵׁם יְיָ אֶקְרָא, אָנָּה יְיָ
מַלְּטָה נַפְשִׁי. חַנּוּן יְיָ וְצַדִּיק, וֵאלֹהֵינוּ מְרַחֵם. שֹׁמֵר פְּתָאִים יְיָ, דַּלּוֹתִי וְלִי יְהוֹשִׁיעַ.
שׁוּבִי נַפְשִׁי לִמְנוּחָיְכִי, כִּי יְיָ גָּמַל עָלָיְכִי. כִּי חִלַּצְתָּ נַפְשִׁי מִמָּוֶת, אֶת עֵינִי מִן
דִּמְעָה, אֶת רַגְלִי מִדֶּחִי. אֶתְהַלֵּךְ לִפְנֵי יְיָ, בְּאַרְצוֹת הַחַיִּים. הֶאֱמַנְתִּי כִּי אֲדַבֵּר,
אֲנִי עָנִיתִי מְאֹד. אֲנִי אָמַרְתִּי בְחָפְזִי, כָּל הָאָדָם כֹּזֵב.

Psalm 116:12-19

מָה אָשִׁיב לַיְיָ, כָּל תַּגְמוּלוֹהִי עָלָי. כּוֹס יְשׁוּעוֹת אֶשָּׂא, וּבְשֵׁם יְיָ אֶקְרָא. נְדָרַי לַיְיָ
אֲשַׁלֵּם, נֶגְדָה נָא לְכָל עַמּוֹ. יָקָר בְּעֵינֵי יְיָ, הַמָּוְתָה לַחֲסִידָיו. אָנָּה יְיָ כִּי אֲנִי
עַבְדֶּךָ, אֲנִי עַבְדְּךָ בֶּן אֲמָתֶךָ, פִּתַּחְתָּ לְמוֹסֵרָי. לְךָ אֶזְבַּח זֶבַח תּוֹדָה, וּבְשֵׁם יְיָ
אֶקְרָא. נְדָרַי לַיְיָ אֲשַׁלֵּם, נֶגְדָה נָא לְכָל עַמּוֹ. בְּחַצְרוֹת בֵּית יְיָ, בְּתוֹכֵכִי
יְרוּשָׁלַיִם, הַלְלוּיָהּ.

(Congregation then Reader)

Psalm 117

הַלְלוּ אֶת יְיָ, כָּל גּוֹיִם, שַׁבְּחוּהוּ, כָּל הָאֻמִּים. כִּי גָבַר עָלֵינוּ חַסְדּוֹ, וֶאֱמֶת יְיָ
לְעוֹלָם, הַלְלוּיָהּ.

Hallelu et Adonai kal goyim, shab'huhu, kal ha-umim.

Ki gavar aleinu ḥas'do, v'emet Adonai l'olam, Halleluyah.

(Reader recites aloud each verse, after which the Congregation responds.
On Sukkot the Four Species are waved - the blessing Netilat Lulav is found on page 204)

Psalm 118:1-4

(Reader) : הוֹדוּ לַיְיָ כִּי טוֹב, כִּי לְעוֹלָם חַסְדּוֹ.

(Cong) : הוֹדוּ לַיְיָ כִּי טוֹב, כִּי לְעוֹלָם חַסְדּוֹ.   *Hodu L'Adonai ki tov, Ki l'olam ḥasdo*

(Reader) : יֹאמַר נָא יִשְׂרָאֵל, כִּי לְעוֹלָם חַסְדּוֹ.

(Cong) : הוֹדוּ לַיְיָ כִּי טוֹב, כִּי לְעוֹלָם חַסְדּוֹ.   *Hodu L'Adonai ki tov, Ki l'olam ḥasdo*

(Reader) : יֹאמְרוּ נָא בֵית אַהֲרֹן, כִּי לְעוֹלָם חַסְדּוֹ.

(Cong) : הוֹדוּ לַיְיָ כִּי טוֹב, כִּי לְעוֹלָם חַסְדּוֹ.   *Hodu L'Adonai ki tov, Ki l'olam ḥasdo*

(Reader) : יֹאמְרוּ נָא יִרְאֵי יְיָ, כִּי לְעוֹלָם חַסְדּוֹ.

(Cong) : הוֹדוּ לַיְיָ כִּי טוֹב, כִּי לְעוֹלָם חַסְדּוֹ.   *Hodu L'Adonai ki tov, Ki l'olam ḥasdo*

Psalm 115:12-18

The Lord has been mindful of us; He will bless us. He will bless the house of Israel; He will bless the house of Aaron. He will bless them that fear the Lord, both small and great. The Lord increase you more and more, you and your children. Blessed are You, Oh Lord, who made heaven and earth. The heavens are the heavens of the Lord, but the earth has He given to the children of men. The dead do not praise the Lord, neither any that are silent, but we will bless the Lord from this time forth and for evermore. Praise the Lord!

(Psalm 116:1-11 is omitted on Rosh Ḥodesh and the last six days of Passover. Continue with Psalm 116:12-19)

Psalm 116:1-11

I love the Lord, because He hears my voice and my supplications. Because He has inclined His ear to me, I will call upon Him as long as I live. The cords of death compassed me, and the pains of Sheol held onto me; I found trouble and sorrow. Then I called upon the name of the Lord. Oh Lord, I beg you, deliver my soul! Gracious is the Lord, and righteous; yes, our God is merciful. The Lord preserves the simple. I was brought low, and He saved me. Return unto your rest, O my soul, for the Lord has dealt bountifully with you. For You have delivered my soul from death, my eyes from tears, and my feet from falling. I will walk before the Lord in the land of the living. I believe, for I will speak. I was greatly afflicted, and I said in my distress, all men are liars.

Psalm 116:12-19

What shall I render unto the Lord for all His benefits toward me? I will take the cup of salvation, and call upon the name of the Lord. I will pay my vows unto the Lord, yes, in the presence of all His people. Precious in the sight of the Lord is the death of His holy ones. Oh Lord, truly I am Your servant, I am Your servant, the son of Your handmaid. You have loosed my bonds. I will offer to You the sacrifice of thanksgiving, and I will call upon the name of the Lord. I will pay my vows to the Lord in the presence of all His people, in the courts of the Lord's house, in the midst of You, Oh Jerusalem. Praise the Lord!

(Congregation then Reader)

Psalm 117

Oh praise the Lord, all you nations; Laud him, all you peoples. For His lovingkindness is great toward us, and the truth of the Lord endures forever. Praise the Lord!

*(Reader recites aloud each verse, after which the Congregation responds.
On Sukkot the Four Species are waved - the blessing Netilat Lulav is found on page 205)*

Psalm 118:1-4

(Reader) : Give thanks to the Lord, for He is good;   His mercy endures forever.

(Cong) : **Give thanks to the Lord, for He is good; His mercy endures forever.**

(Reader) : Let Israel say; His mercy endures forever.

(Cong) : **Give thanks to the Lord, for He is good; His mercy endures forever.**

(Reader) : Let the house of Aaron say; His mercy endures forever.

(Cong) : **Give thanks to the Lord, for He is good; His mercy endures forever.**

(Reader) : Let those who fear the Lord say; His mercy endures forever.

(Cong) : **Give thanks to the Lord, for He is good; His mercy endures forever.**

Psalm 118:5-29

מִן הַמֵּצַר קָרָאתִי יָּה, עָנָנִי בַמֶּרְחָב יָה. יְיָ לִי לֹא אִירָא, מַה יַּעֲשֶׂה לִי אָדָם.
יְיָ לִי בְּעֹזְרָי, וַאֲנִי אֶרְאֶה בְשֹׂנְאָי. טוֹב לַחֲסוֹת בַּיְיָ, מִבְּטֹחַ בָּאָדָם. טוֹב
לַחֲסוֹת בַּיְיָ, מִבְּטֹחַ בִּנְדִיבִים. כָּל גּוֹיִם סְבָבוּנִי, בְּשֵׁם יְיָ כִּי אֲמִילַם. סַבּוּנִי
גַם סְבָבוּנִי, בְּשֵׁם יְיָ כִּי אֲמִילַם. סַבּוּנִי כִדְבֹרִים דֹּעֲכוּ כְּאֵשׁ קוֹצִים, בְּשֵׁם יְיָ
כִּי אֲמִילַם. דָּחֹה דְחִיתַנִי לִנְפֹּל, וַיְיָ עֲזָרָנִי. עָזִּי וְזִמְרָת יָה, וַיְהִי לִי לִישׁוּעָה.
קוֹל רִנָּה וִישׁוּעָה בְּאָהֳלֵי צַדִּיקִים, יְמִין יְיָ עֹשָׂה חָיִל. יְמִין יְיָ רוֹמֵמָה, יְמִין יְיָ
עֹשָׂה חָיִל. לֹא אָמוּת כִּי אֶחְיֶה, וַאֲסַפֵּר מַעֲשֵׂי יָה. יַסֹּר יִסְּרַנִּי יָּה, וְלַמָּוֶת לֹא
נְתָנָנִי. פִּתְחוּ לִי שַׁעֲרֵי צֶדֶק, אָבֹא בָם אוֹדֶה יָה. זֶה הַשַּׁעַר לַיְיָ, צַדִּיקִים
יָבֹאוּ בוֹ.

(Each verse is recited twice)

אוֹדְךָ כִּי עֲנִיתָנִי, וַתְּהִי לִי לִישׁוּעָה.

אֶבֶן מָאֲסוּ הַבּוֹנִים, הָיְתָה לְרֹאשׁ פִּנָּה.

מֵאֵת יְיָ הָיְתָה זֹּאת, הִיא נִפְלָאת בְּעֵינֵינוּ.

זֶה הַיּוֹם עָשָׂה יְיָ, נָגִילָה וְנִשְׂמְחָה בוֹ.

(Reader and Congregation recite the next four lines responsively. On Sukkot the Four Species are waved now through the end of this section.)

Ana Adonai hoshiah na	אָנָּא יְיָ הוֹשִׁיעָה נָּא.
Ana Adonai hoshiah na	אָנָּא יְיָ הוֹשִׁיעָה נָּא.
Ana Adonai hats'liḥa na	אָנָּא יְיָ הַצְלִיחָה נָּא.
Ana Adonai hats'liḥa na	אָנָּא יְיָ הַצְלִיחָה נָּא.

(Each verse is recited twice)

בָּרוּךְ הַבָּא בְּשֵׁם יְיָ, בֵּרַכְנוּכֶם מִבֵּית יְיָ.

אֵל יְיָ וַיָּאֶר לָנוּ, אִסְרוּ חַג בַּעֲבֹתִים עַד קַרְנוֹת הַמִּזְבֵּחַ.

אֵלִי אַתָּה וְאוֹדֶךָּ, אֱלֹהַי אֲרוֹמְמֶךָּ.

הוֹדוּ לַיְיָ כִּי טוֹב, כִּי לְעוֹלָם חַסְדּוֹ.

יְהַלְלוּךָ יְיָ אֱלֹהֵינוּ כָּל מַעֲשֶׂיךָ, וַחֲסִידֶיךָ צַדִּיקִים עוֹשֵׂי רְצוֹנֶךָ, וְכָל עַמְּךָ
בֵּית יִשְׂרָאֵל בְּרִנָּה יוֹדוּ וִיבָרְכוּ וִישַׁבְּחוּ וִיפָאֲרוּ וִירוֹמְמוּ וְיַעֲרִיצוּ וְיַקְדִּישׁוּ
וְיַמְלִיכוּ אֶת שִׁמְךָ מַלְכֵּנוּ. כִּי לְךָ טוֹב לְהוֹדוֹת וּלְשִׁמְךָ נָאֶה לְזַמֵּר, כִּי
מֵעוֹלָם וְעַד עוֹלָם אַתָּה אֵל. בָּרוּךְ אַתָּה יְיָ, מֶלֶךְ מְהֻלָּל בַּתִּשְׁבָּחוֹת.

(Turn to page 92 for the Torah service)

Psalm 118:5-29

Out of my distress I called to the Lord. The Lord answered me and set me in a good place. The Lord is on my side; I will not fear: What can man do unto me? The Lord is on my side among them that help me, therefore shall I see my success against those that hate me. It is better to take refuge in the Lord than to put confidence in man. It is better to take refuge in the Lord than to put confidence in princes. The nations surrounded me. In the name of the Lord I will cut them off. They encircled me again. In the name of the Lord I will cut them off. They surrounded me about like bees, attacking like fiery thorns. In the name of the Lord I will cut them off. They attacked heavily at me that I might fall, but the Lord helped me. The Lord is my strength and song, and He has become my salvation. The voice of rejoicing and salvation is in the tents of the righteous. The right hand of the Lord does valiantly. The right hand of the Lord is exalted. The right hand of the Lord does valiantly. I shall not die, but live and declare the works of the Lord. The Lord has disciplined me severely, but He has not given me over to death. Open to me the gates of righteousness and I will enter into them to give thanks to the Lord. This is the gate of the Lord; the righteous shall enter into it.

(Each verse is recited twice)

I will give thanks unto You for You have answered me, and You are my salvation.

The stone which the builders rejected, is become the chief cornerstone.

This is the Lord's doing, it is marvellous in our eyes.

This is the day which the Lord has made, we will rejoice and be glad in it.

(Reader and Congregation recite the next four lines responsively. On Sukkot the Four Species are waved now through the end of this section.)

We beg Lord, please save us now!
We beg Lord, please save us now!
We beg Lord, please prosper us now!
We beg Lord, please prosper us now!

(Each verse is recited twice)

Blessed be he that comes in the name of the Lord,
we bless you from the House of the Lord.

The Lord is God and He has given us light,
so bind the offering to the horns of the altar.

You are my God and I will give You thanks,
You are my God and I will exalt you.

Oh give thanks to the Lord for He is good,
for His lovingkindness endures forever.

All Your works praise You, Lord our God. Your righteous followers of the House of Israel seeking to do Your will joyously thank and bless, praise and glorify, extol and honor, sanctify and proclaim Your name our King. It is good indeed to give You thanks, it is pleasant to sing praises to Your name, for You are God from eternity to eternity. Blessed are You Lord, King who is worthy of praise.

(Turn to page 93 for the Torah service)

תפלת גשם

(The prayer for rain is recited in the Amidah during the Shemini Atseret morning service)

(Reader) : אֱלֹהֵינוּ וֵאלֹהֵי אֲבוֹתֵינוּ,

(Reader) זְכוֹר אָב נִמְשַׁךְ אַחֲרֶיךָ כַּמַּיִם, בֵּרַכְתּוֹ כְּעֵץ שָׁתוּל עַל פַּלְגֵי מָיִם, גְּנַנְתּוֹ הִצַּלְתּוֹ מֵאֵשׁ וּמִמַּיִם, דְּרַשְׁתּוֹ בְּזָרְעוֹ עַל כָּל מָיִם.

(Cong) בַּעֲבוּר אַבְרָהָם אַל תִּמְנַע מָיִם.

(Reader) זְכוֹר הַנּוֹלָד בִּבְשׂוֹרַת יֻקַּח נָא מְעַט מַיִם, וְשַׂחְתָּ לְהוֹרוֹ לְשַׁחֲטוֹ לִשְׁפָּךְ דָּמוֹ כַּמַּיִם, זִהֵר גַּם הוּא לִשְׁפָּךְ לֵב כַּמַּיִם, חָפַר וּמָצָא בְּאֵרוֹת מָיִם.

(Cong) בַּעֲבוּר יִצְחָק אַל תִּמְנַע מָיִם.

(Reader) זְכוֹר טָעַן מַקְלוֹ וְעָבַר יַרְדֵּן מַיִם, יִחַד לֵב וְגָל אֶבֶן מִפִּי בְּאֵר מַיִם, כְּנֶאֱבַק לוֹ שַׂר בָּלוּל מֵאֵשׁ וּמִמַּיִם, לָכֵן הִבְטַחְתּוֹ הֱיוֹת עִמּוֹ בָּאֵשׁ וּבַמָּיִם.

(Cong) בַּעֲבוּר יַעֲקֹב אַל תִּמְנַע מָיִם.

(Reader) זְכוֹר מָשׁוּי בְּתֵבַת גֹּמֶא מִן הַמַּיִם, נָמוּ דָּלֹה דָלָה וְהִשְׁקָה צֹאן מַיִם, סְגוּלֶיךָ עֵת צָמְאוּ לְמַיִם, עַל הַסֶּלַע הָךְ וַיֵּצְאוּ מָיִם.

(Cong) בַּעֲבוּר מֹשֶׁה אַל תִּמְנַע מָיִם.

(Reader) זְכוֹר שְׁנֵים עָשָׂר שְׁבָטִים שֶׁהֶעֱבַרְתָּ בִּגְזָרַת מַיִם, שֶׁהִמְתַּקְתָּ לָמוֹ מְרִירוּת מַיִם, תּוֹלְדוֹתָם נִשְׁפַּךְ דָּמָם עָלֶיךָ כַּמַּיִם, תֵּפֶן כִּי נַפְשֵׁנוּ אָפְפוּ מָיִם.

(Cong) בַּעֲבוּר יִשְׂרָאֵל אַל תִּמְנַע מָיִם.

(Reader) זְכוֹר מָשִׁיחַ יֵשׁוּעַ וְהִכְרִיז בַּיּוֹם הַגָּדוֹל שֶׁל הֶחָג הַסֻּכּוֹת: מִי שֶׁצָּמֵא יָבוֹא נָא אֵלַי וְיִשְׁתֶּה הַמַּאֲמִין בִּי כִּדְבַר הַכָּתוּב, נְהָרוֹת שֶׁל מַיִם חַיִּים יִזְרְמוּ מִקִּרְבּוֹ.

(Cong) בְּצִדְקַת מָשִׁיחַ יֵשׁוּעַ חֵן חֶשְׁרַת מָיִם.

(Reader) שָׁאַתָּה הוּא יְיָ אֱלֹהֵינוּ, מַשִּׁיב הָרוּחַ וּמוֹרִיד הַגֶּשֶׁם.

(Congregation then Reader) לִבְרָכָה וְלֹא לִקְלָלָה.   *Liv'rakhah v'lo lik'lalah.*

(Cong. responds: Amen) אָמֵן

(Congregation then Reader) לְחַיִּים וְלֹא לְמָוֶת.   *L'ḥayim v'lo l'mavet.*

(Cong. responds: Amen) אָמֵן

(Congregation then Reader) לְשׂוֹבַע וְלֹא לְרָזוֹן.   *Les'vo'va v'lo l'razon.*

(Cong. responds: Amen אָמֵן

(Return to מְכַלְכֵּל חַיִּים בְּחֶסֶד *on page 166 in the Festival Amidah)*

Tefilat Geshem

(The prayer for rain is recited in the Amidah during the Shemini Atseret morning service)

(Reader) Our God and God of our Fathers,

(Reader) Remember Abraham who followed You like water, whom You did bless like a tree planted near streams of water. You protected him and saved him from fire and water. You cared for him when he sowed by streams of water.

(Cong) For Abraham's sake, do not refuse water.

(Reader) Remember Isaac whose birth was foretold over water. You told his father to offer his blood like water. Isaac was obedient in pouring out his heart like water. Digging wells he did discover water.

(Cong) For Isaac's sake, do not refuse water.

(Reader) Remember Jacob who with staff in hand crossed the Jordan's water. His heart trusted when he rolled the stone off of the well of water, when he wrestled with the prince of fire and water. You promised to be with him through fire and water.

(Cong) For Jacob's sake, do not refuse water.

(Reader) Remember Moses who was drawn out from the water, who drew for us and for our sheep water. When Your chosen people thirsted for water he struck the rock and out came water.

(Cong) For Moses' sake, do not refuse water.

(Reader) Remember the Twelve Tribes You brought across the water. You sweetened for them the bitter water. For Your sake was the blood of their descendents spilled like water. Turn to us, for our lives are encircled by our enemies like water.

(Cong) For Israel's sake, do not refuse water.

(Reader) Remember Messiah Yeshua who cried out on the last great day of the Festival of Sukkot, saying: If any man is thirsty, let him come to Me and drink. He that believes in Me, from within him shall flow rivers of living water.

(Cong) For Messiah Yeshua's righteousness sake, grant abundant water.

(Reader) For You are the Lord our God,
who causes the wind to blow and the rain to fall.

(Congregation then Reader) For a blessing and not a curse.

(Cong responds) Amen

(Congregation then Reader) For life and not for death.

(Cong responds) Amen

(Congregation then Reader) For plenty and not for scarcity.

(Cong responds) Amen

*(Return to **You sustain the living with loving kindness** on page 167 in the Festival Amidah)*

הקפות לשמחת תורה

(The Hakafot for Simhat Torah are recited during the Torah service of the Shemini Atseret morning service. The Torah scrolls are removed from the ark and processed around the reading table seven times)

אַב הָרַחֲמִים, הֵיטִיבָה בִרְצוֹנְךָ אֶת צִיּוֹן, תִּבְנֶה חוֹמוֹת יְרוּשָׁלָיִם. כִּי בְךָ לְבַד בָּטָחְנוּ, מֶלֶךְ אֵל רָם וְנִשָּׂא אֲדוֹן עוֹלָמִים.

הקפה א:

אָנָּא יְיָ הוֹשִׁיעָה נָּא. אָנָּא יְיָ הַצְלִיחָה נָא. אָנָּא יְיָ עֲנֵנוּ בְיוֹם קָרְאֵנוּ. אֱלֹהֵי הָרוּחוֹת הוֹשִׁיעָה נָּא. בּוֹחֵן לְבָבוֹת הַצְלִיחָה נָא. גּוֹאֵל חָזָק עֲנֵנוּ בְיוֹם קָרְאֵנוּ.

הקפה ב:

דּוֹבֵר צְדָקוֹת הוֹשִׁיעָה נָּא. הָדוּר בִּלְבוּשׁוֹ הַצְלִיחָה נָא. וָתִיק וְחָסִיד עֲנֵנוּ בְיוֹם קָרְאֵנוּ.

הקפה ג:

זַךְ וְיָשָׁר, הוֹשִׁיעָה נָּא. חוֹמֵל דַּלִּים, הַצְלִיחָה נָא. טוֹב וּמֵטִיב, עֲנֵנוּ בְיוֹם קָרְאֵנוּ.

הקפה ד:

יוֹדֵעַ מַחֲשָׁבוֹת הוֹשִׁיעָה נָּא. כַּבִּיר וְנָאוֹר, הַצְלִיחָה נָא. לוֹבֵשׁ צְדָקוֹת עֲנֵנוּ בְיוֹם קָרְאֵנוּ.

הקפה ה:

מֶלֶךְ עוֹלָמִים הוֹשִׁיעָה נָּא. נָאוֹר וְאַדִּיר הַצְלִיחָה נָא. סוֹמֵךְ נוֹפְלִים עֲנֵנוּ בְיוֹם קָרְאֵנוּ.

הקפה ו:

עוֹזֵר דַּלִּים הוֹשִׁיעָה נָּא. פּוֹדֶה וּמַצִּיל הַצְלִיחָה נָא. צוּר עוֹלָמִים עֲנֵנוּ בְיוֹם קָרְאֵנוּ.

הקפה ז:

קָדוֹשׁ וְנוֹרָא הוֹשִׁיעָה נָּא. רַחוּם וְחַנּוּן הַצְלִיחָה נָא. שׁוֹמֵר הַבְּרִית עֲנֵנוּ בְיוֹם קָרְאֵנוּ. תּוֹמֵךְ תְּמִימִים הוֹשִׁיעָה נָּא. תַּקִּיף לָעַד הַצְלִיחָה נָא. תָּמִים בְּמַעֲשָׂיו עֲנֵנוּ בְיוֹם עוֹלָמִים.

*(Return to **Shema readings** on page 94 in the Torah Service)*

Hakafot L'Simḥat Torah

(The Hakafot for Simḥat Torah are recited during the Torah service of the Shemini Atseret morning service. The Torah scrolls are removed from the ark and processed around the reading table seven times)

Father of mercy, may it please You to make Tsion prosper; rebuild the walls of Jerusalem, we have trusted only in You, King; high and exalted God, Master of the Universe.

Circle 1:

Please, Lord, please bring salvation. Please, Lord, please bring success. Please, Lord, answer us on the day of our calling out. God of all the living, please bring salvation. Examiner of the hearts, please bring success. Strong Redeemer, answer us on the day of our calling out.

Circle 2:

Proclaimer of righteousness, please bring salvation. Majestic One in your appearance, please bring success. Ancient One and Pious One, answer us on the day of our calling out.

Circle 3:

Pure and upright One, please bring salvation. Compassionate One of the Poor, please bring success. The Good One and the One who does Good, answer us on the day of our calling out.

Circle 4:

Knower of thoughts, please bring salvation. Tremendous and Luminous One, please bring success. You who are clothed in righteousness, answer us on the day of our calling out.

Circle 5:

King of the Universe, please bring salvation. Luminous and Powerful One, please bring success. You who supports the falling, answer us on the day of our calling out.

Circle 6:

Helper of the poor, please bring salvation. Redeemer and Rescuer, please bring success. Rock of the Universe, answer us on the day of our calling out.

Circle 7

Holy and Awesome One, please bring salvation. Merciful and Compassionate One, please bring success. Guardian of the covenant, answer us on the day of our calling out. Supporter of the blameless, please bring salvation. Resolute One forever, please bring success. You, Perfect in your actions, answer us on the day of our calling out.

*(Return to **Shema readings** on page 95 in the Torah Service)*

קידוש לשלש רגלים

(On an Erev Yom Tov which is also a Shabbat begin here and read the portions in parenthesis)

(quietly) וַיְהִי עֶרֶב וַיְהִי בֹקֶר) יוֹם הַשִּׁשִּׁי :

וַיְכֻלּוּ הַשָּׁמַיִם וְהָאָרֶץ וְכָל צְבָאָם. וַיְכַל אֱלֹהִים בַּיּוֹם הַשְּׁבִיעִי מְלַאכְתּוֹ אֲשֶׁר עָשָׂה,
וַיִּשְׁבֹּת בַּיּוֹם הַשְּׁבִיעִי מִכָּל מְלַאכְתּוֹ אֲשֶׁר עָשָׂה. וַיְבָרֶךְ אֱלֹהִים אֶת יוֹם הַשְּׁבִיעִי
וַיְקַדֵּשׁ אֹתוֹ, כִּי בוֹ שָׁבַת מִכָּל מְלַאכְתּוֹ, אֲשֶׁר בָּרָא אֱלֹהִים לַעֲשׂוֹת.

(On a Yom Tov that isn't a Shabbat begin here and omit portions in parenthesis)

בָּרוּךְ אַתָּה יְיָ אֱלֹהֵינוּ מֶלֶךְ הָעוֹלָם, בּוֹרֵא פְּרִי הַגָּפֶן.

Barukh atah Adonai Eloheinu Melekh Ha'Olam, borei p'ri ha'gafen.

בָּרוּךְ אַתָּה יְיָ אֱלֹהֵינוּ מֶלֶךְ הָעוֹלָם, אֲשֶׁר בָּחַר בָּנוּ מִכָּל עָם וְרוֹמְמָנוּ מִכָּל לָשׁוֹן,
וְקִדְּשָׁנוּ בְּמִצְוֹתָיו.

וַתִּתֶּן לָנוּ יְיָ אֱלֹהֵינוּ בְּאַהֲבָה (שַׁבָּתוֹת לִמְנוּחָה וּ) מוֹעֲדִים לְשִׂמְחָה, חַגִּים וּזְמַנִּים
לְשָׂשׂוֹן, אֶת יוֹם (הַשַּׁבָּת הַזֶּה וְאֶת יוֹם)

לְפֶסַח:	חַג הַמַּצּוֹת הַזֶּה, זְמַן חֵרוּתֵנוּ
לְשָׁבֻעוֹת:	חַג הַשָּׁבֻעוֹת הַזֶּה, זְמַן מַתַּן תּוֹרָתֵנוּ
לְסֻכּוֹת:	חַג הַסֻּכּוֹת הַזֶּה, זְמַן שִׂמְחָתֵנוּ
לִשְׁמִינִי עֲצֶרֶת:	הַשְּׁמִינִי חַג הָעֲצֶרֶת הַזֶּה, זְמַן שִׂמְחָתֵנוּ

(בְּאַהֲבָה) מִקְרָא קֹדֶשׁ, זֵכֶר לִיצִיאַת מִצְרָיִם.

כִּי בָנוּ בָחַרְתָּ וְאוֹתָנוּ קִדַּשְׁתָּ מִכָּל הָעַמִּים, (וְשַׁבָּת) וּמוֹעֲדֵי קָדְשֶׁךָ
(בְּאַהֲבָה וּבְרָצוֹן)בְּשִׂמְחָה וּבְשָׂשׂוֹן הִנְחַלְתָּנוּ.
בָּרוּךְ אַתָּה יהוה, מְקַדֵּשׁ (הַשַּׁבָּת וְ) יִשְׂרָאֵל וְהַזְּמַנִּים.

(On Motsei Shabbat add the following for Havdalah)

בָּרוּךְ אַתָּה יְיָ אֱלֹהֵינוּ מֶלֶךְ הָעוֹלָם, בּוֹרֵא מְאוֹרֵי הָאֵשׁ. בָּרוּךְ אַתָּה יְיָ, אֱלֹהֵינוּ מֶלֶךְ
הָעוֹלָם, הַמַּבְדִּיל בֵּין קֹדֶשׁ לְחוֹל, בֵּין אוֹר לְחֹשֶׁךְ, בֵּין יִשְׂרָאֵל לָעַמִּים, בֵּין יוֹם הַשְּׁבִיעִי
לְשֵׁשֶׁת יְמֵי הַמַּעֲשֶׂה. בֵּין קְדֻשַּׁת שַׁבָּת לִקְדֻשַּׁת יוֹם טוֹב הִבְדַּלְתָּ, וְאֶת יוֹם הַשְּׁבִיעִי
מִשֵּׁשֶׁת יְמֵי הַמַּעֲשֶׂה קִדַּשְׁתָּ, הִבְדַּלְתָּ וְקִדַּשְׁתָּ אֶת עַמְּךָ יִשְׂרָאֵל בִּקְדֻשָּׁתֶךָ. בָּרוּךְ אַתָּה
יְיָ, הַמַּבְדִּיל בֵּין קֹדֶשׁ לְקֹדֶשׁ.

(On Sukkot add the following)

בָּרוּךְ אַתָּה יְיָ אֱלֹהֵינוּ מֶלֶךְ הָעוֹלָם, אֲשֶׁר קִדְּשָׁנוּ בְּמִצְוֹתָיו וְצִוָּנוּ לֵישֵׁב בַּסֻּכָּה.

*Barukh atah Adonai, Eloheinu Melekh Ha'Olam, asher kid'shanu b'mitzvotav
v'tzivanu lei'yosheiv basukkah.*

(On the first night of Festivals recite the Sheheheyanu blessing)

בָּרוּךְ אַתָּה יְיָ אֱלֹהֵינוּ מֶלֶךְ הָעוֹלָם, שֶׁהֶחֱיָנוּ וְקִיְּמָנוּ וְהִגִּיעָנוּ לַזְּמַן הַזֶּה.

*Barukh atah Adonai, Eloheinu Melekh Ha'Olam, sheheheyanu, vekiyemanu,
vehigiyanu, lazman hazeh!*

Kiddush L'Shalosh Regalim

(On an Erev Yom Tov which is also a Shabbat begin here and read the portions in parenthesis)

(quietly: And there was evening and there was morning) the sixth day. And thus the heavens, and the earth, and all their hosts were finished. And on the seventh day God completed all the work in which He had been engaged, and on the seventh day He rested from all the work which He had made. And God blessed the seventh day calling it holy, for on it He rested from all of the work which He had created.

(On a Yom Tov that isn't a Shabbat begin here and omit portions in parenthesis)

Blessed are You, Lord our God, King of the universe, who creates the fruit of the vine.

Blessed are You, Lord our God, King of the universe, who has chosen and exalted us above all nations, and has set us apart with your commandments.

And You, Lord our God, have given us (Shabbats for rest,) holidays for gladness and festival seasons for joy, (this Shabbat day and) this:

On Pesaḥ add: Festival of Matsah, our Festival of Freedom,
On Shavuot add: Festival of Shavuot, our Festival of the Gift of the Torah,
On Sukkot add: Festival of Sukkot, our Festival of Rejoicing,
On Shemini Atseret add: Festival of Shemini Atseret, our Festival of Joy,

(in love,) a holy assembly in remembrance of the exodus from Egypt.

Surely You have chosen and set us apart from all other peoples, (and Shabbat) and the holy Festivals (in love and in favor) you have given us in happiness and joy. Blessed are You, Lord, who makes holy (the Shabbat,) Israel and the Festivals.

(On Motsei Shabbat add the following for Havdalah)

Blessed are You, Lord our God, King of the universe, who creates the light of the fire. Blessed are You, Lord our God, You have made a distinction between that which is holy and that which is common; between light and darkness; between Israel and the other nations; between the seventh day and the six days of work. Between sanctity of the Shabbat and the sanctity of the Festivals, distinguishing the sanctity of the seventh day from the six days of labor. You have set apart Israel Your people with Your holiness. Blessed are You, Lord, who has made a distinction between the holy and the profane.

(On Sukkot add the following)

Blessed are You, Lord our God, King of the Universe, who has sanctified us with His commandments and has commanded us to dwell in a sukkah.

(On the first night of Festivals recite the Sheheheyanu blessing)

Blessed are You, Lord our God, King of the Universe, who has kept us, and sustained us, and enabled us to reach this season!

לזכור את מותו של ישוע המשיח

(The following is recited in a spirit of quiet contemplation and self-examination)

1 Corinthians 10:16-17

כּוֹס הַבְּרָכָה שֶׁאָנוּ מְבָרְכִים עָלֶיהָ, הַאֵין הִיא הִתְחַבְּרוּת לְדַם הַמָּשִׁיחַ. הַלֶּחֶם שֶׁאָנוּ בּוֹצְעִים, הַאֵין הוּא הִתְחַבְּרוּת לְגוּף הַמָּשִׁיחַ. מִשׁוּם שֶׁהַלֶּחֶם אֶחָד, אֲנַחְנוּ הָרַבִּים גּוּף אֶחָד; שֶׁכֵּן כֻּלָּנוּ מִשְׁתַּתְּפִים בַּלֶּחֶם הָאֶחָד

1 Corinthians 11:23-29

אָכֵן אֲנִי קִבַּלְתִּי מֵאֵת הָאָדוֹן אֶת אֲשֶׁר גַּם מָסַרְתִּי לָכֶם. שֶׁהָאָדוֹן יֵשׁוּעַ, בַּלַּיְלָה שֶׁהֻסְגַּר בּוֹ, לָקַח אֶת הַלֶּחֶם, בֵּרַךְ, בָּצַע אוֹתוֹ וְאָמַר. זֶה גוּפִי הַנִּבְצָע בַּעֲדְכֶם, זֹאת עֲשׂוּ לְזִכְרִי. כֵּן גַּם לָקַח אֶת הַכּוֹס לְאַחַר הַסְּעוּדָה וְאָמַר. הַכּוֹס הַזֹּאת הִיא הַבְּרִית הַחֲדָשָׁה בְּדָמִי, זֹאת עֲשׂוּ לְזִכְרִי בְּכָל עֵת שֶׁתִּשְׁתּוּ. הֵן בְּכָל עֵת שֶׁאַתֶּם אוֹכְלִים אֶת הַלֶּחֶם הַזֶּה וְשׁוֹתִים מִן הַכּוֹס הַזֹּאת, אַתֶּם מַזְכִּירִים אֶת מוֹת אֲדוֹנֵנוּ, עַד שֶׁיָּבוֹא. לָכֵן מִי שֶׁאוֹכֵל מֵהַלֶּחֶם הַזֶּה אוֹ שׁוֹתֶה מִכּוֹס הָאָדוֹן שֶׁלֹּא כָּרָאוּי, יִהְיֶה אָשֵׁם לְגַבֵּי גּוּף הָאָדוֹן וְדָמוֹ. יִבְחַן נָא אִישׁ אֶת עַצְמוֹ וְכָךְ יֹאכַל מִן הַלֶּחֶם וְיִשְׁתֶּה מִן הַכּוֹס, כִּי הָאוֹכֵל וְהַשּׁוֹתֶה מִבְּלִי לִנְהֹג הַבְחָנָה בְּגוּף הָאָדוֹן, אוֹכֵל וְשׁוֹתֶה דִּין לְעַצְמוֹ.

John 6:35, 48-51

אָמַר לָהֶם יֵשׁוּעַ: אֲנִי הוּא לֶחֶם הַחַיִּים. כָּל הַבָּא אֵלַי לֹא יִרְעַב, וְהַמַּאֲמִין בִּי לֹא יִצְמָא עוֹד. אֲנִי הוּא לֶחֶם הַחַיִּים. אֲבוֹתֵיכֶם אָכְלוּ אֶת הַמָּן בַּמִּדְבָּר וָמֵתוּ. זֶה הוּא הַלֶּחֶם הַיּוֹרֵד מִן הַשָּׁמַיִם כְּדֵי שֶׁיֹּאכְלוּ מִמֶּנּוּ וְלֹא יָמוּתוּ. אֲנִי הַלֶּחֶם הַחַי הַיּוֹרֵד מִן הַשָּׁמַיִם. אִם יֹאכַל אִישׁ מִן הַלֶּחֶם הַזֶּה יִחְיֶה לְעוֹלָם. וְהַלֶּחֶם אֲשֶׁר אֶתֵּן הֲרֵיהוּ בְּשָׂרִי בְּעַד חַיָּיו שֶׁל הָעוֹלָם.

(Recite as a Statement of Personal Faith in Messiah Yeshua's Atonement)

יֵשׁוּעַ הַמָּשִׁיחַ תְּמוּרָתִי, יֵשׁוּעַ הַמָּשִׁיחַ מֵת כְּדֵי לְכַפֵּר עַל חֲטָאַי. דַּרְכּוֹ בִּלְבַד אֲנִי אֵלֵךְ לְחַיִּים טוֹבִים עִם אֱלֹהִים בְּשָׁלוֹם.

Yeshua HaMashiah t'murati; Yeshua HaMashiach meit kh'deiy l'khafeir al hatay. Dar'ko vil'bad ani eileikh l'hayyim tovim im Elohim v'shalom.

מוציא

בָּרוּךְ אַתָּה יְיָ אֱלֹהֵינוּ מֶלֶךְ הָעוֹלָם, הַמּוֹצִיא לֶחֶם מִן הָאָרֶץ.

Barukh atah Adonai Eloheinu Melekh Ha'Olam, hamotsi lehem min ha'arets.

לזכור הלחם החי

בָּרוּךְ אַתָּה יְיָ אֱלֹהֵינוּ מֶלֶךְ הָעוֹלָם, אֲשֶׁר קִדְּשָׁנוּ בְּמִצְוֹתָיו, וְצִוָּנוּ לִזְכּוֹר הַלֶּחֶם הַחַי, מְשִׁיחֵנוּ יֵשׁוּעַ.

Barukh atah Adonai, Eloheinu Melekh Ha'Olam, asher kid'shanu b'mitsvotav, v'tsivanu liz'kor HaLehem HaHai, Meshiheinu Yeshua.

(Eat a piece of bread the size of an olive while soberly reflecting on Messiah Yeshua's death)

Remembering the Death of Messiah Yeshua

(The following is recited in a spirit of quiet contemplation and self-examination)

1 Corinthians 10:16-17

The cup of blessing which we bless, is it not our participation together of the blood atonement of the Messiah? The bread which we break, is it not our participation together of the bodily sacrifice of the Messiah? Because there is one bread, we who are many are united together in one community, for we all partake of the one bread.

1 Corinthians 11:23-29

For I received from the Lord that which also I delivered to you, that the Lord Yeshua during the night in which he was betrayed took bread, and when he had given thanks, he broke it, and said, "This is my body, which is given for you: do this in remembrance of me." In the same way he took also the cup, after the meal, saying, "This cup is the New Covenant in my blood. This do, as often as you drink it, in remembrance of me." For as often as you eat this bread, and drink this cup, you proclaim the Lord's death till he returns. Whoever eats the bread or drinks the cup of the Lord in an unworthy manner, shall be guilty of the body and the blood of the Lord. But let a person examine themself, and then after this examination let them eat of the bread and drink of the cup. For the person who eats and drinks, eats and drinks judgment unto themself, if they do so carelessly, not respecting Messiah's body.

John 6:35, 48-51

Yeshua said to them, I am the bread of life. The person who comes to me will not hunger, and the person who believes in me shall never thirst. I am the bread of life. Your fathers ate the manna in the wilderness, and they died. This is the bread which came down out of heaven, that a person may eat and not die. I am the living bread which came down out of heaven. If any person will eat of this bread, he shall live forever. The bread which I will give is my body, for the life of the world.

(Recite as a Statement of Personal Faith in Messiah Yeshua's Atonement)

Messiah Yeshua is my exchange; Messiah Yeshua is my substitute, dying for the atonement of my sins. By His atonement alone am I able to be in relationship with God in peace.

Motsi

Blessed are You, Lord our God, King of the Universe, who brings forth bread from the earth.

Remembering Messiah's Body

Blessed are You, Lord our God, King of the Universe, who sanctifies us by His commandments and has commanded us to remember the Bread of Life, our Messiah Yeshua.

(Eat a piece of bread the size of an olive while soberly reflecting on Messiah Yeshua's death)

אבינו שבשמים

אָבִינוּ שֶׁבַּשָּׁמַיִם יִתְקַדַּשׁ שְׁמֶךָ.   תָּבֹא מַלְכוּתֶךָ יֵעָשֶׂה רְצוֹנְךָ בָּאָרֶץ כַּאֲשֶׁר נַעֲשָׂ
בַּשָּׁמָיִם.   תֶּן לָנוּ הַיּוֹם לֶחֶם חֻקֵּנוּ.   וּסְלַח לָנוּ אֶת אַשְׁמָתֵנוּ כַּאֲשֶׁר סֹלְחִים אֲנַחְנ
לַאֲשֶׁר אָשְׁמוּ לָנוּ.   וְאַל תְּבִיאֵנוּ לִידֵי מַסָּה כִּי אִם הַצִּילֵנוּ מִן הָרָע.   כִּי לְךָ הַמַּמְלָכָ
וְהַגְּבוּרָה וְהַתִּפְאֶרֶת לְעוֹלְמֵי עוֹלָמִים.

Avinu she'bashamayim yit'kadash sh'mekha. Tavo mal'khutekha ya'ase
ritson'kha ba'arets ka'asher na'asah ba'shamayim. Ten lanu hayom lehem
hu'keinu. Us'lah lanu et ash'matainu ka'asher sol'him anah'nu la'asher
ash'mu lanu. V'al t'vi'einu lidei masah ki im hatsileinu min ha'rah. Ki l'kha
hamam'lacha v'hag'vura v'hatiferet l'olimei olamim.

קדש

בָּרוּךְ אַתָּה יְיָ, אֱלֹהֵינוּ מֶלֶךְ הָעוֹלָם, בּוֹרֵא פְּרִי הַגָּפֶן.
Barukh atah Adonai Eloheinu Melekh Ha'Olam, borei p'ri ha'gafen.

לזכור דם הברית

בָּרוּךְ אַתָּה יְיָ אֱלֹהֵינוּ מֶלֶךְ הָעוֹלָם, אֲשֶׁר קִדְּשָׁנוּ בְּמִצְוֹתָיו, וְצִוָּנוּ לִזְכּוֹר דָּם הַבְּרִית
מְשִׁיחֵנוּ יֵשׁוּעַ.

Barukh atah Adonai, Eloheinu Melekh Ha'Olam, asher kid'shanu b'mitsvotav,
v'tsivanu liz'kor Dam HaBrit Meshiheinu Yeshua.

(Drink a small cup of wine or grape juice while soberly reflecting on Messiah Yeshua's death)

Ephesians 4:1-7

לְפִיכָךְ אֲנִי, הָאָסִיר לְמַעַן הָאָדוֹן, מַפְצִיר בָּכֶם לְהִתְנַהֵג כָּיָאֶה לַיִּעוּד שֶׁנִּקְרֵאתֶם אֵלָיו
הִתְנַהֲגוּ בְּכָל עֲנָוָה וּנְמִיכוּת רוּחַ, וּבְאֹרֶךְ אַפַּיִם. סִבְלוּ אִישׁ אֶת רֵעֵהוּ בְּאַהֲבָה. שִׁקְד
לִשְׁמֹר אֶת אַחְדוּת הָרוּחַ בְּקֶשֶׁר שֶׁל שָׁלוֹם. הִנֵּה: גּוּף אֶחָד וְרוּחַ אַחַת, כְּשֵׁם שֶׁגַּם
אַתֶּם נִקְרֵאתֶם אֶל תִּקְוַת יִעוּדְכֶם הָאַחַת; אָדוֹן אֶחָד, אֱמוּנָה אַחַת, טְבִילָה אַחַת, אֶ
וְאָב אֶחָד לַכֹּל, הוּא אֲשֶׁר מֵעַל כֹּל, פּוֹעֵל בַּכֹּל, וּבְתוֹךְ הַכֹּל. אֲבָל לְכָל אֶחָד וְאֶחָד
מֵאִתָּנוּ הֻעֲנַק חֶסֶד כְּפִי הַמִּדָּה שֶׁהֶעֱנִיק לוֹ הַמָּשִׁיחַ.

Hebrews 12:1-2

לָכֵן גַּם אֲנַחְנוּ, אֲשֶׁר עֲנַן עֵדִים כָּזֶה אוֹפֵף אוֹתָנוּ, נָסִירָה נָא כָּל מַעֲמָסָה וְגַם אֶת
הַחֵטְא הַלּוֹכֵד עַל נְקַלָּה, וּכְסַבְלָנוּת נָרוּצָה אֶת הַמֵּרוֹץ הָעָרוּךְ לְפָנֵינוּ, בְּהַבִּיטֵנוּ אֶל
יֵשׁוּעַ מְכוֹנֵן הָאֱמוּנָה וּמַשְׁלִימָהּ, אֲשֶׁר בְּעַד הַשִּׂמְחָה הָעֲרוּכָה לְפָנָיו סָבַל אֶת הַצְּלָב
וּבָז לַחֶרְפָּה, וַיֵּשֶׁב לִימִין כִּסֵּא הָאֱלֹהִים.

Jude 24-25

וְהוּא אֲשֶׁר יָכוֹל לִשְׁמֹר אֶתְכֶם מִמִּכְשׁוֹל וּלְהַעֲמִיד אֶתְכֶם לִפְנֵי כְּבוֹדוֹ נְקִיִּים מִדֹּפִ
וּמְלֵאֵי שִׂמְחָה, הָאֱלֹהִים הַיָּחִיד, מוֹשִׁיעֵנוּ עַל־יְדֵי יֵשׁוּעַ הַמָּשִׁיחַ אֲדוֹנֵנוּ – לוֹ הַכָּבוֹ
וְהַגְּדֻלָּה וְהָעֹז וְהַשִּׁלְטוֹן לִפְנֵי כָּל עוֹלָם, גַּם עַתָּה גַּם לְכָל הָעוֹלָמִים. אָמֵן.

(Conclude with a reflection on the soon return of Messiah Yeshua and the establishment of His earthly Kingdom)

Avinu Shebashamayim

Our Father in Heaven, holy is Your name. Your kingdom will come; Your will shall be done, on the earth as it is in the heavens. Give us this day our daily bread. Forgive us our debts as we forgive our debtors. And lead us not into temptation, but deliver us from the evil one. For Yours is the kingdom, and the power, and the glory, forever.

Kiddush

Blessed are You, Lord our God, King of the Universe, who creates the fruit of the vine.

Remembering Messiah's Blood

Blessed are You, Lord our God, King of the Universe, who has commanded us to remember the covenant blood of our Messiah Yeshua.

(Drink a small cup of wine or grape juice while soberly reflecting on Messiah Yeshua's death)

Ephesians 4:1-7

I therefore, the prisoner of the Lord, plead with you to walk worthy of the calling to which you were called, with all humility and meekness, with patience, putting up with one another in love; working hard to keep the unity of the Spirit in the bond of peace. There is one Body, and one Spirit, even as you also were called in one hope of your calling; one Lord, one faith, one immersion, one God and Father of all, who is over all, and through all, and in all. But to each one of us has been given the special enablement needed according to the grace of Messiah.

Hebrews 12:1-2

Because of this, seeing that we are surrounded with so great a cloud of witnesses, let us also set aside every distraction and the sin which so easily trips us up, and let us run with endurance the race that is set before us, keeping our eyes fixed on Yeshua who is the author and perfecter of our faith, who for the joy that was set before him endured the cross, disregarding the shame, and has now taken his seat at the right hand of the throne of God.

Jude 24-25

Now to the one who is able to guard you from stumbling, and to cause you to stand with great joy before the presence of His glory without blemish, to the only God our Saviour, through Messiah Yeshua our Lord, be glory, majesty, sovereignty and power, before all time, and now, and for all eternity. Amen.

(Conclude with a reflection on the soon return of Messiah Yeshua and the establishment of His earthly Kingdom)

Tevilah: Faith and Allegiance to Messiah Yeshua

(The act of full-body immersion in living water for ritual purity , known as tevilah, was a well-established practice in the Second Temple era, and it became codified in Jewish law during the late Mishnaic period (200 CE). Today, ritual purity remains a common and important practice among the observant Jewish community. In the first century, Messiah Yeshua commanded his followers, the talmidim, to be immersed as a means of publicly declaring their personal faith in, and their allegiance to, his Messiahship. The significance of this immersion was likely adopted from an existing practice in the late Second Temple period where repentant Jews would immerse themselves in water to publicly demonstrate their renewed commitment to God's Covenant to Israel [see Mark 1:1–8]. The practice of "Messianic" tevilah is a clear declaration of faith by the followers in Messiah Yeshua to symbolize their belief in the crucified, buried, and risen Messiah as well as their own death to sin and resurrection to new life.)

Acts 2:36-38, 41-42

"Let all the house of Israel therefore know assuredly that God has made him both Master and Messiah, this Yeshua whom you crucified." Now when they heard this they were cut to the heart, and said to Kefa and the rest of the emissaries, "Brethren, what shall we do?" And Kefa said to them, "Repent, and be ritually immersed every one of you in the name of Yeshua the Messiah to demonstrate the forgiveness of your sins; and you shall receive the gift of the Ruach HaKodesh. So those who accepted his word were ritually immersed, and there were added that day about three thousand souls. And they devoted themselves to the emissaries teaching and fellowship, to the breaking of bread and to the prayers.

Romans 6:3-5,11

Do you not know that all of us who have been immersed into Messiah Yeshua were immersed into His death? We were buried therefore with Him by immersion into death, so that as Messiah was raised from the dead by the glory of the Father, we too might walk in newness of life. For if we have been united with Him in a death like his, we shall certainly be united with Him in a resurrection like His. So you also must consider yourselves dead to sin and alive to God in Messiah Yeshua.

Matthew 28:18-20

And Yeshua came and said to them, "All authority in heaven and on earth has been given to me. Go therefore and make talmidim from all the nations, ritually immersing them in the name of the Father and of the Son and of the Holy Spirit, teaching them to observe all that I have commanded you; and behold, I am with you always, until the very end of the age."

Statement of Faith: Do you believe in Yeshua the Messiah, and in his death and ressurection?

Yes, I believe that Yeshua is the Messiah, the head, and the representative of our people, Israel. He is also the head over those from among the nations who profess faith in, and allegiance to, Israel's Messiah.
I believe that Messiah Yeshua died to provide complete atonement for all my sin, and that He rose from the dead as the first-fruits of my own resurrection.
I believe that He will return at the end of the age to restore the people of Israel, gather His faithful ones from all the nations, and judge the world in righteousness and truth.

* Elements of this Budoff Siddur tevilah liturgy were adapted from an existing tevilah liturgy of Congregation Zera Avraham in Ann Arbor, Michigan

Statement of Allegience: Will you follow Yeshua and live as His disciple?

Yes, I will follow Yeshua as His talmid, and I will loyally serve, honor and obey Him as long as I live.

(The one immersing recites the following two blessings)

Personal Confession of Faith in Messiah Yeshua

בָּרוּךְ אַתָּה, יְיָ אֱלֹהֵינוּ, מֶלֶךְ הָעוֹלָם, אֲשֶׁר נָתַן לָנוּ דְּבַר הַחַיִּים, מָשִׁיחַ יֵשׁוּעַ.

Barukh atah Adonai Eloheinu Melekh Ha'Olam, asher natan lanu d'var haḥayim, Mashiaḥ Yeshua.

Blessed are You, Lord our God, King of the Universe, who has given us the Word of Life, Messiah Yeshua.

Personal Confession of Allegiance to Messiah Yeshua

בָּרוּךְ אַתָּה יְיָ אֱלֹהֵינוּ מֶלֶךְ הָעוֹלָם, אֲשֶׁר קִדְּשָׁנוּ בִּדְבָרוֹ, וְנָתַן לָנוּ אֶת יֵשׁוּעַ מְשִׁיחֵנוּ, וְצִוָּנוּ לִהְיוֹת אוֹר לְעוֹלָם.

Barukh atah Adonai Eloheinu Melekh Ha'Olam asher kid'shanu bidvaro, v'natan lanu et Yeshua Meshiḥeinu, v'tsivanu l'hiyot or l'olam.

Blessed are You, Lord our God, King of the Universe, who has sanctified us with His word, and has given us Yeshua our Messiah and commanded us to be His light to the world.

(After sharing for a few minutes of his/her faith in his/her own words, he/she goes into the water and fully immerses themselves once, reciting the Tevilah blessing after this first immersion)

Tevilah Blessing

בָּרוּךְ אַתָּה אֲדֹנָי אֱלֹהֵינוּ מֶלֶךְ הָעוֹלָם אֲשֶׁר קִדְּשָׁנוּ בְּמִצְוֹתָיו וְצִוָּנוּ עַל הַטְּבִילָה

Barukh atah Adonai, Eloheinu Melekh Ha'Olam, asher kideshanu be-mitzvahtav, vitzivanu, al ha-tevilah.

Blessed are You, Lord our God, King of the Universe, who sanctifies us by His commandments and who has commanded us concerning immersion.

(After the Tevilah blessing, he/she fully immerses twice more, reciting the Sheheḥeyanu blessing afterwards)

Sheheḥeyanu

בָּרוּךְ אַתָּה יְיָ אֱלֹהֵינוּ מֶלֶךְ הָעוֹלָם, שֶׁהֶחֱיָנוּ וְקִיְּמָנוּ וְהִגִּיעָנוּ לַזְּמַן הַזֶּה.

Barukh atah Adonai, Eloheinu Melekh Ha'Olam, sheheḥeyanu, vekiyemanu, vehigiyanu, lazman hazeh!

Blessed are You, Lord our God, King of the Universe, who has kept us, and sustained us, and enabled us to reach this season!

Jude 24-25

Now to the one who is able to guard you from stumbling, and to cause you to stand with great joy before the presence of His glory without blemish, to the only God our Saviour, through Messiah Yeshua our Lord, be glory, majesty, sovereignty and power, before all time, and now, and for all eternity. Amen.

Mi Shebeirakh for an Oleh

מִי שֶׁבֵּרַךְ אֲבוֹתֵינוּ, אַבְרָהָם יִצְחָק וְיַעֲקֹב, הוּא יְבָרֵךְ אֶת ___ בֶּן ___ שֶׁעָלָה
לִכְבוֹד הַמָּקוֹם לִכְבוֹד הַתּוֹרָה *add on festivals)* וְלִכְבוֹד הָרֶגֶל). הַקָּדוֹשׁ בָּרוּךְ הוּא
יִשְׁמְרֵהוּ וְיַצִּילֵהוּ מִכָּל צָרָה וְצוּקָה וּמִכָּל נֶגַע וּמַחֲלָה, וְיִשְׁלַח בְּרָכָה וְהַצְלָחָה
בְּכָל מַעֲשֵׂה יָדָיו בְּשֵׁם יֵשׁוּעַ עַבְדּוֹ הַצַּדִּיק, מְשִׁיחֵנוּ, *add on festivals)* וְיִזְכֶּה
לַעֲלוֹת לָרֶגֶל) עִם כָּל יִשְׂרָאֵל אֶחָיו. וְנֹאמַר אָמֵן.

Prayer for the Israeli Defense Forces

מִי שֶׁבֵּרַךְ אֲבוֹתֵינוּ אַבְרָהָם יִצְחָק וְיַעֲקֹב הוּא יְבָרֵךְ אֶת חַיָּלֵי צְבָא הַגַּנָּה
לְיִשְׂרָאֵל הָעוֹמְדִים עַל מִשְׁמַר אַרְצֵנוּ וְעָרֵי אֱלֹהֵינוּ מִגְּבוּל הַלְּבָנוֹן וְעַד מִדְבַּר
מִצְרַיִם וּמִן הַיָּם הַגָּדוֹל עַד לְבוֹא הָעֲרָבָה בַּיַּבָּשָׁה בָּאֲוִיר וּבַיָּם יִתֵּן יְיָ אֶת
אוֹיְבֵינוּ הַקָּמִים עָלֵינוּ נִגָּפִים לִפְנֵיהֶם הַקָּדוֹשׁ בָּרוּךְ הוּא יִשְׁמֹר וְיַצִּיל אֶת חַיָּלֵינוּ
מִכָּל צָרָה וְצוּקָה וּמִכָּל נֶגַע וּמַחֲלָה וְיִשְׁלַח בְּרָכָה וְהַצְלָחָה בְּכָל מַעֲשֵׂה יְדֵיהֶם
יַדְבֵּר שׂוֹנְאֵינוּ תַּחְתֵּיהֶם וִיעַטְּרֵם בְּכֶתֶר יְשׁוּעָה וּבַעֲטֶרֶת נִצָּחוֹן וִיקַיֵּם בָּהֶם
הַכָּתוּב. כִּי יְיָ אֱלֹהֵיכֶם הַהֹלֵךְ עִמָּכֶם לְהִלָּחֵם לָכֶם עִם אֹיְבֵיכֶם לְהוֹשִׁיעַ אֶתְכֶם.
וְנֹאמַר אָמֵן

Birkat HaGomel

(The Birkat HaGomel Thanksgiving blessing is recited by those following their Torah aliyah who have survived a
life-threatening event, including serious illness and extensive travel)

(Oleh) בָּרוּךְ אַתָּה יְיָ אֱלֹהֵינוּ מֶלֶךְ הָעוֹלָם, הַגּוֹמֵל לְחַיָּבִים טוֹבוֹת, שֶׁגְּמָלַנִי כָּל טוֹב.

Barukh atah Adonai Eloheinu Melekh Ha'Olam, hagomeil l'ḥayavim tovot,
sheg'malani kol tov.

(Congregation) אָמֵן. מִי שֶׁגְּמָלְךָ טוֹב, הוּא יִגְמָלְךָ כָּל טוֹב סֶלָה.

Amen. Mi sheg'malkha tov, hu yig'malkha kol tov selah.

Mi Shebeirakh on the Birth of a Son

מִי שֶׁבֵּרַךְ אֲבוֹתֵינוּ אַבְרָהָם יִצְחָק וְיַעֲקֹב, מֹשֶׁה וְאַהֲרֹן דָּוִד וּשְׁלֹמֹה, שָׂרָה רִבְקָה
רָחֵל וְלֵאָה, הוּא יְבָרֵךְ אֶת הָאִשָּׁה הַיּוֹלֶדֶת ___ בַּת ___ וְאֶת בְּנָהּ
שֶׁנּוֹלַד לָהּ בְּשֵׁם יֵשׁוּעַ עַבְדּוֹ הַצַּדִּיק, מְשִׁיחֵנוּ. יִזְכּוּ לְהַכְנִיסוֹ בִּבְרִיתוֹ שֶׁל
אַבְרָהָם אָבִינוּ וּלְגַדְּלוֹ לְתוֹרָה וּלְחֻפָּה וּלְמַעֲשִׂים טוֹבִים. וְנֹאמַר אָמֵן.

Mi Shebeirakh on the Birth of a Daughter

מִי שֶׁבֵּרַךְ אֲבוֹתֵינוּ אַבְרָהָם יִצְחָק וְיַעֲקֹב, מֹשֶׁה וְאַהֲרֹן דָּוִד וּשְׁלֹמֹה, שָׂרָה רִבְקָה
רָחֵל וְלֵאָה, הוּא יְבָרֵךְ אֶת הָאִשָּׁה הַיּוֹלֶדֶת ___ בַּת ___ וְאֶת בִּתָּהּ
שֶׁנּוֹלְדָה לָהּ בְּשֵׁם יֵשׁוּעַ עַבְדּוֹ הַצַּדִּיק, מְשִׁיחֵנוּ. וְיִקָּרֵא שְׁמָהּ בְּיִשְׂרָאֵל ___
בַּת ___. יִזְכּוּ לְגַדְּלָהּ לְתוֹרָה וּלְחֻפָּה וּלְמַעֲשִׂים טוֹבִים. וְנֹאמַר אָמֵן.

Mi Shebeirakh For an Oleh

May He who blessed our ancestors Abraham, Isaac and Jacob, bless ___________
son of _______ who has come up to honor God and the Torah (*add on festivals:*
and the festival). May the Holy One, blessed be He, protect and deliver him from
all distress and illness, and bless all his efforts with success in the name of Yeshua
His righteous Servant, our Messiah, (*add on festivals:* celebrating the festival in
Jerusalem) among all Israel his brethren, and let us say, Amen.

Prayer for the Israeli Defense Forces

May He who blessed our ancestors Abraham, Isaac and Jacob, bless the soldiers of
the Israel Defense Forces, in their standing guard upon our land and the cities of
our God from the border of the Lebanon to the Wilderness of Egypt and from the
Great Sea to the approach of the Arava - on land, in the air, and in the sea. May the
Lord give our enemies that rise against us plagues in front of them. May the Holy
One, blessed be He, guard and rescue our soldiers from all trouble and distress and
from all affliction and illness; and send blessing and success in all the work of their
hands. May He crush those that hate us below them and crown them with the
crown of salvation and with the crown of victory. And through them let the verse
be fulfilled that says,"For it is the Lord, your God, that walks with you to fight for
you against your enemies to save you." And let us say, Amen.

Birkat HaGomel

*(The Birkat HaGomel Thanksgiving blessing is recited by those following their Torah aliyah who have survived a
life-threatening event, including serious illness and extensive travel)*

(Oleh) Blessed are You, Lord our God, King of the Universe, who provides good
for the undeserving, and who has provided abundant goodness for me.

(Congregation) Amen! May He who has provided good for you continue to
provide abundant goodness for you.

Mi Shebeirakh on the Birth of a Son

May He who blessed our ancestors Abraham, Isaac and Jacob, Moses and Aaron,
David and Solomon, Sarah, Rebekah, Rachel and Leah, bless the mother who has
given birth __________ daughter of __________ and her new-born son who has
been born to her in the name of Yeshua His righteous Servant, our Messiah. May
his parents bring him into the covenant of Abraham and to live a life observing
G-d's Instruction, to the marriage canopy and for a life of good deeds. And let us
say, Amen.

Mi Shebeirakh on the Birth of a Daughter

May He who blessed our ancestors Abraham, Isaac and Jacob, Moses and Aaron,
David and Solomon, Sarah, Rebekah, Rachel and Leah, bless the mother who has
given birth ________ daughter of ________ and her new-born daughter in the
name of Yeshua His righteous Servant, our Messiah. She shall be called in Israel
__________ daughter of _________ . May her parents raise her to the marriage
canopy and for a life of good deeds. And let us say, Amen.

Mi Shebeirakh for a Bar Mitzvah

מִי שֶׁבֵּרַךְ אֲבוֹתֵינוּ, אַבְרָהָם יִצְחָק וְיַעֲקֹב, הוּא יְבָרֵךְ אֶת _________ בֶּן _________ שֶׁמָּלְאוּ לוֹ שְׁלֹשׁ עֶשְׂרֵה שָׁנָה וְהִגִּיעַ לְמִצְוֹת, וְעָלָה לַתּוֹרָה, לָתֵת שֶׁבַח וְהוֹדָיָה לַיְיָ יִתְבָּרַךְ עַל כָּל הַטּוֹבָה שֶׁגָּמַל אִתּוֹ. יִשְׁמְרֵהוּ הַקָּדוֹשׁ בָּרוּךְ הוּא וִיחַיֵּהוּ, וִיכוֹנֵן אֶת לִבּוֹ בְּשֵׁם יֵשׁוּעַ מְשִׁיחֵנוּ, לִהְיוֹת שָׁלֵם עִם יְיָ וְלָלֶכֶת בִּדְרָכָיו וְלִשְׁמֹר מִצְוֹתָיו כָּל הַיָּמִים. וְנֹאמַר אָמֵן.

Mi Shebeirakh for a Bat Mitzvah

מִי שֶׁבֵּרַךְ אֲבוֹתֵינוּ אַבְרָהָם יִצְחָק וְיַעֲקֹב, שָׂרָה רִבְקָה רָחֵל וְלֵאָה, הוּא יְבָרֵךְ אֶת _________ בַּת _________ שֶׁמָּלְאוּ לָהּ שְׁתֵּים עֶשְׂרֵה שָׁנָה וְהִגִּיעָה לְמִצְוֹת, וְעָלְתָה וְנָתְנָה שֶׁבַח וְהוֹדָיָה לַיְיָ יִתְבָּרַךְ עַל כָּל הַטּוֹבָה שֶׁגָּמַל אִתָּהּ. יִשְׁמְרָהּ הַקָּדוֹשׁ בָּרוּךְ הוּא וִיחַיֶּהָ, וִיכוֹנֵן אֶת לִבָּהּ בְּשֵׁם יֵשׁוּעַ מְשִׁיחֵנוּ, לִהְיוֹת שָׁלֵם עִם יְיָ וְלָלֶכֶת בִּדְרָכָיו וְלִשְׁמֹר מִצְוֹתָיו כָּל הַיָּמִים. וְנֹאמַר אָמֵן.

Blessing by the Father of a Bnai Mitzvah

בָּרוּךְ אַתָּה יְיָ אֱלֹהֵינוּ מֶלֶךְ הָעוֹלָם, שֶׁפְּטָרַנִי מֵעָנְשׁוֹ שֶׁלָּזֶה.

Barukh atah Adonai Eloheinu Melekh Ha'Olam, shep'tarani meian'sho shelaze.

מי שברך

(The following prayer for healing is traditionally recited after the reading of the Torah during the Shabbat or Festival morning service. Those who have sick friends or relatives, when so directed, may mention the name of the sick, either in Hebrew or in English, as part of this prayer)

מִי שֶׁבֵּרַךְ אֲבוֹתֵינוּ אַבְרָהָם יִצְחָק וְיַעֲקֹב, שָׂרָה רִבְקָה רָחֵל וְלֵאָה, הוּא יְבָרֵךְ וִירַפֵּא אֶת כָּל הַחוֹלִים:

(the Reader invites people to mention the names of the sick at this time)

הַקָּדוֹשׁ בָּרוּךְ הוּא יִמָּלֵא רַחֲמִים עֲלֵיהֶם, לְהַחֲזִיקָם וּלְרַפְּאוֹתָם, וְיִשְׁלַח לָהֶם מְהֵרָה רְפוּאָה שְׁלֵמָה מִן הַשָּׁמַיִם, לְכָל אֵבְרֵיהֶם וְגִידֵיהֶם, בְּתוֹךְ שְׁאָר חוֹלֵי יִשְׂרָאֵל, רְפוּאַת הַנֶּפֶשׁ, וּרְפוּאַת הַגּוּף.

שַׁבָּת הִיא \ יוֹם טוֹב הִיא

מִלִּזְעֹק וּרְפוּאָה קְרוֹבָה לָבוֹא, הַשְׁתָּא בַּעֲגָלָא וּבִזְמַן קָרִיב, בְּשֵׁם יֵשׁוּעַ עַבְדּוֹ הַצַּדִּיק, מְשִׁיחֵנוּ, שֶׁחֳלָיֵנוּ נָשָׂא וּמַכְאוֹבֵינוּ סְבָלָם. וְנֹאמַר אָמֵן.

Mi Shebeirakh for a Bar Mitzvah

May He who blessed our ancestors Abraham, Isaac and Jacob, bless __________ son of __________ who has completed thirteen years and attained the age of the commandments, who has been called to the Torah to give praise and thanks to the Lord for all the good he has bestowed on him. May the Holy One, blessed be He, protect and sustain him and direct his heart in the name of Yeshua our Messiah, to be perfect with the Lord, to walk in his ways and keep his commandments all the days of his life. And let us say, Amen.

Mi Shebeirakh for a Bat Mitzvah

May He who blessed our ancestors Abraham, Isaac and Jacob, bless __________ daughter of __________ who has completed twelve years and attained the age of the commandments, and gives praise and thanks to the Lord for all the good he has bestowed on her. May the Holy One, blessed be He, protect and sustain her and direct her heart in the name of Yeshua our Messiah, to be perfect with the Lord, to walk in His ways and keep His commandments all the days of her life. And let us say, Amen.

Blessing by the Father of a Bnai Mitzvah

Blessed is He who has relieved me from the responsibility for this child.

Prayer for Healing

(The following prayer for healing is traditionally recited after the reading of the Torah during the Shabbat or Festival morning service. Those who have sick friends or relatives, when so directed, may mention the name of the sick, either in Hebrew or in English, as part of this prayer)

May He who blessed our ancestors Abraham, Isaac, and Jacob,
Sarah, Rebecca, Rachel, and Leah, bless all those near to us who are sick:

(the Reader invites people to mention the names of the sick at this time)

May the Holy One be filled with compassion, and heal and strengthen them.
May He grant a quick and complete healing for all their bodily parts,
among the other sick people of Israel, a healing of soul and of body.

It is a Shabbat \ Festival

when it is traditionally forbidden to plead; yet we believe healing will come soon in the name of Yeshua His righteous Servant, our Messiah, who bore our sickness and endured our suffering.
And let us say: Amen.

קדיש שלם

יִתְגַּדַּל וְיִתְקַדַּשׁ שְׁמֵהּ רַבָּא. (אָמֵן - Cong) בְּעָלְמָא דִּי בְרָא כִרְעוּתֵהּ,
וְיַמְלִיךְ מַלְכוּתֵהּ בְּחַיֵּיכוֹן וּבְיוֹמֵיכוֹן וּבְחַיֵּי דְכָל בֵּית יִשְׂרָאֵל. בַּעֲגָלָא וּבִזְמַן
קָרִיב, וְאִמְרוּ אָמֵן. (אָמֵן - Cong)

*Yitgadal v'yitkadash sh'mei rabah. B'almah di v'rah khi'rutei, v'yamlikh
mal'khutei b'ḥayeikhon uv'yomeikhon uv'ḥayei d'khol beit Yisraeil. Ba'agalah
uviz'man kariv v'imru, Amen. (Cong - Amen)*

(Together)

יְהֵא שְׁמֵהּ רַבָּא מְבָרַךְ לְעָלַם וּלְעָלְמֵי עָלְמַיָּא.

Y'hei sh'mei rabah m'varakh l'alam ul'al'mei al'mayah.

יִתְבָּרַךְ וְיִשְׁתַּבַּח, וְיִתְפָּאַר וְיִתְרוֹמַם וְיִתְנַשֵּׂא וְיִתְהַדָּר וְיִתְעַלֶּה וְיִתְהַלָּל שְׁמֵהּ
דְּקֻדְשָׁא, בְּרִיךְ הוּא, (בְּרִיךְ הוּא - Cong)

*Yit'barakh v'yish'tabakh, v'yit'paar v'yit'romam v'yit'naseh v'yit'hadar
v'yit'aleh v'yit'halal sh'mei d'kudshah b'rikh hu, (Cong - b'rikh hu)*

*לְעֵלָּא מִן כָּל *l'ela min kol*

בִּרְכָתָא וְשִׁירָתָא, תֻּשְׁבְּחָתָא וְנֶחֱמָתָא, דַּאֲמִירָן בְּעָלְמָא,
וְאִמְרוּ אָמֵן. (אָמֵן - Cong)

*bir'khatah v'shiratah, tush'bikhatah v'neḥematah, da'amiran b'alma,
v'imru, Amen. (Cong - Amen)*

תִּתְקַבֵּל צְלוֹתְהוֹן וּבָעוּתְהוֹן דְּכָל בֵּית יִשְׂרָאֵל קֳדָם אֲבוּהוֹן דִּי בִשְׁמַיָּא,
וְאִמְרוּ. אָמֵן.

*Tit'kabel ts'lot'hon uva'ut'hon d'khol beit Yisraeil kadam avuhon di
vish'mayah, v'imru, Amen. (Cong - Amen)*

יְהֵא שְׁלָמָא רַבָּא מִן שְׁמַיָּא וְחַיִּים עָלֵינוּ וְעַל כָּל יִשְׂרָאֵל,
וְאִמְרוּ אָמֵן. (אָמֵן - Cong)

*Y'hei sh'lamah rabah min sh'mayah v'ḥayim aleinu v'al kol Yisraeil, v'imru,
Amen. (Cong - Amen)*

עֹשֶׂה שָׁלוֹם בִּמְרוֹמָיו הוּא יַעֲשֶׂה שָׁלוֹם עָלֵינוּ וְעַל כָּל יִשְׂרָאֵל,
וְאִמְרוּ אָמֵן. (אָמֵן - Cong)

*Oseh shalom bim'romav Hu ya'aseh shalom aleinu, v'al kol Yisraeil v'imru,
Amen. (Cong - Amen)*

Full Kaddish

Magnified and sanctified may God's great Name *(Cong - Amen)* be throughout the world which He has created according to His will. May He establish His kingdom in our lifetime, and during our days, and within the life of the entire house of Israel, speedily and soon; and say, *Amen. (Cong - Amen)*

(Together)

May the greatness of His Name be blessed forever and ever.

Let the Name of the Holy One, *blessed is He, (Cong - blessed is he)* be blessed and praised, glorified and exalted, extolled and honored, adored and lauded,

*beyond all

From Rosh Hashanah to Yom Kippur substitute: **exceedingly* beyond all

of the blessings and songs, praises and consolations that are ever spoken in this world, and say, *Amen. (Cong - Amen)*

May the prayers and supplications of the whole house of Israel be acceptable to our Heavenly Father, and say, *"Amen." (Cong - Amen)*

May there be abundant peace from heaven, and life for us and for all Israel, and say, *"Amen." (Cong - Amen)*

May He who creates peace in His high heavens create peace for us and for all Israel, and say, *"Amen." (Cong - Amen)*

נטילת לולב

יְהִי רָצוֹן מִלְפָנֶיךָ, יְיָ אֱלֹהַי וֵאלֹהֵי אֲבוֹתַי, בִּפְרִי עֵץ הָדָר, וְכַפּוֹת תְּמָרִים, וַעֲנַף עֵץ עָבוֹת, וְעַרְבֵי נָחַל, אוֹתִיּוֹת שְׁמֶךָ. בָּרִיךְ הוּא וּשְׁכִינְתֵהּ, בִּדְחִילוּ וּרְחִימוּ, לְיַחֵד שֵׁם, בְּשֵׁם כָּל יִשְׂרָאֵל. אָמֵן. בָּרוּךְ יְיָ לְעוֹלָם, אָמֵן וְאָמֵן.

Proper procedure for taking up the Lulav and Etrog

(It is a mitsvah to wave the lulav on each of the first seven days of Sukkot, except Shabbat. The proper time is in the morning, both in one's own sukkah and during the special Sukkot liturgy in the morning service. While reciting the blessing, the etrog is held with the pittam (stem) pointed down in the left hand. The lulav is held in the right hand. After the blessing, the etrog is turned around so that it is held with the pittam facing up)

Blessing for Taking up the Lulav

בָּרוּךְ אַתָּה יְיָ אֱלֹהֵינוּ מֶלֶךְ הָעוֹלָם, אֲשֶׁר קִדְּשָׁנוּ בְּמִצְוֹתָיו, וְצִוָּנוּ עַל נְטִילַת לוּלָב.

Barukh atah Adonai, Eloheinu Melekh Ha'Olam,
asher kid'shanu b'mitzvotav v'tzivanu al netilat lulav.

(On the first use of the lulav for the year recite the Sheheheyanu blessing)

בָּרוּךְ אַתָּה יְיָ אֱלֹהֵינוּ מֶלֶךְ הָעוֹלָם, שֶׁהֶחֱיָנוּ וְקִיְּמָנוּ וְהִגִּיעָנוּ לַזְּמַן הַזֶּה.

Barukh atah Adonai, Eloheinu Melekh Ha'Olam, sheheḥeyanu, vekiyemanu,
vehigiyanu, lazman hazeh!

Netilat Lulav

May it be Your will, Lord my God and the God of my Fathers, that through my taking up the fruit of the etrog tree, the date palm branches, the branches of the myrtle and the willow, that I grow closer to You. Blessed are You and Your presence in this world, and in awe and in love do we seek to make holy Your name as Your people Israel. Blessed is the Lord forever and ever. Amen and Amen.

Proper procedure for taking up the Lulav and Etrog

(It is a mitsvah to wave the lulav on each of the first seven days of Sukkot, except Shabbat. The proper time is in the morning, both in one's own sukkah and during the special Sukkot liturgy in the morning service. While reciting the blessing, the etrog is held with the pittam (stem) pointed down in the left hand. The lulav is held in the right hand. After the blessing, the etrog is turned around so that it is held with the pittam facing up)

Blessing for Taking up the Lulav

Blessed are You, Lord our God, King of the Universe, who has sanctified us with His commandments and has commanded us to take up the lulav.

(On the first use of the lulav for the year recite the Sheheheyanu blessing)

Blessed are You, Lord our God, King of the Universe, who has kept us, and sustained us, and enabled us to reach this season!

(After the blessing you wave/shake the lulav in the following manner)

- Stand facing east.

- Hold the lulav out to the east (in front of you) and shake it three times. Each time the motion of shaking should be a drawing in to you: reach out and draw in, reach out and draw in, reach out and draw in.

- Repeat the same motion three times to your right (south), behind and over your shoulder (west), to your left (north), raising it up above you (the heavens), and lowering it down toward your feet (the earth).

- All of these should be done slowly and deliberately concentrating on the symbolisms and intentions of the act.

- The lulav is also waved during Hallel while saying: Give thanks to the Lord for He is good, for His lovingkindness endures forever.

- The lulav is again waved while saying: Let Israel say that His lovingkindness endures forever.

- And it is waved again while saying: We implore You, Lord, save us.

Ḥanukah Blessings & Readings

(Using the lit shammash candle, light each new candle first, starting on the extreme right of the Ḥanukah Menorah on the first night, then adding the daily candle to the left of the previous night's candle, thus lighting the candles from left to right, while reciting the following blessings. On Erev Shabbat light the Ḥanukah Menorah before the Shabbat candles. On Saturday night traditions vary whether to light the Havdalah candle before the Ḥanukah Menorah or afterward. Maoz Tsur is traditionally sung each night of Ḥanukah)

בָּרוּךְ אַתָּה יְיָ אֱלֹהֵינוּ מֶלֶךְ הָעוֹלָם, אֲשֶׁר קִדְּשָׁנוּ בְּמִצְוֹתָיו,
וְצִוָּנוּ לְהַדְלִיק נֵר שֶׁל חֲנֻכָּה.

Barukh atah Adonai, Eloheinu Melekh Ha'Olam,

asher kideshanu be-mitzvahtav, vitzivanu, le-hadniḥ ner, shel Ḥanukah.

Blessed are you, Lord our God, King of the Universe, who has sanctified us with His commandments, and commanded us to light the Ḥanukah lights.

בָּרוּךְ אַתָּה יְיָ אֱלֹהֵינוּ מֶלֶךְ הָעוֹלָם, שֶׁעָשָׂה נִסִּים לַאֲבוֹתֵינוּ בַּיָּמִים הָהֵם
בַּזְּמַן הַזֶּה.

Barukh atah Adonai, Eloheinu Melekh Ha'Olam,

she-asa nisim la-voteinu, ba-yamim ha-hem, bazman ha-zeh.

Blessed are You, Lord our God, King of the Universe who has done miraculous deeds for our forefathers, in those days at this season.

(Only Recite on the First Night of Ḥanukah)

בָּרוּךְ אַתָּה יְיָ אֱלֹהֵינוּ מֶלֶךְ הָעוֹלָם, שֶׁהֶחֱיָנוּ וְקִיְּמָנוּ וְהִגִּיעָנוּ לַזְּמַן הַזֶּה.

Barukh atah Adonai, Eloheinu Melekh Ha'Olam, sheheḥeyanu, vekiyemanu, vehigiyanu, lazman ḥazeh!

Blessed are You, Lord our God, King of the Universe, who has kept us, and sustained us, and enabled us to reach this season!

John 8:12

הַמָּשִׁיחַ יֵשׁוּעַ הוֹסִיף לְדַבֵּר אֲלֵיהֶם וְאָמַר: אֲנִי אוֹר הָעוֹלָם. אִישׁ הַהוֹלֵךְ
אַחֲרַי לֹא יִתְהַלֵּךְ בַּחֹשֶׁךְ, אֶלָּא אוֹר הַחַיִּים יִהְיֶה לוֹ.

Messiah Yeshua spoke unto them, saying: I am the light of the world. A person that follows after me shall not walk in the darkness, but shall have the light of life.

Blessing of the Light of Messiah Yeshua

בָּרוּךְ אַתָּה יְיָ אֱלֹהֵינוּ מֶלֶךְ הָעוֹלָם, אֲשֶׁר קִדְּשָׁנוּ בִּדְבָרוֹ, וְנָתַן לָנוּ אֶת
יֵשׁוּעַ מְשִׁיחֵנוּ, אוֹר הָעוֹלָם.

Barukh atah Adonai Eloheinu Melekh Ha'Olam,

asher kid'shanu bidvaro, v'natan lanu et Yeshua Meshiḥeinu, Or l'Olam.

Blessed are You, Lord our God, King of the Universe, who has sanctified us with his word, and has given us Yeshua our Messiah, the Light of the World.

עַל הַנִּסִּים וְעַל הַפֻּרְקָן וְעַל הַגְּבוּרוֹת וְעַל הַתְּשׁוּעוֹת וְעַל הַמִּלְחָמוֹת שֶׁעָשִׂיתָ
לַאֲבוֹתֵינוּ בַּיָּמִים הָהֵם בַּזְּמַן הַזֶּה.

Al hanisim v'al hafurkan, v'al hag'vurot, v'al hat'shu-ot, v'al hamil'ḥamot sheh-asitah
la-avoteinu bayameem hahem baz'man hazeh

We thank you for the miracles, for the redemption, for the mighty deeds, for the saving acts, and for the battles which You have done for our ancestors in those days, at this time

In the days of the Hasmonean Matityahu son of Yoḥanan the High Priest, and his sons, when stood the wicked kingdom of the Hellenists against Your people Israel to cause them to abandon Your Torah and to turn from the statutes of will, You in Your great compassion stood for them in their time of tribulation. You contended for them in their fight, judged for them in their judgment, avenged them in their vengeance, and delivered them by means of heros when they were weak; the many into the hands of the few, the unclean into the hands of the clean, the wicked into the hands of the righteous, and the deceiver into the hands of they who practiced Your Torah. Your great and holy name is established in Your world, and You have established a great salvation for Your people Israel, and have relieved them from that day to this. Indeed, after this Your children came into the Holy Place of Your House, we cleared Your Temple of defilement, and purified Your holy sanctuary, and lit the lights in Your holy court, and established the lighting of the lights in the eight days of Ḥanukah, to thank and to praise the greatness of Your name, all in preparation for the coming of Israel's Messiah, Yeshua, the Light of the World.

Ma'oz Tsur

מָעוֹז צוּר יְשׁוּעָתִי לְךָ נָאֶה לְשַׁבֵּחַ,

תִּכּוֹן בֵּית תְּפִלָּתִי וְשָׁם תּוֹדָה נְזַבֵּחַ,

לְעֵת תָּכִין מַטְבֵּחַ מִצָּר הַמְנַבֵּחַ,

אָז אֶגְמֹר בְּשִׁיר מִזְמוֹר חֲנֻכַּת הַמִּזְבֵּחַ.

Ma'oz tsur Yeshuati, lekha na'eh le-shabe'aḥ
Tikon beit tefilati, vesham todah nezabe'aḥ
Le'eit takhin matbei'aḥ, mitsar hamna-bei'aḥ
Az egmor beshir mizmor, ḥanukat hamiz-bei'aḥ
Az egmor beshir mizmor, ḥanukat hamiz-bei'aḥ

Rock of Ages let our song praise Thy saving power
Thou amidst the raging foes, wast our sheltering tower
Furious they assailed us, but Thine arm availed us
And Thy word broke their sword, when our own strength failed us
And Thy word broke their sword, when our own strength failed us

Rock of Ages, stumbling stone, whom the builders rejected
You've become the cornerstone, whom the Lord selected
Lift Yeshua up and praise Him, worship God who raised Him
Shine His light through the night, til the day we gaze on Him
Shine His light through the night, til the day we gaze on Him

(Strict Translation of the first verse: A refuge, my rock of salvation, it is pleasant to sing Your praises.
Let our house of prayer be restored, and there we will offer You thanks.
When You have slaughtered the cursing foe, then we will celebrate with song and psalm the altar's dedication.)

Blessing for the Counting of the Omer

בָּרוּךְ אַתָּה יְיָ אֱלֹהֵינוּ מֶלֶךְ הָעוֹלָם, אֲשֶׁר קִדְּשָׁנוּ בְּמִצְוֹתָיו, וְצִוָּנוּ עַל סְפִירַת הָעוֹמֶר.

Barukh atah Adonai, Eloheinu Melekh Ha'Olam, asher kid'shanu b'mitsvotav v'tsivanu al sefirat haOmer.

Blessed are You, Lord our God, King of the Universe who sanctifies us by His commandments and who has commanded us to count the Omer.

(For the first week you count just the days. After a complete week, you count both the number of days and the number of weeks)

Today is ___________ (total) day(s), which are ________ week(s) and ________ day(s), of the Omer.

Blessings before Reading the Megillah

בָּרוּךְ אַתָּה יְיָ אֱלֹהֵינוּ מֶלֶךְ הָעוֹלָם, אֲשֶׁר קִדְּשָׁנוּ בְּמִצְוֹתָיו וְצִוָּנוּ עַל מִקְרָא מְגִלָּה.

Barukh atah Adonai, Eloheinu Melekh Ha'Olam, asher kideshanu be-mitzvahtav, vitzivanu, al mikrah megillah.

Blessed are You, Lord our God, King of the Universe who sanctifies us by His commandments and who has commanded us to read the Megillah.

בָּרוּךְ אַתָּה יְיָ אֱלֹהֵינוּ מֶלֶךְ הָעוֹלָם, שֶׁעָשָׂה נִסִּים לַאֲבוֹתֵינוּ בַּיָּמִים הָהֵם בַּזְּמַן הַזֶּה.

Barukh atah Adonai, Eloheinu Melekh Ha'Olam, she-asa nisim la-voteinu, ba-yamim ha-hem, bazman ha-zeh.

Blessed are You, Lord our God, King of the Universe who has done miraculous deeds for our forefathers, in those days at this season.

בָּרוּךְ אַתָּה יְיָ אֱלֹהֵינוּ מֶלֶךְ הָעוֹלָם, שֶׁהֶחֱיָנוּ וְקִיְּמָנוּ וְהִגִּיעָנוּ לַזְּמַן הַזֶּה.

Barukh atah Adonai, Eloheinu Melekh Ha'Olam, sheheḥeyanu, vekiyemanu, vehigiyanu, lazman hazeh!

Blessed are You, Lord our God, King of the Universe, who has kept us, and sustained us, and enabled us to reach this season!

Prayer for the United States of America

Our God and God of our ancestors, we ask Your blessings for our country, for the government of this Republic, for our military leaders and armed forces, for the President of the United States, and for all who exercise just and rightful authority. Teach them insights of Your Scriptures, that they administer all affairs of state fairly, that peace and security, happiness and prosperity, justice and freedom may forever abide in our midst.

May this land submit to Your Sovereignty and be an influence for good throughout the world, promoting peace and freedom, and helping to fulfill the vision of Your prophets that all the nations will be one in Your name, knowing the truth of Messiah Yeshua's atonement.

Nation shall not lift up sword against nation, neither shall they experience war any more. For all people, both great and small, shall know the Lord and his Messiah. And let us say: *Amen.*

Prayer for the State of Israel

Our Father in Heaven, Rock and Redeemer of the people Israel,
Bless the State of Israel, with its promise of redemption.
Shield it with Your love; spread over it the shelter of Your peace.

Guide its leaders and advisors with Your light and Your truth.
Help them with Your good counsel and open the eyes of Your Chosen People to the full understanding of Messiah Yeshua and Your salvation in him.

Strengthen the hands of those who defend our Holy Land. Deliver them; crown their efforts with triumph. Bless the land with peace, and its inhabitants with lasting joy as we await the return of our Messiah Yeshua. And let us say: *Amen.*

A Jewish Poem

I want to write a Jewish poem. It will be in the form of an old man praying in the Orthodox synagogue across the street from the gas station, and kitty corner from the Yeshiva where boys with dangling ribbons of hair and stern eyes learn the Talmud. This old man is my grandfather, Aaron. A strong man, a farmer in White Russia, who lifted heavy bushels of wheat on his back. He came to America to flee the Cossacks. I can see him now, riding his horse drawn cart through the alleys, collecting valuables from garbage cans. He never spoke English; He seldom spoke Yiddish. His eyes turned inward to an earlier time when prophets and poets, invoked the words he whispers now. Standing to the side of the sacred Ark, covered by his zebrastriped tallit; his yarmulke on his head. He is one of a tribe of ancient worshippers touched by sacred garments, scrolls and words; men and women who lifted their faces toward the burning bush, the parting sea, Moses receiving the tablets of the Law on Mount Sinai. For my grandfather there is a burning light of holiness. So let the sun go down; let the darkness come. Let the other more worldly Jews, some of whom have become rich, leave the synagogue. There is no place for my grandfather in America, but his synagogue stands; confronting me with his sad, intense eyes staring through his spectacles. "So Gehshon, you think you are a poet? Yet you have not listened to the poetry of your fathers. Come and worship with me now." (Gary Pacernick)

יִגְדַּל

יִגְדַּל אֱלֹהִים חַי וְיִשְׁתַּבַּח, נִמְצָא, וְאֵין עֵת אֶל אֶל מְצִיאוּתוֹ.

אֶחָד וְאֵין יָחִיד כְּיִחוּדוֹ, נֶעְלָם, וְגַם אֵין סוֹף לְאַחְדוּתוֹ.

אֵין לוֹ דְמוּת הַגּוּף וְאֵינוֹ גוּף, לֹא נַעֲרוֹךְ אֵלָיו קְדֻשָּׁתוֹ.

קַדְמוֹן לְכָל דָּבָר אֲשֶׁר נִבְרָא, רִאשׁוֹן וְאֵין רֵאשִׁית לְרֵאשִׁיתוֹ.

הִנּוֹ אֲדוֹן עוֹלָם לְכָל נוֹצָר, יוֹרֶה גְדֻלָּתוֹ וּמַלְכוּתוֹ.

שֶׁפַע נְבוּאָתוֹ נְתָנוֹ, אֶל אַנְשֵׁי סְגֻלָּתוֹ וְתִפְאַרְתּוֹ.

לֹא קָם בְּיִשְׂרָאֵל כְּמֹשֶׁה עוֹד, נָבִיא וּמַבִּיט אֶת תְּמוּנָתוֹ.

תּוֹרַת אֱמֶת נָתַן לְעַמּוֹ אֵל, עַל יַד נְבִיאוֹ נֶאֱמַן בֵּיתוֹ.

לֹא יַחֲלִיף הָאֵל וְלֹא יָמִיר דָּתוֹ, לְעוֹלָמִים, לְזוּלָתוֹ.

צוֹפֶה וְיוֹדֵעַ סְתָרֵינוּ, מַבִּיט לְסוֹף דָּבָר בְּקַדְמָתוֹ.

גּוֹמֵל לְאִישׁ חֶסֶד כְּמִפְעָלוֹ, נוֹתֵן לְרָשָׁע רָע כְּרִשְׁעָתוֹ.

יִשְׁלַח לְקֵץ הַיָּמִין מְשִׁיחֵנוּ יֵשׁוּעַ, לִפְדּוֹת מְחַכֵּי קֵץ יְשׁוּעָתוֹ.

מֵתִים יְחַיֶּה אֵל בְּרֹב חַסְדּוֹ, בָּרוּךְ עֲדֵי עַד שֵׁם תְּהִלָּתוֹ.

Yigdal Elohim ḥai veyishtabaḥ nimtza, ve'ein et el metzi'uto.
Eḥad ve'ein yaḥid ke'yiḥ'udoh ne'elam, ve'gam ein sof le'aḥduto.
Ein lo de'mut haguf ve'eino guf, lo na'arokh elav ke'dushato.
Kadmon le'khal davar asher nivra, rishon ve'ein reishit lerey'shito.
Hino Adon Olam l'khal notzar, yoreh ge'dulato u'malkhuto.
Shefa ne'vuato netano, el anshei segu'lato vetif'arto.
Lo kam b'Yisraeil ke'Moshe od, navi umabit et te'munato.
Torat emet natan l'amo El, al yad n'vio ne'eman bei'to.
Lo yaḥalif haEl v'lo yamir dato, l'olamim, l'zulato.
Tsofeh veyodea s'tareinu mabit l'sof davar b'kadmato.
Gomeil l'ish ḥesed k'mifalo, notein l'rasha ra k'rishato.
Yishlaḥ l'ketz hayamim m'shiḥeinu Yeshua, lif'dot m'hakei keits yeshuato.
Meitim yeḥayeh El berov ḥasdo, barukh a'dei aḥd shem tehillato.

Shir Hamalot (Transliteration of Psalm 126)

Shir Hama'alot, B'shuv Adonai et shivat Tsiyon hayinu k'ḥol'mim.
Az Yimalei s'ḥok pinu ul'shoneinu rinah.
Az yom'ru vagoyim hig'dil Adonai la'asot im eileh.
hig'dil Adonai la'asot imanu, hayinu s'meiḥim.
Shuvah Adonai et sh'viteinu, ka'afikim banegev.
Hazor'im b'di'mah, b'rinah yik'tsoru.
Halokh yelekh uvakho nosei meshekh hazarah,
bo yavo v'rinah nosei alumotayv.

Yigdal

Exalted and praised be the Living God, He exists unbounded by time.

He is One - and there is no oneness like His Oneness.

Inscrutable and infinite is His Oneness.

He has no semblance of a body; His holiness is without comparison.

He preceded every being that was created, and nothing preceded Him.

**Behold! He is Master of the Universe for all;
He demonstrates His   greatness and His sovereignty.**

He granted His flow of prophecy to His treasured splendorous people.

**In Israel there was no man like Moses,
a prophet who perceived His vision clearly.**

God gave His people a Torah of truth, by means of His most trusted prophet.

**God will never amend nor exchange His law for any other one,
for all eternity.**

He scrutinizes and knows our hidden most secrets; He perceives a matter's outcome at its inception.

**He recompenses man with kindness according to his deed;
He places evil on the wicked according to his wickedness.**

By the End of Days He will send our Messiah Yeshua, to redeem those longing for His final salvation.

**God will revive the dead in His abundant kindness,
blessed forever is His praised Name.**

Shir Hamalot (Translation of Psalm 126)

When the Lord restored the fortunes of Zion, we were like those who dream. Then our mouth was filled with laughter, and our tongue with shouts of joy; then they said among the nations, "The Lord has done great things for them." The Lord has done great things for us; we are glad. Restore our fortunes, O Lord, like the watercourses in the Negeb! May those who sow in tears reap with shouts of joy! He that goes forth weeping, bearing the seed for sowing, shall come home with shouts of joy, bringing his sheaves with him.

עֲקֵדָה – *Genesis 22:1-19*

וַיְהִי אַחַר הַדְּבָרִים הָאֵלֶּה וְהָאֱלֹהִים נִסָּה אֶת־אַבְרָהָם וַיֹּאמֶר אֵלָיו אַבְרָהָם וַיֹּאמֶר
הִנֵּנִי: וַיֹּאמֶר קַח־נָא אֶת־בִּנְךָ אֶת־יְחִידְךָ אֲשֶׁר־אָהַבְתָּ אֶת־יִצְחָק וְלֶךְ־לְךָ אֶל־אֶרֶץ
הַמֹּרִיָּה וְהַעֲלֵהוּ שָׁם לְעֹלָה עַל אַחַד הֶהָרִים אֲשֶׁר אֹמַר אֵלֶיךָ: וַיַּשְׁכֵּם אַבְרָהָם בַּבֹּקֶר
וַיַּחֲבֹשׁ אֶת־חֲמֹרוֹ וַיִּקַּח אֶת־שְׁנֵי נְעָרָיו אִתּוֹ וְאֵת יִצְחָק בְּנוֹ וַיְבַקַּע עֲצֵי עֹלָה וַיָּקָם
וַיֵּלֶךְ אֶל־הַמָּקוֹם אֲשֶׁר־אָמַר־לוֹ הָאֱלֹהִים: בַּיּוֹם הַשְּׁלִישִׁי וַיִּשָּׂא אַבְרָהָם אֶת־עֵינָיו
וַיַּרְא אֶת־הַמָּקוֹם מֵרָחֹק: וַיֹּאמֶר אַבְרָהָם אֶל־נְעָרָיו שְׁבוּ־לָכֶם פֹּה עִם־הַחֲמוֹר וַאֲנִי
וְהַנַּעַר נֵלְכָה עַד־כֹּה וְנִשְׁתַּחֲוֶה וְנָשׁוּבָה אֲלֵיכֶם: וַיִּקַּח אַבְרָהָם אֶת־עֲצֵי הָעֹלָה וַיָּשֶׂם
עַל־יִצְחָק בְּנוֹ וַיִּקַּח בְּיָדוֹ אֶת־הָאֵשׁ וְאֶת־הַמַּאֲכֶלֶת וַיֵּלְכוּ שְׁנֵיהֶם יַחְדָּו: וַיֹּאמֶר יִצְחָק
אֶל־אַבְרָהָם אָבִיו וַיֹּאמֶר אָבִי וַיֹּאמֶר הִנֶּנִּי בְנִי וַיֹּאמֶר הִנֵּה הָאֵשׁ וְהָעֵצִים וְאַיֵּה הַשֶּׂה
לְעֹלָה: וַיֹּאמֶר אַבְרָהָם אֱלֹהִים יִרְאֶה־לּוֹ הַשֶּׂה לְעֹלָה בְּנִי וַיֵּלְכוּ שְׁנֵיהֶם יַחְדָּו: וַיָּבֹאוּ
אֶל־הַמָּקוֹם אֲשֶׁר אָמַר־לוֹ הָאֱלֹהִים וַיִּבֶן שָׁם אַבְרָהָם אֶת־הַמִּזְבֵּחַ וַיַּעֲרֹךְ אֶת־הָעֵצִים
וַיַּעֲקֹד אֶת־יִצְחָק בְּנוֹ וַיָּשֶׂם אֹתוֹ עַל־הַמִּזְבֵּחַ מִמַּעַל לָעֵצִים: וַיִּשְׁלַח אַבְרָהָם אֶת־יָדוֹ
וַיִּקַּח אֶת־הַמַּאֲכֶלֶת לִשְׁחֹט אֶת־בְּנוֹ: וַיִּקְרָא אֵלָיו מַלְאַךְ יְיָ מִן־הַשָּׁמַיִם וַיֹּאמֶר אַבְרָהָם
אַבְרָהָם וַיֹּאמֶר הִנֵּנִי: וַיֹּאמֶר אַל־תִּשְׁלַח יָדְךָ אֶל־הַנַּעַר וְאַל־תַּעַשׂ לוֹ מְאוּמָה כִּי עַתָּה
יָדַעְתִּי כִּי־יְרֵא אֱלֹהִים אַתָּה וְלֹא חָשַׂכְתָּ אֶת־בִּנְךָ אֶת־יְחִידְךָ מִמֶּנִּי: וַיִּשָּׂא אַבְרָהָם
אֶת־עֵינָיו וַיַּרְא וְהִנֵּה־אַיִל אַחַר נֶאֱחַז בַּסְּבַךְ בְּקַרְנָיו וַיֵּלֶךְ אַבְרָהָם וַיִּקַּח אֶת־הָאַיִל
וַיַּעֲלֵהוּ לְעֹלָה תַּחַת בְּנוֹ: וַיִּקְרָא אַבְרָהָם שֵׁם־הַמָּקוֹם הַהוּא יְיָ יִרְאֶה אֲשֶׁר יֵאָמֵר הַיּוֹם
בְּהַר יְיָ יֵרָאֶה: וַיִּקְרָא מַלְאַךְ יְיָ אֶל־אַבְרָהָם שֵׁנִית מִן־הַשָּׁמָיִם: וַיֹּאמֶר בִּי נִשְׁבַּעְתִּי
נְאֻם־יְיָ כִּי יַעַן אֲשֶׁר עָשִׂיתָ אֶת־הַדָּבָר הַזֶּה וְלֹא חָשַׂכְתָּ אֶת־בִּנְךָ אֶת־יְחִידֶךָ:
כִּי־בָרֵךְ אֲבָרֶכְךָ וְהַרְבָּה אַרְבֶּה אֶת־זַרְעֲךָ כְּכוֹכְבֵי הַשָּׁמַיִם וְכַחוֹל אֲשֶׁר עַל־שְׂפַת
הַיָּם וְיִרַשׁ זַרְעֲךָ אֵת שַׁעַר אֹיְבָיו: וְהִתְבָּרְכוּ בְזַרְעֲךָ כֹּל גּוֹיֵי הָאָרֶץ עֵקֶב אֲשֶׁר שָׁמַעְתָּ
בְּקֹלִי: וַיָּשָׁב אַבְרָהָם אֶל־נְעָרָיו וַיָּקֻמוּ וַיֵּלְכוּ יַחְדָּו אֶל־בְּאֵר שָׁבַע וַיֵּשֶׁב אַבְרָהָם
בִּבְאֵר שָׁבַע:

רִבּוֹנוֹ שֶׁל עוֹלָם יְהִי רָצוֹן מִלְּפָנֶיךָ יְיָ אֱלֹהֵינוּ וֵאלֹהֵי אֲבוֹתֵינוּ שֶׁתִּזְכֹּר לָנוּ בְּרִית
אֲבוֹתֵינוּ כְּמוֹ שֶׁכָּבַשׁ אַבְרָהָם אָבִינוּ אֶת רַחֲמָיו מִבֶּן יְחִידוֹ וְרָצָה לִשְׁחֹט אוֹתוֹ כְּדֵי
לַעֲשׂוֹת רְצוֹנֶךָ כֵּן יִכְבְּשׁוּ רַחֲמֶיךָ אֶת־כַּעַסְךָ מֵעָלֵינוּ וְיִגֹּלּוּ רַחֲמֶיךָ עַל מִדּוֹתֶיךָ, וְתִתְנַהֵג
אִתָּנוּ לִפְנִים מִשּׁוּרַת דִּינֶךָ וְתִתְנַהֵג עִמָּנוּ יְיָ אֱלֹהֵינוּ בְּמִדַּת הַחֶסֶד וּבְמִדַּת הָרַחֲמִים
וּבְטוּבְךָ הַגָּדוֹל יָשׁוּב חֲרוֹן אַפֶּךָ מֵעַמְּךָ וּמֵעִירְךָ וּמֵאַרְצֶךָ וּמִנַּחֲלָתֶךָ וְקַיֶּם לָנוּ יְיָ
אֱלֹהֵינוּ אֶת־הַדָּבָר שֶׁהִבְטַחְתָּנוּ עַל יְדֵי מֹשֶׁה עַבְדֶּךָ כָּאָמוּר: וְזָכַרְתִּי אֶת־בְּרִיתִי
יַעֲקוֹב וְאַף אֶת־בְּרִיתִי יִצְחָק וְאַף אֶת־בְּרִיתִי אַבְרָהָם אֶזְכֹּר וְהָאָרֶץ אֶזְכֹּר:

The Akeidah - *Genesis 22:1-19*

And it came to pass after these things, that God tested Abraham, and said to him, Abraham; and he said, Here am I. And He said, Take now your son, your only son, whom thou love, Isaac, and go to the land of Moriah; and offer him there for a burnt-offering upon one of the mountains which I will show you. And Abraham rose early in the morning, and saddled his donkey, and took two of his young men with him, and Isaac his son. And he carried the wood for the burnt-offering, and rose up, and went to the place which God had told him to go. On the third day Abraham lifted up his eyes, and saw the place in the distance. And Abraham said unto his young men, Wait here with the donkey, and I and the young man will go and worship, and come again to you. And Abraham took the wood of the burnt-offering, and placed it upon Isaac his son; and he took in his hand the fire and the knife; and they both went on together. And Isaac spoke to Abraham his father, and said, My father: and he said, Here am I, my son. And he said, Behold, the fire and the wood, but where is the lamb for a burnt-offering? And Abraham said, God will provide himself the lamb for a burnt-offering, my son. So they both went on together.

And they came to the place which God had told him, and Abraham built the altar there, and laid the wood in order, and bound Isaac his son, and laid him on the altar on the wood. And Abraham stretched out his hand and took the knife to slay his son. And the Angel of the Lord called to him out of heaven and said: Abraham, Abraham. And he said: Here am I. And He said: Lay not your hand upon the young man, neither do anything to him, for now I know that you fear God, seeing you would not withhold your son, your only son, from Me. And Abraham lifted up his eyes, and looked, and, behold, behind him a ram was caught in the thicket by his horns. And Abraham went and took the ram, and offered him up for a burnt-offering in place of his son. And Abraham called the name of that place Adonai-Yireh, as it is said to this day, In the mount of the Lord it will be provided. And the Angel of the Lord called to Abraham a second time out of heaven, and said: By Myself have I sworn, says the Lord, because you have done this thing, and have not withheld your son, your only son, that in blessing I will bless you, and in multiplying I will multiply your seed as the stars of the heavens, and as the sand which is upon the seashore. And your seed shall possess the gate of his enemies and in your seed will all the nations of the earth be blessed, because you obeyed My voice. So Abraham returned to his young men, and they rose up and went together to Beersheba, and Abraham dwelt at Beersheba.

Master of the Universe! May it be Your will, Lord our God and God of our fathers, to remember for our sake the covenant of our fathers. Even as our father, Abraham held back his compassion for his only son and would have slain him to do Your will, so may Your compassion hold back Your anger against us; let Your compassion prevail over Your justice. Deal with us leniently. Deal with us, Lord our God, kindly and in mercy. In Your great goodness, turn Your fierce anger away from Your people and from Your city, from Your land and from Your heritage. Fulfill for us, Lord our God, the promise You made through Your servant Moses, as it is said, "I will remember My covenant with Jacob, and My covenant with Isaac, and also My covenant with Abraham. I will remember the land."

Psalm 27

(Recited daily just before the kiddush according to Ashkenai Jewish tradition from Rosh Hodesh Elul through Hoshanah Rabbah)

לְדָוִד.

יְיָ אוֹרִי וְיִשְׁעִי מִמִּי אִירָא, יְיָ מָעוֹז חַיַּי מִמִּי אֶפְחָד.

בִּקְרֹב עָלַי מְרֵעִים, לֶאֱכֹל אֶת בְּשָׂרִי צָרַי וְאֹיְבַי לִי הֵמָּה כָּשְׁלוּ וְנָפָלוּ.

אִם תַּחֲנֶה עָלַי מַחֲנֶה לֹא יִירָא לִבִּי, אִם תָּקוּם עָלַי מִלְחָמָה בְּזֹאת אֲנִי בוֹטֵחַ.

אַחַת שָׁאַלְתִּי מֵאֵת יְיָ, אוֹתָהּ אֲבַקֵּשׁ שִׁבְתִּי בְּבֵית יְיָ, כָּל יְמֵי חַיַּי לַחֲזוֹת בְּנֹעַם יְיָ וּלְבַקֵּר בְּהֵיכָלוֹ.

כִּי יִצְפְּנֵנִי בְּסֻכֹּה בְּיוֹם רָעָה, יַסְתִּרֵנִי בְּסֵתֶר אָהֳלוֹ בְּצוּר יְרוֹמְמֵנִי.

וְעַתָּה יָרוּם רֹאשִׁי, עַל אֹיְבַי סְבִיבוֹתַי וְאֶזְבְּחָה בְאָהֳלוֹ זִבְחֵי תְרוּעָה, אָשִׁירָה וַאֲזַמְּרָה לַיְיָ.

שְׁמַע יְיָ קוֹלִי אֶקְרָא, וְחָנֵּנִי וַעֲנֵנִי.

לְךָ אָמַר לִבִּי, בַּקְּשׁוּ פָנָי.

אֶת פָּנֶיךָ יְיָ אֲבַקֵּשׁ.

אַל תַּסְתֵּר פָּנֶיךָ מִמֶּנִּי, אַל תַּט בְּאַף עַבְדֶּךָ.

עֶזְרָתִי הָיִיתָ, אַל תִּטְּשֵׁנִי וְאַל תַּעַזְבֵנִי אֱלֹהֵי יִשְׁעִי.

כִּי אָבִי וְאִמִּי עֲזָבוּנִי, וַיְיָ יַאַסְפֵנִי.

הוֹרֵנִי יְיָ דַּרְכֶּךָ, וּנְחֵנִי בְּאֹרַח מִישׁוֹר, לְמַעַן שׁוֹרְרָי.

אַל תִּתְּנֵנִי בְּנֶפֶשׁ צָרָי, כִּי קָמוּ בִי עֵדֵי שֶׁקֶר וִיפֵחַ חָמָס.

לוּלֵא הֶאֱמַנְתִּי, לִרְאוֹת בְּטוּב יְיָ בְּאֶרֶץ חַיִּים.

קַוֵּה אֶל יְיָ, חֲזַק וְיַאֲמֵץ לִבֶּךָ וְקַוֵּה אֶל יְיָ.

Psalm 27

(Recited daily just before the kiddush according to Ashkenai Jewish tradition from Rosh Hodesh Elul through Hoshanah Rabbah)

By David.

The Lord is my light and my salvation, who *else* shall I hold in awe? The Lord is the strength of my life, of whom shall I be afraid?

When the wicked rose up against me to eat at my flesh, and my enemies and adversaries came to me growling, it is they who stumbled and fell.

If he were encamped all around me, my heart would not be afraid. If war should rise up against me, I would still be confident.

One thing I would ask of the Lord; one thing I will seek after, that I might dwell in the House of the Lord all the days of my life; to behold the beauty of the Lord, and to inquire in His temple.

In the day of trouble He will hide me in His tabernacle. He will hide me under the cover of His tent, setting me safe upon the Rock.

And so shall my head be lifted above my enemies who have surrounded me, so I will offer a sacrifice with the sound of the trumpet, and the voice of the singer, singing to the Lord.

Lord, hear my voice when I call, be gracious and answer me.

You said of my heart, "Seek My face."

Lord, I will seek Your face.

Do not hide Your face from me; do not turn Your servant away in anger.

You have been my help. Do not cast me away and do not abandon me, for You are the God who saves.

Though my father and my mother have abandoned me, the Lord will lift me up.

Teach me Your way, O Lord, and let me rest in the path of righteousness, in spite of those who would rule over me.

Do not give me up to the will of my enemy, for false witnesses have stood up against me, breathing violence.

Were it not that I believe, I will see the goodness of the Lord in the land of the living...

Trust in the Lord; be strong and be encouraged in your heart, and trust in the Lord.

אשת חיל

אֵשֶׁת חַיִל מִי יִמְצָא וְרָחֹק מִפְּנִינִים מִכְרָהּ: בָּטַח בָּהּ לֵב בַּעְלָהּ וְשָׁלָל לֹא
יֶחְסָר: גְּמָלַתְהוּ טוֹב וְלֹא־רָע כֹּל יְמֵי חַיֶּיהָ: דָּרְשָׁה צֶמֶר וּפִשְׁתִּים וַתַּעַשׂ
בְּחֵפֶץ כַּפֶּיהָ: הָיְתָה כָּאֳנִיּוֹת סוֹחֵר מִמֶּרְחָק תָּבִיא לַחְמָהּ: וַתָּקָם בְּעוֹד
לַיְלָה וַתִּתֵּן טֶרֶף לְבֵיתָהּ וְחֹק לְנַעֲרֹתֶיהָ: זָמְמָה שָׂדֶה וַתִּקָּחֵהוּ מִפְּרִי כַפֶּיהָ
נָטְעָה כָּרֶם: חָגְרָה בְעוֹז מָתְנֶיהָ וַתְּאַמֵּץ זְרוֹעֹתֶיהָ: טָעֲמָה כִּי־טוֹב סַחְרָהּ
לֹא־יִכְבֶּה בַלַּיְלָה נֵרָהּ: יָדֶיהָ שִׁלְּחָה בַכִּישׁוֹר וְכַפֶּיהָ תָּמְכוּ פָלֶךְ: כַּפָּהּ
פָּרְשָׂה לֶעָנִי וְיָדֶיהָ שִׁלְּחָה לָאֶבְיוֹן: לֹא־תִירָא לְבֵיתָהּ מִשָּׁלֶג כִּי כָל־בֵּיתָהּ
לָבֻשׁ שָׁנִים: מַרְבַדִּים עָשְׂתָה־לָּהּ שֵׁשׁ וְאַרְגָּמָן לְבוּשָׁהּ: נוֹדָע בַּשְּׁעָרִים
בַּעְלָהּ בְּשִׁבְתּוֹ עִם־זִקְנֵי־אָרֶץ: סָדִין עָשְׂתָה וַתִּמְכֹּר וַחֲגוֹר נָתְנָה
לַכְּנַעֲנִי: עוֹז־וְהָדָר לְבוּשָׁהּ וַתִּשְׂחַק לְיוֹם אַחֲרוֹן: פִּיהָ פָּתְחָה בְחָכְמָה
וְתוֹרַת־חֶסֶד עַל־לְשׁוֹנָהּ: צוֹפִיָּה הֲלִיכוֹת בֵּיתָהּ וְלֶחֶם עַצְלוּת לֹא
תֹאכֵל: קָמוּ בָנֶיהָ וַיְאַשְּׁרוּהָ בַּעְלָהּ וַיְהַלְלָהּ: רַבּוֹת בָּנוֹת עָשׂוּ חָיִל וְאַתְּ
עָלִית עַל־כֻּלָּנָה: שֶׁקֶר הַחֵן וְהֶבֶל הַיֹּפִי אִשָּׁה יִרְאַת־יְיָ הִיא תִתְהַלָּל:
תְּנוּ־לָהּ מִפְּרִי יָדֶיהָ וִיהַלְלוּהָ בַשְּׁעָרִים מַעֲשֶׂיהָ:

Eshet ḥayil mi yimtza v'raḥok mip'ninim mikhrah.
Bataḥ bah lev ba'lah v'shalam lo yeḥsar.
G'malatu tov v'lo ra kol y'mei ḥayeiha.
Darshah tzemer ufishtim vata'as b'ḥefetz kapeiha.
Haitah ko'oniyot soḥer mimerḥak tavi laḥmah.
Vatakom be'od lailah vatiten teref l'vetah v'ḥok l'na'aroteiha.
Zamah sadeh vatikaḥehu mipri khapeiha nat'ah karem.
ḥagrah v'oz mot'neiha vat'amets zro'oteiha.
Ta'amah ki tov saḥ'rah lo yikhbeh ba'lailah nerah.
Yadeha shilḥah vakishor v'khapeiha tamkhu felekh.
Kapah parsah le'ani v'yadeiha shil'ḥah la'evyon.
Lo tira l'vetah mishaleg ki khol beitah lavush shanim.
Marvadim as'tah lah shesh v'argaman l'vushah.
Noda bash'arim ba'lah b'shivto im ziknei arets.
Sadin astah vatimkor vaḥagor na'tenah lak'na'ani.
Oz v'hadar l'vushah vatishak l'yom aharon.
Piha pa'teḥah v'ḥochmah v'torat ḥesed al l'shonah.
Tzofi'ah halikhot be'tah v'leḥem atslut lo tokhel.
Kamu vaneha vayash'ruha ba'lah vay'halelah.
Rabot banot asu ḥayil v'at aliyt al kulanah.
Sheker haḥen v'hevel hayofiy ishah yir'at Adonai hi tit'halal.
Tenu lah mip'ri yadeha viyahaleluha vash'arim ma'asehah.

Eishet Ḥayil

A woman of valor, who can find? Her value is far beyond pearls.

Her husband's heart relies on her and he shall lack no fortune.

She does him good and not evil, all the days of her life.

She seeks wool and flax, and works with her hands willingly.

She is like the merchant ships in bringing her bread from afar.

She gets up while it is still night, and gives food to her household and a portion to her maidservants.

She plans for a field, and buys it. With the fruit of her hands she plants a vineyard.

She girds her loins in strength, and makes her arms strong.

She knows that her merchandise is good. Her candle does not go out at night.

She sets her hands to the spindle, and holds the spinning wheel in her hands.

She extends her hands to the poor, and reaches out her hand to the needy.

She fears not for her household because of snow, because her whole household is warmly dressed.

She makes covers for herself, her clothing is fine linen and purple.

Her husband is known at the gates and he sits among the elders of the land.

She makes a coat and sells it, and she delivers clothing to the merchant.

Strength and honor are her clothing and she smiles at the future.

She opens her mouth with wisdom, and kindness is on her tongue.

She watches over the ways of her household, and does not eat the bread of idleness.

Her children rise up and praise her, her husband lauds her.

Many women have acted in a worthy manner, but you surpass them all.

Charm is deceptive and beauty is vain,

but a woman who fears God shall be praised.

Give her of the fruit of her hands, and let her works praise her in the gates.

אֵל אָדוֹן

אֵל אָדוֹן עַל כָּל הַמַּעֲשִׂים. בָּרוּךְ וּמְבֹרָךְ בְּפִי כָּל נְשָׁמָה,

El Adon al kol hama'asim, barukh um'vorakh befi kol neshamah.

גָּדְלוֹ וְטוּבוֹ מָלֵא עוֹלָם, דַּעַת וּתְבוּנָה סֹבְבִים אֹתוֹ.

Gad'lo vetuvo malei olam, da'at ut'vunah sov'vim oto.

הַמִּתְגָּאֶה עַל חַיּוֹת הַקֹּדֶשׁ וְנֶהְדָּר בְּכָבוֹד עַל הַמֶּרְכָּבָה,

Hamit'ga'eh al ḥayot hakodesh veneh'dar bekhavod al hamer'kavah.

זְכוּת וּמִישׁוֹר לִפְנֵי כִסְאוֹ, חֶסֶד וְרַחֲמִים לִפְנֵי כְבוֹדוֹ.

Z'khut umishor lifnei khis'o, ḥesed veraḥamim lifnei k'vodo.

טוֹבִים מְאוֹרוֹת שֶׁבָּרָא אֱלֹהֵינוּ, יְצָרָם בְּדַעַת בְּבִינָה וּבְהַשְׂכֵּל,

Tovim me'orot shebara Eloheinu, yetsaram beda'at bevinah uvhas'kel.

כֹּחַ וּגְבוּרָה נָתַן בָּהֶם, לִהְיוֹת מוֹשְׁלִים בְּקֶרֶב תֵּבֵל.

Ko'aḥ ug'vurah natan bahem, lih'yot mosh'lim bekerev teiveil.

מְלֵאִים זִיו וּמְפִיקִים נֹגַהּ, נָאֶה זִיוָם בְּכָל הָעוֹלָם,

M'lei-im ziv um'fikim nogah, na'eh zivam b'khal ha'olam.

שְׂמֵחִים בְּצֵאתָם וְשָׂשִׂים בְּבוֹאָם, עֹשִׂים בְּאֵימָה רְצוֹן קוֹנָם.

S'meiḥim b'tsetam v'sasim b'vo'am, osim b'eimah retson konam.

פְּאֵר וְכָבוֹד נוֹתְנִים לִשְׁמוֹ, צָהֳלָה וְרִנָּה לְזֵכֶר מַלְכוּתוֹ,

P'eir v'khavod not'nim lish'mo, tsahalah v'rinah l'zeikher mal'khuto.

קָרָא לַשֶּׁמֶשׁ וַיִּזְרַח אוֹר, רָאָה וְהִתְקִין צוּרַת הַלְּבָנָה.

Kara lashemesh vayiz'raḥ or, ra'ah v'hit'kin tsurat ha-l'vanah.

שֶׁבַח נוֹתְנִים לוֹ כָּל צְבָא מָרוֹם, תִּפְאֶרֶת וּגְדֻלָּה, שְׂרָפִים וְאוֹפַנִּים וְחַיּוֹת הַקֹּדֶשׁ.

Shevaḥ not'nim lo kal ts'va marom, tif'eret u-g'dulah, s'rafim ve'ofanim v'ḥayot hakodesh.

לָאֵל אֲשֶׁר שָׁבַת מִכָּל הַמַּעֲשִׂים, בַּיּוֹם הַשְּׁבִיעִי הִתְעַלָּה, וְיָשַׁב עַל כִּסֵּא כְבוֹדוֹ, תִּפְאֶרֶת עָטָה לְיוֹם הַמְּנוּחָה, עֹנֶג קָרָא לְיוֹם הַשַּׁבָּת. זֶה שֶׁבַח שֶׁל יוֹם הַשְּׁבִיעִי, שֶׁבּוֹ שָׁבַת אֵל מִכָּל מְלַאכְתּוֹ, וְיוֹם הַשְּׁבִיעִי מְשַׁבֵּחַ וְאוֹמֵר, מִזְמוֹר שִׁיר לְיוֹם הַשַּׁבָּת, טוֹב לְהוֹדוֹת לַיְיָ, לְפִיכָךְ יְפָאֲרוּ וִיבָרְכוּ לָאֵל כָּל יְצוּרָיו, שֶׁבַח יְקָר וּגְדֻלָּה וְכָבוֹד יִתְּנוּ לָאֵל מֶלֶךְ יוֹצֵר כֹּל, הַמַּנְחִיל מְנוּחָה לְעַמּוֹ יִשְׂרָאֵל בִּקְדֻשָּׁתוֹ, בְּיוֹם שַׁבַּת קֹדֶשׁ, שִׁמְךָ יְיָ אֱלֹהֵינוּ יִתְקַדַּשׁ, וְזִכְרְךָ מַלְכֵּנוּ יִתְפָּאַר, בַּשָּׁמַיִם מִמַּעַל וְעַל הָאָרֶץ מִתָּחַת.

El Adon

God is Lord of all creation. He is, and will be, blessed by the mouth of every soul. His great goodness fills the universe; knowledge and understanding surround Him.

He is exalted above the holy beings and adorned with majestic glory. Purity and uprightness are before His throne, and in His presence are compassion and mercy.

Good are the luminaries which our God has created; they were made with knowledge, wisdom and insight. Strength and power were given them that they might rule over the world.

Full of splendor and radiating brightness, their light brings beauty to all the world. Rejoice in their rising and be exultant in their setting, performing with reverence the will of the Creator.

They give glory and honor to His Name, singing joyously at the fame of His Kingdom. He spoke to the sun, and it began to shine; He looked to regulate the form of the moon.

Give Him praise all you hosts on high; Seraphim and Ophanim and all the holy beings, render glory and grandeur...

... to God who, on the seventh day, ascended to sit upon His throne of glory, and rested from all the work of creation. He gave the day of rest beauty, and He called the Shabbat a delight. Such is the distinction of the seventh day, that on it, God rested from all His work. And so, the seventh day offers praise, saying, "A song for the Shabbat day. It is good to give thanks to the Lord." Therefore, let all God's creatures glorify and bless Him, and render honor, glory and grandeur to God, the King and the Creator of all things. He has, in His holiness, given rest to His people Israel, on the holy Shabbat day. Lord our God, Your Name will be sanctified, and Your fame, our King, will be glorified in the heavens above and on the earth beneath.

Avinu Malkeynu

*(Avinu Malkeynu is recited before an open Ark from Rosh Hashanah through Yom Kippur and on fast days after
the Amidah at Shaḥarit and Minḥa services, but not on Shabbat)*

אָבִינוּ מַלְכֵּנוּ, חָטָאנוּ לְפָנֶיךָ.

אָבִינוּ מַלְכֵּנוּ, אֵין לָנוּ מֶלֶךְ אֶלָּא אָתָּה.

אָבִינוּ מַלְכֵּנוּ, עֲשֵׂה עִמָּנוּ לְמַעַן שְׁמֶךָ.

אָבִינוּ מַלְכֵּנוּ, חַדֵּשׁ עָלֵינוּ שָׁנָה טוֹבָה.

אָבִינוּ מַלְכֵּנוּ, בַּטֵּל מֵעָלֵינוּ כָּל גְּזֵרוֹת קָשׁוֹת.

אָבִינוּ מַלְכֵּנוּ, בַּטֵּל מַחְשְׁבוֹת שׂוֹנְאֵינוּ.

אָבִינוּ מַלְכֵּנוּ, הָפֵר עֲצַת אוֹיְבֵינוּ.

אָבִינוּ מַלְכֵּנוּ, כַּלֵּה כָּל צַר וּמַשְׂטִין מֵעָלֵינוּ.

אָבִינוּ מַלְכֵּנוּ, סְתוֹם פִּיּוֹת מַשְׂטִינֵנוּ וּמְקַטְרִיגֵנוּ.

אָבִינוּ מַלְכֵּנוּ, כַּלֵּה דֶּבֶר וְחֶרֶב וְרָעָב וּשְׁבִי וּמַשְׁחִית וְעָוֹן וּשְׁמַד מִבְּנֵי בְרִיתֶךָ.

אָבִינוּ מַלְכֵּנוּ, מְנַע מַגֵּפָה מִנַּחֲלָתֶךָ.

אָבִינוּ מַלְכֵּנוּ, סְלַח וּמְחַל לְכָל עֲוֹנוֹתֵינוּ.

אָבִינוּ מַלְכֵּנוּ, מְחֵה וְהַעֲבֵר פְּשָׁעֵינוּ וְחַטֹּאתֵינוּ מִנֶּגֶד עֵינֶיךָ.

אָבִינוּ מַלְכֵּנוּ, מְחוֹק בְּרַחֲמֶיךָ כָּל שִׁטְרֵי חוֹבוֹתֵינוּ.

אָבִינוּ מַלְכֵּנוּ, הַחֲזִירֵנוּ בִּתְשׁוּבָה שְׁלֵמָה לְפָנֶיךָ.

אָבִינוּ מַלְכֵּנוּ, שְׁלַח רְפוּאָה שְׁלֵמָה לְחוֹלֵי עַמֶּךָ.

אָבִינוּ מַלְכֵּנוּ, קְרַע רוֹעַ גְּזַר דִּינֵנוּ.

אָבִינוּ מַלְכֵּנוּ, זָכְרֵנוּ בְּזִכָּרוֹן טוֹב לְפָנֶיךָ.

אָבִינוּ מַלְכֵּנוּ, כָּתְבֵנוּ בְּסֵפֶר חַיִּים טוֹבִים.

אָבִינוּ מַלְכֵּנוּ, כָּתְבֵנוּ בְּסֵפֶר גְּאֻלָּה וִישׁוּעָה.

אָבִינוּ מַלְכֵּנוּ, כָּתְבֵנוּ בְּסֵפֶר פַּרְנָסָה וְכַלְכָּלָה.

אָבִינוּ מַלְכֵּנוּ, כָּתְבֵנוּ בְּסֵפֶר זְכֻיּוֹת.

אָבִינוּ מַלְכֵּנוּ, כָּתְבֵנוּ בְּסֵפֶר סְלִיחָה וּמְחִילָה.

אָבִינוּ מַלְכֵּנוּ, הַצְמַח לָנוּ יְשׁוּעָה בְּקָרוֹב.

אָבִינוּ מַלְכֵּנוּ, הָרֵם קֶרֶן יִשְׂרָאֵל עַמֶּךָ.

אָבִינוּ מַלְכֵּנוּ, הָרֵם קֶרֶן מְשִׁיחֶךָ יְשׁוּעַ.

Avinu Malkeynu

(Avinu Malkeynu is recited before an open Ark from Rosh Hashanah through Yom Kippur and on fast days after the Amidah at Shaharit and Minha services, but not on Shabbat)

Our Father, our King, our sins are before You.

Our Father, our King, we have no other King but You.

Our Father, our King, deal with us *kindly* for Your name's sake.

Our Father, our King, renew for us a good year.

Our Father, our King, annul from upon us all harsh decrees.

Our Father, our King, annul the intentions of our enemies.

Our Father, our King, bring to nothing the counsel of our foes.

Our Father, our King, destroy from upon us every foe and adversary.

Our Father, our King, stop the mouth of our adversaries and our accusers.

Our Father, our King, bring an end to pestilence, and drought, and hunger, and captivity, and destruction, and offence, and persecution of the children of Your covenant.

Our Father, our King, hold back the plague from Your heritage.

Our Father, our King, pardon and forgive all our offenses.

Our Father, our King, wipe away and remove our iniquity and our sins from before Your eyes.

Our Father, our King, in Your compassion erase all records of our guilt.

Our Father, our King, bring us back in perfect repentance, before You.

Our Father, our King, send perfect healing to the sick among Your people.

Our Father, our King, tear up the evil judgement decreed against us.

Our Father, our King, remember us before You, with good memories.

Our Father, our King, inscribe us in the Book for a good life.

Our Father, our King, inscribe us in the Book for redemption and salvation.

Our Father, our King, inscribe us in the Book for sustenance and support.

Our Father, our King, inscribe us in the Book for acquittal.

Our Father, our King, inscribe us in the Book for forgiveness and pardon.

Our Father, our King, in the near future cause salvation to bloom for us.

Our Father, our King, raise up the Horn of Israel, Your people.

Our Father, our King, raise up the Horn of Your Messiah Yeshua.

אָבִינוּ מַלְכֵּנוּ, מַלֵּא יָדֵינוּ מִבִּרְכוֹתֶיךָ.

אָבִינוּ מַלְכֵּנוּ, מַלֵּא אֲסָמֵינוּ שָׂבָע.

אָבִינוּ מַלְכֵּנוּ, שְׁמַע קוֹלֵנוּ חוּס וְרַחֵם עָלֵינוּ.

אָבִינוּ מַלְכֵּנוּ, קַבֵּל בְּרַחֲמִים וּבְרָצוֹן אֶת תְּפִלָּתֵנוּ.

אָבִינוּ מַלְכֵּנוּ, פְּתַח שַׁעֲרֵי שָׁמַיִם לִתְפִלָּתֵנוּ.

אָבִינוּ מַלְכֵּנוּ, זְכוֹר כִּי עָפָר אֲנָחְנוּ.

אָבִינוּ מַלְכֵּנוּ, נָא אַל תְּשִׁיבֵנוּ רֵיקָם מִלְּפָנֶיךָ.

אָבִינוּ מַלְכֵּנוּ, תְּהֵא הַשָּׁעָה הַזֹּאת שְׁעַת רַחֲמִים וְעֵת רָצוֹן מִלְּפָנֶיךָ.

אָבִינוּ מַלְכֵּנוּ, חֲמוֹל עָלֵינוּ וְעַל עוֹלָלֵינוּ וְטַפֵּנוּ.

אָבִינוּ מַלְכֵּנוּ, עֲשֵׂה לְמַעַן הֲרוּגִים עַל שֵׁם קָדְשֶׁךָ.

אָבִינוּ מַלְכֵּנוּ, עֲשֵׂה לְמַעַן טְבוּחִים עַל יִחוּדֶךָ.

אָבִינוּ מַלְכֵּנוּ, עֲשֵׂה לְמַעַן בָּאֵי בָאֵשׁ וּבַמַּיִם עַל קִדּוּשׁ שְׁמֶךָ.

אָבִינוּ מַלְכֵּנוּ, נְקוֹם לְעֵינֵינוּ נִקְמַת דַּם עֲבָדֶיךָ הַשָּׁפוּךְ.

אָבִינוּ מַלְכֵּנוּ, עֲשֵׂה לְמַעַנְךָ אִם לֹא לְמַעֲנֵנוּ.

אָבִינוּ מַלְכֵּנוּ, עֲשֵׂה לְמַעַנְךָ וְהוֹשִׁיעֵנוּ.

אָבִינוּ מַלְכֵּנוּ, עֲשֵׂה לְמַעַן רַחֲמֶיךָ הָרַבִּים.

אָבִינוּ מַלְכֵּנוּ, עֲשֵׂה לְמַעַן שִׁמְךָ הַגָּדוֹל, הַגִּבּוֹר וְהַנּוֹרָא שֶׁנִּקְרָא עָלֵינוּ.

אָבִינוּ מַלְכֵּנוּ, חָנֵּנוּ וַעֲנֵנוּ, כִּי אֵין בָּנוּ מַעֲשִׂים, עֲשֵׂה עִמָּנוּ צְדָקָה וָחֶסֶד וְהוֹשִׁיעֵנוּ.

Our Father, our King, fill our hands with Your blessings.

Our Father, our King, fill our storehouses with abundance.

Our Father, our King, hear our cry for mercy and have compassion upon us.

Our Father, our King, accept our prayer with compassion and with favor.

Our Father, our King, open the gates of heaven to our prayer.

Our Father, our King, remember that we are but dust.

Our Father, our King, in times to come do not turn us away empty from before You.

Our Father, our King, may this time be a time of compassion and of favor before You.

Our Father, our King, have pity upon us, and upon our infants and our little children.

Our Father, our King, act for those slain for the sake of Your holy name.

Our Father, our King, act for those slaughtered for the sake of Your Oneness.

Our Father, our King, act for the sake of those who have gone through fire and water for the sanctification of Your name.

Our Father, our King, take vengeance before our eyes, and avenge the spilt blood of Your servant.

Our Father, our King, do it for Your sake, not for our sake.

Our Father, our King, do it for Your sake, and save us.

Our Father, our King, do it for the sake of Your abundant compassion.

Our Father, our King, do for the sake of Your great, mighty and awesome name that will be proclaimed upon us.

Our Father, our King, be gracious and answer us, though there is nothing of merit in us, deal with us in justice and in loving kindness, and save us.

Blessings before Food or Drink

Beginning of every blessing: ...בָּרוּךְ אַתָּה יְיָ אֱלֹהֵינוּ מֶלֶךְ הָעוֹלָם
Barukh atah Adonai Eloheinu Melekh Ha'Olam...
Blessed are You, Lord our God, King of the Universe...

Before eating bread: ...הַמּוֹצִיא לֶחֶם מִן הָאָרֶץ.
...hamotsi lehem min ha'arets. ...who brings forth bread from the earth.

Before eating products of wheat, barley, rye, oats, or spelt: ...בּוֹרֵא מִינֵי מְזוֹנוֹת.
...borei minei m'zunot. ...who creates species of nourishment.

Before drinking grape wine or grape juice: ...בּוֹרֵא פְּרִי הַגָּפֶן.
...borei p'ri ha'gafen. ...who creates the fruit of the vine.

Before eating tree-grown fruit: ...בּוֹרֵא פְּרִי הָעֵץ.
...borei p'ri ha'eits. ...who creates the fruit of the tree.

Before eating produce that grew directly from the earth: ...בּוֹרֵא פְּרִי הָאֲדָמָה.
...borei p'ri ha'adamah. ...who creates the fruit of the ground.

Before eating or drinking any other foods: ...שֶׁהַכֹּל נִהְיָה בִּדְבָרוֹ.
...shehakhol niyeh bid'varo. ...through whose word everything came to be.

Birkat HaMazon - Brief Version

(This very short Birkat follows the traditional minimal requirement to mention the Food, the Land of Israel, Jerusalem's sanctity and G-d's Goodness after eating)

בָּרוּךְ אַתָּה יְיָ, אֱלֹהֵינוּ מֶלֶךְ הָעוֹלָם, הַזָּן אֶת הַכֹּל.
נוֹדֶה לְךָ יְיָ אֱלֹהֵינוּ, עַל הָאָרֶץ וְעַל הַמָּזוֹן.
וּבְנֵה יְרוּשָׁלַיִם עִיר הַקֹּדֶשׁ בִּמְהֵרָה בְיָמֵינוּ.
הַמֶּלֶךְ הַטּוֹב, וְהַמֵּטִיב לַכֹּל. וּמִכָּל טוֹב לְעוֹלָם אַל יְחַסְּרֵנוּ.

Barukh atah Adonai, Eloheinu Melekh Ha'Olam, hazan et hakol.
Nodeh l'kha, Adonai Eloheinu, al ha'arets v'al hamazon.
Uv'neih Y'rushalayim ir hakodesh bimheirah v'yameinu.
HaMelekh hatov v'hameitiv lakol. Umikol tov l'olam al y'has'reinu.

Blessed are You, Lord our God, King of the Universe, who provides food for all.
We thank You Lord our God, for the Land and for its produce.
Rebuild Jerusalem as a holy city very soon, even in our day.
The Good King is good to all. May You, who knows our need, always provide us with good.